INTERNATIONAL COMMODITY MARKET MODELS AND POLICY ANALYSIS

ADVANCED STUDIES IN THEORETICAL AND APPLIED ECONOMETRICS
VOLUME 13

For a complete list of volumes in this series see final page of this volume.

International Commodity Market Models and Policy Analysis

edited by

O. Guvenen

Université de Paris, France

KLUWER ACADEMIC PUBLISHERS
DORDRECHT / BOSTON / LONDON

Library of Congress Cataloging in Publication Data

International commodity market models and policy analysis.

Papers from an international conference organized by the Applied Econometric Association, held at the University of Zaragoza, in Spain.
1. Commodity exchanges--Econometric models--Congresses. I. Guvenen, O. II. Applied Econometric Association.
HG6046.I456 1988 332.64'4'0724 88-13511

ISBN 90-247-3768-0

Published by Kluwer Academic Publishers,
P.O. Box 17, 3300 AA Dordrecht, The Netherlands.

Kluwer Academic Publishers incorporates
the publishing programmes of
D. Reidel, Martinus Nijhoff, Dr W. Junk and MTP Press.

Sold and distributed in the U.S.A. and Canada
by Kluwer Academic Publishers,
101 Philip Drive, Norwell, MA 02061, U.S.A.

In all other countries, sold and distributed
by Kluwer Academic Publishers Group,
P.O. Box 322, 3300 AH Dordrecht, The Netherlands.

Printed in The Netherlands

TABLE OF CONTENTS

PART II: APPLICATIONS

PART III: STABILISATION POLICY

PART IV: TRADE ASPECTS

PREFACE

O. Guvenen, *University of Paris IX–Dauphine*

The aim of this publication is to present recent developments in international commodity market model building and policy analysis.

This book is based mainly on the research presented at the XIIth International Conference organised by the Applied Econometric Association (AEA) which was held at the University of Zaragoza in Spain. This conference would not have been possible without the cooperation of the Department of Econometrics of the University of Zaragoza and its Chairman A.A. Grasa. I would like to express my thanks to all contributors.

I am grateful to J.H.P. Paelinck, J.P. Ancot, A.J. Hughes Hallett and H. Serbat for their constructive contributions and comments concerning the structure of the book.

INTRODUCTION

O. Guvenen

The challenge of increasing complexity and global interdependence at the world level necessitates new modelling approaches and policy analysis at the macroeconomic level, and for commodities. The evaluation of economic modelling follows the evolution of international economic phenomena. In that interdependent context there is a growing need for forecasting and simulation tools in the analysis of international primary commodity markets.

Quantitative techniques, often backed by engineering concepts, have been used to elaborate new generations of models and policy analysis through institutional and structural analysis. In that spirit, this book attempts to cover theoretical and empirical research by model builders and users arising to improve economic policy analysis through better understanding and forecasting of international primary commodity markets in an increasingly interdependent system. This content is presented in four sections:

i) Modelling methodologies
ii) Applications
iii) Stabilisation policy
iv) Trade aspects

In the first section Radetzki and Labys present, at theoretical and empirical level, a model capable of analysing long run exhaustible resource market behaviour with the inclusion of intermediate and short run phenomena. Gilbert's paper derives a number of approximations to the competitive storage function in commodity market models. The study has implications for both policy and modelling. Davutyan analyses in his paper the impact of price and stabilisation on producers' revenue and consumers' expenditure. As a complementary methodology in explaining the conflictual characteristics of the commodity markets and the potential coalitions, Richard uses the game theory approach for the representation of active strategies.

In part two, which deals with modelling applications, Mitchell describes the world grain and soybean model currently used by the World Bank for medium term annual projections of world prices, trade, production, consumption and ending stocks for each country or region. It is a non–spatial, partial–equilibrium, net–trade model.

The paper by Field, Bush and Clark develops an engineering simulation model of the world magnesium market. The demand sector consists of statistical and engineering analysis of the relationship between consumption, technical requirements, market growth, price and the availability of magnesium and substitute materials. The supply side is represented by engineering–based cost functions and a set of alternative pricing mechanisms to translate the cost–output relationships into price–output functions.

How many and which variables should be considered in the final specifcation in analysing gasoline demand? To answer this question, Aznar and Castrillo use a three–stage methodology: (a) determination of the set of admissable models, (b) determination of the set of most informative models, and (c) tests of structural change in order to measure the closeness of different models to new observed facts. Carlevaro proposes a conceptual framework describing the impact of technological changes affecting the stock of fuel burning equipment, on the level and pattern of energy demand. This conceptual framework is used for the simulation of energy demand.

The third section is on stabilisation policy. The paper by Sengupta discusses the complexity of the robustness problem in the context of static and dynamic stabilisation policies in general and particularly in the case of the world coffee market. Conflict and non–cooperation, unequal degrees of risk aversion and the difficulty of specifying an optimal size of variable export quota are mentioned as factors which make it difficult to formulate stabilisation policies in world commodity markets with dominant producers.

Primary commodities being vitally important to the less developed economies, commodity stabilisation agreements have become a major issue in in international commodity policy. In that context, the paper by Hughes Hallett contains a comprehensive analysis based on theoretical and empirical approaches, and considering market stabilisation as a dnamic optimisation problem when there are also speculators operating in the market. He shows that stabilisation of the market is still possible but it is more expensive than in the absence of speculators with forward looking (rational) expectations. The author examines, in the context of a single market, the changes to the intervention patterns needed, the potential costs of reaching the desired goals and the income distribution aspects.

The final section deals with the trade aspects. The paper by Gonzalez–Romero and Kanbur analyses the impact of the price of oil on the terms of trade between North and South. Two alternative frameworks are used: (a) a structural, three–region model which shows that an increase in the price of oil will tend to worsen the terms of trade of the

South vis–a–vis the North, and (b) the neoclassical model which produces the opposite result with its full employment assumptions.

Endogenising commodity prices in OECD's world macro model INTERLINK is the main purpose of the paper by Holtham. The author concludes that estimated equations have standard errors at least as low as other similar ones in the literature, and the results do not suggest that the use of such aggregate equations would be much of an improvement. In the light of the growing interdependence of the world economy, the paper by Adams analyses the ability of econometric approaches to deal with commodities in international economic market model building.

Models which represent an abstraction of a complex real world do have obvious limitations. For many developing economies, more than 50 to 90 percent of earnings are derived from a single commodity. Considering that the aggregate commodity price index shows declining prices since 1950, with the exception of the Korean boom in 1950 and the oil boom in 1973, and adding to that the instability in most commodity markets, the failure of multilateral and unilateral stabilisation policies and increasing protectionist pressures, the importance of the problem solving approach in model building and policy analysis becomes more apparent in the context of an interdependent world economy. As model builders and policy analysts, our role is to have a problem solving approach and to minimise uncertainty.

PART I

MODELLING METHODOLOGIES

CHAPTER 1

AN INTEGRATED MARKET MODEL OF EXHAUSTIBLE RESOURCE BEHAVIOUR

Marian Radetzki , *University of Stockholm, Sweden*
Walter Labys*, *University of West Virginia, USA*

1. INTRODUCTION

The purpose of this paper is to design a theoretically sound and empirically realistic model capable of analysing long run exhaustible resource market behaviour with the inclusion of intermediate and short run phenomena. Such a model would attempt to reproduce and to predict resource quantity and price behaviour over time. Surprisingly, the history of such long run models which would explain resource quantity and price adjustments is almost completely missing from the literature. The standard commodity model (SCM) employed in most econometric representations of exhaustible resource markets focuses on the short run and is typically void of long run considerations, e.g., see Labys (1973). The rational extraction model (REM) derived from Hotelling's (1931) seminal analysis does address the long run. However, it faces very serious empirical problems because of its many simplifying assumptions. While theoreticians have shown the advantages of relaxing some of these assumptions, no overall or integrated model structure has emerged which could serve as a basis for empirical model testing and application. Similarly, econometricians have not yet developed modelling methods which can overcome some of the serious problems encountered because of the structural changes in resource markets over time.

Our study starts out from the basic Hotelling model construct, but synthesises and advances some of the more recent research results in this area so as to develop a more realistic exhaustible resource model. In our attempt to add realism to the REM, we borrow heavily from the SCM. Some of the features which are seen as essential to incorporate in advancing the REM include: additions to reserves, recycling of scrap, changes

O. Guvenen (ed.), International Commodity Market Models and Policy Analysis, 3–26.

in mining capacity, and the behaviour of inventories of the finished exhaustible resource product.

This paper begins by describing the research problem in the context of recent developments in the literature. A model framework is then proposed, based on disequilibrium theory describing linkages between long and short run flow and stock adjustment processes. The specification of the model then takes place primarily through the synthesis of the different theoretical approaches which have been taken to relax the Hotelling assumptions. The theoretical solution of the optimal control formulation of the problem required to provide the model's equilibrium conditions is given in the Appendix. Possibilities for an appropriate modelling methodology and model verification are also discussed. In a concluding section we point to the significance of the present effort for future empirical modelling applications and policy analysis.

2. THE PROBLEM

The present research problem consists of determining whether the basic Hotelling model and its rational extraction versions can be extended to specify a realistic model capable of explaining and forecasting mineral market behaviour over time. As emphasised by Pindyck (1979), rational extraction modelling has not received the kinds of empirical applications and verifications which would make it a useful long run modelling approach similar to that employed in short run modelling efforts.

The basic Hotelling (1931) theory is well known: the rate of extraction of a mining deposit should be such that the present value of rent or net price must be the same in all periods. To convert this insight into a theory of price where net price must rise at the rate of interest, Hotelling made many simplifying assumptions. These include: (1) a strictly competitive or at least a fixed market structure, (2) homogeneous mineral reserves, (3) constant extraction costs, (4) no fixed input factors, (5) uncertainty about the size of the resource base, resource demand, and consequent future prices, (6) instantaneous output adjustment with no transactions or adjustment costs, (7) no recycling activity, (8) no technological change, and (9) no joint production.

There would appear to be several drawbacks in implementing this theory in the form of a model. To begin with, the theory as stated and its extensions assume that resource producers determine production rates from the dynamic maximisation of the equity value of their reserve holdings. Whether or not producers do this is an empirical question that is difficult to answer, and Pindyck (1979), Barnett and Morse (1963), and Frank and Babunovic (1984) suggest that there is a strong possibility that they do not. Furthermore, studies by Heal and Burrows (1980, 1981), Smith (1981), and Feige and

Gewecke (1979) offer only very limited support. Explaining resource market behaviour would thus suggest that the strong maximisation conditions of optimal control theory underlying the REM be supplanted by the less strong maximisation conditions underlying the SCM. There also would appear to be too many assumptions in the Hotelling model that are not valid for mineral markets. Solving the problem of specifying a positive model, therefore, requires that we adopt, modify, or reject some of these assumptions.

As a starting point, we adopt Hotelling's assumption of a competitive market structure, as is appropriate for many of the mineral markets found in the real world. For those markets which are monopolistic, a theoretical basis can be found elsewhere in the work of Stiglitz (1976), Weinstein and Zeckhauser (1975) and others; more complex oligopolistic formulations have been described in Lewis and Schmalensee (1979), Salant (1976) and others.

Homogeneous mineral reserves had been assumed by Hotelling to the extent that extraction costs would increase only where such reserves become less accessible either in location or in depth. We relax this assumption and follow the results of Solow and Wan (1976) and others; that is, when deposits are ranked by quality and hence scarcity rent and costs, the lower cost resource would be extracted first. As this resource is exhausted, the next lower quality deposits are removed from the 'shelf' and placed into production. While costs can only rise discretely, arbitrage assures that prices vary continuously.

The assumption of costs being constant over extraction levels is replaced by the assumption of non–constant costs. Possibilities for more complex market behaviour now arise, as has been shown by Solow and Wan (1976), Fisher (1979), Cremer (1979) and Pindyck (1978b). The possibility of rising costs may ultimately affect prices and hence resource demand. The possibility of declining costs will also affect market equilibrium as analysed by Eswaren, Lewis and Heaps (1983). Mineral prices are thus likely to rise or fall depending on the declining quality of existing reserves, the relative quality of newly discovered reserves, changes in demand, market structure, and technical progress (Schulze, 1974). This new assumption brings considerable change to the REM. As shown by Lonoff (1983), the natural consequence of these price fluctuations is likely to be above–ground inventory holding of finished exhaustible resource product. This permits the proposed model analysis to be enriched by including shorter run mineral product inventories, as well as longer run capacity and mineral reserve stock adjustments.

Hotelling also assumed fixed input costs in all cases. While our model specification does explicitly consider input costs to be fixed in the short run, we do permit variations in the input of factors like capital or mineral reserves in the long run.

Relaxing the assumption of certainty with respect to supply and demand also adds considerably to the model revision. Supply and sometimes demand uncertainty affect the rate at which a deposit can be depleted. If deposits are of uniform quality, although of unknown size, they will be depleted at a slower rate than if the size of stock is known. Kemp (1976), Gilbert (1979), and Loucry (1978) have estimated how the deposit owner will act when he wants to avoid running out of a resource unexpectedly. To some extent, Hotelling did acknowledge supply uncertainty as embodied in exploration uncertainty. Herfindahl (1955) has shown that one can reduce the risk of such uncertainty through offsetting reserve depletion by augmenting reserves through exploration and consequent reserve additions. Hoel (1978) examines the case where owners learn about the size of a second stock by depleting a known stock. Pindyck (1979) instead has explained discoveries from exploration as following a continuous stochastic process. Later it will be shown how the recognition of exploration as an investment by Adelman (1970) and others has enabled us to cast reserves into a capital stock adjustment process.

The importance of uncertainty on the demand side stems from research such as that of Tilton (1980) who shows that short run instability in resource market and price behaviour stems mostly from unexpected fluctuations in demand. Weinstein and Zeckhauser (1979) have shown that the behaviour of risk neutral firms is unaffected by uncertain demand but that risk averters extract very rapidly. Pindyck (1979) treats uncertainty by allowing demand to fluctuate as a continuous stochastic process. Future demand may also be uncertain because of unanticipated technological change. Nordhaus (1974) and Heal (1976) have considered this possibility through the concept of a 'backstop' technology which causes a substitute commodity to appear at an unknown date. Dasgupta and Heal (1974) make this uncertain date an exogenous random variable. In the present case, demand is allowed to vary stochastically to reflect the uncertainty of fluctuations in industrial activity.

Next, the relaxing of uncertainty and the introduction of transactions costs provides speculative, precautionary and transactions motives for holding finished exhaustible resource product inventories. Van Duyne (1981) showed that the 'supply of storage' theory which embodies these motives represents an alternative approach for explaining medium and short run resource price movements. As well as explained later, motivation to borrow from the SCM specification and to include inventories increases the flexibility of the REM to explain adjustments in market equilibrium. This adaptation has also been considered separately by Eswaren, Lewis and Heaps (1983) in their study of resource market behaviour.

The remaining important Hotelling assumption to be relaxed is that of the neglect of recycling. Supply based on recycled scrap derived from metal containing products, similar to inventories, can cause adjustments in the rate of primary production. Schulze (1974), Weinstein and Zeckhauser (1974), and Pindyck (1979) have included scrap in their REM formulations as we do here.

It would be important to relax the assumptions which abstract from technical change and joint production. While we have considered the implications of technical change indirectly, it would be unduly difficult to include joint production effects in the present modelling effort.

3. THE MODEL

The presentation of the model begins with an explanation of the dynamic adjustment process required to extend the long run REM model by including medium and short run SCM considerations. An overall dynamic disequilibrium model framework is proposed and then each of the model's components is explained.

3.1. The Adjustment Process

The attempt to explain the relation between the long run and the short run adjustment process in commodity markets has a distinguished although somewhat neglected history in economic theory in general and in exhaustible resource theory in particular. The possibility for linking the long and short run based on stock and flow considerations has received attention from Keynes (1936), Harrod (1964), and more recently Hicks (1979). Particularly in the markets for extractive industries this approach can explain market adjustments where extractive capacity cannot be varied immediately. Price movements are a result of fluctuations in demand (and the extent of these movements depends on the ability of the market to release or to absorb the finished product inventories). If there is an upward price move from an earlier long run equilibrium level, then investment in extractive production capacity will result and will eventually enable the price to return to its initial equilibrium value. There will also be an upward adjustment in reserves, since mineral firms attempt to maintain reserve levels in proportion to their extractive production capacity. This will occur through investment in exploration which increases the level of reserves.

A simplified explanation of this adjustment process can be obtained by referring to Figure 1. Quadrant 1 features short term inventory demand ID and short term inventory supply IS curves. Price is assumed to adjust instantaneously to attain a short term equilibrium price $\overline{p}$ that is consistent with the existing stock level i^{o}. Quadrant 2 contains the long term flow demand D and flow supply S curves. The intersection of these

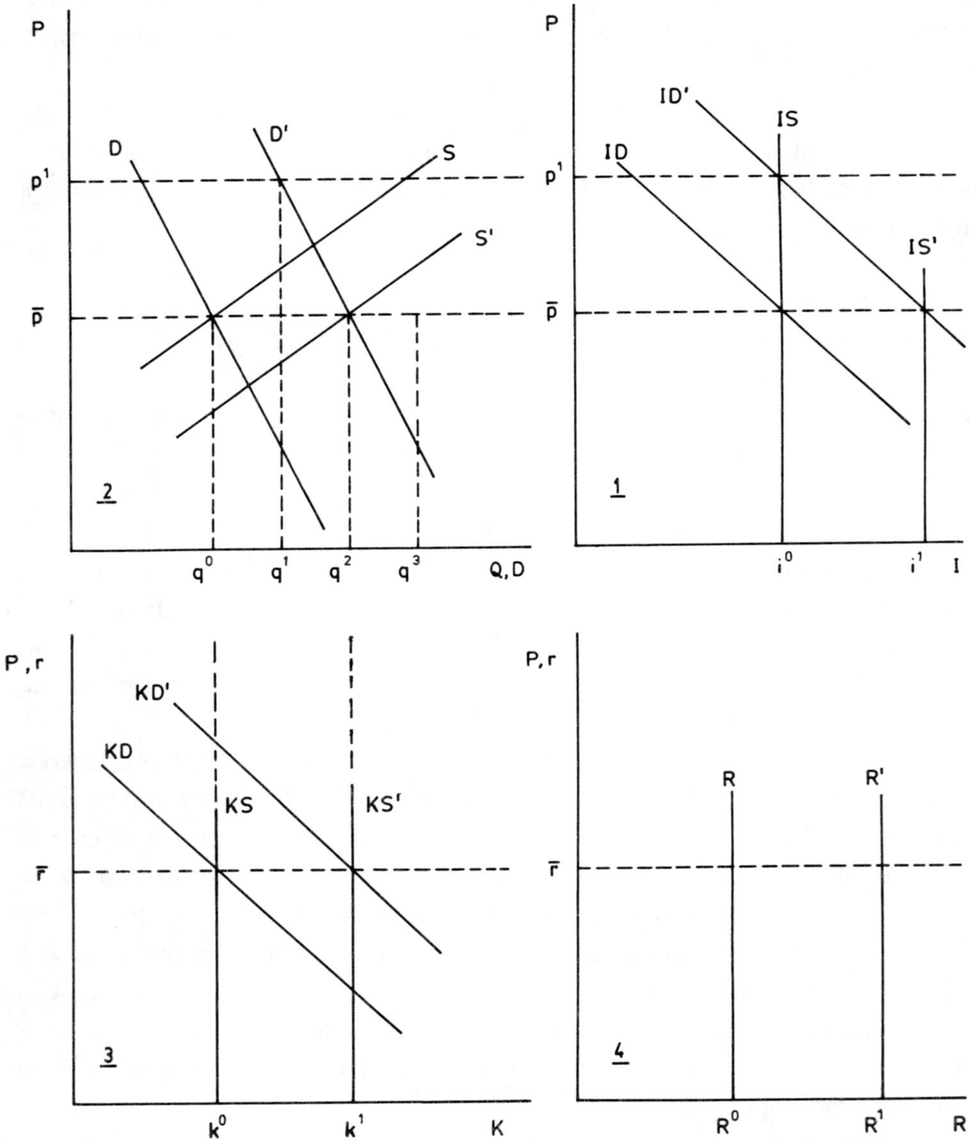

Figure 1. Combined long and short run flow and stock adjustments

curves determines the long term equilibrium price $\overline{p}$ and the quality demanded for current use, q^0. Both stock equilibrium in quadrant 1 and flow equilibrium in quadrant 2 hold for price $\overline{p}$. In long term equilibrium the quantity of inventories, given by the intersection between ID and IS in quadrant 1, is assumed to be directly proportional to the quantity demanded for current use.

It is assumed that the flow supply curve S is dependent on the level of production capacity K. Thus, the equilibrium level of capacity k^0 is defined in quadrant 3 at the rate of interest $\overline{r}$, which represents the intersection of the long term capacity supply curve KS and demand curve KD. The latter curve can be considered similar to the marginal efficiency of capital curve. The capacity level k^0 and the production level q^0 can be considered roughly equivalent. In quadrant 4, reserve levels are assumed to expand as the long run price exceeds the prevailing rate of interest which is consistent with extraction theory. That is, firms continue to extract as long as the net resource price exceeds the rate of interest. Should this differential extend over a sufficiently long period of time to cause exhaustion of the current deposit, firms will tend to expand reserves to bring additional deposits into extraction.

The linkages between flow equilibrium conditions in quadrant 2 and stock equilibrium conditions in quadrants 1, 3 and 4 can be shown to reflect the long and short run adjustment processes. Assume initially that an exogenous shift in demand occurs, such as that resulting from an increase in industrial activity, and that it causes the demand curve in quadrant 2 to shift from D to D′. As a consequence, inventory demand shifts from ID to ID′, raising price to p^1. At this price level, consumption rises to q^1, while the quantity supplied shifts to q^3. The excess of supply over consumption $q^3 - q^1$ is added to inventories. The higher price level creates an incentive to increase production capacity. This is represented by an upward shift of the demand for extractive capacity from KD to KD′ in quadrant 3.

The process of dynamic adjustment to the initial shift in demand involves a gradual fall in price as inventories increase from i^0 to K^1 in quadrant 3. A new equilibrium is reached when prices have fallen back to $\overline{p}$, and the capacity additions have expanded supply to S′. Additions to inventories will then cease, and consumption will equal the quantity supplied at q^2 in quadrant 2, given by the intersection between D′ and S′. Since producers attempt to maintain their reserves in proportion to extractive capacity, the reserve stock curve will have shifted from R to R′ in the course of the adjustment process.

3.2. Disequilibrium Model Framework

Possibilities for embodying the above long and short run adjustment process into a single model framework which constitutes a hybrid between the REM and SCM framework have been suggested from time to time. For example, Frank and Babunovic (1984) have combined long and medium run adjustment phenomena into their exhaustible resource investment model. Labys (1980a), Richard (1978), and Wagenhals (1984) have approached this problem at an empirical level by constructing econometric models of the copper market which incorporate adjustments in mining capacity but do not explicitly consider reserve formation. The latter consideration has been included in a model study of the same market conducted by Charles River Associates (CRA) (1978).

An appropriate model framework corresponding to these adjustments has been suggested in Figure 2. One essential feature of the proposed integrated model structure is that stock and flow market adjustments are represented at three levels: (1) longer term mineral reserve stock with flow depletion and additions, (2) intermediate to long term stocks in the form of primary production capacity with flow depletion and additions, and (3) shorter term inventories of finished products determined by consumption and production. Scrap could also be considered a stock which leads to secondary production flows, but we have selected the simpler formulation of scrap and secondary production as a flow process. A second distinguished feature of the framework is the linkages between these stock and flow variables in the model representation.

To embody these various considerations into a consistent model, we begin with Solow's recasting of Hotelling's theory into one more closely related to mineral market behaviour. While Hotelling thought of optimal exhaustibility as a condition of flow equilibrium in the market for ore, Solow considered it also as a condition of stock equilibrium in the asset market. Resource market quantity and price adjustments are thus a consequence of simultaneous flow equilibrium adjustments in the market for the ore and of stock equilibrium adjustments in the market for deposits. This important insight can be employed to transform the exhaustible resource model from one based on market equilibrium adjustment to one of disequilibrium adjustment, where stock adjustments work to move flow adjustments into equilibrium. While various aspects of this approach have been hinted at in the literature, this is to our knowledge the first time that they will all be integrated into a single model framework.

Among previous endeavours in this area, Lonoff (1982) and Heal (1976) have employed disequilibrium analysis to examine the linkages between resource prices, interest rate movements, and futures market activity. Attempts to include inventories in resource, or more particularly, mineral models have been numerous, as reviewed by

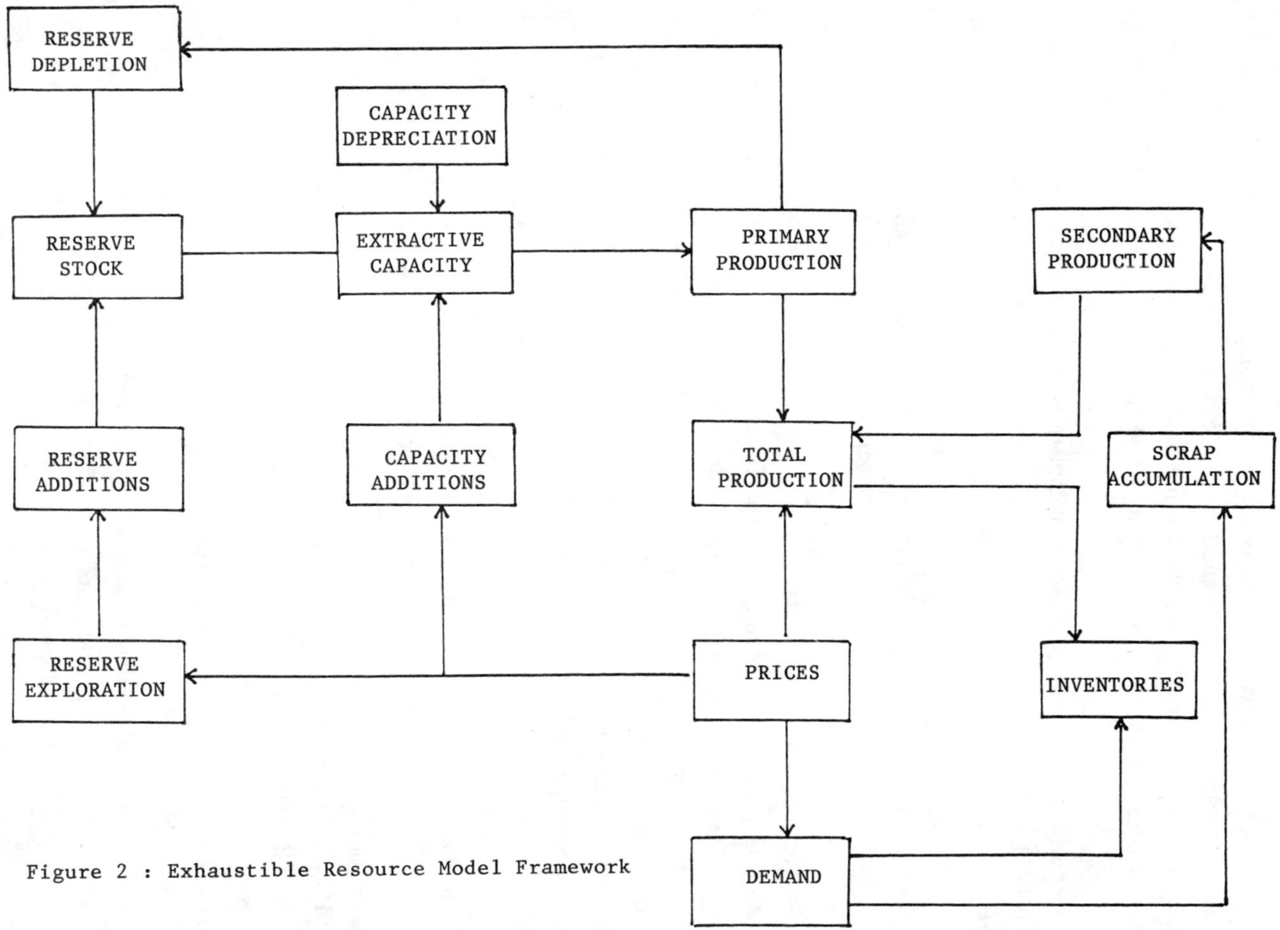

Figure 2 : Exhaustible Resource Model Framework

Burrows and Lonoff (1977) and Labys, Church and Clark (1984). The theoretical basis for specifying the stock relationship has also been advanced in the form of the 'supply of storage' theory by Burrows (1971) and Lonoff (1982). Attempts to include both long run primary production capacity and short run inventory relationships in mineral models have also been successfully made by Labys (1980b), Richard (1978), and Wagenhals (1984).

We now turn to a description of the complete set of components required to specify a model of this type. In establishing the model, the specification is restricted to the typical resource exhaustion model based on mineral extraction. To explain the different forms of stock adjustment in a single model, it is preferable to regard mineral extraction and mineral processing as a single production process yielding refined metal, and to assume that the market exchange takes place only at the refined metal stage.

3.3. Reserves, Output and Capacity

The starting point for explaining resource exhaustion in any modelling context is the REM. The solution of the optimal reserve depletion problem is normally reached by applying the continuous maximum principle of optimal control theory, e.g., see Clark (1976). The result of this effort provides the basic structure of the equations required to specify the proposed model. In the present case, the solution of the original Hotelling model for example, as described by Clark, is not sufficient for our specification. An appropriate solution, too detailed to describe at this point, is provided in the Appendix. The nature of this solution depends on maximising an objective function which defines the basic characteristics of the resource market configuration of interest.

$$\text{Max} \int e^{-rt}[P\cdot(Q+S-\Delta I) + B_1(I,I/Q) - C_1Q - C_2(W) - C_3((V,S) - C_4(J)]dt \quad (1)$$

Definition of variables:

P = Price of refined metal

Q = Primary output based on resource extraction

S = Secondary output based on recycling of scrap

$\Delta I = \dot{I}$, change in refined metal inventories I

W = Exploration effort

V = Stock of recoverable metal contained in finished products in use

J = Investment in primary production capacity

B_1, C_1, C_2, C_3, C_4 = Benefits and costs of various activities

Net producer benefits are obtained as the difference between sales revenue and the additional benefit derived from inventory holdings on the one hand, and the costs of primary production, exploration, secondary production, and investment on the other. The solution to this optimisation problem as provided in the Appendix, indicates the levels of the different variables required to achieve market equilibrium.

We begin model specification with the definition of the reserve level R existing at any point in time as being equal to the initial reserve level R_o minus cumulative differences between resource extraction Q and reserve additions $\dot{X}$.

$$R_t = R_o + \sum_o^T(\dot{X}_t - Q_t) \tag{2}$$

The theoretical background for explaining reserve additions or discoveries can be found in several sources such as Peterson (1978), Pindyck (1978b), and CRA (1978). Mineral producers have a preferred reserves/production capacity ratio. The desired stock of reserves should be large enough to reduce uncertainty by permitting rational long term production planning. Hence, as their stocks of reserves are used up in the process of extraction, producers will invest in exploration so as to maintain a desired reserve level. In some cases, there may be an incentive to invest in exploration even when the stock of reserves exceeds the desired level. This will occur when the producer expects the sum total of exploration and production costs in the deposits he hopes to discover to be lower than the production costs alone in the known deposits that constitutes his current stock of reserves. Finally, there will be a tendency for the producer to expand his reserve stock (as well as his primary production capacity) when he expects high future price and profit levels.

New reserve additions can be postulated to depend on expected profitability Π^* which includes expected prices as well as expected costs of the exploration effort, the ratio K/R which implies that firms attempt to maintain a given relation between primary production capacity and reserves, and the level of cumulative primary output A. The latter is justified by the premise that additions to reserves will grow more expensive the more the resource has been used up. The difference between prices and costs is an important determinant of investment in reserve additions, particularly since it reflects the declining returns which may occur as exploratory effort extends to lower quality deposits. According to Devarajan and Fisher (1981), the efforts of rising extraction costs occur not only in relation to the stock remaining in the ground but also to the amount of cumulative primary production. Since the influence of the reserves is imposed in relation to the the capacity decision, we thus include cumulative production as an independent variable to reflect the fact that the best quality ores get depleted first.

Reserve additions are thus explained by:

$$\dot{X}_t = e(\Pi^*_{t-\theta}, K_t/R_t, A_t) \qquad (3)$$

where X_t is defined as cumulative reserve additions and A is defined by:

$$A_t = \sum_{o}^{T} Q_t \qquad (4)$$

where $\frac{\delta\dot{X}}{\delta\Pi^*}$ and $\frac{\delta\dot{X}}{\delta K/R} > 0$ and $\frac{\delta\dot{X}}{\delta A} < 0$.

The lag θ represents the period required between the time of exploration and the time of actually bringing a mine on stream (normally a lag of about 10–20 years for basic metal mining). Stochastic disturbance terms and additional exogenous influences have been omitted here and elsewhere to simplify presentation.

The functional relationship describing the primary output of mineral producers, as confirmed in studies such as that of Eswaren, Lewis and Heaps (1983), Gordon (1967), and Weinstein and Zeckhauser (1975), can be expressed as:

$$Q_t = q(P_t, K_t, R_t) \qquad (5)$$

where

$$\frac{\delta Q}{\delta P}, \frac{\delta Q}{\delta K}, \text{ and } \frac{\delta Q}{\delta R} > 0. \qquad (6)$$

The primary supply function (5) has been simplified by omitting labour and energy inputs, because the latter are of less consequence for the present analysis. While some researchers have included cumulative output in their supply function, the implied effect of decreasing returns can be accounted for with the included reserve variable. At the same time, we believe that any such cost effect of depletion is likely to be balanced by cost reducing technological progress. The consequences of including cumulative output in the analysis, nonetheless, are considered in the Appendix.

Primary production capacity adjustments can be explained on the basis of investment theories such as that of net present value or the desire of mineral producers to keep capacity in proportion to reserves. Let us begin with the definition of capital formation.

$$K_t = K_{t-1} + IN_t - dk_{t-1} \qquad (7)$$

where $IN_t = \Delta K_t$ is investment or change in new capacity and d is the rate of depreciation of existing capacity. Investment can then be explained by expanding the accelerator principle to include the producer goals of profitability and of maintaining capacity in proportion to reserves.

$$IN_t = n(Y_t, \Pi^*_{t-\phi}, K_t/R_t) \qquad (8)$$

where

$$\frac{\delta IN}{\delta Y}, \frac{\delta IN}{\delta P^*}, \frac{\delta K/R}{\delta IN} > 0.$$

Industrial output Y as the prime accelerator variable reflects aggregate industry behaviour; profitability occurs only at the end of the gestation period ϕ required to complete investments in primary production facilities (normally 5 – 7 years for basic metal mining); and investment is assumed to vary in relation to the K/R proportion.

3.4. Secondary Production

It has been common practice in constructing SCM for metal markets to consider secondary supply and demand, e.g., Mikesell (1979) and Labys and Pollak (1984). Attempts to include recycling in the REM have been made by Schulze (1974), Weinstein and Zeckhauser (1975), and Pindyck (1984b). More recently, Radetzki and Van Duyne (1983a) have demonstrated that declining economic growth increases the importance of secondary supply and reduces the rate of growth of primary production. Among the assumptions necessary to specify the recycling component are the following: (1) all metal products are used for a number of years after which they are scrapped; (2) a proportion of scrapped products recovered and supplied to the market varies with scrap prices; (3) the market for scrap adjusts continually so that scrap demand equals scrap supply; and (4) primary and secondary supplies at the finished metal stage are perfect substitutes.

The first two of these assumptions provide a basis for specifying a secondary supply relationship. Consider that all metal products available for recycling exist in the form of a flow or recoverable material M based on past demand D, as suggested by Radetzki and Van Duyne (1983a).

$$M_t = \theta D_{t-\alpha} \tag{9}$$

where θ is the recoverable share of scrap and α is the average age of durability of the metal products under consideration. If S represents the level of secondary supply in a given year, then it can be said to vary with the recoverable share M and with the price of scrap PS relative to that of the refined metal P.

$$S_t = s(M_t, PS_t/P_t) \tag{10}$$

Substitution for M yields secondary supply as a function of only past demand and scrap prices.

$$S_t = s(D_{t-\alpha}, PS_t) \tag{11}$$

3.5. Consumption

Mention has been made of the role of demand in explaining resource market adjustments. Particularly the influence of uncertainty on resource demand has been studied by Weinstein and Zeckhauser (1975). The specification of a relationship explaining resource demand follows from that of the SCM. Demand in this case is a derived demand and depends on the consumption of the resource in its final metal product use. That is, consumption D depends on the resource price P, industrial activity Y, other (cross) commodity prices P^C reflecting possible substitution from other commodities, and U represents stochastic demand influences.

$$D_t = d(P_t, Y_t, P_t^C, U_t) \tag{12}$$

where $\frac{\delta D}{\sigma P} < 0$, $\frac{\delta D}{\delta P^C} > 0$, and $\frac{\delta D}{\delta Y} > 0$. Since consumption is measured at the refined stage, we do not distinguish between primary or secondary sources of materials; the refined products from both are assumed to be perfect substitutes.

3.6. Inventories, Prices and Model Closure

The important step of introducing inventories into the present model requires that we consider the market disequilibrium approach in closing the model structure. This differs from the equilibrium approach where supply and demand are in equilibrium at all points in time. We justify the inclusion of inventories for the following reasons: (1) The presence of rising (or falling) marginal primary production costs give rise to corresponding price changes and hence demand adjustments. (2) Given typically inelastic short term supply adjustability, these demand fluctuations will induce the holding of inventories. With rising demand, there is a tendency to reduce them. (3) The cost of varying primary production capacity utilisation is high because of the deterioration of systems and equipment which would follow from capacity closure. There will, therefore, be a tendency for firms to continue to operate in excess of consumption during recession and below consumption during boom. This too, will result in inventory additions over the business cycle. (4) The introduction of uncertainty gives rise to transactions costs and inventories help to reduce these costs. (5) Finally, inventories can help to restore displacements from market equilibrium as is required for the adjustment process of the combined model. Eswaren, Lewis and Heaps (1983) have pointed to the importance of including inventories in the REM as a buffer to prevent discontinuous jumps in prices that would result from sudden reserve declines as reserve depletion becomes imminent.

Embodying inventory adjustments in disequilibrium also requires that we consider stock equilibrium as well as flow equilibrium conditions, the former facilitating the explanation of the latter, i.e., see Hicks (1979). Most importantly, the existence of inventories implies that one time period may be related to the next time period by the expectations which may occur between them or which serve to link them. Since actual consumption or supply will normally differ at the end of a period from what it was expected to be at the beginning, inventories must either be held or the underlying primary production capacity must be adjusted. The market clearing process as specified by disequilibrium theory is thus seen as a combination of long term adjustments involving changes in reserves and primary production capacity and short term adjustments involving changes in inventories.

These considerations have been included in the theoretical model formulation in the Appendix in the form of the benefit to be derived from inventory holding. The solution of that model would confirm the inclusion of a model component typical of the SCM which would explain the demand for and the supply of inventories. Inventory demand behaviour is normally explained by appropriate economic theories such as the accelerator, or more recently the 'supply of storage'. The significance of the latter theory for describing inventory adjustments has been stated earlier. Transactions, precautionary and speculative motives are now formalised in a theory which equates marginal inventory holding costs to marginal storage costs minus insurance costs against stockout (or stockout yield) and the insurance costs against over or under coverage (or coverage yield), i.e., see Van Duyne (1981). Consumers will thus increase or decrease their inventory levels to the point where their marginal inventory holding costs equal the rate at which they expect the refined metal price to appreciate. This nonlinear relationship implies that the aggregate demand for inventories is a function of expected price changes; the desired inventory size increases as the expected price difference widens.

$$I_t = i\left(\frac{P_t^* - P_t}{h}\right) \tag{13}$$

where the expected price P* refers to a particular horizon point in the near future, the horizon interval equalling h.

Since inventories in the SCM are often defined endogenously in the closing identity as given by (14), a normal procedure is to invert equation (13) and to express resource prices as a function of the ratio between inventories and demand I/D.

$$P_t = p(P_t^*, I_t/D_t) \tag{14}$$

One final equation is needed to close the model, and this is specified to represent the supply of inventories.

$$I_t = I_{t-1} + Q_t + S_t - D_t \tag{15}$$

Inventories are thus stated to exist because of the consistent differences occurring between the sum total of primary and secondary supply on the one hand, and consumption on the other.

3.7. The Complete Model and Its Verification

One possible specification for the complete model implied by the above equations would be as follows. It consists of equations (2), (3), (4), (5), (6), (7), (11), (12), (14) and (15), and these have been linearised to suggest a model form suitable for empirical analysis.

$$R_t = R_o + \sum_{o}^{T}(RA_t - Q_t)$$

$$\dot{X}_t = b_o + b_1 P^*_{t-\theta} + b_2(K_t/R_t) + b_3 A_t$$

$$Q_t = b_o + b_1 P_t + b_2 K_t + b_3 R_t$$

$$K_t = K_{t-1} + IN_t - dK_{t-1}$$

$$IN_t = b_o + b_1 Y_t + b_2 P^*_{t-\phi} + b_3(K_t/R_t)$$

$$S_t = b_o + b_1 D_{t-\theta} + b_2(PS_t)$$

$$D_t = b_o + b_1 P_t + b_2 Y_t + b_3 P^c_t + U_t$$

$$P_t = b_o + b_1 P^*_t + b_2(I_t/D_t)$$

$$I_t = I_{t-1} + Q_t + S_t - D_t$$

All three of the price expectations variables have different time structures and would require different expectations equivalents.

A major problem confronting the empirical verification of a model which integrates long, medium and short run adjustments is that of selecting an appropriate modelling methodology and related data for the exercise. It is obvious that the long time period needed to explain resource exhaustibility tends to be too long to permit the structural stability of the estimated parameters of typical econometric commodity models. We thus see future modelling possibilities to include experimental market simulations (e.g., Lonoff (1982) and Nordhaus (1985)), system dynamic model simulations (e.g., Barsotti (1978) and Suzuki and Shoji (1977)), and differential or spectral methods of time series analysis (e.g., Afrasiabi (1985) and Richard (1978)).

4. CONCLUSIONS

The model designed above integrates the key features from the Rational Extraction models of the Hotelling tradition, on the one hand, and from the Standard Commodity Models commonly employed in short run econometric analyses of base material markets, on the other. The major long run influences in the model are exhaustible resource depletion and the possibility of rising extraction costs which would provide an incentive for establishing new reserves. The major short run influences are those determining current market developments, such as business cycles and inventory behaviour. Other factors frequently neglected both in the REM and the SCM appoaches, such as production capacity and the role of scrap in supply, are also important components of the integrated model structure.

Because it is more comprehensive, the integrated model in our view provides a better and more realistic representation of exhaustible resource markets than either the REM or the SCM. The model provides a view of long run market adjustments by bringing supply and demand into equilibrium at what can be considered the long run equilibrium price. Investment in exploration and in mine capacity are matched with expected changes in demand to achieve this balance. Since capacity adjustments are of a long run nature and demand fluctuations are of an intermediate and short run nature, deviations between supply and demand must be dealt with by establishing linkages dynamically over time. We have thus employed a disequilibrium approach which involves coupling long run and short run flow equilibrium adjustments through the voluntary ownership of above–ground inventories. Investment in inventories whose value–added differs from under ground reserves are thus related to any short run imbalances between capacity and unanticipated changes in demand. The model thus emulates a mineral market in which capacity and stock adjustments represent a groping towards an elusive, yet attainable price equilibrium.

There would appear to be several opportunities for employing the model as an improved tool for the empirical analysis of such markets. This is especially true of the medium and long run, when considerations additional to those contained in the SCM play a significant role. A forthcoming task on our research agenda is to select a mineral market where appropriate empirical tests can be performed. An important issue in this regard concerns the choice of a modelling methodology which would be suitable for such a model verification. We have mentioned several possibilities in this regard in the previous section.

In the end we expect these empirical exercises to improve our understanding of the forces that cause dynamic adjustments and that shape developments in exhaustible resource markets. This in turn should provide a more reliable basis for market and policy analysis which must span periods where the capital stock of an industry including mining reserves and capacity is variable, e.g., somewhere between 20 and 50 years. Among issues suitable for model analysis government policy makers can investigate the impacts of exploration, tax policies, or investment in state mining companies. Decision makers in private industry can analyse the timing and the extent of capacity expansion, the determination of production volumes and inventories, possible material substitution, or indeed whether a particular mineral market is worth entering into in the long run.

In either case the model can advance our capabilities in the area of medium to long run planning. We would hope that it forces the analyst to be aware of all the factors that ensure that mineral supply equals demand through time. If nothing else, this should help reduce the instability that has been so characteristic of mineral market behaviour.

APPENDIX

OPTIMAL RESOURCE EXTRACTION MODEL SOLUTION[1]

The purpose of this Appendix is to present an extension of the optimal REM model solution to include several of the variables of present interest. This requires introducing several of the REM modifications made separately, but not simultaneously, by researchers such as Pindyck (1978b) and Peterson (1978) to include reserve formation; Pindyck (1981) and Weinstein and Zeckhauser (1975) to make extraction costs a function of output; and Pindyck (1979) and Schulze (1974) to introduce resource recycling.

The starting point is with the statement of the objective function given by (1) as an optimal control problem in which a Pareto optimum is obtained by maximising the present value over an unconstrained interval of net benefits (gross revenue and inventory holding benefits minus the various costs of importance).

$$\text{Max} \int_0^\infty e^{-rt}[P\cdot(Q+S-\Delta I) + B(I,I/Q) - C_1Q - C_2(W) - C_3(V,S) - C_4(J)]dt \tag{A.1}$$

Definition of variables:

P = Price of refined metal

Q = Primary output based on resource extraction

A = Accumulated extraction, $A(0) = A_0$

S = Secondary output based on recycling of scrap

ΔI = Change in finished metal inventories I

R = Reserves, $R(0) = R_0$

$\dot{X}$ = Reserve additions due to exploration

X = Accumulated reserves from reserve additions

V = Stock of recoverable metal contained in finished products in use

K = Primary production capacity

IN = Investment in primary production capacity

J = Capacity expansion effort

W = Exploration effort

The revenue and cost expressions contained in the objective function follow from these definitions:

$$P \cdot (Q + S - \Delta I) = \text{Gross revenue}$$

where primary output is defined to vary with capital, reserve levels and cumulated output

$$Q = f(Q, R, A)$$

$$C_1 \cdot Q = \text{Primary output operating costs}$$

$$C_2(W) = \text{Exploration costs}$$

$$C_3(V,S) = \text{Secondary output recovery costs}$$

$$B(I,IQ) = \text{Net benefit of above–ground inventory holding}$$

$$C_4(J) = \text{Investment costs}$$

The behaviour of costs is such that operating costs of primary output, $C_1 \cdot Q$ increase linearly with output Q(t), that exploration costs $C_2(W)$ increase with exploration effort W(t) where $\ddot{C}_2(W) \geq 0$, and that costs of secondary output $C_3(V,S)$ decrease with the stock of recoverable metal V(t) and increase with secondary output S(t) where $\ddot{C}_3(V) \geq 0$.

The formulation of the optimal control problem requires that the system be further defined in terms of its dynamic properties and constraints. The control variables of the system are given by W, Q, ΔI, S, and J; and the state variables are A, R, X, V, I, and K. Changes in reserves are defined as the difference between reserve additions $\dot{X}$ and the quantity extracted Q during a period.

$$\dot{R} = \dot{X} - Q \tag{A.2}$$

We simplify the explanation of reserve additions from (3) to make them a function of exploration effort W and cumulative reserve additions.

$$\dot{X} = g(W, X) \tag{A.3}$$

Changes in the stock of recoverable material are equal to the total stock less secondary output.

$$\dot{V} = (1-\alpha)(Q+S) - S \qquad (A.4)$$

where α represents the portion not recoverable. The remaining dynamic relations are identities of the form:

$$\dot{K} = IN - \delta K_{-1} \qquad (A.5)$$

where investment varies with the cost of capital

$$IN = h(J) \qquad (A.6)$$

$$\dot{A} = Q \qquad (A.7)$$

and where δ is the rate of depreciation of existing capacity. The following non–zero conditions must also hold.

$$P, Q, A, S, I, R, V, K, IN, J, W, \geq 0$$

Commodity market equilibrium conditions can be applied to this extractive model by defining stocks in terms of changes in demand and supply.

$$\Delta I = Q + S - D \qquad (A.8)$$

Primary output Q and secondary output S are assumed to be perfect substitutes. Hence, the total demand for the product facing the resource industry is the combined demand for primary and secondary output, which varies with prices P and time t.

$$D = d(P,t) \qquad (A.9)$$

This relation can also be considered in its inverted form yielding prices.

$$P = d^{-1}(D,t) \qquad (A.10)$$

The model solution depends on the optimisation of the control problem expressed in the form of a Hamiltonian.

$$\begin{aligned} H = {} & [P\cdot(Q - \Delta I + S) + B(I,I/Q) - C_1 Q - C_2(W) \qquad (A.11) \\ & - C_3(V,S) - C_4(J)]e^{-rt} + \lambda_A Q + \lambda_R[g(W,X) - Q] \\ & + \lambda_x g(W,X) + \lambda_V[(1-\alpha)(Q+S) - S] + \lambda_I \Delta I + \lambda_K(IN-\delta K_{-1}) \\ & + \mu[f(K,A,R) - Q] \end{aligned}$$

Differentiation of H with respect to the state variables and rearranging gives the following set of differential equations governing the co–state variables. These are termed the adjoining equations, and the costate variables λ and μ are multipliers' on the constraints and have the usual interpretation of shadow prices.

$$\dot{\lambda}_A = r\lambda_A - \frac{\partial H}{\partial A} = r\lambda_A - \mu\frac{\partial f}{\partial A} \qquad (A.12)$$

$$\dot{\lambda}_R = r\lambda_R - \frac{\partial H}{\partial R} = r\lambda_R - \mu\frac{\partial f}{\partial R} \qquad (A.13)$$

$$\lambda_X = r\lambda_X - \frac{\partial H}{\partial X} = r\lambda_X - (\lambda_R + \lambda_X)\frac{\partial g}{\partial x} \tag{A.14}$$

$$\lambda_V = r\lambda_V - \frac{\partial H}{\partial V} = r\lambda_V - \frac{\partial C_3}{\partial V} \tag{A.15}$$

$$\lambda_I = r\lambda_I - \frac{\partial H}{\partial I} = r\lambda_I - \frac{\partial B}{\partial I} - \frac{\partial B}{\partial (I/Q)} \cdot \frac{1}{Q} \tag{A.16}$$

$$\lambda_K = r\lambda_K - \frac{\partial H}{\partial K} = r\lambda_K + \lambda_K \delta - \mu \frac{\partial f}{\partial K} \tag{A.17}$$

The Hamiltonian can also be differentiated directly with respect to the control variables to yield the first order conditions that define the optimal solution of the model in equilibrium.

$$\frac{\partial H}{\partial Q} = P + \frac{\partial B}{\partial (I/Q)} \frac{\Delta I}{Q^2} - C_1 + \lambda_A - \lambda_R + \lambda_V(1-\alpha) - \mu = 0 \tag{A.18}$$

$$\frac{\partial H}{\partial \Delta I} = -P + \lambda_I = 0 \tag{A.19}$$

$$\frac{\partial H}{\partial s} = P - \frac{\partial C_3}{\partial s} - \lambda_V \alpha = 0 \tag{A.20}$$

$$\frac{\partial H}{\partial W} = C \frac{\partial C_2}{\partial W} + (\lambda_R + \lambda_X) \frac{\partial f}{\partial W} = 0 \tag{A.21}$$

$$\frac{\partial H}{\partial J} = -\frac{\partial C_4}{\partial J} + \lambda_K \leq 0 \tag{A.22}$$

$$\mu \geq 0 \tag{A.23}$$

$$\mu\,[f(K, A, R) - Q] \tag{A.24}$$

NOTES

* Institute for International Economic Studies, University of Stockholm, and Department of Mineral and Energy Resource Econonomics, West Virginia University, respectively. This is a working paper subject to revision. Draft No. 5, January 1985.

1) This Appendix has been prepared with the assistance of Michael Hoel, Institute of Economics, Univesity of Oslo; and Karl Irwin and John Pierce, Department of Mathematics, West Virginia University.

REFERENCES

Adelman, M.A. (1970), "Economics of Exploration for Petroleum and other Minerals', *Geoexploration* 8, pp. 131–50.

Afrasiabi, M.A. (1985), 'Dynamics of Long Term Adjustments in Mineral Markets', Ph.D. Dissertation, West Virginia University.

Burrows, J.C. (1971), *Tungsten: An Industry Analysis*, Heath Lexington Books, Lexington, MA.

Burrows, J.C. and M.J. Lonoff (1977), 'Models of Metal Markets', Ford Foundation Conference on Stabilizing World Commodity Markets, Airlie, VA.

Charles River Associates (1978), 'The Economics and Geology of Mineral Supply: An Integrated Framework for Long Run Policy Analysis', CRA Report No. 327, Charles River Associates, Boston, MA.

Clark, C.W. (1976), *Mathematical Bioeconomics: The Optimal Management of Renewable Resources*, John Wiley & Sons, New York.

Cox, J.C. and A.W. Wright (1976), 'The Determinants of Investment in Petroleum Reserves and their Implications for Public Policy', *American Economic Review*, 66, pp. 153–67.

Cremer, J. (1979), 'On Hotelling's Formula and the Use of Permanent Equipment in the Extraction of Natural Resources', *International Economic Review*, 20, pp. 317–24.

Cremer, J. and M. Weitzman (1976), 'OPEC and the Monopoly Price of World Oil', *European Economic Review*, 8, pp. 155–64.

Dasgupta, P. and G. Heal (1979), *Economic Theory and Exhaustible Resources*, Cambridge University Press, Cambridge, MA.

Dasgupta, P. and G. Heal (1974). 'The Optimal Depletion of Exhaustible Resources', *The Review of Economic Studies*, Symposium, pp. 3–28.

Devarajan, S. and A.C. Fisher (1981), 'Hotelling's Economics of Exhaustible Resources: Fifty Years Later', *Journal of Economic Literature*, 19, pp. 65–73.

Eswaren, M., T.R. Lewis and T. Heaps (1983), 'On the Nonexistence of Market Equilibria in Exhaustible Resource Markets with Decreasing Costs, *Journal of Political Economy*, 91, pp. 154–67.

Feige, E. and J. Gewecke (1979), 'Testing the Empirical Implications of Hotelling's Principle', Mimeograph, University of Wisconsin, Madison.

Fisher, A.C. (1979), 'Measures of Natural Resource Scarcity', in V.K. Smith (ed.), *Scarcity and Growth Reconsidered*, John Hopkins University Press, Baltimore, MD.

Frank, J. and M. Babunovic (1984), 'An Investment Model of Natural Resource Markets', *Economica*, 51, pp. 83–95.

Gilbert, R.J. (1979), 'Optimal Depletion of an Uncertain Stock', *Review of Economics Studies*, 46, pp. 47–57.

Gilbert, R.J. (1978), 'Dominant Firm Pricing Policy in a Market for an Exhaustible Resource', *Bell Journal of Economics*, 9, pp. 385–95.

Gordon, R.L. (1967), 'A Reinterpretation of the Pure Theory of Exhaustion', *Journal of Political Economy*, 75, pp. 274–86.

Harrod, R.F. (1964), *Towards a Dynamic Economics*, MacMillan, London.

Heal, G. (1976), 'The Relationship Between Price and Extraction Cost for a Resource with a Backstop Technology', *Bell Journal of Economics*, 7, pp. 371–78.

Heal, G. and M. Burrow (1980), 'The Relationship Between Interest Rates and Metal Price Movements', *Review of Economic Studies*, 47, pp. 161–81.

Heal, G. and M. Burrow (1981), 'Empirical Investigation of the Long Term Movement of Resource Prices', *Economic Letters*, 7, pp. 95–103.

Hicks, J. (1979), *Causality in Economics*, Basic Books, Inc., New York.

Hoel, M. (1984), 'Extraction of a Resource with a Substitute for Some of its Uses', *Canadian Journal of Economics*, 17, pp. 593–602.

Hoel, M. (1978), 'Resource Extraction, Uncertainty, and Learning', *Bell Journal of Economics*, 9, pp. 642–45.

Hotelling, H. (1931), 'The Economics of Exhaustible Resources', *Journal of Political Economy*, 39, pp. 137–75.

Hynilicza, E. and R.S. Pindyck (1976), 'Pricing Policies for a Two–Part Exhaustible Resource Cartel', *European Economic Review*, 8, pp. 139–47.

Kemp, M.C. (1976), 'How to Eat a Cake of Unknown Size', in M. Kemp (ed.), *Three Topics in the Theory of International Trade*, North–Holland Publishing Company, Amsterdam.

Keynes, J.M. (1936), *The General Theory of Employment, Interest and Money*, MacMillan, London.

Labys, W.C. (1973), *Dynamic Commodity Models: Specification, Estimation and Simulation*, Heath Lexington Books, Lexington, MA.

Labys, W.C. (1980a), 'A Model of Disequilibrium Adjustments in the Copper Market', *Materials and Society*, 4, pp. 153–64.

Labys, W.C. (1980b), 'Dynamics of Market Adjustment and Stabilization in the Minerals Industry', Report submitted to the National Science Foundation under Grant No. DAT 78–08810, Department of Mineral and Energy Resource Economics, West Virgina University, Morgantown, WV.

Labys, W.C. (1982), 'A Critical Review of International Energy Modeling Methodologies', MIT Energy Laboratry Working Paper No. MIT–EL 82–034WP, Massachusetts Institute of Technology, Cambridge, MA.

Labys, W.C., F. Church and J. Clark (1984), 'Mineral Modeling', in W. Vogeley (ed.), *Economics of the Mineral Industries*, AIME, New York.

Labys, W.C. and P. Pollack (1984), *Commodity Models for Forecasting and Policy Analysis*, Croom–Helm, London.

Lewis, T.R. and R. Schmalensee (1979), 'Cartel and Oligopoloy Pricing of Non–Renewable Natural Resources', in P.T. Liu (ed.), *Dynamic Optimization and Mathematical Economics*, Plenum Press, New York.

Levhari, D. and R.S. Pindyck (1979), 'The Pricing of Durable Exhaustible Resources', MIT Energy Laboratory Working Paper No. MIT–EL 79–053WP, Massachusetts Institute of Technology. Cambridge, MA.

Lonoff, M. (1982), 'Economic Aspects of the Copper Market', Ph.D. Dissertation, Massachusetts Institute of Technology, Cambridge, MA.

Lourcy, G.C. (1978), 'The Optimum Exploitation of an Unknown Reserve', *Review of Economic Studies*, 45, pp.621–36.

Mackinnon,J. and N. Olewiler (1980), 'Disequilibrium Estimation of the Demand for Copper', *Bell Journal of Economics and Management*, 11, pp. 197–211.

Mikesell, R.F. (1979), *The World Copper Industry*, John Hopkins University Press, Baltimore, MD.

Nordhaus, W.D. (1985), 'Long Run Dynamics of the Copper Industry', Working Paper, Department of Economics, Yale University, New Haven, CT.

Peterson, F.M. (1978), 'A Model of Mining and Exploring for Natural Resources', *Journal of Environmental Economics and Management*, 5, pp. 236–51.

Peterson, F.M. and A.C. Fisher (1977), 'The Exploitation of Natural Resources: A Survey', *Economic Journal*, 87, pp. 681–721.

Pindyck, R.S. (1981), 'The Optimal Production of an Exhaustible Resource When Price is Exogenous and Stochastic', *Scandinavian Journal of Economics*, 10, pp. 277–87.

Pindyck, R.S. (1979), 'Models of Resource Markets and the Explanation of Resource Price Behaviour', MIT Working Paper No. MIT–EL 79–062WP, Massachusetts Institute of Technology, Cambridge, MA.

Pindyck, R.S. (1979). 'Uncertainty and Exhaustible Resource Markets', MIT Energy Laboratory Working Paper No. MIT–EL 79–021WP, Massachusetts Institute of Technology, Cambridge, MA.

Pindyck, R.S. (1978a), 'Gains to Producers from the Cartelization of Exhaustible Resources', *Review of Economics and Statistics*, 60, pp. 238–51.

Pindyck, R.S. (1978b), 'The Optimal Exploration and Production of Non–Renewable Resources', *Journal of Political Economy*, 86, pp. 841–62.

Radetzki, M. (1975), 'Metal Mining Resource Exhaustion and the Threat to Material Progress: The Case of Copper', *World Development*, 3, pp. 123–36.

Radetzki, M. and C. Van Duyne (1983a), 'The Demand for Scrap and Primary Metal Ores after a Decline in Secular Growth', Seminar Paper No. 246, Institute for International Economic Studies, Stockholm, Sweden.

Radetzki, M. and C. Van Duyne (1983b), 'The Response of Mining Investment to a Decline in Economic Growth: The Case of Copper in the 1970s', Research Memo No. 86, Williams College, Williams, MA.

Richard, D. (1978), 'A Dynamic Model of the World Copper Industry', *IMF Staff Papers*, 25, pp. 779–833.

Salant, S.N. (1976), 'Exhaustible Resources and Industrial Structure: A Nash–Cournot Approach to the World Oil Market', *Journal of Political Economy*, 84, pp. 1079–94.

Salant, S.N., F. Miercort, A. Sanghvi and M. Wagner (1981), *Imperfect Competition in the World Energy Market*, Heath Lexington Books, Lexington, MA.

Schulze, W.D. (1974), 'The Optimal Use of Non–Renewable Resources: The Theory of Extraction', *Journal of Environmental Economics and Management*, 1, pp. 53–74.

Smith, V.K. (1981), 'The Empirical Relevance of Hotelling's Model for Natural Resources', *Resources and Energy*, 3, pp. 105–17.

Solow, R.M. (1974), 'The Economics of Resources or the Resources of Economics', *American Economic Review*, 64, pp. 1–14.

Solow, R.M. and F.Y. Wan (1976), 'Extraction Costs in the Theory of Exhaustible Resources', *Bell Journal of Economics*, 7, pp. 359–70.

Stiglitz, F.E. (1976), 'Monopoly and the Rate of Extraction of Exhaustible Resources', *American Economic Review*, 66, pp. 655–61.

Suzuki, Y. and K. Shoji (1977), 'Global Metallic Resources Model', in G. Bruckman (ed.), *Input–Output Approaches in Global Modeling*, Pergamom Press, New York.

Tilton, J. (1981), 'Market Instability in the Metal Industries', *Materials and Society*, 5. pp. 243–45.

Van Duyne, C. (1981), 'Price Determination in Markets for Storable Commodities', Seminar Paper No. 176, Institute for International Economic Studies, Stockholm.

Wagenhals, G. (1984), *The World Copper Market*, Lecture Notes in Economics and Mathematical Systems No. 233, Springer Verlag, Berlin.

Weinstein, M.C. and R.J. Zeckhauser (1975), 'The Optimal Consumption of Depletable Natural Resources', *Quarterly Journal of Economics*, 89, pp. 371–82.

CHAPTER 2

OPTIMAL AND COMPETITIVE STORAGE RULES: THE GUSTAFSON PROBLEM REVISITED

Christopher L. Gilbert*

1. INTRODUCTION

A country benefits from an abnormally good harvest of a crop. What proportion of this crop should be carried forward to be consumed in future years? If the storage decision were left to the market, would the optimal carryover result? And is it possible to provide an explicit representation of the competitive storage function?

These questions were analyzed in two pioneering contributions by Gustafson (1958a, 1958b). He showed that, under specified conditions, the private sector will make the optimal stockpiling decision. He also provided a characterization of the storage rule. It turns out to be difficult to provide a closed form representation of the storage function, essentially because of nonlinearities forced by the non–negativity constraint on stocks. Gustafson showed that under certainty equivalence the storage fuction is piecewise linear, and further demonstrated that, in the absence of certainty equivalence, a continuous function is obtained with the same general shape, but implying a higher level of storage at any level of supply.

There have only been two major published contributions to this literature subsequent to 1958. Newbery and Stiglitz (1981, ch. 30; 1982) discuss approximation techniques for deriving the optimal stock rule; and Wright and Williams (1982) use numerical methods to characterize the stock function in a wide variety of stuations. In particular, Wright and Williams find that lagged supply response substantially increases the optimal and competitive marginal propensity to stock. In this paper we develop the approximation methods discussed by Newbery and Stiglitz in an attempt to provide a theoretical underpinning of the Wright and William results. We argue that analysis of this problem is facilitated by adopting functional supply and demand specifications which eliminate all non–essential nonlinearities, and this indicates use of semilogarith-

O. Guvenen (ed.), International Commodity Market Models and Policy Analysis, 27–52.

mic functions. The certainty equivalence stock function then assumes a very simple form, derived prior to Gustafson's work by Samuelson (1957), who drew upon an earlier contribution of Williams (1936).

The plan of this paper is as follows: in section 2 we consider competitive stockholding, and in section 3 we demonstrate its optimality properties; section 4 derives the certainty equivalence approximation to the storage function; in section 5 we generalize this approximation to allow lagged supply and demand responses; and in section 6 we attempt to provide bounds to the storage function once certainty equivalence has been dropped; section 7 compares the storage functions derived by these methods to those given by Wright and Williams; and section 8 contains brief conclusions.

2. CHARACTERIZATION OF THE COMPETITIVE STORAGE RULE

Stocks may be held by any market agent, and typically producers and consumers will both have reasons for wishing to hold stock. Analogously with the macroeconomic classification of money demand into transactions, precautionary and speculative components, we may think of transactions (working stocks), precautionary and speculative stock demands. The competitive storage rule is concerned only with speculative stockholdings, which arbitrage current and expected future prices – transactions and precautionary stocks, which will not depend on expected future prices, may be aggregated into consumption demand.[2]

Consider the decision to hold stock for a single period. The agent purchases at the current spot price p_t and expects to sell at the price $p^e_{t+1|t}$ in period t+1. In the case of soft commodities we need to take into account the rate of deterioration δ of stock over the period, and for all commodities there will be a warehousing (storage) cost of w_t. The expected gain from holding one unit of the stock is therefore $(1-\delta)p^e_{t+1|t}-p_t-w_t$, and if a risk neutral agent is to be willing to hold this unit of stock this gain must exceed or be equal to the return R_t he would return from investing the same amount of money elsewhere. Thus

$$s_t > 0 \Rightarrow (1-\delta)p^e_{t+1|t}-p_t - w_t \geqq R_t p_t \qquad (1)$$

(1) gives the condition for a risk neutral agent being willing to hold stock, but an inequality in (1) is not compatible with supply and demand equilibrium. So long as the expected return from stockholding exceeds the return obtainable elsewhere, the price p_t will be bid up until equality obtains. Thus two outcomes are possible. The first is positive stockholding with equality in returns, but a situation in which the expected return form holding stock falls short of R_t is also consistent with equilibrium so long as no

stock is carried. We may write this joint condition as

$$(1-\delta)p^e_{t+1|t} - p_t - w_t \leqq R_t p_t : s_t \geqq 0 \tag{2}$$

This complementary slackness condition asserts both inequalities together with the assertion that one or other (or both) must hold as an equality. For simplicity, suppose that storage costs are proportional to value

$$w_t = wp_t$$

which allows us to approximate (2) as

$$\ln p^e_{t+1|t} - \ln p_t \leqq r_t : s_t \geqq 0 \tag{3}$$

where

$$r_t = R_t + \delta + w$$

may be interpreted as the total carrying cost of the commodity from period t to period t+1.[2]

This relationship implicitly defines the competitive stockholding rule. Writing current demand for stock as s_t, market clearing implies

$$s_t = (1-\delta)s_{t-1} + y_t - x_t \tag{4}$$

where y_t is production and x_t consumption in period t. Either or both of production and consumption must be dependent on price, implying $s_t = s(p_t)$. Similarly in period t+1, we obtain $E_t s_{t+1} = E_t s(p_{t+1})$. Substitution into (3) gives s_t as a function of $E_t s_{t+1}$, which itself must be a function of $E_t s_{t+2}$, and so forth. Elimination of the future expected stocks in principle allows current stock demand to be expressed in terms of expected future levels of production and consumption. However, this solution procedure is complicated by the non–negativity requirement that $s_t \geqq 0$ in every period, which results in loss of linearity. We discuss characterization of the solution in section 4.

Equation (3) has been derived under the assumption of risk neutrality, but it will hold as a limiting proposition under risk aversion. The existence of an excess rate of return will lead to a demand by the investor for a quantity of stock, but not for an unlimited demand. This may be seen within a standard model. Write the excess return from holding a unit of stock for one period and discounted to the purchase date as $e_{t+1} = \frac{p_{t+1}}{(1+r_t)} - p_t$. Consider an individual maximizing his expected utility Eu(A+se), where s is his stock purchase and A is his initial wealth. We consider a pure speculator who neither derives income from production of the commodity nor utility from its consumption, so that both his initial wealth A_t and his marginal utility $u'(A_t)$ at that wealth level may be regarded as independent of the sequence of commodity prices. The first order condition is

$$E[u'(A_t+s_t e_{t+1}).e_{t+1}] = 0 \tag{5}$$

Substituting for e_{t+1}, we obtain

$$(1+r)p_t Eu'(A_t+s_t e_{t+1}) = E[u'(A_t+s_t e_{t+1}).p_{t+1}] \tag{6}$$

In the case of risk neutrality, marginal utility u′ is constant, and (5) reduces to (3). For a risk averse speculator, on the other hand, marginal utility will decline as the return e_{t+1} rises. Taking a first order expansion

$$u'(A_t+s_t e_{t+1}) \simeq u'(A_t) + u''(A_t)s_t e_{t+1} = u'(A_t)\left[1 - \frac{\rho s_t}{A_t}\right]$$

where ρ is the standard coefficient of relative risk aversion $\frac{Wu''}{u'}$. Writing $Ee_{t+1}=\bar{e}$ and $Var(e_{t+1})=\sigma_e^2$, this gives

$$\frac{s_t}{A_t} = \frac{\bar{e}}{\rho(\bar{e}^2+\sigma_e^2)} \tag{7}$$

The speculator's demand for stock is therefore positively related to the expected excess return $\bar{e}$, with the relationship tending to linearity as $\bar{e}$ tends to zero. Write this linear relationship as

$$\frac{s_t}{A_t} = \frac{\bar{e}}{\rho(\bar{e}^2+\sigma_e^2)}$$

Now suppose that there are n speculators with, for simplicity, identical wealth A_t. Competition by these speculators will reduce the expected excess return $\bar{e}$, and so we may write $\bar{e}=\epsilon(n)$ where $\epsilon(.)$ satisfies $\epsilon'<0$. Total demand for stock is therefore $\alpha n\epsilon(n)A_t$. This is bounded above at some level $\bar{s}$ by total availability of the commodity, and below at zero (since negative stock levels are physically impossible). Letting n tend to infinity, the quantity $n\epsilon(n)$ must remain within the range $[0,\bar{s}]$, and this implies $lim_{n\to\infty}\epsilon(n)=0$. Thus (3) will hold as a limiting proposition as the number of speculators becomes very large, and we may consider a market composed of a large number of risk averse speculators as being near risk neutral.

An alternative, and in some cases more attractive, justification of the risk neutrality assumption is to note that for commodities in which it is possible to trade on unbiased forward or futures markets, stockholding becomes a near riskless activity. This is because the stockholder can sell his stock forward, if necessary rolling over his hedge at (or towards) the contract maturity date. To the extent that the basis (the spot–forward differential) is predictable, this eliminates the risk in stockholding; and, if the market is unbiased, it does not add to the costs of stockholding. Futures trading effectively separates the stockholding and speculative functions, and allows us to proceed as if stockholders were risk neutral.

3. EQUIVALENCE OF OPTIMAL AND COMPETITIVE STORAGE RULES

The competitive storage rule (3) may equally well be derived as the optimal storage rule in a planned environment. This is straightforward within a market economy in which the planning authority wishes to maximize the sum of consumers' surplus, producers' surplus and intervention profits. Let the inverse demand function be $p=f(x)$, and the inverse supply function be $p=g(y)$. Then consumers' surplus is

$$CS(x) = \int_0^x (f(z) - f(x))dz \tag{8}$$

and producers' surplus

$$PS(y) = \int_0^y (g(y) - g(z))dz \tag{9}$$

Let net buffer stock purchases in period t be b_t. The authority wishes to maximize

$$\sum_{t=0}^{T} \psi_t \left\{ CS(x_t) + PS(y_t) - b_t p_t \right\} \tag{10}$$

where ψ_t is a discount factor defined by

$$\psi_t = \frac{\psi_{t-1}}{1+R_t} \tag{11}$$

and $\psi_0=1$. Maximization is subject to

$$b_t = y_t - x_t = s_t - (1-\delta-w)s_{t-1} \tag{12}$$

where as previously δ is the rate of deterioration (shrinkage) of stock, and w is the warehousing cost (where measured a proportion of the stock held). We also require

$$s_t \geqq 0 \tag{13}$$

Noting that

$$\frac{dCS(x)}{dx} = -x\frac{\partial p}{\partial x} = -\frac{\partial p}{\partial s} \tag{14}$$

and

$$\frac{dPS(y)}{dy} = y\frac{\partial p}{\partial y} = y\frac{\partial p}{\partial s} \tag{15}$$

and linearizing $\frac{1+R_t}{1-\delta-w} = 1+r_t$ as previously, we may write the first order condition for this problem as

$$(1+r_t)(p_t - \Delta s_t \frac{\partial p}{\partial s}) \geqq E_t(p_{t+1} - \Delta s_{t+1} \frac{\partial p}{\partial s}) : s_t \geqq 0 \tag{16}$$

This differs from (3) only by the presence of the terms $\frac{\partial p}{\partial s}$, which represent the extent to which the buffer stock intervention moves the price against itself. Provided we take a sufficiently short time period, the terms Δs_t and Δs_{t+1} will become negligibly small, and (16) reduces to (3).

An alternative approach is to consider a planning authority which is concerned only with quantities. Suppose the authority's welfare function is simply $W(x_t)$ ($W'>0$, $W''<0$), where x_t is consumption, as previously. The authority wishes to maximize

$$\sum_{t=1}^{T} \psi_t W(x_t) \tag{17}$$

subject to the (12) and (13). The first order condition for this new problem is

$$s_t \geqq 0 \Rightarrow (1-\delta-w)E_t W'(x_{t+1}) = (1+R_t)W'(x_t) \tag{18}$$

But if we now define $p_t=W'(x_t)$, the shadow price of consumption in period t, then taking logs and again linearizing $(1-\delta-w)^{-1}(1+R_t)$ we obtain (3). Thus with prices reinterpreted as shadow prices, the same stockpiling rule holds.

This equivalence of the competitive and optimal stockpiling rules was first noted by Gustafson (1958a). It allows us to interpret the explicit stockholding function we shall derive in section 4 either as the foundation for econometric study of commodity stockholding relationship in free market economies, or as the planning rule for stockholding in planned economies.

4. CERTAINTY EQUIVALENCE APPROXIMATION OF THE STORAGE FUNCTION

The competitive storage function is implicitly defined by (3), and we have seen that same relationship, suitably reinterpreted, can also represent the optimal storage function in a planned environment. The non–negativity constraint on the stock, which must hold in the current and in every future period, makes it impossible to obtain an exact closed form representation for the current stock except in the most simple cases. Gustafson (1958a) used dynamic programming methods to solve for the carryover on the assumption of no supply response, and demonstrated that these exact solutions may be well approximated by a piecewise linear function through application of certainty equivalence to the size of future harvests. The nonlinearity of the storage function makes certainty equivalence inappropriate to this problem, and the Gustafson approach therefore amounts to supposing that agents ignore the randomness in future harvests in dealing with the consequences of the randomness of the current harvest. Gustafson's certainty equivalence approximation has been discussed by Newbery and Stiglitz (1979, ch. 30, and 1982).

The purpose of this section is to derive the Gustafson linear approximation to the competitive storage rule in a way which clearly exhibits its simple structure. In addition, we are able to provide a continuous approximation to the piecewise linear function. The essential nonlinearity of the storage function arises from the non–negativity constraint on the carryover. Representation of the storage rule is simplified if this is the only source of nonlinearity. Since we are aiming only to approximate the storage function, we may choose to take our supply and demand functions to be linear in any reasonable metric. Here, as elsewhere in commodity market analysis,[3] the semilogarithmic specification is most convenient, since this simultaneously accommodates the levels linearity of the stock identity (12), and the loglinearity of the intertemporal price path (3). It is this functional choice allows simple representation of the storage function.

We specify consumption $x_t = x(p_t, q_t, v_t)$, where q_t is a vector of exogenous variables and v_t is a white noise disturbance, and adopt the semilogarithmic specification

$$x(p_t, q_t, v_t) = \bar{x}\left[1 - e(ln p_t - ln\bar{p}) - a'(q_t - \bar{q}) + v_t\right] \tag{19}$$

where e is the demand elasticity $\frac{-px_p}{x}$ evaluated at $\bar{x}$, and $\bar{p}$ is the geometric mean of the price distribution, defined by $ln\bar{p} = E ln p_t$. Similarly, we specify production y_t as

$$y(p_t, q_t, w_t) = \bar{y}\left[1 + \epsilon(ln p_t - ln\bar{p}) + \alpha'(q_t - \bar{q}) + w_t\right] \tag{20}$$

where ϵ is the supply elasticity $\frac{py_p}{y}$ evaluated at $\bar{y}$. Market clearing ensures that $\bar{x} = \bar{y}$. Without loss of generality, we take $\bar{q} = 0$, and normalize $\bar{y} = 1$ (so that all quantities are measured as multiples or proportions of the 'normal harvest'). This allows us to write aggregate excess supply z_t as

$$z_t = y_t - x_t = \bar{x}(e+\epsilon)(ln p_t - ln\bar{p}) + (a+\alpha)'q_t + u_t \tag{21}$$

where $u_t = v_t - w_t$. Substitution of (21) into the instantaneous market clearing relationship (12) gives

$$ln p_t - ln\bar{p} = \frac{1}{e+\epsilon}\left[s_t - s_{t-1} - (a+\alpha)'q_t - u_t\right] \tag{22}$$

From the normality assumption on v and w, it follows that $u_t \sim N(o, \sigma_u^2)$ where

$$\sigma_u^2 = \sigma_v^2 - 2\sigma_{vw} + \sigma_w^2 \tag{23}$$

and this implies that, in the absence of any private stockholding, the commodity price p is lognormally distributed as

$$ln p_t - ln\bar{p} \sim N\left[\frac{(a+\alpha)'q_t}{e+\epsilon}, \frac{\sigma_u^2}{(e+\epsilon)^2}\right] \tag{24}$$

The unconditional price variance σ_p^2 is given by

$$\sigma_p^2 = \frac{\sigma_u^2 + (a+\alpha)'\Psi(a+\alpha)}{(e+\epsilon)^2} \tag{25}$$

where $\Psi = E(q_t q_t')$. If $q^e_{t+1|t}=0$, it follows from the properties of the lognormal distribution that

$$p^e_{t+1|t} = \bar{p}(1+\tfrac{1}{2}\sigma_p^2) \tag{26}$$

Conditional upon a planned carryover s_t, the current price p_t is given by (22). Similarly, if agents expect to hold the stock $s^e_{t+1|t}$

$$E_t(\ln p_{t+1}) - \ln\bar{p} = \left[\frac{1}{e+\epsilon}\, s^e_{t+1|t} - s_t - (a+\alpha)' q^e_{t+1|t}\right] \tag{27}$$

To obtain the certainty equivalence approximation to the storage function, we replace uncertain variables by their certainty equivalents (denoted by superscript 'c'). This gives

$$\ln p^c_{t+1|t} - \ln\bar{p} = \frac{1}{e+\epsilon}\left[s^c_{t+1|t} - s_t - (a+\alpha)' q^c_{t+1|t}\right] \tag{28}$$

Subtracting (22) from (28), we obtain the expected return on the carryover as

$$\ln p^c_{t+1|t} - \ln p_t = \frac{1}{e+\epsilon}\left[s^c_{t+1|t} - 2s_t + s_{t-1} + \left[\zeta_t - \zeta^c_{t+1|t}\right]\right] \tag{29}$$

where

$$\zeta_t = (a+\alpha)' q_t + u_t$$

If s_t is to be positive, this rate of return must solve (3) as an equality. Thus

$$\frac{1}{e+\epsilon}\left[s^c_{t+1|t} - 2s_t + s_{t-1} + \left[\zeta_t - \zeta^c_{t+1|t}\right]\right] \leqq r_t : s_t \geqq 0 \tag{30}$$

Solving for s_t conditional upon the expected carryover $s^c_{t+1|t}$

$$s_t = \tfrac{1}{2}\left[s^c_{t+1|t} + s_{t-1} + \left[\zeta_t - \zeta^c_{t+1|t}\right] - (e+\epsilon) r_t\right]^+ \tag{31}$$

where

$$[x]^+ = \max(x,0).$$

We may obtain a lower bound for the current period carryover by supposing that agents expect with certainty zero carryover at the end of the next period ($s^c_{t+1|t}=0$):

$$s_t \geqq \tfrac{1}{2}\left[s_{t-1} + \left[\zeta_t - \zeta^c_{t+1|t}\right] - (e+\epsilon) r_t\right]^+ \tag{32}$$

Taking (32) as an equality defines a myopic storage rule, in which agents carry stock forward in the current period, but never anticipate doing so in subsequent periods. In the simple case in which $q^c_{t+1|t}=0$ implying $\zeta^c_{t+1|t}=0$, this gives

$$s_t = \tfrac{1}{2}\left[Z_t - Z_t^*\right]^+ \tag{33}$$

where

$$Z_t = s_{t-1} + \zeta_t = s_{t-1} + (a+\alpha)'q_t + u_t$$

and $\quad Z_t^* = (e+\epsilon)r_t$

Z_t may be interpreted as the price–independent component of current excess supply. (33) states that precisely one half of the total available supply in excess of the quantity Z_t^* will be stocked, the remainder being consumed in the current period. The storage propensity of one half arises because, under the myopic rule, with excess supply greater than this critical value, agents plan to consume this quantity over precisely two years, and, as the consequence of our linearity assumptions, this supply will be spread equally over the two years. This is exactly the conclusion reached in Samuelson (1957):

> However, if today's Harvest is *super*abundant, we may have to modify our conclusion about the independence of crop–years. Suppose today's crop were big enough to depress this year's price so as to make its Harvest Eve price *lower* than next year's post–Harvest price would have been? Then obviously, it would become advisable to carry over some crop from this year to next. The two years then become a single unit with positive storage going on all the time. Hence, price must rise throughout the two years ..." (*ibid*, author's italics).

Equation (33) defines the first segment of Gustafson's piecewise linear approximation to the competitive storage function. The second segment is obtained by taking $s^c_{t+1|t}>0$ and using (30), asserted for period t+1, to obtain an expression for $s^c_{t+1|t}$ in terms of s_t and $s^c_{t+2|t}$. We again suppose that this latter expectation is held with certainty. Analogously to (29), we obtain

$$\mathit{ln}p^c_{t+2|\,t} - \mathit{ln}p^c_{t+1|t} = \frac{1}{e+\epsilon}\left[s^c_{t+2|t} - 2s^c_{t+1|t} + s_t + \left[\zeta^c_{t+1|t} - \zeta^c_{t+2|t}\right]\right] \tag{34}$$

Substituting this into (3), we find, analogously with (31)

$$s^c_{t+1|t} = \tfrac{1}{2}\left[s^c_{t+2|t} + s_t + \left[\zeta^c_{t+1|t} - \zeta^c_{t+2|t}\right] - (e+\epsilon)r^c_{t+1|t}\right]^+ \tag{35}$$

We now substitute (35) into (31) to obtain

$$s_t = \frac{2}{3}\left[s_{t-1} + \tfrac{1}{2}s^c_{t+2|t} + \left[\zeta_t - \tfrac{1}{2}\left[\zeta^c_{t+1|t} + \zeta^c_{t+2|t}\right]\right] - (e+\epsilon)\left[r_t + \tfrac{1}{2}r^c_{t+1|t}\right]\right]^+ \tag{36}$$

The structure of the function is more apparent if we again consider the simple case in which $\zeta^c_{t+1|t}=0$ for i>0 and if we impose $r^c_{t+i|t}=r_t$ for i>0. If agents expect with certainty that there will be no carry over at the end of period t+2, then, under these conditions, (36) simplifies to

$$s_t = \frac{2}{3}\left[Z_t - \frac{3}{2}Z^*_t\right] \tag{37}$$

with Z_t and Z^*_t defined as in (33). (37) defines the second segment of the piecewise linear approximation to the storage function. The marginal propensity to store is two thirds since, over this range, agents expect with certainty to consume the excess supply over a three year period.[4] From (35), the lowest value for excess supply Z such that $s^c_{t+2|t}=0$ is $Z=3Z^*$, and this is also the value of Z at which (33) and (37) intersect. (33) therefore applies in the range $Z^* \leqq Z \leqq 3Z^*$.

We may obtain the third section of the approximation by exactly the same steps. This results in a section of the function with marginal propensity to store of three quarters:

$$s_t = \frac{3}{4}\Big[s_{t-1} + \frac{1}{3}s_{t+3|t} + \Big[\zeta_t - \frac{1}{3}\big[\zeta_{t+1|t}+\zeta_{t+2|t}+\zeta_{t+3|t}\big]\Big] - (e+\epsilon)\Big[r_t + \frac{2}{3}r_{t+1|t} + \frac{1}{3}r_{t+2|t}\Big]\Big]^+ \tag{38}$$

Assuming $\zeta^c_{t+i|t}=0$ and $r^c_{t+i|t}=r_t$ all i>0, this reduces to

$$s_t = \frac{3}{4}\left[Z_t - 2Z^*_t\right] \tag{39}$$

which intersects (37) at $Z=6Z^*$ implying that (37) holds over the range $3Z^* \leqq Z \leqq 6Z^*$.

Reverting to the general case, successive substitution allows expression of the *n*th segment of the approximation as

$$s_t = \frac{n}{n+1}\left[s_{t-1} + \frac{1}{n}s^c_{t+n|t} + (\zeta_t - \frac{1}{n}\sum_{i=1}^{n}\zeta_{t+i|t}) - \frac{1}{n}(e+\epsilon)\sum_{i=0}^{n}(n-i)r^c_{t+i|t}\right]^+ \tag{40}$$

In the special case of $\zeta^c_{t+i|t}=0$ and $r^c_{t+i|t}=r_t$ all i>0 this simplifies to

$$s_t = \frac{n}{n+1}\left[Z_t - \tfrac{1}{2}(n+1)Z^*_t\right] \tag{41}$$

and this segment applies in the range

$$\tfrac{1}{2}n(n+1)Z^* \leqq Z \leqq \tfrac{1}{2}(n+1)(n+2)Z^* \tag{42}$$

There are a number of features of the certainty equivalence storage function (39) that are worthy of note, and which we summarize for subsequent reference:

(i) storage depends on total supply (carryover plus inherited stock);

(ii) the function is piecewise linear;

(iii) the marginal propensity to store is dependent only on total supply, and is independent of both the interest rate and the supply and demand elsticities;

(iv) the initial storage point (horizontal intercept) is a multiplicative function of the interest rate and the sum of the supply and demand elasticities.

The function defined by (41) is graphed in Figure 1. It is apparent that the nonlinearity in the storage rule is not very acute after one moves from zero to positive carryover. For certain purposes a smooth approximation to the function may be useful. A function with identical derivatives to (41) at the midpoints of the ranges defined by (42) is

$$\frac{s_t}{Z_t} = \left[1 - \left[\frac{Z_t^*}{2Z_t}\right]^{\frac{1}{2}}\right]^2 \tag{43}$$

This is graphed as the broken line in Figure 2 with the piecewise linear function (41) reproduced for comparison. The approximation is very close except over the range $Z^* < Z < 2Z^*$. An improved approximation is therefore obtained by substituting (31) for (43) over this range. The resulting splined function has continuous first derivatives, except at $Z^*=1$, and continuous second derivatives except at $Z^*=1$ and $Z^*=2$.

How dependent are these results on the particular choice of functional form? The two obvious alternatives to the semilogarithmic function are the linear and loglinear specifications. Unfortunately, it is not possible to obtain analytic results for the storage function in the loglinear case. This is because of acute nonlinearities which result when supply and demand from the loglinear functions are substituted into the necessarily linear market clearing identity (12). However, it is relatively easy to relate our analysis to that obtained from the linear supply and demand specification adopted by both Gustafson (1958a) and Newbery and Stiglitz (1981, 1982).

Assuming both linearity and certainty equivalence, (3) is replaced by

$$p_{t+1|t}^c \leqq (1+r_t)p_t : s_t \geqq 0 \tag{44}$$

and this implies

$$\left[s_{t+1|t}^c - s_t + \zeta_{t+1|t}^c\right] - (1+r_t)\left[s_t - s_{t-1} + \zeta_t\right] \leqq (b+\beta)r_t\bar{p} : s_t \geqq 0 \tag{45}$$

where $\beta = y_p$ and $b = -x_p$. Putting $\zeta_{t+1|t}^c = 0$, taking the interest rate to be constant, and

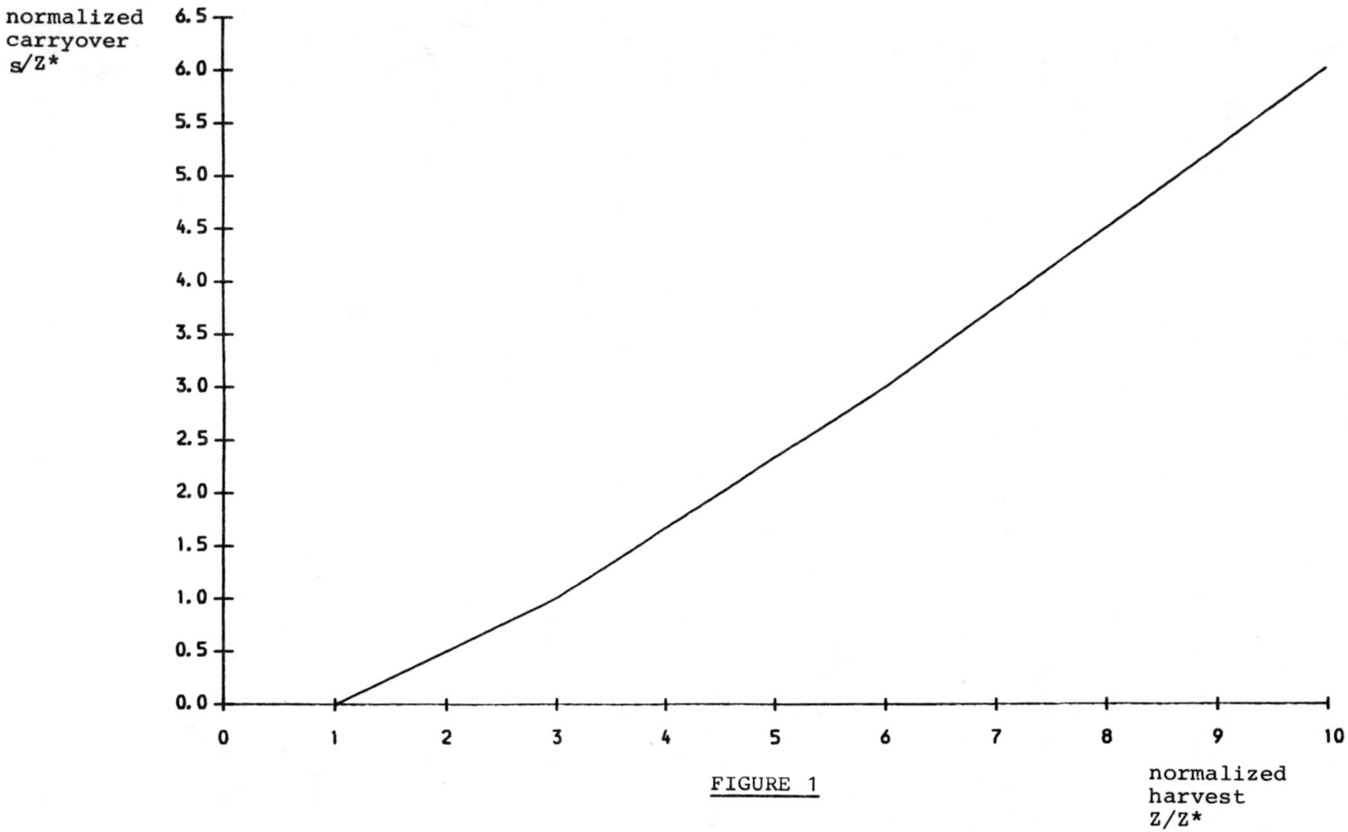
normalized
carryover
s/Z*
6.5
6.0
5.5
5.0
4.5
4.0
3.5
3.0
2.5
2.0
1.5
1.0
0.5
0.0
0
1
2
3
4
5
6
7
8
9
10
normalized
harvest
Z/Z*

FIGURE 1

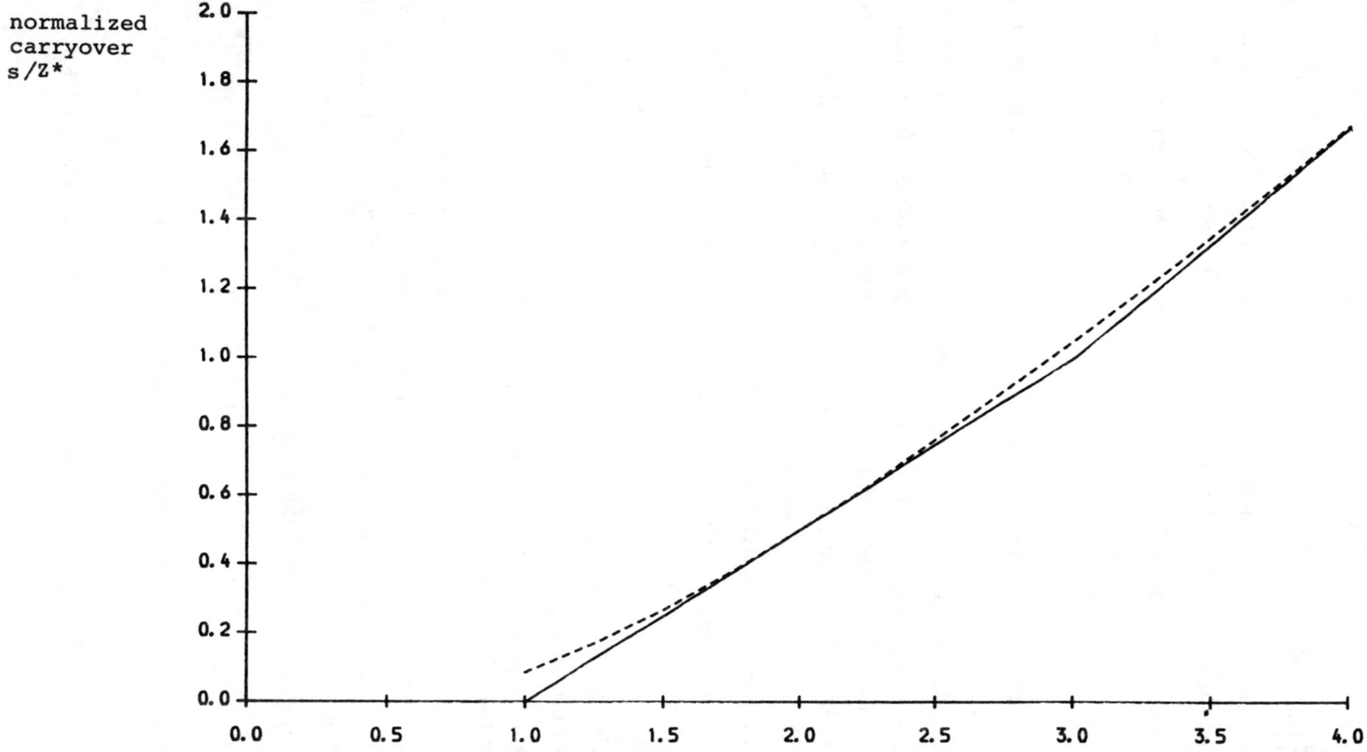
normalized
carryover
s/Z*
2.0
1.8
1.6
1.4
1.2
1.0
0.8
0.6
0.4
0.2
0.0
0.0
0.5
1.0
1.5
2.0
2.5
3.0
3.5
4.0
normalized
harvest
Z/Z*

<u>FIGURE 2</u>

again normalizing $\bar{x}=\bar{y}=1$, we may solve for the first section of the storage function as

$$s_t = \frac{1+r}{2+r}\left[Z_t - \frac{1}{1+r} Z_t^*\right]^+ \tag{46}$$

where $Z^* = (e+\epsilon)r$ as in (33), but where the elasticities e and E are point equivalents of the corresponding slope coefficients b and β. Similarly, if the rate of interest is sufficiently low that terms in r^2 may be neglected, the second section of the function is given by

$$s_t = \frac{2+r}{3+3r}\left[Z_t - \frac{3+5r}{2+r} Z_t^*\right]^+ \tag{47}$$

Derivation of the subsequent sections of the function is straightforward, but the expressions become increasingly complicated.

As in the semilogarithmic case, the storage function is piecewise linear and depends only on total available supply, but the separability property of that function, whereby the interest rate affected only the initial storage point and not the marginal propensity to stock, is lost, although it remains the case that the marginal propensity to stock is independent of the supply and demand elasticities. The loss of separability with respect to the interest rate results in a significantly more complicated storage function once the initial section is past, and this complexity highlights the advantage of adopting the semi–logarithmic specification.

5. LAGGED SUPPLY RESPONSE

It is a feature of production of most primary commodities, and certainly of agricultural crops, that production decisions must be made prior to knowledge of the cash price that the product will fetch. The supply–demand model (19,20) of section 4, which only allows contemporaneous price response, omits this feature. Generalization of this model while still maintaining certainty equivalence gives rise to a storage function which preserves the same general features of the function defined by (41) and (42), but which results in a higher marginal propensity to store.

With this objective, we extend the supply function (20) to

$$y(p_t, p_{t|t-1}, q_t, w_t) = \bar{y}\left[1+\epsilon(\ln p_t - \ln\bar{p}) + \gamma(\ln p^e_{t|t-1} - \ln\bar{p}) + \alpha'(q_t - \bar{q}) + w_t\right] \tag{48}$$

We can also introduce lagged price effects symmetrically into the demand function (19) which becomes

$$x(p_t, p_{t|t-1}, q_t, v_t) = \bar{x}\left[1 - e(\ln p_t - \ln\bar{p}) - g(\ln p^e_{t|t-1} - \ln\bar{p}) + a'(q_t - \bar{q}) + v_t\right] \tag{49}$$

The specification issue relates to the way $p^e_{t|t-1}$ is modelled. The most attractive assumption is that producers are fully informed and, in the private context, share the same price expectations as speculators.[5] Under certainty equivalence, this will imply $p^e_{t|t-1}=p^c_{t|t-1}$. This will also be the outcome in a planned environment where production and stockholding decisions are made jointly. Excess supply (21) is replaced by

$$z_t = (e+\epsilon)(\ln p_t - \ln\bar{p}) + (g+\gamma)(\ln p^c_{t|t-1} - \ln\bar{p}) + (a+\alpha)' q_t + u_t \tag{50}$$

The current period price (22) is now

$$\ln p_t - \ln\bar{p} = \frac{1}{e+\epsilon}\left[s_t - s_{t-1} - (g+\gamma)(\ln p^c_{t|t-1} - \ln\bar{p}) - (a+\alpha)' q_t - u_t\right] \tag{51}$$

and we also have

$$\ln p^c_{t+1|t} - \ln\bar{p} = \frac{1}{e+\epsilon+g+\gamma}\left[s^c_{t+1|t} - s_t - (a+\alpha)' q^c_{t+1|t}\right] \tag{52}$$

Then, analogously with (29)

$$\ln p^c_{t+1|t} - \ln p_t = \frac{1}{e+\epsilon}\left[\frac{1}{1+\theta} s^c_{t+1|t} - \left(1 + \frac{1}{1+\theta}\right) s_t + s_{t-1} + (a+\alpha)'\left[q_t - q^c_{t+1|t} + u_t\right] + (g+\gamma)\left[\ln p^c_{t|t-1} - \ln\bar{p}\right]\right] \tag{53}$$

where $\theta=\frac{(g+\gamma)}{(e+\epsilon)}$. Setting $q^c_{t+1|t}=0$ and solving for the current period stock gives

$$s_t = \frac{1+\theta}{2+\theta}\left[\frac{1}{1+\theta} s^c_{t+1|t} + s_{t-1} + \zeta_t + (g+\gamma)(\ln p_{t|t-1} - \ln\bar{p}(e+\epsilon) r_t\right]^+ \tag{54}$$

Setting $s^c_{t+1|t}=0$ gives the first segment of the Gustafson piecewise linear function:

$$s_t = \frac{1+\theta}{2+\theta}\left[Z_t - Z^*_t\right]^+ \tag{55}$$

where Z_t is now redefined as

$$Z_t = s_{t-1} + \zeta_t + (g+\gamma)(\ln p_{t|t-1} - \ln\bar{p})$$

and Z^*_t is as defined in (33). The storage function defined by (55) differs from (33) only in the higher marginal propensity to store.

Similarly, the second segment of the function is defined by

$$s_t = \frac{2(1+\theta)}{3+2\theta}\left[Z_t - Z^*_t\right]^+ \tag{56}$$

Repeated substitution gives the *n*th segment as

$$s_t = \frac{n(1+\theta)}{n(1+\theta)+1}\left[Z_t - \tfrac{1}{2}(n+1)Z_t^*\right]^+ \tag{57}$$

which again differs from its non–dynamic counterpart (40) only in the higher marginal storage propensity. The *n*th segment, defined by (57), applies over the range

$$\left[\tfrac{1}{2}n(n-1)(1+\theta)+n\right]Z_t^* \leqq Z_t \leqq \left[\tfrac{1}{2}n(n+1)(1+\theta)+(n+1)\right]Z_t^* \tag{58}$$

It unfortunately does not appear possible to provide a satisfactory closed form continuous approximation to this function.

The effect of the lagged response is to increase the marginal propensity to stock, but leaves the horizontal intercept of the storage function unaffected provided that aggregate excess supply Z_t is appropriately defined.[6] The higher storage propensity arises because storage may be viewed as a substitute for future production: from a social point of view, storage is preferable to increasing future production only if this yields a higher return. In terms of the market mechanism, a decision to carry over a greater proportion of this year's crop will reduce the price expected for next year, and will thereby reduce the incentive to produce – part of the increased carryover therefore goes to replace the anticipated reduction in the level of future production, and it will be necessary to carry forward a higher level of stock than would be appropriate if there were no lagged response.

An alternative assumption is that producers are unable to obtain, either directly or indirectly, information on current stock levels, and their expectations are based on historic prices. The most simple assumption of this class is that the current price expectation is always equal to the previous period's price, and we briefly explore this possibility. This assumption gives exactly the same stock function as the full information assumption adopted above. The reason for this coincidence of stockholding under rational expectations and myopic expectations is that efficient stockholding arbitrages the current price to the expected future prices less the carrying cost (see Gilbert (1985)). Thus the current price and the RE expectation of next period's price become informationally equivalent. Note that this result does not extend to adaptive expectations, which results in a considerably more complicated stockholding function.

Excess supply (50) is replaced by

$$z_t = \bar{x}\left[(e+\epsilon)(\ln p_t - \ln\bar{p}) + (g+\gamma)(\ln p_{t-1} - \ln\bar{p}) + (a+\alpha)'q_t + u_t\right] \tag{59}$$

The current period price (22) is now

$$\ln p_t - \ln \bar{p} = \frac{1}{e+\epsilon}\left[s_t - s_{t-1} - (g+\gamma)(\ln p_{t-1} - \ln \bar{p}) - (a+\alpha)' q_t - u_t\right] \tag{60}$$

Moving forward one period

$$(\ln p^c_{t+1|t} - \ln \bar{p}) + \theta(\ln p_t - \ln \bar{p}) = \frac{1}{e+\epsilon}\left[s^c_{t+1|t} - s_t - (a+\alpha)' q^c_{t+1|t}\right] \tag{61}$$

This allows us to derive, analogously to (53)

$$\ln p^c_{t+1|t} - \ln p_t = \frac{1}{e+\epsilon}\Big[s^c_{t+1|t} - (2+\theta)s_t + (1+\theta)s_{t-1}$$

$$+ \left[(1+\theta)\zeta_t - \zeta^c_{t+1|t}\right] + (1+\theta)(g+\gamma)(\ln p_{t-1} - \ln \bar{p})\Big] \tag{62}$$

Setting $\zeta^c_{t+1|t} = s^c_{t+1|t} = 0$ and solving for the current carryover gives the initial segment of the RE stock function (56). It may be confirmed that this identity continues with regard to subsequent segments.

We conclude that the same storage function applies in the case of myopic expectations to that in the full information case. However, the explanations for the higher marginal propensity to store differ between the two cases. In the full information case, the increased storage propensity arose from the reduced incentives to produce as the result of the higher carryover. In the myopic case the producers are unaware of the lower incentives. Nevertheless, next period's production is reduced to the same extent as the consequence of the lower price received this period which producers extrapolate into the next period. Excess supply this year results, in this model, in a higher probability of excess demand next year, and thereby increases the need for storage. The high marginal propensity to stock in this case therefore results from the need to offset the production decisions resulting from ill–informed expectations.

6. THE STORAGE FUNCTION WITHOUT CERTAINTY EQUIVALENCE

Gustafson (1958a) calculated the exact storage function by using dynamic programming without invoking certainty equivalence, but this method did not permit supply response, and could not give a closed form expression for storage. He found that, in practice, the certainty equivalent approximation gave an accurate representation of the shape of the exact solution, but that the approximation was displaced a small way to the right, implying too low a level of storage at any level of excess supply. This accords with our observation that (30) defines a lower bound to the amount that will be stored.

We first consider the storage function in the absence of supply response. Certainty equivalence allowed simplification of the storage function in two respects: it firstly allowed substitution of $p^c_{t+1|t}$ for $p^e_{t+1|t}$, and secondly allowed substitution of $s^c_{t+1|t}$ for $s^e_{t+1|t}$. These simplifications both occur in the move from (27) to (28). First consider $p^e_{t+1|t}$: if $q^e_{t+1|t}=0$ then, from (26),

$$\ln p^e_{t+1} = E_t \ln p_{t+1} + \tfrac{1}{2}\sigma^2_p$$

This allows us to replace (3) by

$$E_t \ln p_{t+1} - \ln p_t \leqq r_t - \tfrac{1}{2}\sigma^2_p : s_t \geqq 0 \tag{63}$$

Note however that the price variance drops out of subsequent rates of return

$$E_t\left[\ln p_{t+i} - \ln p_{t+i-1} | s_{t+i-1} > 0\right] \leqq E_t r_{t+i-1} \qquad \forall i > 1 \tag{64}$$

Using (63), (30) is replaced by

$$\frac{1}{e+\epsilon} s^e_{t+1|t} - 2s_t + s_{t-1} + \zeta_t \leqq r_t - \tfrac{1}{2}\sigma^2_p : s_t \geqq 0 \tag{65}$$

This substitution is therefore equivalent to a reduction in the rate of interest obtainabale on alternative investments. It arises as a consequence of the semi–logarithmic functional specification: at any price level, a given positive shock to excess demand will raise price by more than the same negative shock will reduce it, and this raises the expected return from holding stock. This feature will be absent from a linear supply–demand specifiction

Now consider substitution of the expected stock level $s^e_{t+1|t}$ for its certainty equivalent $s^c_{t+1|t}$. Because the distribution of the stock is truncated below at zero, we have

$$s^e_{t+1|t} \geqq s^c_{t+1|t} \tag{66}$$

and since the current carryover is positively related to the expected carryover in the next period (31), this substitution leads to an underestimate of the current optimal stock. Making the same substitutions in (35) and using (64), the carryover in period t+1 satisfies

$$s_{t+1} = \tfrac{1}{2}\left[+ s_t + s^e_{t+2|t} + \zeta_{t+1} + u_{t+1} - (e+\epsilon)r_{t+1}\right]^+ \tag{67}$$

Consider any variable $x \sim N(0,\sigma^2)$: from the properties of the truncated normal distribution

$$\begin{aligned} E[a+x]^+ &= aPr(x>-a) + E(x|x>-a).Pr(x>-a) \\ &= a\left[1 - \phi\left[-\frac{a}{\sigma}\right]\right] + \sigma\Phi\left[-\frac{a}{\sigma}\right] \\ &= a\phi\left[\frac{a}{\sigma}\right] + \sigma\Phi\left[\frac{a}{\sigma}\right] \end{aligned} \tag{68}$$

where $\phi(.)$ and $\Phi(.)$ are respectively the standard normal distribution and density functions. It follows that

$$s^e_{t+1|t} = \tfrac{1}{2}\left[\phi h_t + \Phi\sigma_\zeta\right] \tag{69}$$

where

$$h_t = s_t + s^e_{t+2|t} - (e+\epsilon)r_{t+1}$$
$$\sigma^2_\zeta = \sigma^2_u + (a+\alpha)'\varphi(a+\alpha) = (e+\epsilon)^2\sigma^2_p$$

and where $\phi = \phi\left[\frac{h_t}{\sigma_\zeta}\right]$ and $\Phi = \Phi\left[\frac{h_t}{\sigma_\zeta}\right]$.

Solution for s_t is complicated by the fact that $s^e_{t+1|t}$ depends upon $s^e_{t+2|t}$ through (69). We may obtain a lower bound on the storage function by setting $s^e_{t+2|t}=0$. Substituting into (37) (with $s^e_{t+1|t}$ replacing $s^c_{t+1|t}$) and rearranging, one obtains

$$s_t = \frac{2}{4-\phi}\left[s_{t-1} + \zeta_t + \tfrac{1}{2}\Phi\sigma_\zeta - \left[1+\tfrac{1}{2}\phi\right](e+\epsilon)r + \tfrac{1}{2}(e+\epsilon)\sigma^2_p\right]^+$$

$$= \frac{2}{4-\phi}\left[Z_t + \tfrac{1}{2}\Phi\sigma_\zeta + \tfrac{1}{2}(e+\epsilon)\sigma^2_p - \left[1+\tfrac{1}{2}\phi\right]Z^*_t\right]^+ \tag{70}$$

Certainly equivalence amounts to allowing σ_ζ to tend to zero. From the definition of h_t in (69) it is clear that $\sigma_\zeta \to 0$ implies $\Phi \to 0$ and, at least for low values of the carryuover, $h_t \to -\infty$ and thus $\phi \to 0$. In any case, $\sigma_\zeta \to 0$ implies $\sigma^2_p \to 0$. It may be confirmed that insertion of these limits specializes (70) to (31), the expression obtained in section 4 for the first section of the storage function under certainty equivalence.

It is tempting to infer the marginal propensity to store from (69) as $\frac{2}{4-\phi}$, and perhaps even to note that at the central value of $\phi=\frac{1}{2}$, this gives a value of 4/7. This inference is however incorrect since ϕ and Φ are functions of s and hence of Z. The analytic representation of the marginal propensity to store from (70) is, as a consequence, complicated and unhelpful.

It is also difficult to make clear inferences about the horizontal intercept in (70). At this point, $\phi=\phi\left[\frac{Z^*}{\sigma_\zeta}\right]$. Write $\phi^* = \phi\left[\frac{Z^*}{\sigma_\zeta}\right] = 1 - \phi$ and $\Phi^* = \Phi\left[\frac{Z^*}{\sigma_\zeta}\right] = \Phi$. The point of intersection Z^- is given by

$$Z^- = \frac{3-\phi^*}{2} Z^* - \tfrac{1}{2}\Phi^* \sigma_\zeta - \tfrac{1}{2}(e+\epsilon)\sigma_p^2 \tag{71}$$

The function defined by (70) provides a lower bound to the storage function, implying that (71) provides an upper bound to the horizontal intercept. An upper bound to the storage function is obtained by setting $s^e_{t+2|t} = s^e_{t+1|t}$ in (69), since on these assumptions, a proportion of the stock carried forward in period t must be consumed in each subsequent period. In this case, one obtains

$$s_t = \frac{2-\phi}{4-3\phi}\left[Z_t + \frac{1}{2-\phi}\phi\sigma_\zeta + \tfrac{1}{2}(e+\epsilon)\sigma_p^2 - \frac{2}{2-\phi}Z_t^*\right]^+ \tag{72}$$

The intersection of (72) with the Z axis, which gives a lower bound to the initial storage point, is at

$$Z^- = \frac{2Z^* - \Phi^*\sigma_\zeta}{1+\phi^*} - \tfrac{1}{2}(e+\epsilon)\sigma_p^2 \tag{73}$$

We now re–introduce lagged supply (and demand) response, adopting the full information approach. Corresponding to (54) we obtain

$$s_t = \frac{1+\theta}{2+\theta}\Big[\frac{1}{1+\theta}s^e_{t+1|t} + s_{t-1} + \zeta_t + (g+\gamma)(\ln p^e_{t|t-1} - \ln\bar{p})$$

$$- (e+\epsilon)r_t + \tfrac{1}{2}(e+\epsilon)\sigma_p^2\Big]^+ \tag{74}$$

where $s^e_{t+1|t}$ is given, as above, by (69). To obtain the lower bound storage function, we set $s^e_{t+2|t}=0$. This gives, analogously with (76),

$$s_t = \frac{2(1+\theta)}{2(2+\theta)-\phi}\Big[s_{t-1} + \zeta_t + (g+\gamma)(\ln p^e_{t|t-1} - \ln\bar{p})$$

$$+ \frac{1}{s(1+\theta)}\Phi\sigma_\zeta - (1+\tfrac{1}{2}\phi)(e+\epsilon)r_t + \tfrac{1}{2}(e+\epsilon)\sigma_p^2\Big]^+$$

$$= \frac{2(1+\theta)}{2(2+\theta)-\phi}\left[Z_t + \frac{1}{2(1+\theta)}\Phi\sigma_\zeta + \tfrac{1}{2}(e+\epsilon)\sigma_p^2 - \left[1+\tfrac{1}{2}\phi\right]Z_t^*\right] \tag{75}$$

The upper bound for the horizontal intercept therefore becomes

$$Z^- = \frac{3-\phi^*}{2} Z^* - \frac{1}{2(1+\theta)}\Phi\sigma_\zeta - \tfrac{1}{2}(e+\epsilon)\sigma_p^2 \tag{76}$$

Setting $\theta=0$ specializes (75) to (70), and allowing $\sigma_\zeta \to 0$ gives (55), the initial section of the certainty equivalence storage function obtained in section 5.

As previously, we obtain an upper bound to the storage function by putting $s^e_{t+2|t}=s^e_{t+1|t}$. This gives

$$s_t = \frac{(2-\phi)(1+\theta)}{2(2+\theta)-(3+\theta)\phi}\Big[s_{t-1} + \zeta_t + (g+\gamma)(\ln p^e_{t|t-1} - \ln\bar{p})$$

$$+ \frac{1}{(2-\phi)(1+\theta)}\phi\sigma_\zeta - \frac{1}{1-\frac{1}{2}\Phi}(e+\epsilon)r_t + \tfrac{1}{2}(e+\epsilon)\sigma^2_p\Big]^+$$

$$= \frac{(2-\phi)(1+\theta)}{2(2+\theta)-(3+\theta)\phi}\Big[Z_t + \frac{1}{(2-\phi)(1+\theta)}\phi\sigma_\zeta + \tfrac{1}{2}(e+\epsilon)\sigma^2_p - \frac{2}{2-\phi}Z^*_t\Big]^+ \tag{77}$$

giving a lower bound to the horizontal intercept at

$$Z^- = \frac{1}{1+\phi^*}\Big[2Z^* - \frac{1}{1+\theta}\phi\sigma_\zeta\Big] - \frac{1}{2}(e+\epsilon)\sigma^2_p \tag{78}$$

As previously, we may confirm that setting $\theta=0$ specializes (77) to the upper bound function (72) in the absence of supply response, and allowing $\sigma_\zeta \to 0$ gives the first section of the certainty equivalence function (55).

It is possible to obtain analogous expressions to those developed in this section for the linear supply and demand specification explored briefly at the end of section 4. These expressions are however considerably more complicated than those obtained from the semi–logarithmic specification, and we therefore confine attention to the case of no lagged supply or demand response. Using the same procedures and notation as above, the lower bound function corresponding to (70) is

$$s_t = \frac{(1+r)(2+r)}{(2+r)^2-(1+r)\phi}\Big[Z_t + \frac{1}{2+r}\phi\sigma_\zeta - \frac{r(2+r)}{(1+r)^2}(e+\epsilon)\phi\Big]^+ \tag{79}$$

Similarly, the upper bound function, corresponding to (72) is

$$s_t = \frac{(1+r)(2+r)-(1+r)^2\phi}{(2+r)^2-(1+r)(3+r)\phi}\Big[Z_t + \frac{1}{(2+r)-(1+r)\phi}\phi\sigma_\zeta$$

$$- \frac{r}{1+r}\Big[1 + \frac{\phi}{(2+r)-(1+r)\phi}\Big](e+\epsilon)\Big]^+ \tag{80}$$

Comparison of these expressions with their semi–logarithmic counterparts illustrates the benefit from adopting this latter specification.

7. NUMERICAL ILLUSTRATIONS

For many practical purposes the crucial features of the storage functions are the horizontal intercept (point of initial storage) and initial slope. Wright and Williams (WW, 1980, p. 600) report estimates of these values, obtained from polynomial approximation of the exact solutions derived from stochastic dynamic programming solution. It is interesting to compare the estimates implied by our approximation methods to their solutions. However, there are two problems in this exercise:

(i) For the estimates we consider, WW adopt the loglinear specification for the supply and demand functions. As we noted in section 4, it is not possible to obtain analytic expressions for the storage function under this specification. We compare the WW estimates with those obtained from our semi–logarithmic specification.

(ii) Using the semi–logarithmic specification, estimation of the storage function requires a value for the price variance σ_p^2. In the absence of any stockholding, this variance is given by (25), but stockholding will reduce this variance, which is therefore jointly determined with the stock function. We have ignored this problem and taken a value for σ_p of 0.1 throughout. The slope estimates are insensitive to variation of this parameter, but there is a major influence on the estimates of the intercept (71, 73, 76, 78). It is straightforward to adjust our estimates of this intercept for alternative values of the parameter.

In Table 1 we provide estimates of the parameters of the storage function in the absence of any lagged supply response. Respectively considering the horizontal intercept and the initial slope, we list the certainty equivalence (ce) estimates, the estimates from the lower bound function (lbf), the estimates from the upper bound function (ubf) together with the estimates provided by WW. The slopes of the lower bound functions uniformly take the value of .57 (4/7) while those of the upper bound function range between .59 and .62. The WW estimates vary more considerably, and we conjecture that this is due to the logarithmic specification. The initial carryover points show greater sensitivity to parameter variation, but depart considerably less from the normal carryover harvest level of 100 than do their certainty equivalent counterparts. It seems reasonable to conclude from these estimates that, if the semi–logarithmic specification is acceptable and if there is no lagged supply or demand response, then a sensible rule is to store four sevenths of current year supply (harvest plus inherited stock) in excess of the normal harvest level.

These conclusions require substantial modification in the presence of lagged supply

Table 1: The Storage Function in the Absence of Lagged Supply Response

Data				Initial carryover point				Initial slope			
#	σ_ζ	e+ϵ	r	ce	lbf	ubf	WW	ce	lbf	ubf	WW
3	.05	.2	.05	101.0	99.6	99.4	99.1	.50	.57	.59	.60
5	.05	.5	.05	102.5	100.4	100.4	101.2	.50	.57	.62	.52
7	.05	1.0	.05	105.0	101.7	101.7	104.5	.50	.56	.61	.44
9	.025	.2	.05	101.0	100.1	100.0	100.4	.50	.57	.61	.56
11	.075	.2	.05	101.0	99.1	98.8	97.7	.50	.57	.59	.61
13	.05	.2	.075	101.5	100.2	100.1	99.8	.50	.57	.60	.58
15	.05	.2	.10	102.0	100.8	100.7	100.6	.50	.57	.61	.54

Table 2: The Storage Function with Lagged Supply Response

Data					Initial carryover point				Initial slope			
#	σ_ζ	e+ϵ	g+γ	r	ce	lbf	ubf	WW	ce	lbf	ubf	WW
4	.05	.2	1.0	.05	101.0	100.4	100.4	100.4	.86	.86	.85	.85
6	.05	.5	1.0	.05	102.5	101.0	101.0	101.9	.75	.76	.77	.75
8	.05	1.0	1.0	.05	105.0	102.0	102.0	104.9	.67	.68	.71	.61
10	.025	.2	1.0	.05	101.0	100.5	100.5	100.8	.86	.84	.82	.87
12	.075	.2	1.0	.05	101.0	100.4	100.3	100.0	.86	.87	.86	.87
16	.05	.2	.2	.05	101.0	100.1	100.0	99.8	.67	.72	.72	.73

Notes: The specification # relates to Wright and Williams (WW, 1982, p. 600); ce = certainty equivalence; lbf = lower bound function; ubf = upper bound function; the 'normal' harvest is 100.

or demand responses. In Table 2 we provide the same information as in Table 1 for functions relating to this situation. With the exception of the final specification (#16) these examples follow WW and take a lagged response of typically much greater in the magnitude than the contemporaneous response. This gives rise to very high marginal propensities to store. The dependence of the slope coefficient on the value of $\theta = \frac{(g+\gamma)}{(e+\epsilon)}$ makes generalization difficult, but the certainty equivalence slope of $\frac{(1+\theta)}{(2+\theta)}$ appears to provide a reasonable guide. Comparison of the horizontal intercepts between analogous specifications in Tables 1 and 2 suggests that the effects of lagged response on this feature of the function are relatively slight.

8. CONCLUSIONS

In this paper we have derived a number of approximations to the competitive storage function. These derivations have been aided by adoption of the semi–logarithmic specification for the supply and demand relationships. Use of this formulation also enabled us to demonstrate the simple structure of the storage rule. Under certainty equivalence, the storage decision may be seen as a decision to pool the current year's harvest with the anticipated harvest for the next and perhaps even succeeding years. If pooling is over n years, then it will be both socially optimal and the outcome of the competitive process that exactly 1/nth of the current harvest in excess of a specified quantity will be consumed this year, and the remaining fraction $\frac{(n-1)}{n}$ of the harvest will be consumed over the next n–1 years. Under cetainty equivalence, therefore, the storage problem requires solution for the number of years carryover (n), and the base consumption level for the current year.

The certainty equivalence solution to the storage problem, discovered by Gustafson (1958a, 1958b), may be fairly easily extended to allow for lagged responses in production or consumption. This is important in agricultural commodity markets where production decisions must be made well in advance of knowledge of delivery prices. Storage is competitive with future consumption in the sense that a given increase in supply next year may either be generated through increased production next year, or through a higher carryover from this year's crop. It follows that a decision to store more of the current crop will both reduce the necessity for increased production next year, and, if price expectations take this storage into account, will reduce the incentive to produce for next year. Somewhat remarkably, the same result holds although for different reasons if expectations are solely based on the current year's price. This gives rise to functions with considerably higher marginal propensities to store than in the absence of lagged response: the crucial parameter here is the ratio of the sum of the lagged supply and demand elasticitiies to the sum of the contemporaneous elasticities.

It is also possible to move some way towards analytic representation of the storage function in the absence of certainty equivalence by providing analytic upper and lower bounds. Numerical calculations indicate that these bounds relate fairly closely to other authors' estimates of the function.

A notable feature of the storage functions developed using the semi–logarithmic functional specification is the separation of factors which affect the marginal propensity to store from those that effect the horizontal intercept of the storage function. Under certainty equivalence, the storage propensity depends on the number of years over which the carryover is to be consumed and the ratio of the lagged to the contemporaneous elasticities, while the intercept depends on the product of the interest rate and the (sum of the) contemporaneous elasticities. These features are still apparent once certainty equivalence is dropped, but the story is complicated by the fact that all the parameters will enter into agent's expectations as to the probability of their being a further carry-over in subsequent years.

This study has implications for both policy and for modelling. For policy purposes it is important to note that when there are lagged supply and demand responses to current prices, it will in general be optimal to store considerably more than one half of the excess of the current harvest relative to the normal level,[7] and even in the absence of lagged response a figure of four sevenths provides a better guide than one half. The implications for modelling relate to the possibility of including analytic approximations to the competitive storage function in commodity market models. This will enable the modeller to examine the effects of public sector intervention schemes on private sector storage. It is widely recognized that the carrying of private sector stocks constitutes a major cost of commodity market intervention, but in the absence of closed form private sector stock functions, it has not previously been possible to examine this issue rigorously.

NOTES

* This paper was written while I was visiting Queen's University, Kingston, Canada.

1. The transactions and precautionary demands for stocks are analyzed in Ghosh, Gilbert and Hughes Hallett (1986, ch. 2).
2. This requires that R_t, δ and w be sufficiently small to allow a first order approximation. More generally, the carrying cost r_t will be given by

$$r_t = \left[R_t + w - \tfrac{1}{2}\left[R_t + w\right]^2\right] + \left[\delta + \tfrac{1}{2}\delta^2\right]$$

3. The semi–logarithmic specification was adopted by Ghosh, Gilbert and Hughes Hallett (1986, ch. 4), in their model of the World copper market, in order to obtain a linear structure within which optimal control methods could be simply applied. The specification is tested against the liner and loglinear specifications in Ghosh, Gilbert and Hughes Hallett (1983) and found to be broadly acceptable.
4. "Subsequent years are unaffected unless today's superabundance is so colosally great as to make for positive carryover into the third year or later." (Samuelson (1957, p. 189)).
5. Full information, in the required sense, will be facilitated if producers have access to efficient forward or futures markets.
6. In the absence of dynamic responses, aggregate excess supply Z_t is defined as $s_{t-1}+z(\bar{p},q_t,u_t)$. In the dynamic generalization, the appropriate definition is $s_{t-1}+z(\bar{p},p_{t-1},q_t,u_t)$.
7. Wright and Williams (1982, pp.601–602 make a similar comment.

REFERENCES

Ghosh, S., C.L. Gilbert and A.J. Hughes Hallett (1984): "Tests of Functional Form in Dynamic Econometric Models: some empirical experience", *Empirical Economics*, 8, 63–69.

Ghosh, S., C.L. Gilbert and A.J. Hughes Hallett (1986): *Stabilizing Speculative Commodity Markets*, Oxford University Press, Oxford (forthcoming).

Gilbert, C.L. (1985): "Efficient Market Commodity Price Dynamics", Commodity Studies and Projections Division, Division Working Paper 1985–4, The World Bank, Washington D.C.

Gustafson, R.L. (1958a): "Carryover Levels for Grains: a method for determining amounts that are optimal under specified conditions", US Department of Agriculture *Technical Bulletin*, 1178.

Gustafson, R.L. (1958b): "Implications of Recent Research on Optimal Storage Rules", *Journal of Farm Economics*, 40, 290–300.

Newbery, D.M.G. and J.E. Stiglitz (1981): *The Theory of Commodity Price Stabilization*, Oxford, Oxford University Press.

Newbery, D.M.G. and J.E. Stiglitz (1982): "Optimal Commodity Stockpiling Rules", *Oxford Economic Papers*, 34, 403–427.

Samuelson, P.A. (1957): "Intertemporal Price Equilibrium: a prologue to the theory of speculation", *Weltwirthschaftliches Archiv*, 79, 181–219; reprinted in P.A. Samuelson: *Collected Scientific Papers* (J.E. Stiglitz ed.), 2, 946–984.

Williams, J.B. (1936): "Speculation and the Carryover", *Quarterly Journal of Economics*, 50, 436–455.

Wright, B.D., and J.C. Williams (1982): "The Economic Role of Commodity Storage", *Economic Journal*, 92, 596–614.

CHAPTER 3

THE IMPACT OF PRICE STABILISATION ON PRODUCERS' REVENUE AND CONSUMERS' EXPENDITURE

N. Davutyan, *University of California, Santa Barbara*

1. INTRODUCTION

Despite its obvious relevance, price stabilisation with multiplicative errors has not received the attention it deserves. In this paper, the model developed in section 2 is used to assess the impact of complete price stabilisation on producer's revenue and consumer's expenditure. Using a theorem[1] due to Turnovsky, some rather strong analytical results are presented in sections 4 and 5. In particular, it is shown that demand and supply elasticities acquire a strategic importance. The conclusions, together with the assumptions implicit in the treatment are presented in section 6.

2. THE MODEL

Let the market for a commodity be represented by:

$$D = AP^{-\alpha}U \qquad \alpha > 0 \tag{1}$$

$$S = BP^{\beta}V \qquad \beta > 0 \tag{2}$$

$$D = S \tag{3}$$

where α and β are price elasticities of demand and supply respectively. Furthermore, it is assumed that U and V are lognormally distributed random variables such that

$$\ell n U = u \sim N(0,\sigma_u^2),\ \ell n V = v \sim N(0,\sigma_v^2),\ Cov(u,v) = 0\ .$$

Using the above model, we can see that equilibrium requires:

$$P = \left[\frac{A}{B}\frac{U}{V}\right]^{1/\alpha+\beta} \tag{4}$$

When we substitute (4) into (2) we get the equilibrium level of supply

$$S = BV\left[\frac{A}{B}\frac{U}{V}\right]^{\frac{\beta}{\alpha+\beta}} \tag{5}$$

Multiplying (4) and (5) we get the equilibrium level of revenue R,

O. Guvenen (ed.), International Commodity Market Models and Policy Analysis, 53–61.

$$R = BV\left[\frac{A}{B}\frac{U}{V}\right]^{\frac{\beta+1}{\alpha+\beta}} \tag{6}$$

Proceeding in a completely analogous fashion we can derive the equilibrium level of expenditures X,

$$X = AU\left[\frac{B}{A}\frac{V}{U}\right]^{\frac{\alpha+1}{\alpha+\beta}} \tag{7}$$

Taking the natural logs of equations (6) and (7) we get:

$$\ell nR = r \sim N\left[\frac{a(\beta+1) + b(\alpha-1)}{\alpha+\beta}, \frac{(\beta+1)^2\sigma_u^2 + (\alpha-1)^2\sigma_v^2}{(\alpha+\beta)^2}\right] \tag{8}$$

$$\ell nX = x \sim N\left[\frac{a(\beta-1) + b(\alpha+1)}{\alpha+\beta}, \frac{(\beta-1)^2\sigma_u^2 + (\alpha+1)^2\sigma_v^2}{(\alpha+\beta)^2}\right] \tag{9}$$

where a and b are the natural logarithms of A and B respectively.

Therefore R and X are lognormal random variables, such that

$$E(R) = \exp[E(r) + \tfrac{1}{2}Var(r)] \tag{10}$$

$$Var(R) = \exp[2E(r) + 2Var(r)] - \exp[2E(r) + Var(r)] \tag{11}$$

$$E(X) = \exp[E(x) + \tfrac{1}{2}Var(x)] \tag{12}$$

$$Var(X) = \exp[2E(x) + 2Var(x)] - \exp[2E(x) + Var(x)] \tag{13}$$

3. PRICE STABILISATION

Now, let us assume that a buffer stock authority stabilises the price at that level where expected demand equals expected supply. It can easily be verified that (see, for instance, Turnovsky, p. 137–38) this price level is given by

$$P^* = \left[\frac{A}{B}\frac{\overline{U}}{\overline{V}}\right]^{\frac{1}{\alpha+\beta}}, \overline{U} = E(U) = \exp\left[\tfrac{1}{2}\sigma_u^2\right], \overline{V} = E(V) = \exp\left[\tfrac{1}{2}\sigma_v^2\right] \tag{14}$$

It should be recalled that at this price, the stabilising authority can expect to break even on average.

Substituting (14) into (12) we get

$$S^* = BV\left[\frac{A}{B}\frac{\overline{U}}{\overline{V}}\right]^{\frac{\beta}{\alpha+\beta}} \tag{15}$$

Multiplication of P^* with S^* gives

$$R^{*} = BV\left[\frac{A\ \bar{U}}{B\ \bar{V}}\right]^{\frac{\beta+1}{\alpha+\beta}} \tag{16}$$

Similarly it can be readily shown that

$$X^{*} = AU\left[\frac{B\ \bar{V}}{A\ \bar{U}}\right]^{\frac{\alpha+1}{\alpha+\bar{b}}} \tag{17}$$

As the reader has probably observed, a star denotes the post stabilisation equilibrium level of the corresponding variable.

It can be easily established that both R^{*} and X^{*} are lognormal, because

$$\ell nR^{*} = r^{*} \sim N\left[\frac{a(\beta+1)\ +\ b(\alpha-1)}{\alpha+\beta} + \tfrac{1}{2}\left[\frac{\beta+1}{\alpha+\beta}\right](\sigma_u^2 - \sigma_v^2),\ \sigma_v^2\right]$$

$$\ell nX^{*} = x^{*} \sim N\left[\frac{a(\beta-1)\ +\ b(\alpha+1)}{\alpha+\beta} + \tfrac{1}{2}\left[\frac{\alpha+1}{\alpha+\beta}\right](\sigma_v^2 - \sigma_u^2),\ \sigma_u^2\right]$$

Therefore we can state that

$$E(R^{*}) = \exp[E(r^{*}) + \tfrac{1}{2}Var(r^{*})] \tag{18}$$

$$Var(R^{*}) = \exp[2E(r^{*}) + 2Var(r^{*})] - \exp[2E(r^{*}) + Var(r^{*})] \tag{19}$$

$$E(X^{*}) = \exp[E(x^{*}) + \tfrac{1}{2}Var(x^{*})] \tag{20}$$

$$Var(X^{*}) = \exp[2E(x^{*}) + 2Var(x^{*})] - \exp[2E(x^{*}) + Var(x^{*})] \tag{21}$$

We may now compare the pre and post stabilisation means and variances.

4. MEAN–VARIANCE ANALYSIS OF PRODUCER'S REVENUE

When we look at equation (18), we can see that $E(R^{*})$ can also be written as

$$E(R^{*}) = B\bar{V}\left[\frac{A\ \bar{U}}{B\ \bar{V}}\right]^{\frac{\beta+1}{\alpha+\beta}} \tag{22}$$

Comparing equations (6) and (16) we note that $E(R^{*})$ has the same functional form as R, with all the random variables being replaced by their respective means. Therefore we may invoke Turnovsky's theorem to compare E(R) with $E(R^{*})$.

Let the matrix of second partial derivatives of R be denoted by

$$R'' = \begin{bmatrix} R_{UU} & R_{UV} \\ R_{UV} & R_{VV} \end{bmatrix}$$

Then $E(R) \gtrless E(R^{*})$ according to whether the matrix R" is positive or negative semi-definite. After some tedious algebra, it can be verified that when:

i) $\alpha < 1$, R" is positive semi–definite and $E(R) > E(R^{*})$

ii) $\alpha > 1$, R" is negative semi–definite and $E(R) < E(R^{*})$

iii) $\alpha = 1$, R" is degenerate and $E(R) = E(R^*)$.

Namely, when demand is inelastic stabilisation decreases mean revenue, while the opposite is true for the elastic case. It may be worthwhile to stress that this result is independent of the values of all the other parameters of the model. Interestingly, this is the revenue analogue of a similar result, obtained by Turnovsky, for producer's surplus.

As for the pre and post stabilisation variances, the following results can be stated (the demonstration is rather messy and is relegated to the Appendix).

iv) $\alpha \leq 1$ and[2] $\sigma_v^2 \leq \sigma_u^2$, then $Var(R^*) < Var(R)$

v) $\alpha \geq 1$ and[2] $\sigma_v^2 \geq \sigma_u^2$, then $Var(R^*) > Var(R)$

vi) $\alpha = 1$ and $\sigma_v^2 = \sigma_u^2$, then $Var(R^*) = Var(R)$

vii) On the other hand, when $\underset{(<)}{\alpha > 1}$ and $\sigma_u^2 \underset{(<)}{>} \sigma_v^2$, the outcome is indeterminate. As shown in the Appendix, price stabilisation may or may not stabilise revenue depending on the values of all the parameters.

5. MEAN–VARIANCE ANALYSIS OF CONSUMER'S EXPENDITURE

Proceeding in a completely analogous fashion let us look at equations (7) and (17). We can immediately see that the preconditions to invoke Turnovsky's theorem are there. Let X" denote the matrix of second partial derivatives of X with respect to U and V

$$X'' = \begin{bmatrix} X_{UU} & X_{UV} \\ X_{UV} & X_{VV} \end{bmatrix} \tag{24}$$

As one would anticipate, when $\beta < 1$ (>1) X" is positive (negative) semi–definite. Hence the following results can be stated:

viii) when $\beta < 1$, $E(X) > E(X^*)$

ix) when $\beta > 1$, $E(X) < E(X^*)$

x) when $\beta = 1$, $E(X) = E(X^*)$

Contrasting those results with the corresponding ones for mean revenue we can see that the roles are reversed. Namely, when supply is (in)elastic, stabilisation (decreases) increases mean expenditure.

As for the variances, results analogous to the ones obtained for revenue can be stated. (The demonstration which is completely symmetric to the one presented in the Appendix is omitted). When:

xi) $\beta \leq 1$ and[3] $\sigma_v^2 \geq \sigma_u^2$, implies $Var(X) > Var(X^*)$

xii) $\beta \geq 1$ and[3] $\sigma_v^2 \leq \sigma_u^2$, implies $Var(X) < Var(X^*)$

xiii) $\beta = 1$ and $\sigma_v^2 = \sigma_u^2$, implies $\mathrm{Var}(X) = \mathrm{Var}(X^*)$

xiv) $\beta \underset{(>)}{<} 1$ and $\sigma_v^2 \underset{(>)}{<} \sigma_u^2$, the outcome depends on the particular numerical values of α, β, σ_u^2 and σ_v^2. It should be recalled that this is analogous to case vii.

6. CONCLUSIONS

A full treatment of the implications of the foregoing results would require a case by case approach. Nevertheless the following remarks are in order.

a) To the extent that both demand and supply are inelastic, complete price stabilisation will reduce both mean revenue and mean expenditure. On this ground alone, it is beneficial to consumers.

b) To the extent that preconditions (iv) and (v) are valid, producers face a trade off between (increased) decreased but (de)stabilised revenues.

c) On the other hand, consumers face a different kind of trade off. Namely, when supply is inelastic (elastic) and supply disturbances outweigh (are outweighed by) demand disturbances, price stabilisation is an unmixed blessing (evil) for consumers, assuming expenditures to be an adequate measure of welfare.

d) Referring to cases (vii) and (xiv), we can say that there exists a set of values for α, β, σ_u^2, σ_v^2, where price stabilisation benefits both the producers and consumers, again assuming revenue and expenditure to be adequate measures of welfare for those two groups.

We finish by reviewing some of the restrictions of the foregoing analysis. Firstly, we assume that the probability of the buffer stock running out over the period of stabilisation is zero. We also assume that the storage and administrative costs associated with the buffer stock are zero. Secondly, by operating within an equilibrium framework, we implicitly endow all decision makers with perfect anticipation. Finally and obviously, we also assume that a partial equilibrium framework provides an adequate basis of analysis.

NOTES

*) I am grateful to Prof. Jati K. Sengupta for his generous help. Nevertheless, I alone am responsible for all the errors.

1) To be more precise, Turnovsky extended the well–known Jensen's inequality to the multivariate case (see S.J. Turnovsky (1976)). This result will henceforth be referred to as Turnovsky's theorem.

2) The inequality being true for at least one of them.

3) Where the inequality holds for at least one of them.

REFERENCES

Turnovsky, S.J. (1976), 'The Distribution of Welfare Gains from Price Stabilisation: The Case of Multiplicative Disturbances', *International Economic Review*, Vol. 17, No. 1, pp. 133–48.

APPENDIX

Cases iv–vi

Step 1: Rewrite E(R) and E(R^*), i.e., equations (12) and (16)

$$E(R) = \exp[k]\,\exp\left[\frac{(\beta+1)^2\sigma_u^2 + (\alpha-1)^2\sigma_v^2}{2(\alpha+\beta)^2}\right]$$

$$E(R^*) = \exp[k]\,\exp\left[\tfrac{1}{2}\left[\frac{\beta+1}{\alpha+\beta}\right](\sigma_u^2 - \sigma_v^2) + \tfrac{1}{2}\sigma_v^2\right]$$

where $E(R) = k = \dfrac{a(\beta+1) + b(\alpha-1)}{\alpha+\beta}$

Step 2: We know that when $\alpha \underset{(>)}{<} 1$, $E(R) \underset{(<)}{>} E(R^*)$ dividing both sides by exp[k] and then taking logs we get,

$$\alpha \underset{(>)}{<} 1 \text{ implies } \frac{(\beta+1)^2\sigma_u^2 + (\alpha-1)^2\sigma_v^2}{2(\alpha+\beta)^2} \underset{(<)}{>} \tfrac{1}{2}\left[\frac{\beta+1}{\alpha+\beta}\right](\sigma_u^2 - \sigma_v^2) + \tfrac{1}{2}\sigma_v^2$$

Multiplying both sides by 2 we get

$$\frac{(\beta+1)^2\sigma_u^2 + (\alpha-1)^2\sigma_v^2}{(\alpha+\beta)^2} \underset{(<)}{>} \frac{\beta+1}{\alpha+\beta}(\sigma_u^2 - \sigma_v^2) + \sigma_v^2$$

or

$$m = \frac{(\beta+1)^2\sigma_u^2 + (\alpha-1)^2\sigma_v^2}{(\alpha+\beta)^2} \underset{(<)}{>} n = \frac{\beta+1}{\alpha+\beta}(\sigma_u^2 - \sigma_v^2) + \sigma_v^2$$

Step 3: Rewrite Var(R) and Var(R*)

$$\mathrm{Var(R)} = \exp\left[\frac{2a(\beta+1) + 2b(\alpha-1)}{\alpha+\beta} + \frac{2(\beta+1)^2\sigma_u^2 + 2(\alpha-1)^2\sigma_v^2}{(\alpha+\beta)^2}\right] -$$

$$-\exp\left[\frac{2a(\beta+1) + 2b(\alpha-1)}{a+\beta} + \frac{(\beta+1)^2\sigma_u^2 + (\alpha-1)^2\sigma_v^2}{(\alpha+\beta)^2}\right]$$

Using the previously defined notation and taking the common terms out we get:

$$\mathrm{Var(R)} = \exp(2k)[\exp(m)[\exp(m)-1]]$$

$$\mathrm{Var(R^*)} = \exp\left[\frac{2a(\beta+1) + 2b(\alpha-1)}{\alpha+\beta} + \frac{\beta+1}{\alpha+\beta}(\sigma_u^2 - \sigma_v^2) + 2\sigma_v^2\right] -$$

$$-\exp\left[\frac{2a(\beta+1) + 2b(\alpha-1)}{\alpha+\beta} + \frac{\beta+1}{\alpha+\beta}(\sigma_u^2 - \sigma_v^2) + \sigma_v^2\right]$$

Using the simplifying notation introduced above and taking out the common terms we get:

$$\mathrm{Var(R^*)} = \exp[2k][\exp(n)[\exp(\sigma_v^2)-1]$$

Step 4: Recall that $\underset{(>)}{\alpha < 1}$ implied

$$m = \frac{(\beta+1)^2\sigma_u^2 + (\alpha-1)^2\sigma_v^2}{(\alpha+\beta)^2} \underset{(<)}{>} n = \frac{\beta+1}{\alpha+\beta}(\sigma_u^2 - \sigma_v^2) + \sigma_v^2$$

Now when $\sigma_u^2 \underset{(<)}{>} \sigma_v^2$, it is obvious that $m \underset{(<)}{>} \sigma_v^2$.

Step 5: Now let us compare Var(R) with Var(R*)

$$\mathrm{Var(R)} = \exp(2k)[\exp(m)[\exp(m)-1]]$$
$$\mathrm{Var(R^*)} = \exp(2k)[\exp(n)[\exp(\sigma_v^2)-1]]$$

Dividing both of them with exp[2k] leaves their relationship unchanged and we end up with

$$\exp(m)[\exp(m)-1] \quad \text{versus} \quad \exp(n)[\exp(\sigma_v^2)-1]$$

Now referring to steps 2 and 4 we can state that:

$\alpha \underset{(>)}{<} 1$ implies $\mathrm{E(R)} \underset{(<)}{>} \mathrm{E(R^*)}$. By step 2 this means $m \underset{(<)}{>} n$ which in its turn implies

$m \underset{(<)}{>} \sigma_v^2$ (from step 4). Hence both of the terms of Var(R) $\underset{(<)}{>}$ than those of Var(R^*).
Therefore when $\alpha \underset{(>)}{<} 1$ and $\sigma_u^2 \underset{(<)}{>} \sigma_v^2$, Var(R) $\underset{(<)}{>}$ Var(R^*).

Step 6: When $\sigma_u^2 = \sigma_v^2$ we can easily see that

$$\alpha \underset{(>)}{<} 1 \Rightarrow E(R) \underset{(<)}{>} E(R^*) \Rightarrow m \underset{(<)}{>} n \Rightarrow Var(R) \underset{(<)}{>} Var(R^*)$$

Step 7: When $\alpha = 1$, the two expressions reduce to

$$Var(R) = \exp[2a + 2\sigma_u^2] - \exp[2a + \sigma_u^2]$$

$$Var(R^*) = \exp[2a + \sigma_u^2 + \sigma_v^2] - \exp[2a + \sigma_u^2]$$

Therefore $\sigma_v^2 \underset{(<)}{>} \sigma_u^2 \Rightarrow Var(R^*) \underset{(<)}{>} Var(R)$

Case vii

To compare Var(R) with Var(R^*) when $\alpha \underset{(<)}{>} 1$ and $\sigma_u^2 \underset{(<)}{>} \sigma_v^2$, let us rewrite them in full:

$$Var(R) = \exp(2k)[\exp(m)[\exp(m)-1]]$$

$$Var(R^*) = \exp(2k)[\exp(n)[\exp(\sigma_v^2)-1]]$$

Simplifying both of them by exp(2k), does not affect the relation and leaves us with

$$R \rightarrow \exp(m)[\exp(m)-1] \quad \text{versus} \quad \exp(n)[\exp(\sigma_v^2)-1] \leftarrow R^*$$

When $\alpha \underset{(>)}{<} 1$ then $m \underset{(<)}{>} n$. If m were greater than σ_v^2 then clearly Var(R) $\underset{(<)}{>}$ Var(R^*). Unfortunately, this is not necessarily true when $\sigma_v^2 \underset{(<)}{>} \sigma_u^2$. So in those two cases the result depends on the values of the system parameters, as is shown in the numerical example that follows. Let $\alpha = .9$ $\sigma_v^2 = 2$, $\sigma_u^2 = 1$, $\beta = .1$

$$m = \frac{(\beta+1)^2\sigma_u^2 + (\alpha-1)^2\sigma_v^2}{(\alpha+\beta)^2}, \quad n = \frac{\beta+1}{\alpha+\beta}(\sigma_u^2 - \sigma_v^2) + \sigma_v^2$$

It follows that $m = 1.23$, $n = .9$

$$Var(R) = (C)\ \exp(1.23)[\exp(1.23)-1] = 8.2836C$$

$$Var(R^*) = (C)\ \exp(.9)[\exp(2)-1] = 15.71C$$

Since C is a constant, Var(R^*) > Var(R). Now let $\alpha = .9$, $\sigma_v^2 = 2$, $\sigma_u^2 = 1.9$, $\beta = .1$.

It can easily be verified that $\mathrm{Var(R)} = 90.828\mathrm{C}$, and $\mathrm{Var(R^*)} = 42.29\mathrm{C}$. Hence, despite the fact that $\alpha < 1$, $\sigma_v^2 > \sigma_u^2$ in both cases, for the second example $\mathrm{Var(R)} > \mathrm{Var(R^*)}$.

CHAPTER 4

STABILITY OF BASE PRODUCT MARKETS: A GAME THEORY ANALYSIS

A. Richard, *University II, Grenoble, France*

1. INTRODUCTION

The contributions of econometrics to the study of base products markets are numerous and important. However as Banks (1974) remarks: 'For most base products, econometrics alone cannot reflect moves of the future as much as those of the past'. The projections achieved from such models are at the mercy of outside disturbances or unforeseen structural changes, occurances in which this recent period has been particularly fertile.

The object of this paper is to examine, with the aid of the game theory, the correlation between the existing power ratio in the base products markets and the strategies of the agents concerned. The market's institutional stability is assumed only as long as no agent or agents' union, having the power to challenge functioning guidelines, is interested in doing so.

This approach implies the analysis of, first, the conditions of formation of an exporters' coalition, and second, the conditions of formation of an importers' coalition in response to the common strategy of the exporters. (An example of this is the International Energy Agency (I.E.A.) formed after the fixing of a high OPEC price). The problem, then, is to determine if cooperative solutions exist for quota negotiations between exporters and for price negotiations between exporters and importers.

2. THE CONFLICT CHARACTERISTICS OF THE BASE PRODUCTS MARKETS

The rapid evolution of the petroleum market, from the domination of an oligopoly consisting of a few powerful countries to that of an exporting countries' cartel, raised, in 1973, many questions. Would the creation of such coalitions spread to other base products markets? Although the fears of consuming countries and the hopes of exporting countries are now more realistic, these base products markets are by no means secure

O. Guvenen (ed.), International Commodity Market Models and Policy Analysis, 63–83.

from conflicting strategies. Brown's work (1980) provides multiple evidence of this and illustrates the intervening modalities. Since concerted action from the exporters is an essential condition for the success of these interventions, it is essential to determine if the stakes are sufficient to justify cartelisation.

2.1 The Stakes: The Surplus Sharing

The producers seek to capture a part of the consumer's surplus by fixing a higher price than that of the market's competitive balance. As the theory indicates, they would otherwise only obtain the producer's normal surplus:

- the static rent proportional to the differences in productivity (Ricardian rent);
- the dynamic rent proportional to the intertemporal equalisation of prices, on an actualised base, in the case of exhaustible resources (Hotelling (1931)).

To this surplus is added the extra funds linked to price fluctuation and to high investment costs (entry barrier for marginal producers).

During the recovery of their natural resources, the less developed countries (LDCs) whose import requirements are considerable, are at risk when estimating, on a macro-economic base, the profitability of their base products resources (by defining, for example, a high shadow price for the currency gained in exportation) because the production increases resulting from this would be suicidal if such a behaviour generalised itself to markets in which the elasticity of demand, with regard to price, is very small.

A minimum of planning in concert seems essential for exporting countries if they wish to obtain 'a just and profitable price', according to the terms constantly used in UNCTAD documents. For this, a cartelisation is accepted by the United Nations.[2] In the years succeeding the first petroleum shock, many prospective studies considered price scenarios corresponding to situations of monopoly. The cartel approach is more realistic, as Ezzati (1976) notes, because of the absorption disparities of petroleum resources within OPEC. Cartelisation is therefore not synonymous with monopoly prices due to possible reactions from the consumers.

The cartel approach of the petroleum market has been used in several studies. Hnyilicza and Pindyck (1976) divide the OPEC countries into two groups: the thrifty countries and the spending countries. The proposed Nash solution is unrealistic because it eliminates from the market the first group of countries to the advantage of the second during the first period, and then does the opposite during the second period. This is essentially caused by the choice of constant actualisation rates which are different for each group.

Stoffaes (1981) has an even finer sampling (4 groups). The group of doves (Saudi

Arabia, Kuwait, etc.) can even ally themselves to the consumers. The resulting matrix also integrates the social and political costs of certain strategies.

In this methodological study the accent is placed on the conditions of stability of the coalitions.

2.2 The Potential Coalitions

Following the complete recovery of primary activities, LDCs would have control of their output. Consequently, the existence of rare localised factors and the relative ease with which required technology may be obtained make primary activities chosen targets for LDCs anxious to regain their economic independence. Developed countries also tend to participate in these activities to ensure their own national independence and to protect the revenue of social classes (for example, agricultural policies). Therefore the risk of a reduction in supplies compels states to impose strict controls on private companies and to expand the role of state enterprise. But since risks for private companies differ from those of a state enterprise – financial for the former, national economics for the latter – the emphasis on each varies correspondingly, the value of uncovered reserves in politically stable areas differs in each case.

This leaves the state with two alternatives: to subsidise prospecting in designated areas or to have the prospecting in these areas done by public agencies. In this context, the establishment of guaranteed floor prices is comparable to the granting of a subsidy. Thus the working of local resources helps to free the primary sector from risk. Through increased state intervention, not only in DCs but in LDCs as well, base products will gradually become subject to the influence of national strategies. The choice between confrontation or concerted action then falls under state jurisdiction.

We can consider the various potential markets depicted in the following chart. The policies of the exporters (LDC) are shown horizontally and those of the importers (DC) vertically.

LDC \ DC	No Cartel	Cartel
No Cartel	Competitive market (I)	–
Cartel	Cartel with a producer price (II)	Conflict (III) Agreement (IV)

Situation II differs from situations III and IV only in the consumers' passivity. This is likely to last if the exporters fix a producer price which will not provoke defensive reactions from the consumers.

The following situation corresponds to the solution of relatively simple conflicts:

- the transition from situation I to situation II implies negotiations between exporting countries for common control of the quantities exported, i.e. quota negotiations;
- the transition from situation II to situations III and IV follows negotiations where the cartel of the exporting countries opposes that of the importing countries.

Viewed from another perspective, the homogeneity of products considerably simplifies the formalisation of demands and of possible producers' strategies. These strategies are in fact limited to the choice of quantities or prices which is equivalent in situation II.

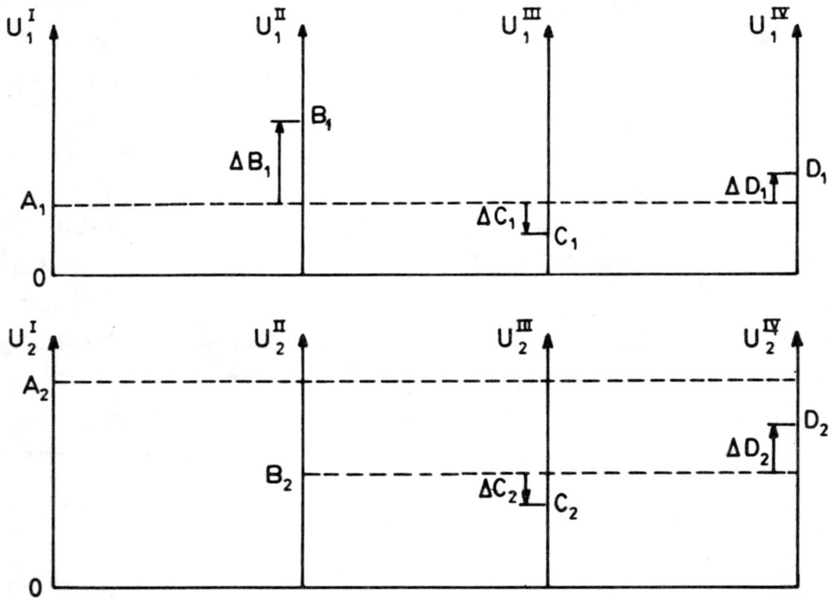

Figure 1

Of the four preceding situations, three are conflictual. Can we foresee, knowing the characteristics of a given market, towards which situation it will evolve? Assuming that these countries behave rationally, their profit in particular situations can be estimated.

The country's choice will be based on its assessment of the risks and advantages involved. Thus, if producers' strategies are compatible, a common strategy may develop within a cartel. The cartel's stability will increase if the estimated risks are small compared to the advantages.

Let U_1^k (U_2^k) be the profit of an exporting (importing) country in the situation k, k ϵ {I, II, III, IV}

The profits are actualised and correspond to the market forecasts in the situation k. However, these forecasts are much more hypothetical in situations other than I, for which drastic structural changes occur with respect to the competitive status quo.

If an exporter at the negotiation table of a developing cartel can estimate his profit in B_1 it will already be difficult for him to accurately estimate the profits in C_1 and D_1; in fact, these profits depend on the strategies chosen by the importers. Such doubts tend to slow down the forming of cartels and the choice of 'hard strategies'.

An exporter whose part of the market is sufficient to halt the forming of a cartel is in a stable positions (A_1). On the other hand, if he accepts such a cartel, then an advantage ΔB_1, he finds himself in B_1, a position only stable in the absence of a consumer's reaction. He also takes the risk of a substantial loss, ΔC_1, and a decreased profit, ΔD_1.

The feasibility of an exporting countries' cartel not only depends on aggregate profits of the coalition, but also on the heterogeneity of the political and economical characteristics within the cartel. The joining of each country would depend on the proposed price and on the quotas granted during the negotiations.

An importer, confronted with a producers' price (B_2) has the alternative of action or passivity. In the first case he risks a loss ΔC_2 against an advantage ΔD_2. The aim of an importers' coalition is to put pressure on the exporting countries to moderate their prices by limiting their imports. The importers can only limit their dependency by accepting far higher local production costs than the world marginal cost. In the case of a price recession, importing countries must then be ready to subsidise these local productions. Failing this, few investors would be ready to take such a risk.

The aim of negotiations between importers would be to define a floor price, guaranteed to investors whatever further prices may be. The higher this price is the greater the subsidies and the more effective the dissuasion facing the exporters.

Let us consider the respective profits of exporters and consumers in situation III. These low profits are due to disastrous production allowances between high cost producers (importers) and low cost producers (exporters). The arbitration consists then to 'exchange' a producer price reduction, to the advantage of importers, with an increase of imports to the advantage of exporters.

3. THE NEGOTIATIONS ON EXPORT QUOTAS

The transposition from quota negotiations to a n–players' cooperative game requires data on the strategies sets Σ_i of each player, as well as on the pay–offs $G_i(\tau_1,...\tau_i,...\tau_n)$, where each player chooses a particular strategy τ_i from Σ_i. Those data reflect the characteristics of the producers and of the demand, up to a chosen horizon, far enough to cover the consumers' and producers' reactions to the price variations. Data uncertainty then increases and the smaller the actualisation rate the greater its reverberations.

The coalition cannot choose any producer price, because some producers would receive lower payments than those of the status quo and this would be against the individual rationality axiom. So, for a given rule of quotas assignment, a producer price interval in which the coalition is possible may exist. If this interval is empty, whatever rules are chosen, no coalition is possible. The existence of such an interval is proven in the case of a simplified model valid for non–exhaustible resources or exhaustible resources with long reserves.

3.1 The Choice of an Allowable Price Interval

The model's data

- Importing countries set: (1, 2,..., i,...n)
- Exporting countries set: (1, 2,..., j,...m)
- Price: P

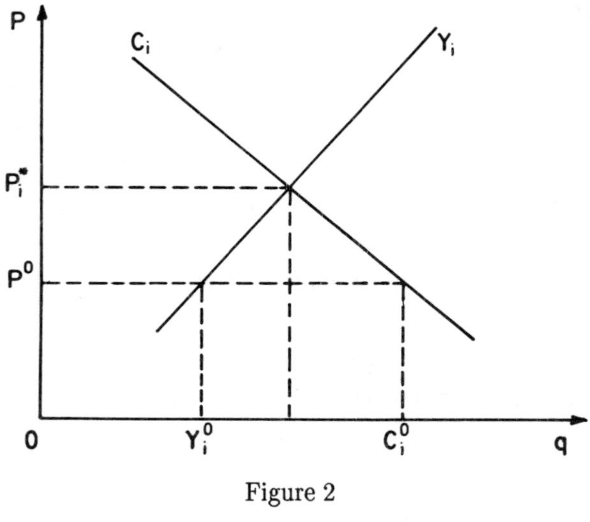

Figure 2

The following data are indexed by i for importers and j for exporters:

C : consumption

Y : production

$M_i = C_i - Y_i$: imports of i

$X_j = Y_j - C_j$: exports of j

η and β are elasticity in consumption and production respectively with regard to the price. The initial data are indexed by ^{o}. This initial state $(C_i^o, Y_i^o, M_i^o, P^o, C_j^o, Y_j^o, X_j^o)$ is balanced: it secures the equality between imports and exports at price P^o.

The n importers' imports calculation

With constant elasticities the offer and demand functions are:

$$\frac{Y_i - Y_i^o}{Y_i^o} = \beta_i \left[\frac{P - P^o}{P^o}\right]$$

$$\frac{C_i - C_i^o}{C_i^o} = \eta_i \left[\frac{P - P^o}{P^o}\right]$$

$$Y_i = Y_i^o(1-\beta_i) + \frac{\beta_i Y_i^o P}{P^o} \tag{1}$$

$$C_i = C_i^o(1+\eta_i) - \frac{\eta_i C_i^o P}{P^o} \tag{2}$$

The autosufficiency point obtained for the price P_i^* is given by their intersection.

$$P_i^* = \frac{P^o\left[C_i^o(1+\eta_i) - Y_i^o(1-\beta_i)\right]}{\beta_i Y_i^o + \eta_i C_i^o} = P^o\left[1 + \frac{C_i^o - Y_i^o}{k_i}\right]$$

with $k_i = \beta_i Y_i^o + \eta_i C_i^o$.

Let M be the imports sum:

$$M = \sum_{i=1}^{n} M_i = \sum_{i=1}^{n} C_i^o(1+\eta_i) - Y_i^o(1-\beta_i) - P/P^o\left[\beta_i Y_i^o + \eta_i C_i^o\right]$$

$$A = \sum_{i=1}^{n} C_i^o(1+\eta_i) - Y_i^o(1-\beta_i) = \sum_{i=1}^{n} M_i^o + k_i = M^o + K$$

$$K = \sum_{i=1}^{n} k_i$$

$$M = A - (PK/P^o) = f(P). \qquad (3)$$

The total imports diminish in a linear manner when P grows. The autosufficiency for this importers set is secured for P^* (M=0):

$$P^* = (AP^o/K) = P^o(1+(M^o/K))$$

The higher K is, the less producers can fix high prices: the participation of each importer to k is made up of two terms:

$\beta_i Y_i^o$: local production aptitude

$\eta_i C_i^o$: consumption sensitiveness to the price

The optimal profit for the exporter j

Let us now try to optimise respectively the exporter j's profit and the coalition's profit, assuming that the assigned export quotas α_j are those of the initial equilibrium:

$$\alpha_j = X_j^o/X^o$$

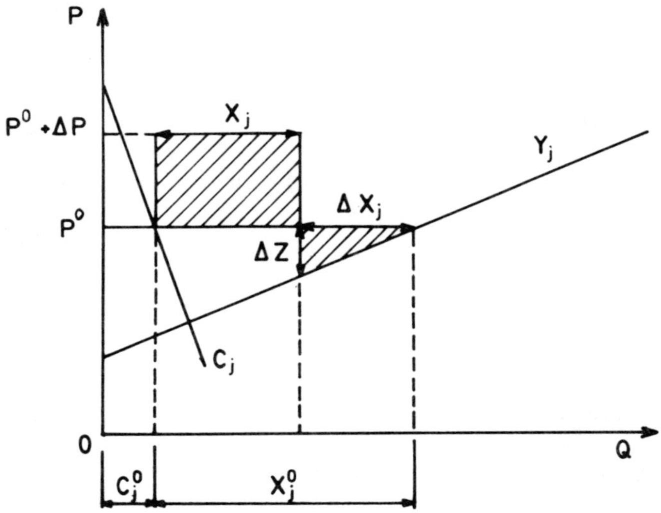

Figure 3

A price increase $\Delta P = P - P^o$ over the initial equilibrium reduces global imports (ΔM) and then j's exports (ΔX_j):

$$\Delta M = -K(\Delta P/P^o) = \Delta X$$

$$\Delta X_j = \alpha_j \Delta X = -\alpha_j K(\Delta P/P^o)$$

$$X_j = X_j^o - \Delta X_j$$

We assume that the price inside the exporting country remains unchanged as well as the consumption C_j^o. This assumption, which is realistic if the use and processing of local base products is widely encouraged in the LDC, can be abandoned without greatly changing the demonstration.

The variation of profit ΔS_j, due to a price increase ΔP, appears in this case as the difference in the diagrams hached areas (Figure 3).

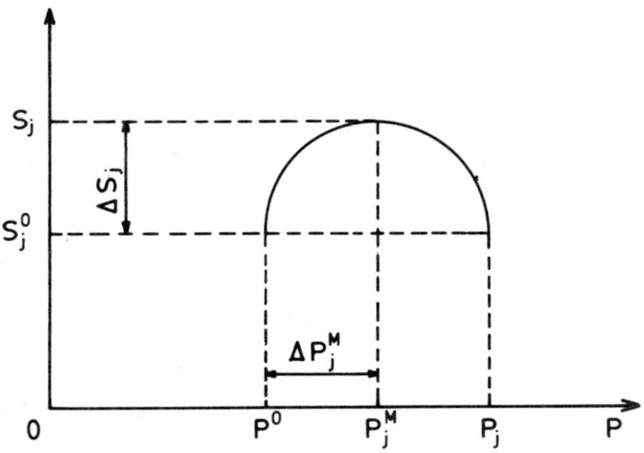

Figure 4

$$\Delta S_j = X_j \Delta P - \left[\frac{\Delta X_j \Delta Z}{2}\right]$$

ΔZ is the cost decrease due to the production decrease ΔX_j.

$$\Delta S_j = \left[X_j^o - \frac{\alpha_j K}{P^o}\Delta P\right]\Delta P - \frac{P^o}{2\beta_j Y_j^o}\left[\frac{\alpha_j K}{P^o}\Delta P\right]^2$$

$$\frac{\partial(\Delta S_j)}{\partial(\Delta P)} = X_j^o - \frac{2\alpha_j K}{P^o}\Delta P - \frac{P^o}{\beta_j Y_j^o} \cdot \left[\frac{\alpha_j K}{P^o}\right]^2 \cdot \Delta P$$

The exporters j's optimal profit is reached in P_j^M (Figure 4).

$$\Delta P_j^M = \frac{P^o X_j^o}{\alpha_j K \left[2 + \frac{\alpha_j K}{\beta_j Y_j^o}\right]}$$

The highest price P_j that j can accept corresponds to the producer price for which his profit is that of the status quo (S_j^o): $\Delta S_j = 0$. Due to the parabolic form of the diagram, P_j is symmetric to P^o with respect to P_j^M:

$$P_j = P^o + 2\Delta P_j^M$$

The Coalition's Maximum Profit (Monopoly Profit)

Let ΔS be the coalition's extra profit due to a price increase ΔP:

$$\Delta S = \sum_{j=1}^{m} \Delta S_j = \sum_{j=1}^{m} \left[X_j^o - \frac{\alpha K}{P^o}\Delta P\right]\Delta P - \frac{P^o}{2\beta_j Y_j^o}\left[\frac{\alpha K}{P^o}\Delta P\right]^2$$

In the same manner we obtain the coalition's maximum profit, at a price P^c:

$$\Delta P^c = \frac{P^o X^o}{2K + \sum_{j=1}^{m} \frac{\alpha_j^2 K^2}{\beta_j Y_j^o}}$$

The coalition's maximum profit cannot be attained if P^c is outside the price interval allowable for the coalition.

The Limits of the Allowable Price Interval

Let us classify the m exporters' set by increasing limit prices P_j. The price interval, allowable by the coalition, is then $[P^o, P_1]$, limited by the first producer's limit price (the most dynamic producer).

in favour of consumers.

The power ratio's sensitivity to substitution possibilities makes the two parameters, costs and delays, intervene. Low costs and short delays give a balanced power ratio: producers have no interest in causing a consumers' coalition by fixing a price which is too high. On their side, consumers cannot hope for more than the equilibrium. The opposite combination (high costs and long delays) leads to a power ratio in favour of producers and helps them to overcome 'political barriers' which are prejudicial to the creation of coalitions.

The model has also been applied in 1975 to the copper market using 1972 data. The results showed a nearly balanced market:

- the Nash solution is the competitive equilibrium if the demand elasticity is 0.6;
- it is very near to it ($\Delta p/p = 2\%$) if this elasticity is 0.4.

The prospects of a durable higher price by cartelisation was not likely, something which the price evolution over the next ten years confirmed.

4.2 The Stability of an Agreement between Exporters and Importers

An agreement between two cartels helps avoid costly independency strategies for both. However, importers, by accepting an increased dependency, expose themselves to an ulterior raising of the negotiated producer price. Different extensions of the model could help simulate concerted policies aimed to stabilise the initial power ratio, without resorting to an increase in substitutions. Three types of action can be envisaged:

- to carry on with studies in research development (RD) to reduce substitution costs. We can integrate RD strategies into substitution strategies if we can establish a relationship between the RD budget and the costs and delays of substitutions;
- to create a strategic stockpiling;
- to increase producers' activities in the concerned sector.

The first two actions improve the consumers' position in the case of a breaking off of the agreement by producers, yet without reducing the exporters' market in the opposite case. The third action increases the added value of exports, as well as it dissuades producers from employing a too aggressive price policy which would harm the profitability of their operations downstream.

By using these different actions it is possible to limit in time the evolution of the initial power ratio and so to increase the agreement's life expectancy. The actions can be simulated on the model if one has estimations of the substitution cost's evolution with respect to the RD budget.

The evolution of floor prices and of the supply and demand functions on the reproduction must be reduced (no producers storing). However this adaptation is limited to obsolescence of the existing capacity, depending on the life expectancy of investments. Beyond this limit excess capacities bear a fixed cost.

For the surplus calculus, capacities evicted by supply restriction policies are not necessarily those whose production costs are the lowest (production quotas system). Then, the supply function distortion leaves the costs' structure invariant.

The Model's Resolution Programme

The following data is necessary for this programme:

- the price and quantity vectors, defining by points the supply and demand functions;
- the producer price and floor price vectors (allowable strategies interval points);
- the substitution capacities matrix;
- the horizon and the actualisation rates;
- the producers' fixed costs;
- the demand growing rate;
- the investments' life expectancies.

The results are:

- the pay–offs bimatrix, which allows to plot the 'isostrategies' in the profits' space;
- the different game solutions;
- the power ratio relative to the Nash solutions with and without substitutions.

$$p = \frac{U_1^N / U_1^o}{U_2^N / U_2^o} \qquad \text{(p = 1 at the competitive equilibrium)}$$

If $p > 1$, cartelisation is profitable for producers. As well if $U_1^{M_1} > U_1^o$ at the optimal threat point M_1, this cartel is stable because it will be profitable whatever may be the importers' reactions.

The Model's Applications

Sensitivity analysis has been carried out on hypothetical models in order to determine how the power ratio changes when the model's parameters are modified.

The consumption surplus and production ratio play a primary role, but only where substitution possibilities are reduced. Producers can then confiscate for their own benefit a large part of the consumers' surplus, this one being unprotected by potential substitutions. The comparison to petroleum is obvious: before 1973, the surplus ratio was largely

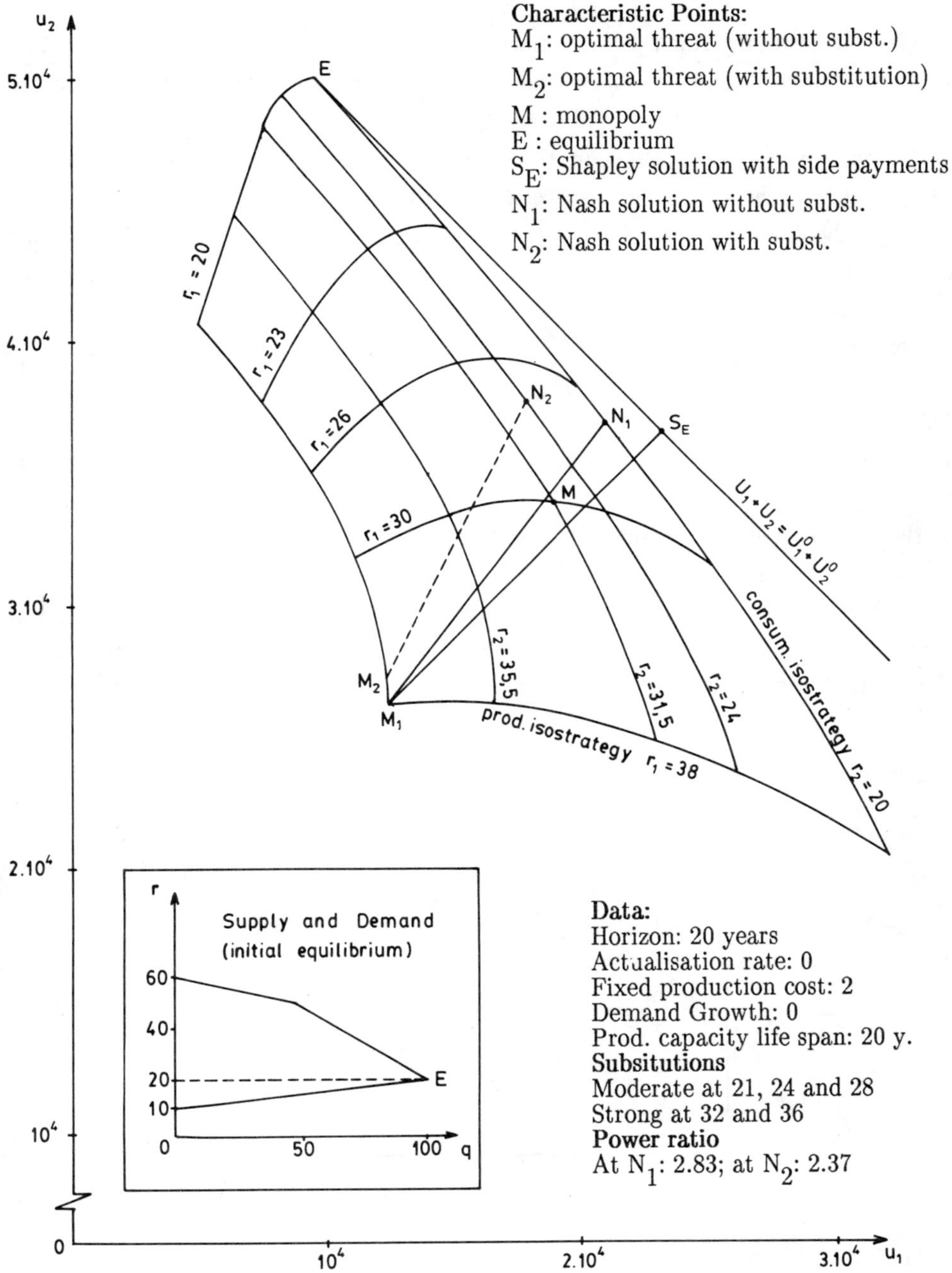

Graph 1. Market Example (Profits' Space)

$N \subset \{((U_1(p_1, p_1), U_2(p_1, p_1))\}, \forall \epsilon \Sigma_1$

One can easily imagine other negotiation sets relative to more severe constraints, for example social constraints of guaranteed agricultural prices, eventually greater than an international negotiated price.

Graph 1 sheds some light on these different concepts in a quantified market example. It represents, in profits' space, the 'isostrategies' of producers and consumers, as well as the characteristic points of the game. The characteristic points on the graph are: M_1: optimal threat (without substitution), M_2: optimal threat (with substitution), M: monopoly, E: equilibrium, S_E: Shapley solution with side payments, N_1: Nash solution without substitution, N_2: Nash solution with substitution.

Model Data

This model seeks to integrate the principal factors of obvious importance in negotiations:

- the substitution possibilities of a consumers' coalition at different prices as well as adaptation lags of consumers, for these substitutions;
- the characteristics of supply and demand functions obtained by econometrical methods, defined here by the set of slope changing points. The evolution of the demand function should be regular at the growing rate τ (invariant demand structure).

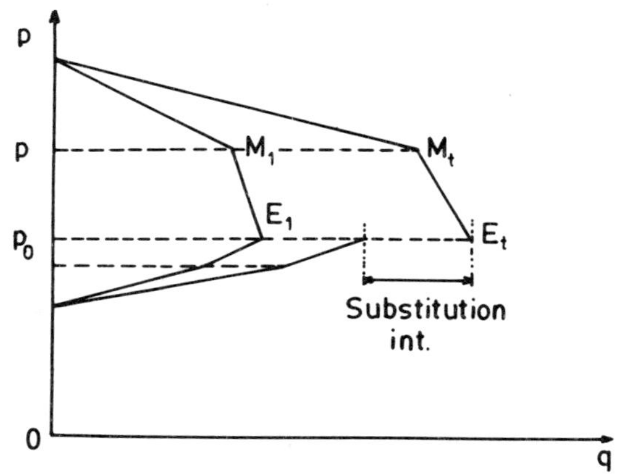

Figure 5

The supply adapts itself to import demand (demand minus substitutions) if the last is greater than the period's initial capacity (hypothesis of perfect anticipation for estimated substitution capacities and for the demand growth). In case of an excess capacity,

4.1 A Negotiation Simulation Model

At a producer price strategy p_1, consumers may oppose that of a price p_2, guaranteed by importers for substitution operations. Respective profits of both coalitions are then:

- $U_1(p_1, p_2)$: exporters' profits minus fixed costs of evinced production capacities.
- $U_2(p_1, p_2)$: consumers' residual surplus (at price p_1) plus the balance of substitution or storing operations.

Game Theory Approach of Negotiations

Such a situation is represented by a two players game, $\Gamma = \{\Sigma_1, \Sigma_2, U_1, U_2\}$, a game in which Σ_i are allowable price intervals for p_1 and p_2. U_i is an application of $\Sigma_1 \times \Sigma_2$ in $\mathbb{R}$. The game possesses a couple of strategies in equilibrium (s_1^o, s_2^o) according to Nash's theorem. These maximin strategies correspond to the prudent behaviour of both players which minimises the risks, whatever adverse strategies there may be. In fact, during negotiations one seeks the best possible starting position in relation to the position of the opponent.

We then use threat strategies. Each couple of starting strategies (p_1, p_2) defines a cooperative Nash solution $(\overline{U}_1 = \overline{U}_1(p_1, p_2), \overline{U}_2 = \overline{U}_2(p_1, p_2))$. The most rational starting point is, according to Nash, the solution of the duel: $\{\Sigma_1, \Sigma_2, \overline{U}_1 - \overline{U}_2\}$. This solution realises the equilibrium of threat strategies $(\overset{*}{p}_1, \overset{*}{p}_2)$ as such:

$$\overline{U}_1(p_1, \overset{*}{p}_2) \leq \overline{U}_1(\overset{*}{p}_1, \overset{*}{p}_2), \forall p_1 \in \Sigma_1$$
$$\overline{U}_2(\overset{*}{p}_1, p_2) \leq \overline{U}_2(\overset{*}{p}_1, \overset{*}{p}_2), \forall p_2 \in \Sigma_2$$

However, the Nash solution must be carefully used. Base products markets are submitted to several constraints which reduce the optimality. One of these constraints arises from the existence of free enterprise. If the power ratio is favourable to producers the negotiated price p_1 will be greater than the equilibrium price p_o. Certain substitution operations in the price area $[p_o, p_1]$ may then prove profitable.

In a capitalist economy those operations will be undertaken in many cases with government approval, for they limit the opportunities for producers to cheat. This constraint leads us to envisage two extreme Nash solutions:

- the first consists of a total absence of substitution from consumers in a successful negotiation.

  $N \subset \{((U_1(p_1, p_o), U_2(p_1, p_o))\}, \forall p_1 \in \Sigma_1$
- the second requires complete substitution for all operations, the cost of this never exceeding the negotiated price

The Model's Extension

The preceding results have been acquired under very strict hypotheses:

- transfer to the state of the responsibilities and risks of base products production,
- measure of the utility of the results in monetary terms, whatever the country,
- negotiations on the sharing of the annual increases in demand.

States, as individuals or firms must remain fairly orthodox in the management of their resources and although the 'player's ruin' phenomenon has different consequences than for firms there is a limit to the proportion of its budget which a state can spend on non–profit production. This is particularly evident for LDCs. DCs have more opportunities to sustain their base products prices artificially, especially in agriculture. In short, there does not exist a true scale for inter–state utility comparison and the negotiation reflects, once again, the power ratio between protagonist states.

As presented, this model shows that small exporting countries should claim much larger shares than they obtain, in the quota allocation mechanism, based principally on the previous year's production. Furthermore, the progressive increase of small exporting countries' shares would favour a better diversification of base products sources. Although the generalisation of this model to an oligopoly is feasible, a simulation approach seems preferable.

4. BASE PRODUCTS PRICE NEGOTIATION BETWEEN EXPORTERS AND IMPORTERS[3]

Faced with an exporting countries' cartel, deciding higher prices thanks to limited quotas, what can importers envisage?

They search for lowest cost base products supply, but with sufficient safety to limit the disastrous consequences of eventual shortages. These two aims are now incompatible: the lowest cost supplying consists of massive base products imports with a reduced safety strategies' cost, compared to that of foreign supplying. The strategies are of two types:

- the stockpiling intended to minimise the consequences of a short term supply; and
- the substitution to limit the effect of more durable shortages.

The use of these strategies also constitutes a dissuasion towards exporters who try to adopt an oligopoly strategy. Failing that, disunited importers would be requested a cartel price by exporters. However, if they coalise they can use retaliation strategies by reenforcing their safety strategies. Concertation alone can avoid ruinous solutions for both coalitions, as in the following model.

$\tilde{U}_2$) corresponds to threat strategies: $\eta_1 = \eta_2 = 1$.

R is the convex area of the possible pay–off couples. The negotiation set N corresponds to the profit couples (U_1, U_2) so that $\eta_1 + \eta_2 = 1$.

The Nash solution is attained by maximising, under the preceding constraint, the expression

$$\underset{\eta_1}{\mathrm{Max}}(U_1 - \tilde{U}_1)(U_2 - \tilde{U}_2)$$

Thus:

$$\eta_1 = \tfrac{1}{2} - \frac{\Delta\rho}{2\Delta q} + \frac{\Delta C\,(p_1 - p_o)}{2(p_o - C_1)(p_o - C_2)}$$

$$+ \frac{1}{2\Delta q}\left[\frac{\rho_1(p_1 - C_1)}{p_o - C_1} - \frac{\rho_2(p_1 - C_2)}{p_o - C_2}\right] = 1 - \eta_2$$

Expressions in which:

$\Delta\rho \;= \rho_1 - \rho_2$

$\Delta C \;= C_1 - C_2$

$p_1 \;= a - b(1+2\Delta q)q_o e^{-\lambda}$ (threat point price)

Influence of Heterogeneity on the Sharing

Inequality in sharing ($\eta_1 \neq \eta_2$) is directly related to the disparities in size and production costs:

a) Size disparity: (at identical costs: $\Delta C = 0$)

Inequality grows with:

$\Delta\rho$: initial inequality in the sharing

C_1: the loss risk grows and so increases the threat.

Inequality diminishes with:

Δq: slowly expanding market

p_1: duopolist combat price

So $\Delta\rho$ tends to progressively reduce the initial inequality in the market sharing. The larger exporter is effectively more vulnerable to the threat of a combat price than is the smaller exporter.

b) *Production cost disparity* (at $\Delta\rho = 0$)

The inequality grows with ΔC and when both C_i are nearing p_o. A lower cost than the competitor's obviously keeps a leading position.

3.2 Quota Allocation

Usually, quota allocation is an n–player's cooperative game. As Eckbo's study, qquoted in Nappi (1979) sshows, cartel stability is short lived: 5.4 years for the average life expectancy, of 51 associations studied in the base products markets.[2] In short, cartelisation must be nearly total to last.

This rule excludes the use of solution concepts which integrate the pay–offs of all the possible coalitions (shapley value, nucleolus). However, the Nash solution to the quota negotiation seems interesting.

The principle of this negotiation is shown in a simply duopoly case which illustrates the influence of the duopolists' heterogeneity.

The Duopoly Characteristics

Let the stake correspond to the demand increase of a growing market, each of the two countries being able to assure, on their own, this increase. The problem is to determine each country's share in this increase, the price being satisfactory (for example, on previous arrangements).

On the markets' initial equilibrium (not always competitive) we have:

p_o : equilibrium price

q_o : imports or exports volume

ρ_i : q_o^i/q_o = initial share of country i, (i=1,2)

p_t : $a - bq_t^s e^{-\lambda t}$ demand equation) where λ is the demand increase rate $(q_t = q_o^t)$ at the price p_o

q_t^s $= q_{1t} + q_{2t}$

C_i : average unit cost

r_i : actualisation rate in country i.

The negotiation's stake is the sharing of the relative demand increase: $\Delta q = e^{\lambda} - 1$.

Σ_i are the strategies' set corresponding to the relative shares in this negotiation: $\eta_i \epsilon [0,1]$.

The game's bimatrix represents all the pay–offs relative to the possible strategy couples: $(U_1(\eta_1 \eta_2), U_2(\eta_1,\eta_2))$ $\forall$ η_1 and $\eta_2 \epsilon [0,1]$.

The Nash Solution

Pay–offs are in monetary terms and represent both countries utilities. No transfer is allowed. The game is defined by the triplet $[R, \breve{U}_1, \breve{U}_2]$ in which the pay–off couple $(\breve{U}_1,$

(a) $|P^o$ ——— P^c ——— $[P^1$ ——— $P^o+2\Delta P^c$ ——— $]P^m_m$ ———

(b) $|P^o$ ——— $[P_1$ ——— P^c ——— $P^o+2\Delta P^c$ ——— $]P_m$ ———

The following two cases are then possible:

– $P^c < P_1$ (a): the maximum profit is feasible

– $P^c > P_1$ (b): the most dynamic producers prevent the coalition from attaining the maximum profit (unless satisfactory side payments in their favour). The coalition's members' heterogeneity can be estimated from the quotient $\Delta P_1/\Delta P^c$

$$\frac{\Delta P_1}{\Delta P^c} = \frac{2K + \dfrac{\alpha_1 K^2}{\beta_j Y_j^o}}{2K + \sum\limits_{j=1}^{m} \dfrac{\alpha_j^2 K^2}{\beta_j Y_j^o}} = \frac{1 + \dfrac{\alpha_1 K}{2\beta_1 Y_1^o}}{1 + \sum\limits_{j=1}^{m} \dfrac{\alpha_j^2 K}{2\beta_j Y_j^o}}$$

with:

$$v_j = \frac{X_j^o}{\beta_j Y_j^o}, \quad \bar{v} = \sum_{j=1}^{m} \alpha_j v_j$$

The dispersion of the coalition's members' extra profits is zero only if:

$$\sum_{j=1}^{m} \alpha_j v_j = v_j, \forall_j \Rightarrow \frac{\Delta P_j}{\Delta P^c} = 1$$

When $\Delta P_j/\Delta P^c < 1/2$ the coalition cannot attain the maximum profit.

The allowable price interval essentially depends on the heterogeneity of the exporters; i.e., of the different values of V_j. Here V_j is the quotient of two terms:

– the exporter's part in the production, in the initial state (X_j^o/Y_j^o);

– the elasticity of production with regard to the price.

However, in reality, producers cannot be described as simply as in this model. Other factors of heterogeneity also intervene, especially reserves and actualisation rates used in dynamic models.

tained horizon (structural changes) requires more serious modifications. However, the difficulty lies more in the collection of the data.

The negotiation presents itself as a conflict between two cartels whose members and characteristics are known. Yet nothing prevents one from considering successively many different coalition possibilities. We can test, for example, two games:

– the first between LDC and DC,
– the second in which exporting DCs would become members of the LDC exporters' cartel.

The result would then permit us to estimate the two situations from the results obtained in both games. Thus we could know if it was more interesting for the bauxite cartel's members (I.B.A.) to welcome Australia at the price of a reduction of their offensive strategies.

The general model also shows clearly the importance of the negotiation's 'game rules'. The choice of rules is without doubt more important than that of the solution concept which is used. The game rules can be in a certain way changed by the players. This is the case of the degree of substitution relative to the concerted solution. By controlling and even nationalising the local base products production sources, consuming countries can choose this degree of substitution, influencing then the negotiation results. In the actual stage of transition towards a New International Economic Order, the fast policy alteration contributes to a revision of the game's rules and it is not one of the least difficulties of the modelisation of markets in a prospective goal. For example, what can one think of the price negotiation for certain metals as long as the legal boundaries of underwater nodule workings are not defined. Such models can, however, be used by simulating markets under different rules. Instead of a unique solution one then obtains, with the same solution concept, a range of solutions. The knowledge of such a range is perhaps one of the means for negotiation of the game's rules.

5. CONCLUSION

The base products markets are the object of multiple interventions as much nationally as internationally. The representation of these active strategies in econometrical studies is difficult. The complementary approach by the game theory as demonstrated in this paper allows one to explore, in the form of scenarios, the likelihood of such strategies, from the value of power ratios prevailing on these markets.

But their success also depends on the homogeneity of a cartel's members, from the political angle too. Policy differences can effectively lead to a refusal of cooperation or a deliberate abandoning of hard strategies, justified though on strictly economical bases.

NOTES

1. "All efforts should be made ... to facilitate the functioning and to further the aims of producer's associations, including their joint marketing arrangements, orderly commodity trading ...' in Prog. of action on the establishment of a new international economic order, No. 3202, 05/01/1974.
2. C. Nappi (1979), p. 187.
3. See A. Richard (1976) for a detailed presentation.

REFERENCES

Banks, F.E. (1974), '*The World Copper Market: An Economic Analysis'*, Ballinger, Cambridge, Mass.

Brown , C.P. (1980), *'The Political and Social Economy of Commodity Control'*, MacMillan, London.

Ezzati, A. (1976), 'Future OPEC Price and Production Strategies as Affected by Its Capacity to Absorb Oil Revenues', *European Economic Review*, 8, pp.107–38.

Hnyilicza, E. and R.S. Pindyck (1976), 'Pricing Policies for a Two–part Exhaustible Resource Cartel: The Case of OPEC', *European Economic Review*, 8, pp.139–54.

Hotelling, H. (1931), 'The Economics of Exhaustible Resources', *Journal of Political Economy*, 39, pp. 137–75.

Levy, B. (1982), 'World Oil Marketing in Transition', *International Organisation*, 36, No. 1, p. 113 ff

Melese, F. (1980), 'Cartel Extraction and Backstop Entry', *Recherche Economique de Louvain*, 46, No. 3, p. 255 ff

Nappi, C. (1979), *Commodity Market Controls*, Lexington, Mass.

Nash, J.F. (1950), 'The Bargaining Problem', *Econometrica*, 18, pp. 155–62.

Richard, A. (1976), 'Les marchés des Produits de Base–Emergence d'un nouvel ordre économique international', Thesis, University of Grenoble II.

Steeg, H. (1984), 'Nouvel accord de l'AIE: les stocks petroliers parade à une baisse des approvisionnements', l'obs. de l'OCDE, No. 130, pp. 28–30.

Stoffaes, C. (1981), 'Quelques applications de la théorie des jeux aux relations économiques internationales', *Revue Economique*, 2, pp. 271–340.

PART II

APPLICATIONS

CHAPTER 5

A WORLD GRAINS AND SOYBEANS MODEL

Donald O. Mitchell, *The World Bank, Washington, DC*

1. INTRODUCTION[1]

This paper describes the recently completed world grains and soybean model currently used by the Commodity Studies and Projections Division. The model is a non–spatial, partial equilibrium, net–trade model. It is global in scope with 15 countries modelled individually and the remaining countries grouped into nine regions.

The commodities included in the model are wheat, rice, coarse grains (maize, oats, barley, sorghum, rye, millett, and mixed grains), soybeans, soymeal, and soyoil. Individual models are estimated for each commodity and country or regions with cross linkages between commodities. Soybeans are modelled as beans on the production side but oil and meal in the consumption and trade components.

Production for each country or region is determined as the product of separately estimated harvested area and yield equations. Harvested area is determined by a two-stage process wherein total area harvested is determined first and then allocated among competing crops on the basis of lagged per acre revenues. Yields are estimated as a function of lagged crop prices, fertilizer prices, the proportion of area planted to high yielding varieties and a linear trend.

Per capita imports of each commodity are estimated directly for importing countries as a function of population, income, domestic supply and prices. Ending stocks are estimated as a share of consumption and prices. Total consumption is obtained as an identity. Net exports are estimated for exporting countries as a function of the level of each commodity available for export and world prices. Consumption in the exporting countries is estimated as a function of population, income and prices.

The model is solved simultaneously for the level of world prices which equate net imports and net exports. A trade hierarchy is assumed which allows small exporters to export as much as they desire while forcing the United States to be the residual supplier.

O. Guvenen (ed.), International Commodity Market Models and Policy Analysis, 87–111.

The primary objective of the model is to provide a basis for medium term (one to ten years) annual projections of world prices, and projections of trade, production, consumption and ending stocks for each country or region. A secondary objective is to provide a flexible global framework within which more detailed policy analysis models can be built and simulated.

2. MODEL DESCRIPTION

The general structure of the global model is shown in Figure 1. Each country model takes the price from the world linkage and returns the level of net trade. This structure allows great flexibility in the design and level of detail in the country models. When a particular policy simulation requires greater country detail than is provided by the standard model, a more detailed model is built and inserted in place of the standard model.

The variables used in the model must satisfy several criteria. First, and most importantly, the variables must be appropriate for capturing the economic relationships within the commodity markets of the countries and regions of the world market. Second, since the variables are to be used in an econometric model, a time series extending over approximately 20 years is desired. Third, the desired output of the model must be satisfied by the variables selected. Finally, forecasts of the exogenous variables used in the model should be available for the relevant future period.

Table 1 contains the list of exogenous and endogenous variables used in the model, along with their sources, definitions and availability of forecasts and updates. One difficulty with commodity data is the distinction between a calendar year and a crop year. Some agriculural data, such as stocks, are only available on a crop year basis. Other macro economic data, such as income, are available only for a calendar year. Regardless of the year definition selected, some incompatibilities will be encountered. If a calendar year is selected, consumption and trade for a single harvest fall in two years. If a crop year is selected, the macroeconomic definitions do not correspond. A crop year basis is used in this model in order to focus on the agricultural aspects of the model.

Every model necessarily involves compromise and simplifications of the real world. This model does not consider a number of topics which are important, but which have not been modelled at this stage. Quality differences within each product are not considered; each commodity is treated as homogeneous and having a single world price. Trade flows between countries are also ignored; trade is assumed to take place in a world market yielding only net trade figures. Resource use for production is also largely ignored with the exception of land and fertilizer. Transportation costs are also not con-

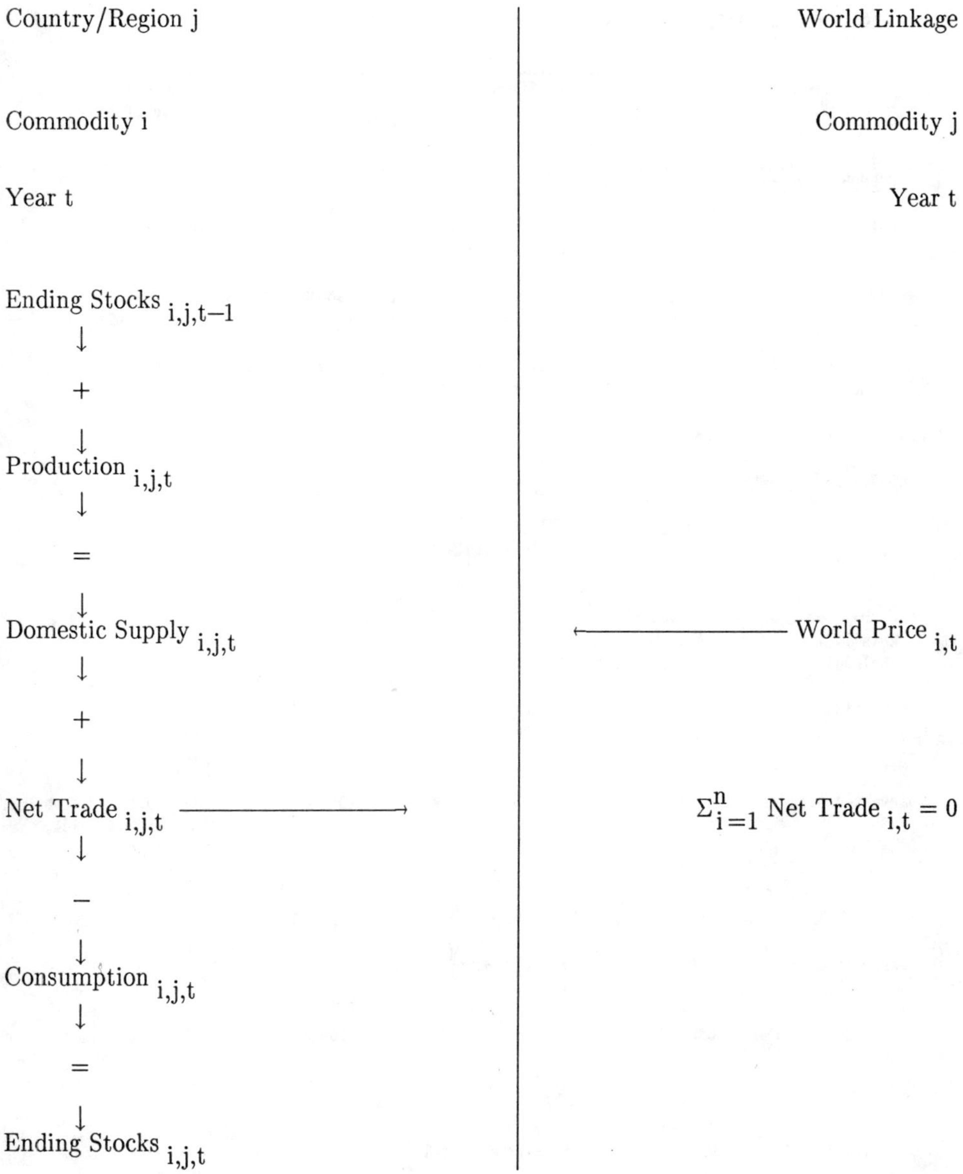

Figure 1. World Grain and Soybeans Model

TABLE 1 : Agricultural Model Variable List*

Variable	Source	Definition	Years	Fore-cast	Frequency & Source of Forecast
EXOGENOUS VARIABLES					
Population	WB, UN	Million People Calendar Year	196-083	2000	Annually, WB, UN
Income - GDP	WB, IFS	Billion Local Currency Calendar Year	1960-83	1995	Quarterly, WB, OECD, WEFA
Exchange Rate to $	WB, IFS	Local Currency/US $ Calendar Year	1960-83	1995	Quarterly, WB, WEFA
Consumer Price Index	WB, IFS	Index, 1975=100 Calendar Year	1960-83		Quarterly, WB, WEFA
ENDOGENOUS VARIABLES					
World Crop Prices	USDA	$/MT, f.o.b., Gulf Simple Monthly Average Crop Year	1960-84		Monthly, USDA
Country Crop Price Retail Wholesale	As available FAO, WB, USDA FAO, WB, USDA				
Production	USDA	Thousand Metric Tons Crop Year	1960-83		Monthly, FAS, USDA, World Grain Situation/Outlook
Harvested Area	USDA	Thousand Hectares Crop Year	1960-83		Semi-Annually, Sept & March, FAS, USDA, Reference Tables on Supply Utilization
Crop Yields	USDA	Tons Per Hectare	1960-83		"
Consumption	USDA	Thousand Metric Tons Crop Year	1960-83		"
Net Trade	USDA	Thousand Metric Tons	1960-83		Monthly, Calendar Year Basis, FAS, USDA
Beginning Stocks	USDA	Thousand Metric Tons	1960-83		Semi-Annually,Sept & March, FAS, USDA, Reference Tables on Supply Utilization.

*Data sources are WB = World Bank; FAO = Food and Agricultural Organization; IFS = International Financial Statistics published by the International Monetary Fund; USDA = US Dept. of Agriculture; WEFA = Wharton Econometric Forecasting Service; FAS = Foreign Agricultural Service of USDA+ OECD = Organization for Economic Cooperation and Development.

sidered at this stage.

Given the size of the model and the important variables which are not included, it is apparent that the model will provide a framework for research, not a rigid forecasting model. The model is constructed so that individual variables, such as yields, can be analysed and modified by expert opinion. In this way the important variables which cannot be explicitly included, can be reflected in model variables. This approach is consistent with the Commodity Studies and Projections Division's approach to forecasting which uses opinion from country experts in the preparation of forecasts.

The model has been estimated primarily with ordinary least squares, using annual data from 1960 to 1981. The equations are linear in the variables. The entire model contains approximately 1200 equations and is solved using the Gauss–Seidel iterative procedure.

The countries and regions defined in the model are shown in Table 2. The selection of countries to model individually was made on the basis of three criteria: 1) similar economic and political structure; 2) geographical location; and 3) importance to global trade for the commodities.

3. SUPPLY

The supply model consists of three separate components corresponding to the decision sequence of producers. First, a total cropland equation is estimated for each country or region to capture the quantity of cropland harvested for the four model commodities; second, the allocation of this land among the commodities is estimated; and third, a yield equation is estimated for each commodity. Production for each commodity is the product of the area harvested and yield equations.

The two–stage specification of the cropland harvested of each crop attempts to separate the short term and long term decisions faced by producers. The short term decision involves allocating cropland among closely competing crops. This decision can be made and implemented very rapidly and the decision can be reversed in a future year at very little cost. Rigidities are imposed on the decision by different machinery requirements for each crop and the competition for a scarce resource such as labour availability at peak load periods, but switching of land between crops is generally possible.

The decision of how much total land to plant to crops is a long term decision because of the capital investment required to prepare land for planting. The decision to expand cropland requires that land be taken out of its alternative use (e.g. forestry) and cleared, ploughed and harrowed so that it can beplanted. This process requires an investment of labour and capital. Once land is prepared for cropping, the subsequent invest-

Table 2. Model Regions

Country/Region	Countries
Industrial Countries	
Australia	Australia
Canada	Canada
EC–10	Belgium, France, Luxembourg, Netherlands, W. Germany, Ireland, United Kingdom, Denmark, Greece
Japan	Japan
Other Industrial Countries	Austria, Finland, Iceland, Malta, Norway, Portugal, Spain, Sweden, Switzerland, New Zealand
United States	United States
Centrally Planned Economies	
Eastern Europe	Albania, Bulgaria, Czechoslovakia, East Germany, Hungary, Poland, Romania, Yugoslavia
USSR	Union of Soviet Socialist Republic
Developing Countries	
Argentina	Argentina
Brazil	Brazil
Central Africa	Botswana, Lesotho, Namibia, Kenya, Swaziland, Malagasy Republic, Malawi Mozambique, Tanzania, Uganda, Zambia, Angola, Burundi, Cameroon, Central African Republic, Chad, Congo, Ethiopia, Djibouti, Benin, Gabon, Gambia, Ghana, Guinea, Equatorial Guinea, Guinea–Bissau, Ivory Coast, Liberia, Mali, Mauritania, Mauritius, Niger, Reunion, Rwanda, Senegal, Sierra Leone, Somalia, Sudan, Togo, Upper Volta, Zaire, Zimbabwe

China	China
East Asia	Burma, Kampuchea, Laos, Vietnam, Hong Kong, Singapore, South Korea, Brunei, Malaysia, Philippines, North Korea, Mongolia, Pacific Islands, Papua New Guinea, Fiji Islands
Egypt	Egypt
India	India
Indonesia	Indonesia
Latin America and Caribbean	Bahamas, Barbados, Bermuda, Belize, Other Caribbean Islands, Cuba, Dominica, Dominican Republic, Jamaica, Trinidad and Tobago, Honduras, Nicaragua, Panama, Costa Rica, El Salvador, Guatemala, Haiti, Bolivia, Chile, Colombia, Ecuador, French Guiana, Guyana, Paraquay, Peru, Surinam, Uruquay, Venezuela
Mexico	Mexico
Nigeria	Nigeria
North Africa and Middle East	Algeria, Bahrain, Cyprus, Iran, Iraq, Israel, Kuwait, Libya, Oman, Qatar, Saudi Arabia, United Arab Emirates, Jordan, Lebanon, Morocco, Syria, Tunisia, Turkey, Yemen A.R., Yemen D.M.
Pakistan	Pakistan
South Asia	Afghanistan, Bangladesh, Bhutan, Nepal, Sri Lanka
Thailand	Thailand

Source: EPDCS.

ment required to keep the land under crop is small. Consequently, the decision to expand cropland involves an initial outlay plus the loss of revenue from the previous land use. The decision is often irreversible in the short run. Timber, for example, is not an annual crop and cannot be interchanged with an annual crop.

3.1. Total Cropland

The expansion of total cropland which a producer will undertake can be viewed as an optimal investment problem. It is assumed that the producer will attempt to maximise the following function

$$\pi_t = f(\Sigma_1 \Delta P_i/(1 + r)^i, C_t)$$

where $\Sigma_1 \Delta P_i/(1 + r)^i$ is the discounted incremental profit flow expected from planting the land to crops rather than its previous use. The one–time capital investment required to prepare the land for crops is denoted by C_t.

This investment function suggests that an estimated total cropland equation should contain variables to measure the profitability of alternative land uses, and the capital cost of land preparation. Based on these assumptions, the cropland equation is specified as follows:

$$TCHA_t = f(TCHA_{t-1}, DTCRV_{t-1}, DBP_{t-1}, TGES_{t-1}, TIME)$$

where

$TCHA_t$ is the harvested area in year t of the model commodities

$DTCRV_{t-1}$ is the weighted revenue per hectare based on world prices of the crops expressed in constant local currency in year t–1.

DBP_{t-1} is the world beef price expressed in constant local currency in year t–1.

$TGES_{t-1}$ is the sum of wheat, coarse grain and rice ending stocks in year t–1.

TIME is a linear trend with 1960 = 1, 1962 = 2, etc.

The lagged total cropland, $TCHA_{t-1}$, is included to reflect the partial adjustment of cropland toward the desired level. The arguments for this specification are well known and date back to Nerlove's work on agricultural supply response (Nerlove, 1958). The variable $DTCRV_{t-1}$ reflects the weighted revenue per hectare received from all crops in the previous year. The prices used to calculate this variable are the international prices. The yields are the actual country yields and the weights are based on the area harvested of each of the crops. This variable does not capture the profitability of crop production since no cost information is included, however, it is a superior specification to prices since it reflects yield increases over time. The lagged form of the variable is included to proxie farmers' expectations of future revenues. This variable may also be measuring capital availability which may be a factor in an investment decision. The variable is converted into local country currency and deflated by the country consumer price index.

The world beef price was included to capture the value of using the land for pasture. Price rather than revenue is used because estimates of beef production has not changed significantly over time. A linear trend is included to capture unknown factors such as government land development programmes which are independent of year–to–year changes in commodity prices or profitability.

A final variable, not suggested by the theoretical model, is also included in the estimated equation. This variable is total grain ending stocks (wheat, coarse grain and rice) in the previous year. It is included to measure local food stock conditions. It is significant in a number of countries. The negative sign indicates that low grain stocks in the previous year result in expanded total cropland in the next year. This result would be consistent with a subsistence type agriculture where low stocks increase the risk of lower food consumption. It is also consistent with an exporting country which attempts to maintain an inventory for exports.

The land preparation costs suggested by the theoretical model were not included because of lack of data. However, at a future time this variable will be explored using wage rates and other proxie variables. Interest rates were included in several preliminary specifications, but were consistently not found to be significant.

An alternative functional form of the total crop revenue and beef price variables which was used in some specifications was to include these variables in ratio form rather than separately. While not the preferred specification, this alternative has the advantage of eliminating the exchange rate and consumer price index from the equation. It worked better for countries which have had very high inflation rates and rapidly falling currency values. An undesirable characteristic of this functional form is the forced equality of the response of area to both total crop revenue and beef prices.

3.2 Harvested Area

The harvested area of each crop is estimated as a function of total cropland harvested and relative commodity revenues. This specification treats the determination of harvested area as a short run allocation decision given that the decision of how much cropland to plant has already been made. The specified equation is:

$$HA_{i,t} = f(TCHA_t, HA_{i,t-1}, RV_{i,t-1}, RV_{j,t-1}, TIME)$$

where

$HA_{i,t}$ is the harvested area of commodity i in year t

$TCHA_t$ is the total cropland harvested in year t of wheat, coarse grains, rice and soybeans

$RV_{i,t}$ is the revenue of commodity i in year

TIME is a linear trend with 1960=1, 1961=2, etc.

The lagged dependent variable, $HA_{i,t-1}$, was included to represent the partial adjustment toward a desired area harvested. The inclusion of this variable is based on theoretical arguments offered by Nerlove and others. The lagged crop revenues are included to represent the relative profitability of competing crops. Revenues rather than prices are used to allow changing crop yields to be reflected in both the historical estimates and in projections. Finally a linear trend, TIME, is included to capture unknown factors or factors which are known to be important, but which cannot be included due to data limitations. One of these known but not included factors is production costs. Ideally, net profits should be used rather than revenues. By excluding production costs, the assumption is being made that costs are growing proportionately to revenues. This is not true. The costs of producing some crops, such as those which require large amounts of fertilizers and chemicals, are growing more rapidly than other crops. A linear trend allows some of these omitted variables to be captured but not identified.

3.3 Crop Yields

Crop yields are assumed to be influenced by seed quality, inputs such as fertilizers, land quality and weather. The estimated yield model necessarily simplifies these factors into variables which can be used to represent the various factors. The model is:

$$YD_{i,t} = f(TIME, RPF_{i,t-1}, HA_{i,t}, HYV_{i,t})$$

where

$YD_{i,t}$ is the yield per hectare in year t of commodity i

TIME is a linear trend with 1960=1, 1961=2, etc.

$RPF_{i,t-1}$ is the lagged ratio of the price of the commodity i to the price of fertilizer

$HA_{i,t}$ is the area harvested of the commodity i in year t

$HYV_{i,t}$ is the percent of total area planted to the high–yielding varieties.

The linear trend, TIME, is included to measure the genetic improvement in seed over time. Doing so assumes that the contribution of plant breeding research to yields is growing at a constant amount per year. An alternative assumption which should be considered is that a yield limit exists and yields increase at a decreasing rate. If this is the case yields would increase along a nonlinear or perhaps log linear path. The selection of the appropriate yield model can be based on both empirical observation and agronomic research. Yield experiments conducted by plant breeders provide some evidence of whether leveling–off of yields is being observed. As reported by Menz and Pardey (1983), agronomic trials do not indicate any plateau in US corn yield gains, and the evidence suggests linear growth.

For many countries data is very difficult to obtain on rates of fertilizer application. In order to capture the contribution of fertilizer to yields, the ratio of world crop price to world fertilizer price was used. This variable attempts to measure the incentives for farmers to apply fertilizer, considering both the price of fertilizer and the price of the crop.

Three different variables are used to measure the influence of fertilizer and crop prices on yields. In one form, the ratio of last year's crops to last year's fertilizer price is used. Secondly, last year's crop price is divided by the current fertilizer prices. The appropriate variable to use depends on two factors, the availability of information and the speed of adjustment. The first variable, last year's crop price divided by the current year's fertilizer price assumes that at the time of fertilizer application, farmers do not know the current crop price but they do know the current year's fertilizer price. The third mentioned form of the variable is only appropriate in Southern Hemisphere countries where crops are planted after the Northern Hemisphere crops are harvested. Consequently, farmers are able to estimate the current year price very well. This specification is applied to crops grown in Argentina, Australia, Brazil and South Africa.

The third factor influencing crop yields is the quality of land. In general, the quality of land should be inversely related to the quantity of land planted. As more and more land is planted, farmers will be using less productive land. Since not all countries have changed their crop area significantly over the last two decades, we would not expect yields to respond to this variable in all countries. Further, it is often statistically difficult to separate the negative influence of lower quality land from the positive influence of genetic yield gains.

The introduction of the high–yielding varieties (HYVs) represents a movement to a higher yield curve. In some cases the new varieties were able to produce twice the amount of the traditional varieties. In order to account for this shift, the HYV variable was included directly in the yield equation. When data was not available on the level of HYV use, a proxie variable was used to represent the adoption of the HYVs.

4. IMPORT DEMAND

The demand for imports can be viewed in general as a function of income, prices and relevant demand shifters

$$M_{i,t} = f(Y_t, P_{i,t}, P_{j,t}, Z_t)$$

where $M_{i,t}$ is per capita imports of commodity i, Y_t is real per capita income, $P_{i,t}$ is the real import price of commodity i, $P_{j,t}$ is the real price of a related commodity j, and Z_t is a set of relevant demand shifters. This basic import demand model has been presented by Leamer and Stern (1970), Labys (1973) and others. The specific functional form, relevant variables and expected results are dependent upon characteristics of the commodity being imported, the nature of use of the imported commodity, the structure both of the international market and the domestic market and many other factors.

In this study the demand for grain imports is treated as the independent demand for each of the primary grain categories – wheat, rice, coarse grains, soymeal and soyoil.[2] In many cases, an importing country both produces and imports the commodity, and in some cases a country will produce, import and export the commodity. This latter case can occur for several reasons. First, a large country may import in one geographic region while exporting from another. This kind of activity occurs between the United States and Canada, with the United States importing feed grains along the Canadian border and exporting through the Gulf. Seasonal supply availabilities may also cause an exporting country to import during certain periods of the year. Finally, differences in grain quality and varieties may cause a country to both import and export grain. The EEC, for example, produces, consumes and exports soft wheat while importing hard wheat. The soft wheat is used primarily for noodles, pastries and quick bread while the hard wheats are used for yeast breads and hard rolls.

An explanation of the occurrence of both imports and exports within the same year will not be pursued here. In order to avoid these issues, other researchers have chosen instead to study the net import demand for grain. This approach has merit to the extent that imported and domestic goods are substitutes. If the imported good does not substitute for the domestically produced good, no amount of change in domestic production will affect the demand for imports. Alternatively, if the imported and domestic good are identical, domestic and imported goods are perfect substitutes and a unit of imported grain will exactly offset a unit of domestically produced grain.

Because of the small size of their imports relative to total world demand, most importing countries can be assumed to face a perfectly elastic supply at a given price. If imports and domestic goods are regarded as perfect substitutes, import demand can be viewed as an excess demand schedule. Consider Figure 2. Domestic demand and supply are shown in Figure 2A as D and S respectively. The difference between D and S below P_1 is the excess demand schedule, ED in Figure 2B, or equivalently the demand for imports. At a price below P_1, domestic demand exceeds domestic supply and ED shows the imports required to satisfy domestic demand. If the imported and domestically produced goods are perfect substitutes and if free trade prevails, then imports, M, will equal ED. Therefore, domestic supply will directly influence imports and the import demand function should include domestic supply variables directly (see Leamer and Stern, 1970, p. 11 for a discussion of this specification).

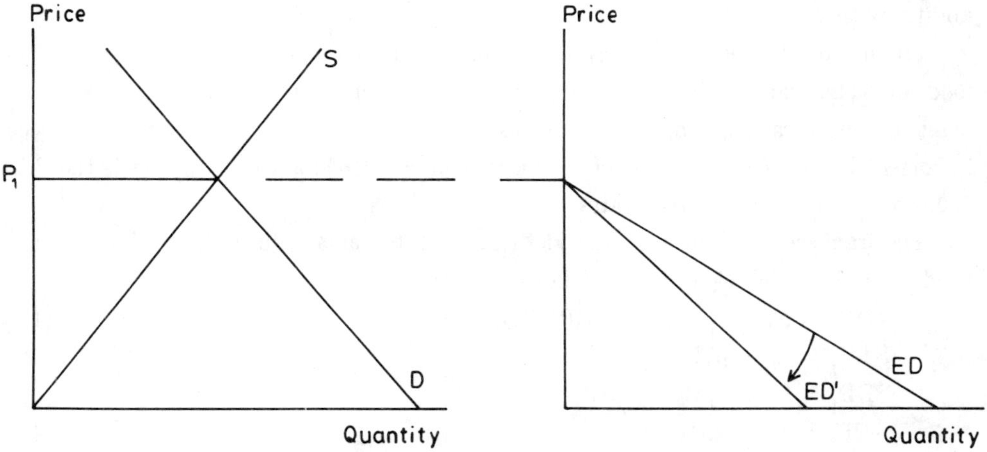

Figure 2a

Figure 2b

Figure 2. Import demand

With trade barriers the excess demand curve will be rotated to ED′. This situation can be written as

$$ED' = F(ED, G)$$

where the excess demand curve depends on the difference between domestic demand and supply and a set of government variables, G. Examples of such government variables could be import duties, foreign exchange constraints or a government budget constraint.

A dynamic specification of import demand is appropriate when demand in any period is assumed to adjust only partially toward desired or equilibrium demand. Government restrictions could also delay the adjustment of demand to changes in the underlying demand determinants. Partial adjustment to some desired level can be modelled using the Koyck lag specification of a lagged dependent variable as an explanatory variable. However, this specification may have another valid interpretation. That is, the use of an imported good as an input into a production process could cause the level of imports to depend on past levels of imports. This occurs when imports have contributed importantly to the size of an end use industry and their continuation is necessary to maintain the industry. The feeding of livestock is an example.

Foreign exchange availability has been suggested as an important determinant by a number of authors including Leamer and Stern (1970), Hemphill (1974), Abbott (1979). The importance of foreign exchange as a constraint may have increased in recent years, at least among the developing countries, following the worsening in debt servicing ability by these countries.

Finally, a variable which may also influence grain import demand is the level of food aid. This variable is relevant for many developing countries and should act as a demand shifter causing imports to increase beyond the levels which would have been imported without food aid. One of the most significant food aid programmes is the P.L. 480 programme of the United States

The framework of the import model can be stated as a reduced form of a standard residual trade model. Consider the following model:

$$PROD_t = \beta_0 + \beta_1 PF_{t-1} + \beta_2 PROD_{t-1} \qquad (1)$$

$$STK_t = \alpha_0 + \alpha_1 PF_{t-1} \qquad (2)$$

$$DD_t = \gamma_0 + \gamma_1 Y_t + \gamma_2 PR_t \qquad (3)$$

$$PF_t = \tau_1 + \tau_2 PW_t \qquad (4)$$

$$PR_t = \delta_1 + \delta_2 PW_t \qquad (5)$$

$$M_t = \pi_0 + \pi_1 (DD_t - PROD_t - STK_t + STK_{t+1}) - \pi_2 G_t \qquad (6)$$

where

$PROD_t$ is production in year t

PF_t is the real farm price in year t

STK_t is the level of beginning stocks in year t

DD_t is the level of domestic demand in year t

Y_t is real per capita income in year t

PR_t is the real retail price in year t

M_t is the level of imports in year t

PW_t is the world price expressed in local currency and deflated by consumer price index in year t

G_t is other factors which influence imports such as a country's balance of payments, in year t

All quantities are assumed to be expressed on a per capita basis and all prices are in real terms. Transportation costs are assumed to be zero. Equation (1) is a simple production model in which production depends on farm prices in the previous period and on last year's production. Equation (2) is a stock equation which specifies the level of stocks available in period t as dependent on prices in year t–1. Domestic demand, equation (3), is a function of income, population and retail price. Equations (4) and (5) reflect the relationship between farm and retail price and the world price. Finally, equation (6) expresses the level of imports as a function of the level of excess demand, the world price and other relevant variables such as the balance of payments. Assume that production and stocks are predetermined in any given year. Substituting equations (1)–(5) into (6) and rewriting, we have:

$$M_t = \pi_0 + \pi_1(\gamma_0 + \gamma_1 Y_t + \gamma_2(\delta_1 + \delta_2 PW_t) \tag{7}$$

$$+ (\overline{PROD}_t + \overline{STK}_t) + \pi_1(\alpha_0 + \alpha_1(\tau_1 + \tau_2 PW_t) - \pi_2 G_t$$

or

$$M_t = \omega_0 + \omega_1 Y_t + \omega_2 PW_t + \omega_3(\overline{PROD}_t + \overline{STK}_t) + \omega_4 G_t \tag{8}$$

where

$$\omega_0 = \pi_0 + \pi_1\gamma_0 + \pi_1\gamma_2\delta_1 + \pi_1\alpha_0 + \pi_1\alpha_1\tau_1$$
$$\omega_1 = \pi_1\gamma_1$$
$$\omega_2 = \pi_1\gamma_2\delta_2 + \pi_1\alpha_1\tau_2$$
$$\omega_3 = \pi_1$$
$$\omega_4 = \pi_2$$

Equation (8) is a reduced form import demand equation which can be estimated directly. It is difficult to interpret the individual coefficients, however, we can infer the sign of most of the variables. Income should have a positive sign, production plus stock should have a negative sign as should current world price. The intercept term and the exogenous variable G_t may have either a positive or negative sign.

The direct estimation of an import equation is not without problems. However in spite of these problems, this approach produces a useful model for forecasting imports of a country or region. Abbott (1979) has pointed out some of the advantages and disadvantages of using this approach. One of the advantages of the import demand approach is that the direct estimation of trading behaviour requires little knowledge of individual country's policies. This is important when a large number of countries are being studied as is the case in building a world model. It is also essential when regions are being considered since the government policies of a region are nearly impossible to define.

A second advantage of the import demand model is that the government is treated endogenously in the determination of the level of imports. This corresponds to the decision making structure regarding the level of imports in the majority of countries. It also indicates that the coefficients of the import demand equation reflect the response of the government importing agency. Variables which would influence a government decision maker can also be explicitly included as explanatory variables. These types of variables cannot be easily included in the more traditional trade models.

The import demand approach does have limitations which need to be recognised. Since the estimated equation is a reduced form, interpretation of the parameters is difficult. The structural form model which yields the reduced form is unknown and incorrect conclusions about the contribution of a particular variable are more likely to occur. Another problem occurs because the parameters also change. As a consequence, estimation of the import demand equation requires stable country policies. At the very least, this problem requires some attention and caution in the use of import equations under unstable policy conditions.

The elasticity of demand for imports taken from the excess demand curve is:

$$E_{ED} = \frac{\delta ED}{\delta P} \cdot \frac{\overline{P}}{\overline{Q}_I}$$

where $\overline{Q}_I$ is the mean quantity imported and $\overline{P}$ is the mean price. This can be stated in terms of domestic demand and supply elasticities as:

$$E_{ED} = E_D \frac{\overline{Q}_D}{\overline{Q}_I} - E_S \frac{\overline{Q}_S}{\overline{Q}_I}$$

Therefore, the elasticities of excess demand is equal to the elasticity of demand times the ratio of quantity demanded to the quantity imported minus the elasticity of domestic supply times the ratio of domestically produced to imported quantities.

The E_{ED} will equal E_D when $Q_s = 0$ or $E_S = 0$ and E_{ED} will be more elastic than E_D in all other cases. Suppose $E_S = 0$, domestic supply is perfectly inelastic – the situation which exists in the short run for production of an annual crop such as wheat. The elasticity of excess demand is then given by

$$E_{ED} = E_D \cdot \frac{\overline{Q}_D}{\overline{Q}_I}$$

or it is equal to domestic demand times the ratio of quantity demanded to imports. If imports represent half of total quantity demanded, E_{ED} would be twice E_D.

The import equation (8) expresses imports as a function of income, domestic supply, the import price and a government variable. An expanded version of the model was estimated for each of the three grain types. The estimated equation allows for cross price effects and domestic substitution between grains and is estimated on net imports. The model is also specified as a dynamic model to allow for a partial adjustment to changes in the independent variables. The estimated model is:

$$NI_{i,t} = f(Y_t, DS_{i,t}, DS_{j,t}, P_{i,t}, P_{j,t}, TB_t, NI_{i,t-1})$$

where

$NI_{i,t}$	is per capita net imports of commodity i in year t
Y_t	is per capita real gross domestic product in year t
$DS_{i,t}$	is per capita domestic supply (production plus beginning period of stocks) of commodity i in year t
$DS_{j,t}$	is domestic supply of a substitute commodity j in year t
$P_{i,t}$	is the world price of commodity in year t in US dollars expressed in the country currency and deflated by the country's consumer price index
$P_{j,t}$	is the price of a substitute commodity j in year t
TB_t	is the per capita merchandise trade balance in year t measured in country currency and deflated by the country's consumer price index

An additional variable, food aid shipments, was included when data were available.

5. EXPORT SUPPLIES

The structure of the world grain export market has been described by various authors as oligopolistic with price leadership provided by one or several of the major exporting countries. McCalla (1967) described the world wheat market as a duopoly with price leadership provided by Canada. Alaouze, Watson and Sturgess (1977) described the wheat market as a triopoly involving the United States, Canada and Australia. Bredahl and Leonardo (1983) tested a US residual supplier model for coarse grain exports.

Grain and soybean exports are dominated by a few countries. The five largest exporters provided 73.3% of the total rice exports, 94.2% of the total wheat exports, 84.4% of the total grain exports and 98% of the total soybean exports over the 1979–81 period. The United States was the largest exporter, providing 65.3% of the coarse grain exports, 45.3% of the wheat exports, 58% of the soy product exports and 23.2% of the rice exports over the 1979–81 period.

Because of the small number of countries which supply the majority of exports, the oligopoly model provides a useful beginning point for analysis of exports. An oligopoly exists when more than one seller can influence the market. Because of the small number of sellers, each seller is expected to be aware of the actions of its rival and of their reactions to changes in policy. Many different market outcomes are possible from an oligoploy model ranging from competition to collusion.

Suppose the market consists of one dominant firm and a number of smaller firms. The dominant firm may or may not be the low cost producer in the market. For political or other reasons, the dominant firm may decide to set the market price and let the small firms sell all they wish at that price. The small firms will behave as perfectly competitive suppliers and regard their demand curve as perfectly elastic at the price set by the dominant firm. The problem facing the dominant firm is to determine the price so as to maximise profits while allowing the small firms to sell as much as they wish. Consider Figure 3. The market demand curve is D, and the marginal cost curve of the dominant firm is MC_d. The summation of the marginal cost curves of all small firms is MC_s.

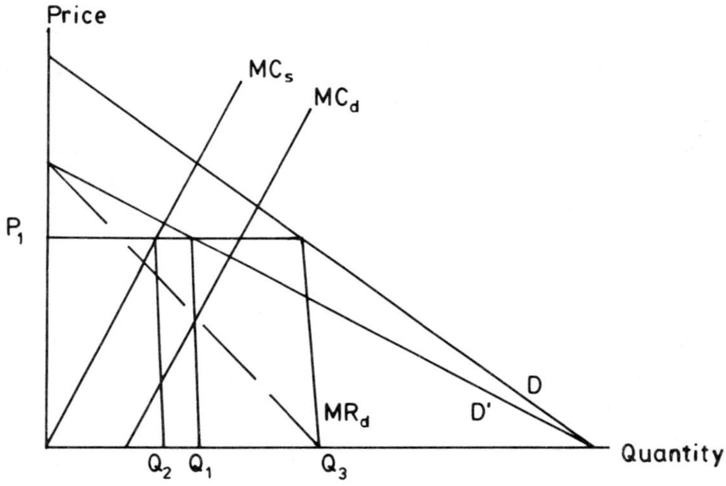

Figure 3. Dominant firm oligopoly model

The dominant firm will maximise profits by equating its marginal cost with its marginal revenue curve, after allowing the small firms to sell their desired amounts. In Figure 3, this occurs by equating MC_d and MR_d to sell a total output of Q_1 at a price of P_1. The small firms will supply Q_2, while the dominant firm provides Q_1. Total sales will be $Q_1 + Q_2 = Q_3$.

This basic model provides a reasonable model of the world grain and soybean markets. Two basic tenants of this model are price leadership and the granting of market access by the dominant firm to the smaller firms. Consider how closely this conforms to the world grain markets. The United States is the dominant exporter and sets price bounds by its government programme allowing price to fall as low as the loan rate after which grain is bid into the government storage programme. If price rises beyond a certain level, the stocks are released back onto the market. Thus, a price band is provided to the world market through the United States' government programme. Other exporting countries can and do export as much as desired, with occasional pressure from the United States. Argentina, for example, increased coarse grain exports from 5.3 million tons in 1979/80 to 14.2 million tons in 1980/81 when the United States embargoed grain sales to the USSR.

In this form of oligopoly the behaviour of the small firms is that of a price taker. The small firm accepts the world price as set by the dominant firm and maximises profits by supplying the quantity where marginal cost equals world price. The application of this model to exports is shown in Figure 4.

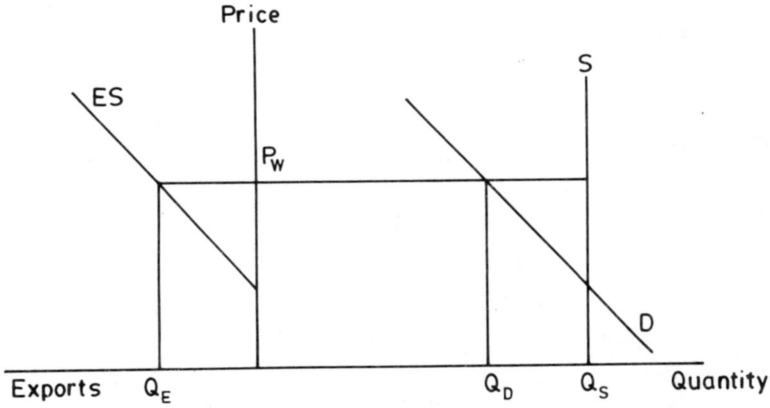

Figure 4. Small country exporter

Domestic supply is shown by S, and is fixed within a given marketing year. Domestic demand is given by D. At an export price above the level where domestic demand is equal to domestic supply, the country will export (ignoring differences between country and world prices). The excess supply curve, ES, is equal to S – D and shows the level of exports. At the world price P_W, domestic demand is given by Q_D, exports are equal to Q_E which is also $Q_S - Q_D$.

The elasticity of export supply can be obtained from examining the elasticity of the ES curve.

$$E_{ES} = \frac{\delta ES}{\delta P} \cdot \frac{\overline{P}}{Q_E}$$

Restating in terms of domestic demand, supply and domestic elasticities, we have:

$$E_{ES} = E_S \frac{\overline{Q}_S}{\overline{Q}_E} - E_D \frac{\overline{Q}_D}{\overline{Q}_E}$$

Therefore the elasticity of the excess supply curve is given by the elasticity of domestic supply weighted by the ration of domestic supply to exports minus the elasticity of domestic demand weighted by the ratio of domestic demand to exports. In the short run, the elasticity of domestic supply is zero and the elasticity of the excess supply curve is

$$E_{ES} = - E_D \frac{\overline{Q}_D}{\overline{Q}_E}$$

The elasticity of excess supply is equal to the negative of the elasticity of domestic demand weighted by the ratio of domestic demand to exports. Since the elasticity of demand is negative, the elasticity of excess supply becomes positive.

Following the dominant firm oligopoly model of the world grain and soybean market, the export supply curves for the exporting countries is:

$$X_{i,t} = DS_{i,t} - DD_{i,t} - STK_{i,t+1}$$

where

$X_{i,t}$	is the exports of commodity i in year t
$DS_{i,t}$	is the domestic supply (production plus beginning of stocks) of commodity i in year t
$STK_{i,t+1}$	is the beginning stocks of commodity i in year t

The functional relationships can be described as

$$DS_{i,t} = PROD_{i,t} + STK_{it}$$
$$DD_{i,t} = f(Y_t, P_{i,t}, P_{j,t})$$
$$STK_{i,t} = f(Y_t, P_{i,t}, P_{j,t}, DD_{i,t-1})$$

where $DS_{i,t}$ is per capita domestic supply and is predetermined; domestic demand, $DD_{i,t}$, is defined as per capita demand which depends on real per capita income, Y_t, and real prices of commodity i and a related commodity j; per capita ending stocks, $STK_{i,t}$, are a function of real per capita income, relative prices and an inventory holding level which depends on domestic demand in the previous year.

All exporters of wheat, rice, coarse grains, soymeal and soyoil are treated as small country exporters, except for the United States. Exports from the United States are equal to the residual required to balance world net imports and exports. This configuration corresponds with actual market behaviour since the early 1970s.

6. CONSUMPTION

In the importing countries and regions, consumption is calculated as the residual with production, net imports and stocks being estimated. For the exporting countries, consumption is estimated directly. In these countries, consumption is disaggregated into two final uses: feed and all other. Per capita consumption is then estimated as a function of income and relevant prices:

$$CF_{i,t} = f(Y_t, P_{i,t}, P_{j,t})$$
$$CO_{i,t} = f(Y_t, P_{i,t}P_{j,t})$$

where $CF_{i,t}$ and $CO_{i,t}$ are per capita food and all other consumption of commodity i respectively. Y_t is real per capita income and $P_{i,t}$ and $P_{j,t}$ are the real prices of the commodity i and a related commodity j.

7. STOCKS

In order to close each country model, the final component which must be estimated is the level of ending stocks (next year's beginning stocks). The ratio of ending stocks to domestic consumption in the previous year is estimated. The equation is:

$$\frac{STK_{i,t}}{DD_{i,t-1}} = f(P_{i,t})$$

where

$STK_{i,t}$ is the level of ending stocks of commodity i in year t

$P_{i,t}$ is the real price of commodity i in year t

Previous experience has shown that this type of model will perform reasonably well, but will not capture totally the volatilability which is frequently present in stock holdings.

8. PRICES

A single world price, the US export price in dollars, is assumed to exist for each of the commodities. Each country's border price is then equal to the world price expressed in constant units of local currency.

$PW_{i,t}$ = US export price of commodity i in year t

$P^k_{i,t}$ = border price of country k for commodity i in year t

$$= PW_{i,t} * XR_{k,t} / CPI_{k,t}$$

where $XR_{k,t}$ is the exchange rate of country i relative to the US dollar, and $CPI_{k,t}$ is the consumer price index of country k in year t.

The model is solved for the world price which equates net imports with net exports. A price equation is used to solve for the equilibrium world price. This approach has been used extensively in recent years. A discussion of the advantages of the use of a price equation can be found in Hein (1977).

The price equation used in the model is designed to reflect the role of US government policy as the determinant of the US and world price floor. This occurs because of the loan rate programmes of the United States which bids grain away from the world market at the price floor or loan rate. Under the current programme, the US government allows farmers enrolled in the programme to place their grain in government storage and receive a low interest loan against the commodity. This loan is made at a rate, the loan rate, which is intended to reflect the cost of production for US farmers. In effect, the loan rate sets the floor on the US and world markets since US farmers will opt for the government programme if the price falls to the level of the loan rate. This places a floor on the price of US exports and unless supplies are extremely large, the floor will also support the world price.

The US export price equation for each grain is estimated as

$$PW_t = f(LR_t, SU_t)$$

where LR_t is the US farm loan rate expressed in nominal dollars, and SU_t is the ending world stocks relative to utilisation in the previous year.

9. ADDITIONAL WORK

A model which is used is constantly evolving and changing. This version of the world grain and soybean model has several features which will be changed in subsequent versions. The first improvement which will be undertaken is to include country specific data to a greater extent. Producer prices of crops and inputs will be included for the largest countries. This will allow a greater range of policy simulations. It hopefully will also permit more accurate price and trade forecasts.

A second change, which would represent a major effort and hopefully a major advanve would be to endogenise the macro economic variable for key countries. This step is essentially important for countries in which agricultural production represents a major component of national income. This activity will be pursued on an individual case basis with the most important countries considered first.

NOTES

1. The estimation of the soybean model was carried out by Mr. T.Y. Pee. Mr. Alan Bowers gave very able research assistance in all aspects of construction of the grains and soybeans model.
2. Although a system of demand equations which estimates the total demand for grains as well as the demand for individual grains is probably desirable, it has not been undertaken in this study.

REFERENCES

Abbott, Philip C., 'Modeling International Grain Trade with Government Controlled Markets', *American Journal of Agricultural Economics*, Vol. 61, No. 1, pp. 22–31, February 1979.

Abbott, Philip C., 'The Role of Government Interference in International Commodity Trade Models', *American Journal of Agricultural Economics*, Vol. 61, No. 1, pp. 135–39, February 1979.

Alaouze, Chris M., A.S. Watson and N.H. Sturgess, 'Oligopoly Pricing in the World Wheat Market, *American Journal of Agricultural Economics*, Vol. 60, No. 2, May 1978, pp. 173–85.

Askari, H. and J. Cummings, *Agricultural Supply Response: A Survey of the Econometric Evidence*, Praeger Publishers, 1976.

Bjarnason, H.F. (1967), 'An Economic Analysis of 1980 International Trade in Feed Grains', unpublished Ph.D. dissertation, University of Wisconsin.

Brandow, A.E. (1958), "A Note on the Nerlove Estimate of Supply Elasticity', *Journal of Farm Economics*, Vol. 40, August.

Bredahl, M.E., W.H. Meyers, and K.J. Collins (1979), 'The Elasticity of Foreign Demand for U.S. Agricultural Products: The Importance of the Price Transmission Elasticity', *American Journal of Agricultural Economics*, 61, pp. 58–63.

Bredahl, M.E. and L. Green (1983), 'Residual Supplies Model of Coarse Grain Trade', *American Journal of Agricultural Economics*, 65:4, pp.785–90.

Capel, R.E. and L.R. Rigaux (1974), 'Analysis of Export Demand or Canadian Wheat', *Canadian Journal of Agricultural Economics*, 22, pp. 1–14.

Chambers, R.G. and R.E. Just (1979), 'Critique of Exchange Rate Treatment in Agricultural Trade Models', *American Journal of Agricultural Economics*, 61:1, pp. 249–57.

Falcon, W.P. and E.R. Monke (1979/80), *Food Research Institute Studies*, XVIII:3, pp. 279–306.

Grennes, T, P.R. Johnson and M. Thursby (1977), "Devaluation, Foreign Controls and Domestic Wheat Prices', *American Journal of Agricultural Economics*, 59, pp. 619–27.

Hemphill, W. (1974), 'The Effects of Foreign Exchange Receipts on Imports of Less Developed Countries', *International Monetary Fund Staff Papers*, 21, pp.637–77.

Jabara, C.L. (1981), 'Trade Restrictions in International Grain and Oilseed Markets', USDA, Foreign Agricultural Economic Report No. 162.

Johnson, P.R. (1977), 'The Elasticity of Foreign Demand for U.S. Agricultural Products', *American Journal of Agricultural Economics*, 59, pp.735–36.

Labys, W.C. (1973), *Dynamic Commodity Models: Specification, Estimation, and Simulation*, Lexington Books.

Leamer, E.E. and R.M. Stern (1970), *Quantitative International Economics*, Aldine Publishing Company.

McCalla, A.F. (1966), 'A Duopoly Model of World Wheat Pricing', *American Journal of Farm Economics*, 48, pp. 711–27.

Menz, K.M. and P. Pardey (1983), 'Technology and U.S. Corn Yields: Plateau and Price Responsiveness', *American Journal of Agricltural Economics*, pp.558–62.

Nerlove, M. (1958), *The Dynamics of Supply: Estimtion of Farmers' Response to Price*, John Hopkins University Press, Baltimore, MD.

Nerlove, M. (1956), 'Estimates of Supply of Selected Agricultural Commodities', *Journal of Farm Economics*, 38, pp. 496–509.

Nerlove, M. (1958), 'On the Nerlove Estimate of Supply Elasticity: A Reply', *Journal of Farm Economics*, 40.

Nerlove, M. and W. Addison (1958), 'Statistical Estimation of Long–Run Elasticities of Supply and Demand', *Journal of Farm Economics*, 40.

Schmitz, A. and D.G. Watts (1970), 'Forecasting Wheat Yields: An Application of

Parametric Time Series Modeling', *American Journal of Agricultural Economics*, 52:2.
Schuh, G.E. (1974), 'The Exchange Rate and U.S. Agriculture', *American Journal of Agricultural Economics*, 56:1, pp.1–13.
Tweeten, L.G. (1967), 'The Demand for United States Farm Output', *Stanford Food Research Institutes Studies*, 7, pp.343–69.
Walsh (1940), 'Response to Price in the Production of Cotton and Cottonseed', *Journal of Farm Economics*, 26, pp.359–72.
Zwart, A.C. and K.D. Meilke (1979), 'The Influence of Domestic Pricing Policies and Buffer Stocks on Price Stability in the World Wheat Industry', *American Journal of Agricultural Economics*, 61, pp.434–47.
USDA (1981), *Alternative Futures For World Food in 1985*, ESS,FAE No. 151.
The World Bank (1984), *World Development Report, 1984*, Oxford University Press.

APPENDIX: Data Sources and Definitions

The primary historical data sources are the World Bank, International Monetary Fund, FAO and the US Department of Agriculture.

A single world rice, wheat and corn and soybean price is used in the model. The wheat price is the US No. 1 HRW, Ordinary Protein, FOB Gulf, July–June year. The rice price is the US No. 2 Long Grained, Milled, Bagged, FOB Houston, August–July year. The corn price (which is a proxy for all coarse grains) is US No. 2 Yellow, FOB Gulf, October–September year. The soybean price is the US No. 2 Yellow, FOB Gulf, October–September year. The real border price for each country is then used for estimation and is defined as the world price multiplied by the exchange rate and deflated by the country's consumer price index.

The grain and soybean data is taken from the Foreign Agriculture Service of the US Department of Agriculture. All data are on a crop year basis and are measured in thousand metric tons or thousand hectares.

The macroeconomic and demographic data are taken from the World Bank data base and the *International Financial Statistics* (International Monetary Fund). Population is in millions, income is gross domestic product measured in billions of local currency. The exchange rate is measured in units of local currency per dollar, and the consumer prices are an index. All these data are taken from the IFS or from the World Bank data base. The trade balance is FOB Exports minus FOB imports in millions of US dollars and is from the IFS.

Finally data for the USSR, Eastern Europe and China are defined differently from the data used for other countries. The exchange rate and consumer price indices were not used. Equations were estimated on real US commodity prices and real income based on World Bank data.

The regional data are obtained by aggregating country data for variables with common units, i.e., tons, hectares, persons. Regional GDP is obtained by converting local currency GDP to US dollars using a 1971–80 average exchange rate and then aggregating. Regional exchange rate and consumer price indices are constructed as a weighted average of the largest countries in each region. Because the exchange rate and consumer price index data are the most incomplete of the data series used in the model, this approach was the only alternative for regions comprised of many small countries. The food aid data was from the FAO publication *Food Aid in Figures*, 1983, and from the USDA for years prior to 1970.

CHAPTER 6

SIMULATION OF SUPPLY, DEMAND AND PRICE INTERACTIONS IN THE MAGNESIUM MARKET

F. Field*, J. Bush+ and J. Clark*

1. INTRODUCTION

Magnesium is the sixth most abundant metal in the earth's crust. It is found both as an oxide in mineral deposits and in salt water as $MgCl_2$, in concentrations up to almost 0.13 percent. The oceans and brine deposits of the world represent an essentially infinite reservoir of magnesium; each cubic kilometer of sea water contains in excess of 1.3 million metric tons of magnesium. Additionally, magnesium is present in the common minerals magnesite and dolomite, at concentrations of 29 and 13 percent, respectively.

The properties of magnesium, particularly its low density, make it a potentially useful material in a wide variety of structural applications. Magnesium is approximately 1.5 and 4.5 times lighter than aluminium and steel, respectively, for equivalent volumes. And the motivations for using it are large. It has been estimated that if 50 pounds of magnesium were substituted for ferrous materials in a fleet of 10 million cars, a saving of 2.1 billion gallons of gasoline would accrue over the assumed 100,000 mile lifetime of the vehicles.

Moreover, there are a number of non–structural applications for magnesium where the demand is essentially price inelastic. Such applications include alloying in cast and wrought aluminium materials in concentrations up to 10%, as a reagent for desulfurising steels and as a constituent in incendiary devices.

Given the availability of the resource and its useful properties, it follows that at some future time the market for magnesium should be large. The question is, why has such a market expansion not already occurred, and when could such an event be reasonably expected to occur? In particular, the following issues are of interest:

1. The level of demand for magnesium that can be expected in future, given assumptions about prices, economic activity, and technical change in the consuming

O. Guvenen (ed.), International Commodity Market Models and Policy Analysis, 113–142.

markets;

2. The profitability of an investment in primary production capacity for magnesium (at varying levels of capacity), given assumptions about demand behaviour, market growth, and pricing mechanisms;
3. The likely path of magnesium prices and the nature of the supply/demand interactions in the future, given assumptions about the market clearing behaviour, market consumption patterns, and changes in production technologies; and
4. The sensitivity of magnesium market behaviour to uncertain variables such as tariffs, recycling, and the costs of factor inputs.

The purpose of this paper is to present a framework for analysis of such issues. This framework was developed in the form of an engineering simulation model.[2] The magnesium industry is particularly amenable for application of such a methodology because of the relatively small number of primary producers and demand sectors. Moreover, there are ample data with which to derive cost functions of the producers on a site specific basis and to derive demand functions of the consumers on an end use specific basis.

The model is composed of two major sectors, as shown in Figure 1. These sectors are supply and demand. The supply sector consists of engineering based cost functions and a set of alternative pricing mechanisms to translate the cost–output relationships into price–output functions. The demand sector consists of statistical and engineering analyses of the relationship between consumption and factors such as technical requirements, market growth, and the price and availability of magnesium and substitute materials. The sectors are discussed in detail below.

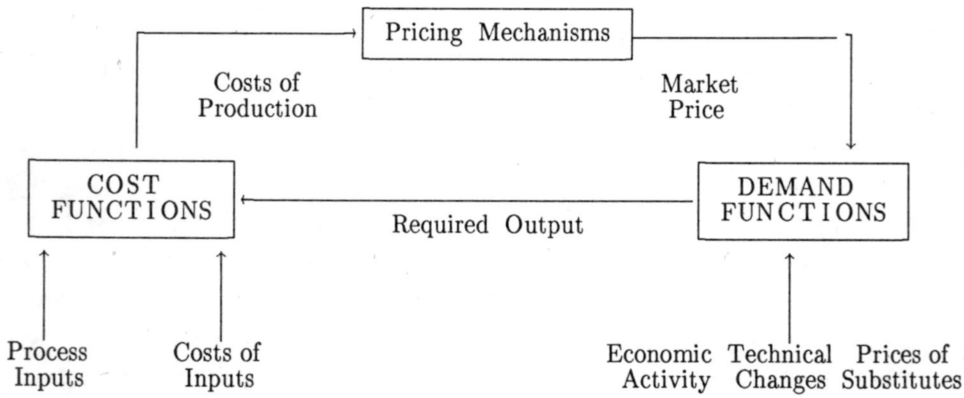

Figure 1. Overview of the Magnesium Simulation Model

Since the market is not competitive, prices determined within the supply sector are fed directly into the demand sector. The reaction to price information is not instantaneous; rather the demand sectors respond to prices after a one year lag.

2. THE DEMAND FOR MAGNESIUM

In the model, the demand for magnesium is separated into two geographical regions and two market classifications.

Categories of Magnesium Demand

US Basic	World Basic
US Incremental	World Incremental

The term 'world' within this study refers to all non communist, non US countries. The first market classification, 'basic', is for those end use sectors which have matured and are expected to behave in the future according to historical trends. The second classification, 'incremental', refers to emerging applications or to those that are expected to diverge from past trends. The demand for magnesium in 'basic' sectors was estimated using standard statistical techniques. In 'incremental' market sectors, a combination of engineering and judgemental analysis was used to formulate demand equations.

2.1 Basic US Demand

The established demand for magnesium in the US is divided into the following end uses:

1. Aluminium alloying
2. Titanium production
3. Military applications
4. Wrought products
5. Cathodic protection

For each of these end uses, regression analysis is used to forecast the future demand. A statistical technique was chosen since these are mature markets and the future performance of these markets will most likely follow historical trends.

All of the regression equations were of the form:

$$\text{Sector Demand}_t = A \times (\text{Price Mg}_t)^B \times (\text{Production Index}_t)^C$$

For the regressions, the production indices and corresponding end uses were:

Production Index	End Use
Total industrial production	Aluminium alloying
Military production	Military applications
Titanium production	Titanium production
Construction	Wrought products
Cross national product	Cathodic protection

Table 1 shows the results of the regressions. T–statistics appear in parantheses.

Table 1. Established Demand Sectors – Regression Results

Demand Sector	Coefficient A		Exponent B		Exponent C	
Allum. Alloy	–.038	(–2.4)	–.213	(–2.3)	2.08	(9.1)
Titanium	91.8	(2.6)	–.170	(–0.9)	0.52	(2.3)
Military	–0.31	(–0.4)	–.569	(–1.6)	2.69	(4.0)
Wrought	3260	(21)	–.184	(–3.3)	0.42	(3.9)
Cathode	3.19	(1.5)	–.707	(–6.3)	2.16	(9.9)

The future demand for magnesium in each end use was estimated using exogenous forecasts of the production indices and annual magnesium prices generated within the model.

2.2 Established Basis Demand

Reliable data on consumption patterns by end use in countries outside the US are not available. Moreover, there is not a complete time series of historical data available for aggregate consumption. Therefore, it was necessary to arrive at estimates of consumption by judgemental methods. Conversations with international consumers and producers of magnesium led to subjective estimates of the price and income elasticities of demand, –0.25 and 1.0, respectively. Established world demand is treated as an aggregate category within the model and forecasts are generated using the following equation:

$$\text{Demand}_t = \text{Demand}_0 \times (\text{IPI}_t/\text{IPI}_0) \times (\text{Price}_t/\text{Price}_0)^{-0.25}$$

2.3 Incremental US Demand

Four end uses were identified as areas where substantial growth in magnesium demand is anticipated. These are:

1. Automotive castings
2. Aluminium cans
3. Desulfurisation of carbon steel

4. Die castings

For each of these, a combination of engineering analysis and judgement were applied to generate forecasts of the future consumption. The methodology used for each sector is described below.

1. *Automotive castings*: Magnesium is used in automobiles primarily as a substitute for aluminium. The viability of a substitution depends on the relative cost effectiveness of each material. To estimate the demand for magnesium in automotive applications, the market was segmented into twenty seven components which have been, or could be fabricated from magnesium. For each of these, the average weight of magnesium required for the particular application was determined (see Table 2). Questionaires and interviews with automotive industry representatives were used to establish the critical magnesium/aluminium price ratio (PR(in)) which would result in the introduction of magnesium. The critical price ratios varied for each component depending on the ease of substitution, the required capital investment, technical barriers, and marketing considerations.

In addition to the critical price ratio for introducing magnesium, a higher price ratio (PR(out)) which would result in a return to aluminium was established for each component. Substitution back to aluminium would occur if magnesium became sufficiently unprofitable to justify abandoning or revamping the magnesium processing equipment. When the price ratio is between the value for introduction and the value for withdrawal, a steady growth (Rate in) towards a targeted market penetration (Pentr.) is assumed to occur.

The lead time (Lead) for the design, development, testing, and production of each component was estimated and incorporated into the model, resulting in a delay between the decision to use magnesium and actual consumption.

For each year, the model calculates the two, three, four, and five year historical averages of the aluminium/magnesium price ratio. The appropriate average is compared to the critical price ratio requirements of each component to determine whether substitution will occur. The number of years over which the price ratio is averaged equals the lead time for each component. This insures that magnesium will not be selected for long lead components until the cost advantage is well established.

Forecasts of the U.S. automotive demand for magnesium appear in Figures 2 and 3. The magnesium/aluminium price ratios which results in these demand projections are also presented. These forecasts are based on separate sets of economic assumptions and are included here to demonstrate the sensitivit of the automotive sector of the model to prices.

Table 2 : X Components Which Could Be Fabricated From Magnesium

Components	PR(in)	PR(out)	Lead	Wgt	Rate In	Pentr.
Steering Lock Housing	1.55	1.86	2	1.25	0.25	50%
Glove Box Door	1.55	1.86	2	0.25	0.25	30%
Brackets (alt,p.str,a/c,pedal)	1.50	1.80	2	5.00	0.25	50%
Window Regulator	1.45	1.74	2	2.00	0.25	50%
W/W Arm Casting	1.45	1.74	2	0.10	0.25	50%
Elec Mot Housing	1.40	1.68	2	2.68	0.25	50%
Distributor Housing	1.40	1.68	2	0.89	0.25	40%
Mirror Housing	1.45	1.74	2	0.17	0.25	40%
Transmission Pan	1.40	1.68	2	5.80	0.25	30%
Valve Cover	1.30	1.56	2	1.70	0.25	10%
Air Cleaner Assy	1.30	1.56	2	2.65	0.25	10%
Oil Pan	1.30	1.56	2	3.36	0.25	10%
Radiator Brace	1.30	1.56	2	1.53	0.25	20%
Air Intake Grill	1.30	1.56	2	1.90	0.25	10%
Pulleys (alt, w.pump, crank, a/c)	1.35	1.62	3	3.76	0.25	20%
Brake Pedals	1.30	1.56	3	2.32	0.25	10%
Steering Box	1.35	1.62	3	1.16	0.25	20%
Master/Slave Cylinder	1.35	1.62	3	3.28	0.25	40%
Fuel Pump Housing	1.40	1.68	3	0.34	0.25	10%
Carburetor Housing	1.35	1.62	3	3.14	0.25	10%
Water Pump Housing	1.35	1.62	3	1.65	0.25	10%
Transmission Housing (manual 30%)	1.40	1.68	4	13.90	0.25	40%
Intake Manifold	1.35	1.62	4	7.26	0.25	40%
Brake Calipers	1.30	1.56	5	2.40	0.25	10%
Cylinder Heads	1.30	1.56	5	10.80	0.25	10%
Pistons	1.20	1.44	5	3.95	0.25	10%
Engine Block	1.20	1.44	5	40.00	0.25	10%
Wheels	1.50	1.80	2	48.00	0.25	5%

Figure 2

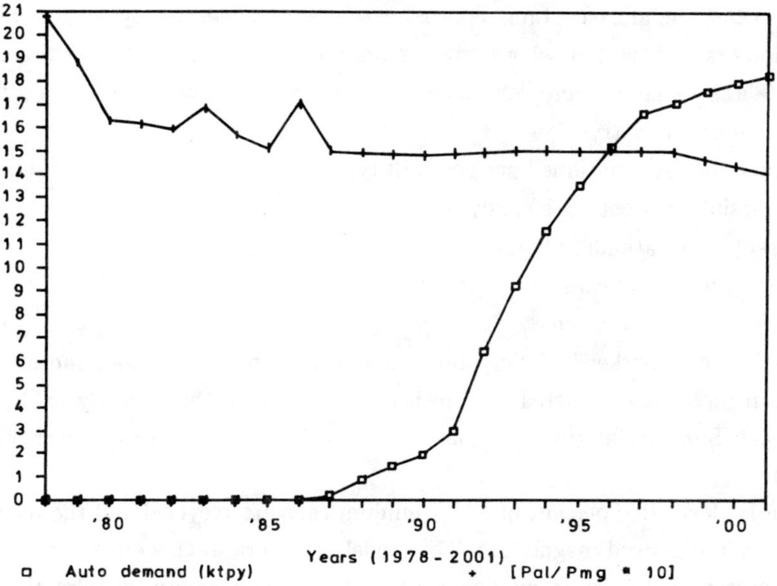

Figures 2 and 3. Correlation Between the Consumption of Magnesium and the Relative Prices of Magnesium and Aluminium

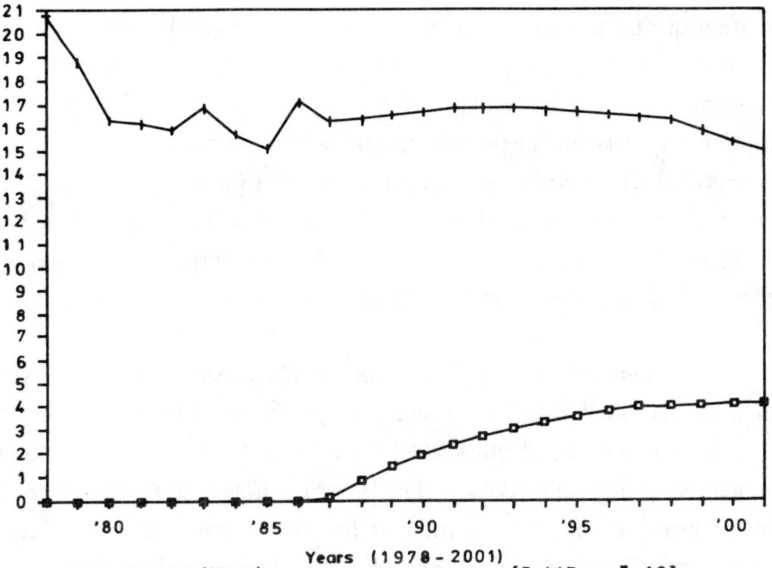

Figure 3.

2. *Aluminium cans*: Magnesium is consumed as an alloying element in the production of aluminium cans; the alloy contains approximately 2% magnesium by weight. Historical data and forecasts of the following variables were obtained from a major US aluminium producer. These variables were combined to generate forecasts of the demand for magnesium by the can industry.

1. Number of cans consumed per year (all types)
2. Magnesium content of the alloy
3. Market penetration of aluminium cans
4. Average weight of cans
5. Percent of cans recycled

The aluminium can market is divided into three sectors: beverage, food, and others. The beverage can sector is considered mature because aluminium has already captured 90% of the market. Substantial growth is forecast for food cans and others (motor oil, tennis balls, etc.).

Currently, forty five percent of all aluminium cans are recycled and the recycle process conserves the alloyed magnesium. The model incorporates this effect by subtracting forty five percent of the previous year's consumption of magnesium from the current year's demand. A one year recycle life is considered typical of the time required to collect and reprocess cans.

Consumption of magnesium in can stock is relatively insensitive to the magnesium price because it is a minor alloying constituent. Therefore, this application is considered to be price insensitive within the model.

Consumption forecasts for magnesium use in cans appear in Figure 4. These projections are shown to indicat a typical consumption pattern that is expected for this sector.

3. *Desulfurisation of carbon steel*: Magnesium is used as a substitute for a variety of materials in steel desulfurisation. The technologies for desulfurising with magnesium are relatively new and their application is expected to become more widespread as they develop.

Forecasts of the demand for magnesium for desulfurisation were obtained through consultation with the major magnesium and steel producers. These forecasts appear in Figure 5. They are based on two factors: steel capacity utilisation and the total potential market for magnesium in desulfurisation. The latter of these factors was estimated from the thermodynamics of steel desulfurisation. It has been found that approximately 300 grams of magnesium is required to produce each ton of desulfurised steel.

Magnesium producers forecast that the desulfurisation demand will reach 25 ktpy when the market matures (assuming full capacity utilisation in the steel industry).

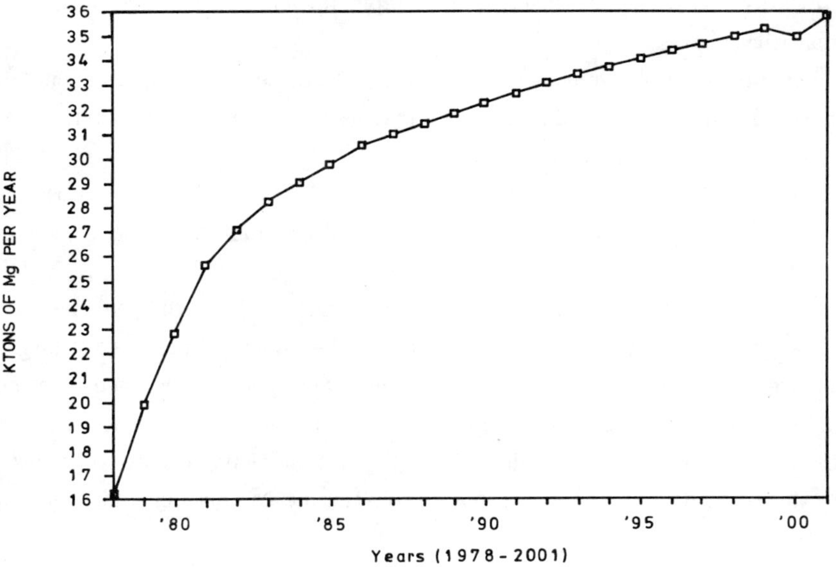

Figure 4. Simulation of the Consumption of Magnesium in Aluminium Alloys Used for Beverages and Food Cans in the US

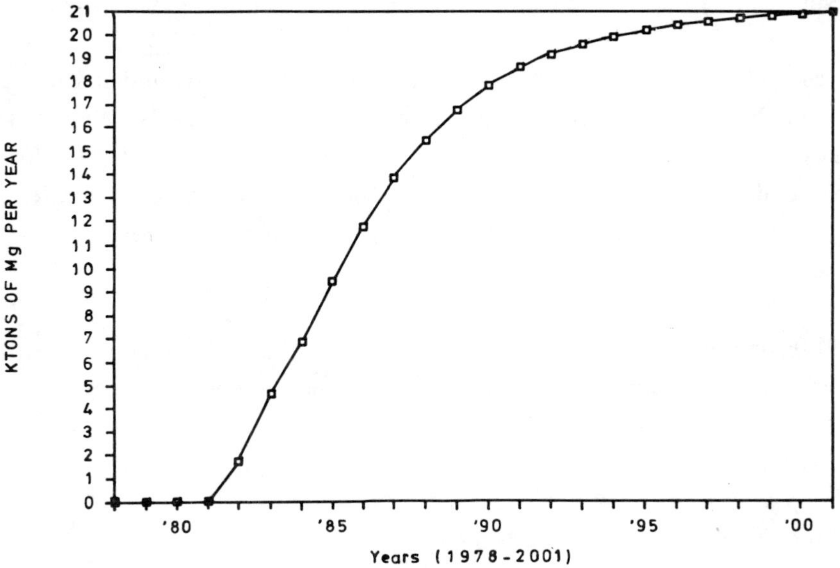

Figure 5. Simulation of Magnesium Consumption for the Desulfurisation of Steel in the US

Growth towards this target is expected to be rapid initially, decreasing as the market reaches maturity.

The demand for magnesium in desulfurisation is not sensitive to price since there are technical advantages to desulfurising with magnesium and since the incremental cost of desulfurisation is relatively small.

4. *Die casting*: The non automotive die casting market is expected to grow substantially over the next twenty years. Potential end uses include computer housings, chain saws, and power tools.

Discussions with potential users led to an estimate of an income elasticity of demand of slightly less than unity. In these sectors, the impact of price is not large, but is also not negligible. The use of magnesium in each application is governed by a unique set of economic considerations which make it difficult to estimate the price where magnesium becomes cost effective. Therefore, a single price elasticity, the same as was used for aggregate world demand, was incorporated in the die casting demand equation, as shown below.

$$\text{Demand}_t = \text{Demand}_o \times (\text{GNP}_t/\text{GNP}_o)^{0.85} \times (\text{PR}_t/\text{PR}_o)^{-0.25}$$

where GNP = Gross National Product
PR = Magnesium/Aluminium Price Ratio
subscript 't' = time 't'
subscript 'o' = baseline

Recycling of magnesium die castings is expected to follow consumption since this is a non–dissipative use. The time lag between production and recycle is estimated to be about ten years and it is assumed that 50% of the castings are recovered. Therefore, an equation was developed to add 50% of consumption in this category, with a ten year time lag, to the available supply, thereby reducing the demand for primary material in the future.

2.4 World Incremental Demand

Four sectors of the international market were identified where the demand for magnesium is expected to grow substantially:

1. Japanese automotive castings
2. European automotive castings
3. European desulfurisation of carbon steel
4. Desulfurisation of carbon steel in other countries.

To forecast consumption, magnesium industry experts were asked to provide estimates of the expected demand in each of these end uses once the markets were fully mature. Growth towards these target values was assumed to be rapid at first and to taper off as each market matured. An asymptotic curve was used to simulate such growth.

For both of the automotive sectors, the target for growth was expressed as pounds of magnesium contained per average automobile. Annual demand was calculated by multiplying forecasts of automotive production with the pounds per car for each year.

The magnesium/aluminium price ratio also has a strong impact on the automotive demand for magnesium in Europe and Japan. Therefore, assumptions similar to thone made for the US market were applied to the European and Japanese markets. The price ratio was assumed to impact the rate of growth of magnesium demand.

For both of the desulfurisation sectors, asymptotic growth towards a target value was again assumed. The rate of growth, however, was fixed. The demand for magnesium for desulfurisation was multiplied by forecasts of the world steel capacity utilisation and was adjusted proportional to the world industrial production index.

2.5 Total World Demand (US and non–US)

Forecasts of the U.S. and world demand for magnesium through the year 2001 appear in Figure 6. These forecasts are comprised of the sum of established and developing end uses. They result from a specific set of economic assumptions and are included to show typical results attainable with the model. They should not necessarily be constructed as the best available forecasts.

3. MAGNESIUM SUPPLY

In 1981, worldwide production capacity of magnesium was nearly 300 ktpy (ktpy: thousands of metric tons per year). Actual production was 244 ktons, representing 81% of capacity utilisation; low for the magnesium industry which normally operates above 90% of capacity.

Three US facilities account for the total domestic production capacity and for 61% of the world capacity. These are:

Dow Chemical in Freeport, TX (120 ktpy), AMAX Speciality Metals in Rowley, UT (38 ktpy), and North West Alloys in Addy, WA (25 ktpy). Norsk Hydro of Norway (55 ktpy capacity) is the only non–US magnesium producer with a significant market share. The remaining 62 ktpy of world capacity is spread among a number of countries including Brazil, Italy, France, Japan, Canada, and India.

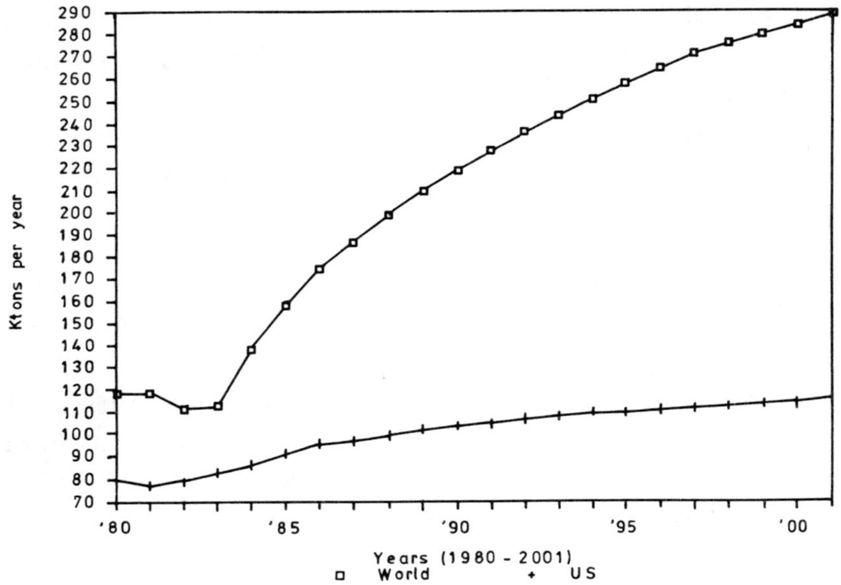

Figure 6. Simulation of Future Magnesium Consumption

As the above statistics indicate, magnesium production is highly concentrated with four producers accounting for 80% of the total world capacity. Most of the remaining world capacity is nationalised and produces according to government policies for captive markets. For this reason, only the four mentioned magnesium producers were incorporated into the model of the world magnesium market.

3.1 Magnesium Production Process

There are three primary magnesium production technologies currently in use worldwide. These are

1. Electrolytic processes
2. Magnethermic processes
3. Silicothermic (Pidgeon) processes

The Pidgeon process is an older technology with limited application in the current market. It was not included in the model because it is not currently, nor likely to be, used in any large scale operation.

The electrolytic process, used at the Dow Chemical and AMAX plants, employs an externally applied electrical potential to separate $MgCl_2$ into its constituent elements. The process can be divided into two operations. The first is feedstock preparation where a brine of magnesium salts and/or magnesium oxide is refined, dehydrated and chemically treated to yield a magnesium chloride powder. The second operation is the actual electrolysis of the powder. A generalised flow sheet of these operations appears in Figure 7.

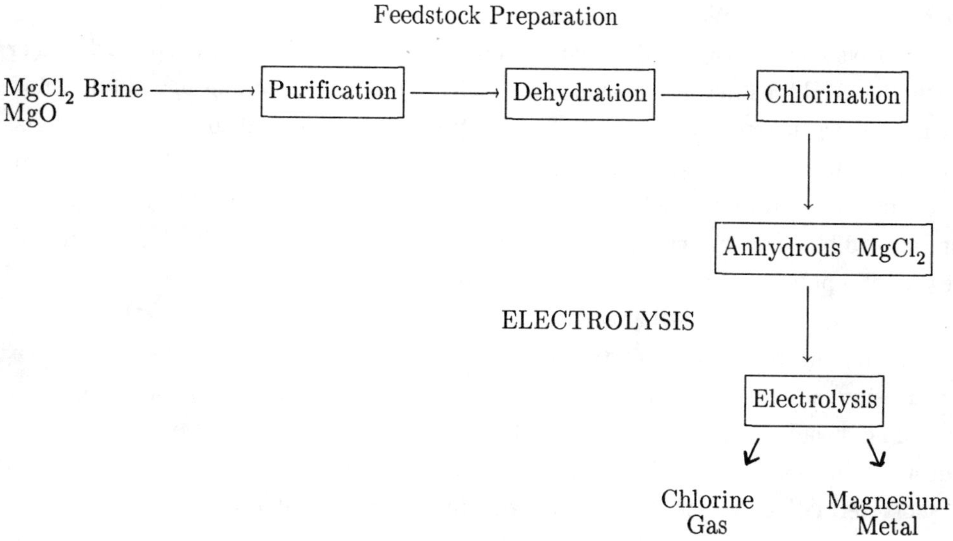

Figure 7. Generalised Flow Sheet for Electrolytic Magnesium Production Processes

Typically, feedstock preparation accounts for half of the expense of producing magnesium electrolytically. Cost reductions are expected to come primarily from technological improvements in feedstock preparation since the electrolysis operation currently operates near the theoretical efficiency limit.

Currently, the electrolytic process is most economical for large production capacities – greater than 25 ktpy. It is employed at three of the four major production facilities and accounts for more than 70% of the worldwide production capacity.

Thermic processes for producing magnesium entail the reduction of magnesium oxide with a compound or alloy of calcium, aluminium, silicon, or carbon. Magnesium oxide can be extracted from magnesite or dolomite or it can be generated from magnesium chloride. The choice of reductant is an instrumental factor in: a) determining the optimum operating conditions of the process (e.g. slag temperature, production rate); b) supplying the heat required to drive the reaction. The thermic process produces a molten slag, oxides, and magnesium vapour.

Thermic processes account for nearly 30% of current Western production capacity. Its advantages include the simplicity of process equipment, ease of feedstock preparation, ease of process operation, less restrictive site selection criteria, economies of scale at low production capacities (<25 ktpy), and lower initial investment requirements.

3.2 Magnesium Production Cost Model

Cost models were constructed by simulating the design and operation of each major production facility. First, each facility was divided into a series of unit operations. Information on the thermodynamics and kinetics of each step was used to estimate material and energy flow streams. Capital and labour requirements were obtained from the producers or they were estimated based on data from similar operations. The raw material, capital, and labour requirements of each unit operation were summed, yielding estimates for the total process. Overhead requirements were added to this total.

Production costs are separated into fixed and variable costs (and a by–product credit if applicable). Fixed costs include maintenance, overheads, taxes, insurance, depreciation, administration and indirect expenses. In addition, 50% of the labour costs (including benefits) were included in the fixed cost category since interviews with industry sources indicated that about half of the labourers would be retained regardless of short term fluctuations in the level of production. Variable costs include process materials, electric and thermal utilities and 50% of labour (including benefits).

Site specific production costs are computed based on the capacity utilisation rate, a value which is calculated endogenously and which is a function of the annual demand for magnesium. The cost of a ton of magnesium is equal to the sum of the fixed cost divided by the number of tons produced and the variable cost.

A sample spreadsheet showing the costs of production at a typical magnesium plant appears in Table 3. These estimates are based on 1980 conditions and are expressed in 1980 dollars.

Forecasts of future production costs were generated by multiplying the factor inputs of the 1980 costs by exogenous cost inflators. The inflators and their forecast values through the year 2001 appear in Table 3.

The site specific cost models provide a framework for estimating present and future magnesium production costs as a function of factor inputs and exogenous cost inflators.

3.3 Potential New Production Capacity

A greenfield electrolytic facility was incorporated into the model as a potential investment by a new entrant into the market. This facility was assumed to be situated in the

Table 3. Cost of Production at an Electrolytic Magnesium Production Facility

Process Materials	Units	$/Unit	$/ton Mg
Quicklime	16,162	32.00	13.61
CaCl2	2,120	32.50	1.81
Oolites	770	32.00	0.65
Kerosene	768,354	0.25	5.05
Iso–octanal	352,540	0.54	5.01
Ferrous Chloride	6,022	100.00	15.85
Iron Oxide	40,560	0.40	0.43
Charcoal	11,018	50.00	14.50
Coke	4,020	100.00	10.58
Flux	448	260.00	3.07
Sulfur Dioxide	122	200.00	0.64
Sulfuric Acid	1,696	58.65	2.62
Calcium Fluoride	238	145.00	0.91
Other	–	–	5.01
Supplies and Expenses			127.89
Cell Rebuild Materials			142.11
Alloying Materials			13.42
			========
			Total $363
Utilities			
Electricity	5.38E + 08	0.02	282.89
Natural Gas	7.72E + 06	1.36	276.29
Fuel Oil	2.38E + 06	0.42	26.31
Propane	3.70E + 04	0.51	0.50
			========
			Total $ 586
Direct Labour			
Operating (50% variable)	132	24,650	85.63
Operating (50% fixed)	132	24,650	85.63
Maintenance (fixed)	285	25,310	189.83
Supervision (fixed)	141	24,400	90.54
Benefits (% of salary)		35%	158.07
			========
			Total $610
Fixed Costs			
Plant Maintenance	–	–	126.32
Overhead (% of wages)	–	60%	365.81
Development Projects	–	–	8.95
Insurance and Taxes	–	–	31.58
Depreciation	–	–	5.26
			========
			Total $538

continental US in proximity to competitively priced sources of energy and raw materials. Production capacities were varied between 15 and 100 ktpy. Improvements in the productivity of labour and energy utilisation as well as an innovative approach to feedstock preparation were assumed.

The model also permits expansion of existing capacity, taking into account capital movement costs and improvements in factor input efficiencies.

3.4 Pricing

Once production costs have been estimated, the market price of magnesium can be inferred, given assumptions about the behaviour of the market. In order to estimate prices, the relationship between the cost of production, the state of the market (e.g. capacity utilisation) and the market price must be assessed. Unfortunately, pricing policies within the magnesium market have varied over the past 15 years; there is no clear cut relationship. Because of this uncertainty, three pricing mechanisms were incorporated in the model in order to explore the implications of alternative scenarios.

Pricing Theory

According to economic theory, in a perfectly competitive market, the price of a commodity is equal to the marginal cost of production. Unfortunately, perfect competition, like most theoretical ideals, is rarely observed. Extensions to the theory of pricing have been devised to characterise some of the more commonly observed market conditions. The theory most pertinent to the magnesium market is that of oligopoly. An oligopolistic market is one in which there are a few producers, each of whom has a degree of market power which can be used to manipulate prices.

There are three classes of oligopolistic behaviour: CournotNash, collusion, and Stackelberg. Of the three, Stackelberg is the most pertinent to the magnesium industry, since it assumes that the market consists of one leader and several followers. Each of these market forms are examined thoroughly in economic literature.

Observed Features of the Magnesium Market

The most important feature of the domestic magnesium market is that magnesium historically has not been sold as a structural metal. Rather, it is sold as a chemical, with unique chemical properties and no perfect substitutes. For this type of application, the demand for magnesium is highly price inelastic.

Coupled with this feature is the distribution of production capacity. Dow Chemical is by far the largest domestic producer of the metal, with a production capacity of 120 ktpy equivalent to nearly $^2/_3$ of the domestic capacity. Furthermore, Dow operates at the lowest cost, owing the economies of scale and to a fully depreciated physical plant. Together, these factors conspire to give Dow considerable power in establishing market price.

Another feature of the market is the observed stability of market share over the years. Some industry observers argue that Dow pursues pricing strategies directed towards maintaining these market shares. According to these observers, this strategy allows the current producers to break even while limiting entry to the market.

Alternative Pricing Schemes

The pricing mechanisms developed must necessarily capture the above described characteristics, especially:

1. the dominance of Dow in the market,
2. stability of market share, and
3. effects of producer costs.

Additionally, the mechanisms must be able to accommodate the structural changes being considered in the analysis, including new producers and new markets.

There is no single mechanism that captures all of these features. However, three mechanisms were found, each of which yields consistent and compelling results under certain of the scenarios being considered. These mechanisms are:

1. Cost plus pricing;
2. Historical pricing; and
3. Marginal cost pricing.

Each of these mechanisms are outlined below. The supply curves derived by combing the cost functions with the appropriate pricing mechanism are shown in Figures 8–10.

Cost Plus Pricing

Cost plus pricing is the simplest of the mechanisms applied. This mechanism assumes that the price of magnesium is equal to the unit cost of production multiplied by a fixed markup, i.e.

$$P_t = a \times C_{t-1}$$

where

P_t = Price of magnesium at time t

C_{t-1} = Average cost of magnesium production at time t–1

a = markup (>1)

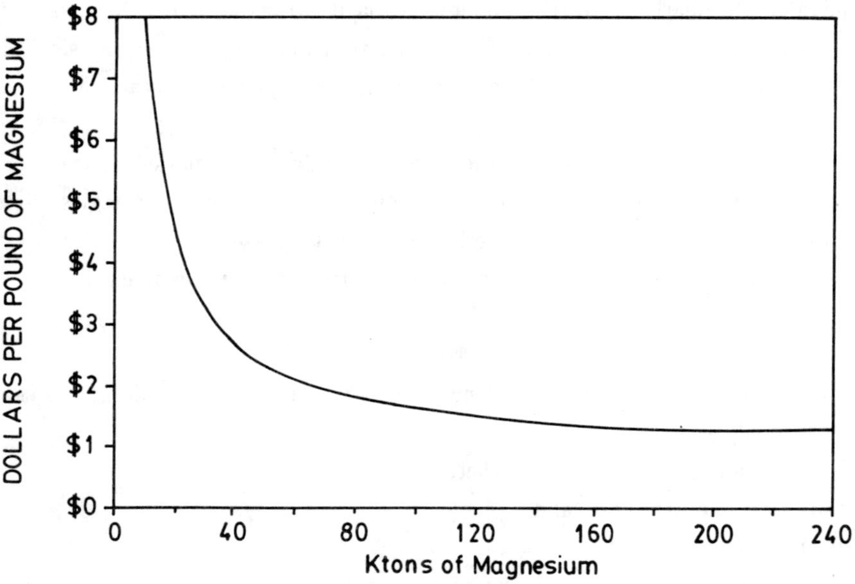

Figure 8. Magnesium Supply Function Under Cost Plus Pricing

In the model, the supply sector yields the costs of production at each US site. based upon the volume of current demand. In the cost plus scheme, Dow's unit costs were used as the basis of price, reflecting Dow's dominance in the market. This mechanism yields a positive and linear relationship between cost and price which is intuitively compelling. However, the mechanism does have some serious weaknesses.

Total cost is the sum of fixed and variable costs. As output increases, the percentage of fixed cost that must be borne by each unit of output is reduced. Thus, as output increases, unit costs decrease. If price is proportional to cost, an increase in output implies a decrease in price.

While this makes sense from the production side, it makes no sense when applied to demand pricing. Basic economic theory states that as price increases, output increases. The results of cost plus pricing are, therefore, counterintuitive as well as economically unsound.

Additionally, while Dow does dominate the market, the costs of the other producers should not be totally ignored in certain situations. It cannot be assumed that Dow's competitors will remain in the market if the price does not cover their costs.

Historical Pricing

The next mechanism examined was the use of regression models to capture the historical relationship between prices, producer cost, and capacity utilisation. The relationship proposed between the three was:

$$\log(P_t) = a \times \log(AC_{t-1}) + b \times \log(CU_{t-1}) + C$$

where

P_t = price of magnesium at time t

AC_{t-1} = cost of production a time t–1

CU_{t-1} = capacity utilisation at time t–1

In order to perform this regression, it was necessary to collect historical data on past prices, capacity utilisation, and producer costs. The model was used to 'back cast' Dow's production costs and these values were used for producer cost data. The regression was limited to the years 1970–82 because major structural changes occurred in the market in 1970.

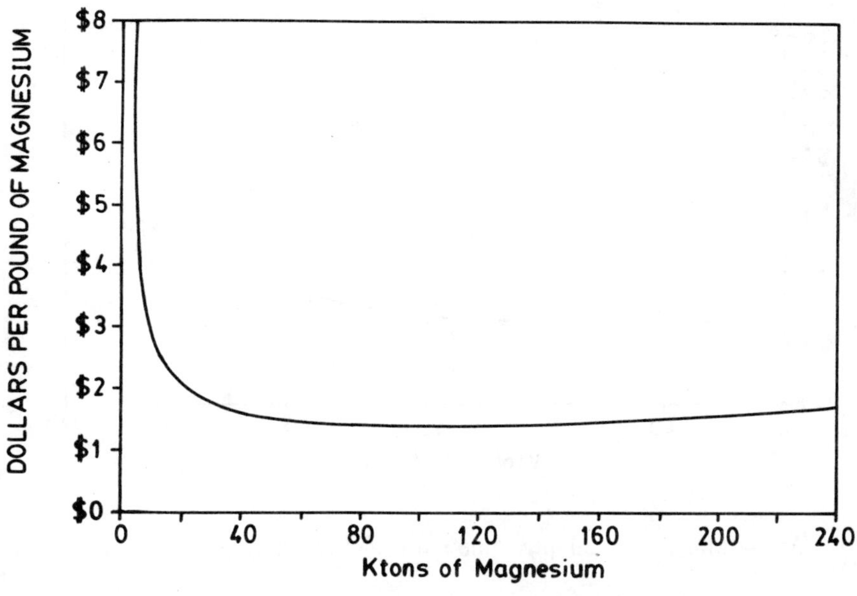

Figure 9. Magnesium Supply Function Under the Historical Pricing Scenario

This pricing mechanism has all the advantages of the cost plus pricing mechanism, with some additional benefits. First, the mechanism identifies the dependence of prices on costs and capacity utilisation in a way that can be validated through statistical analysis. Second, the mechanism does not ignore the effects of capacity utilisation, yielding results consistent with economic theory.

Nevertheless, this pricing mechanism has some serious weaknesses. In particular, regression pricing assumes that the future will be the same as the present. One of the important considerations the magnesium model had to address was what is the impact of a new entry into the market. Regression pricing cannot be trusted to yield meaningful results when major structural changes are being considered.

Marginal Cost Pricing

In marginal cost pricing, a fourth order curve was fit through the full capacity costs of the lowest and highest cost producers. The resulting upward sloping supply curve was multiplied by a scaling factor to incorporate the expected markup above minimum cost.

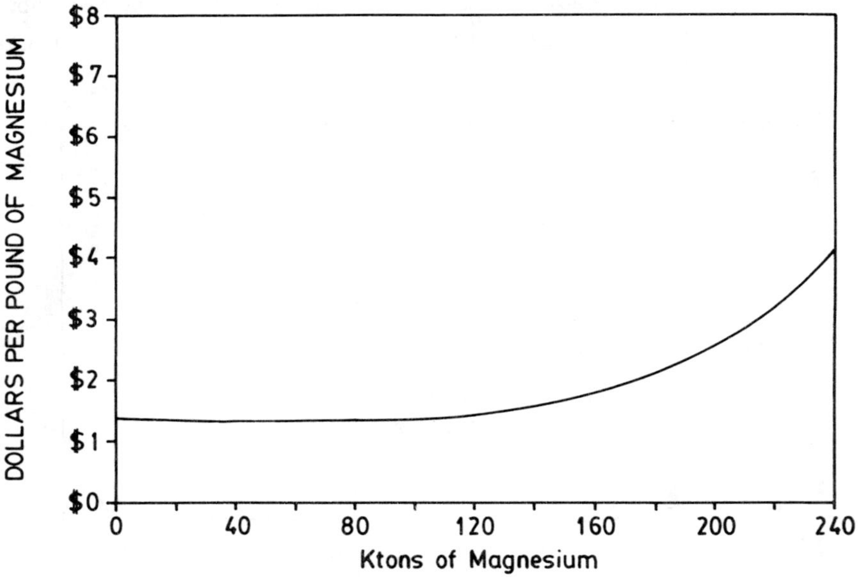

Figure 10. Magnesium Supply Function Under Marginal Cost Pricing

The pricing mechanism may be defined as follows:

$$P = a \times C_1 \qquad (Q < Q_1)$$

$$P = a \times (C_1 + \left[C_1 + (C_2 - C_1) \times \frac{(Q-Q_1)^4}{(Q_2-Q_1)^4} \right] \qquad (Q \geq Q_1)$$

where

P = price of magnesium at time t

Q = output demanded

C_1 = full capacity cost of production at Dow at t–1

C_2 = greatest full capacity cost of production at t–1

Q_1 = 20% of Dow's capacity

Q_2 = total US capacity

a = scaling factor

This mechanism exhibits several interesting features. First, Dow's cost structure defines the minimum price for magnesium. Second, price increases monotonically with demand and in direct relation to the increase in producer cost. Finally, the addition of new producers to the market can be incorporated easily and in a consistent fashion.

3.5 Results of Pricing Scheme

For a large number of the market scenarios, historical pricing and the marginal cost pricing yield almost identical behaviour. Only those scenarios involving the entry of a small (< 15 kton per year) producer yield significantly different results.

Overall, the utility of the three pricing mechanisms depends on the scenario being examined. This dependence is summarised below:

Cost plus pricing – Because of its intensitivity to capacity limitations, this mechanism is best suited to modelling scenarios that assume new capacity will come on line to meet any new demand. Additionally, it assumes that no new producers will operate at costs lower than those of Dow Chemical, and that Dow retains its market advantage.

Historical pricing – This mechanism is best suited to examining the effects of sustaining the status quo of the market. It can also be used for those scenarios that assume the current producers will increase their capacities proportionally or that assume a new entrant into the market will be a small producer. However, its results should be viewed with care under scenarios that examine sweeping changes in the structure of the market.

Marginal cost pricing – This mechanism assumes the existence of a competitive market for the production of magnesium. It can most profitably be used for those scenarios in which significant new capacity comes on line.

4. MAJOR ASSUMPTIONS

As was outlined in the above sections, the behaviour of the model is a direct result of a well defined set of assumptions. These assumptions can be tailored to analyse the behaviour of the magnesium market under a variety of scenarios.

The assumptions available to be modified are:

1. the consumption of magnesium in the developing sectors.

   These sectors are:
   - steel desulfurisation
   - automotive usage
   - aluminium can usage
   - non automotive die casting

2. pricing policies of the industry. Depending on the anticipated market conditions, one of the following pricing mechanisms can be employed:
   - cost plus pricing
   - historical pricing
   - marginal cost pricing

3. the economic growth rates in consumer demand sectors. A variety of economic indicators are used to estimate the consumption of magnesium in the established demand sectors. The value of these indicators may be modified to reflect various economic assumptions.

4. the production capacity of the magnesium industry. Both the size and the distribution of production capacity in the magnesium industry can be modified to reflect assumptions concerning the structure of the magnesium industry.

5. the price of aluminium. The ratio of the price of aluminium to the price of magnesium has been cited by industry observers as the critical decision variable determining the applicability of magnesium in the automotive industry. Forecasts of the price of aluminium can be used to examine a variety of assumptions about the behaviour of the aluminium industry when faced with competition for their markets.

6. the cost of factor inputs. The production costs at each of the sites modelled are based on various cost indices, whose values reflect assumptions that may be modified to examine changing economic environments.

7. process innovation. Improvements in the productivity of various factor inputs can be incorporated into the cost models for any of the production sites modelled.

5. RESULTS

The model of the world magnesium market provides a means of assessing the impacts of technical and economic changes on the markets for magnesium. With this tool, scenario analyses can be performed, examining the implications of changes in the costs of production, process technology, economic activity, pricing policy, etc. The results from four such scenarios are presented below. These scenarios can be described as: base case, high economic growth, low economic growth, and high aluminium price. The last scenario, high aluminium price, was designed to examine the potential for magnesium in automotive applications, since many analysts believe that the price ratio of magnesium/aluminium is the primary variable to affect the use of automotive magnesium.

The major assumptions of each scenario are presented in Table 4.

As shown, only the aluminium price, the production indices, and the pricing policy were varied. Other exogenous variables could be expected to change within each scenario (e.g., capacity utilisation for the steel industry, number of cars produced per year). However, for the purposes of this paper, these were assumed to remain at their base case values.

Additionally, except for the low growth scenario, it was assumed that new magnesium producers, utilising an advanced and efficient production technology, would enter the market in 1987 with a 30 ktpy production capacity. In the high growth scenario, a new producer enters the market every four years with production capacity of 60 ktpy. In the high aluminium price scenario, a 30 ktpy entrant coming at four year intervals is assumed. For these last two scenarios, capacity expansions were based on the levels of the production required to prevent domestic consumption from exceeding domestic supply.

Table 4. Major Assumptions – Scenario Analysis

	Base Case	High Growth	Low Growth	High Al. Price
Al. Price	+5.5%/yr	+8.0%/yr	+4.0%/yr	+9.0%/yr
GNP	+3	+5	+1	+3
IPI	+2	+4	+1	+2
Titanium Consumption	flat	+1.55	–1	flat
Military Expenditures	+5 to 1988 → flat	+5 to 1988 → +2	+5 to 1988 → –2	+5 to 1988 → flat
Construction Costs	+3 to 1988 → +1	+3	flat	+3 to 1988 → +1
Pricing Policy	cost (+)	marg. cost	historical	marg. cost

Projections of domestic consumption, market price, and production capacity that result from each of these scenarios are presented graphically in Figures 11–14.

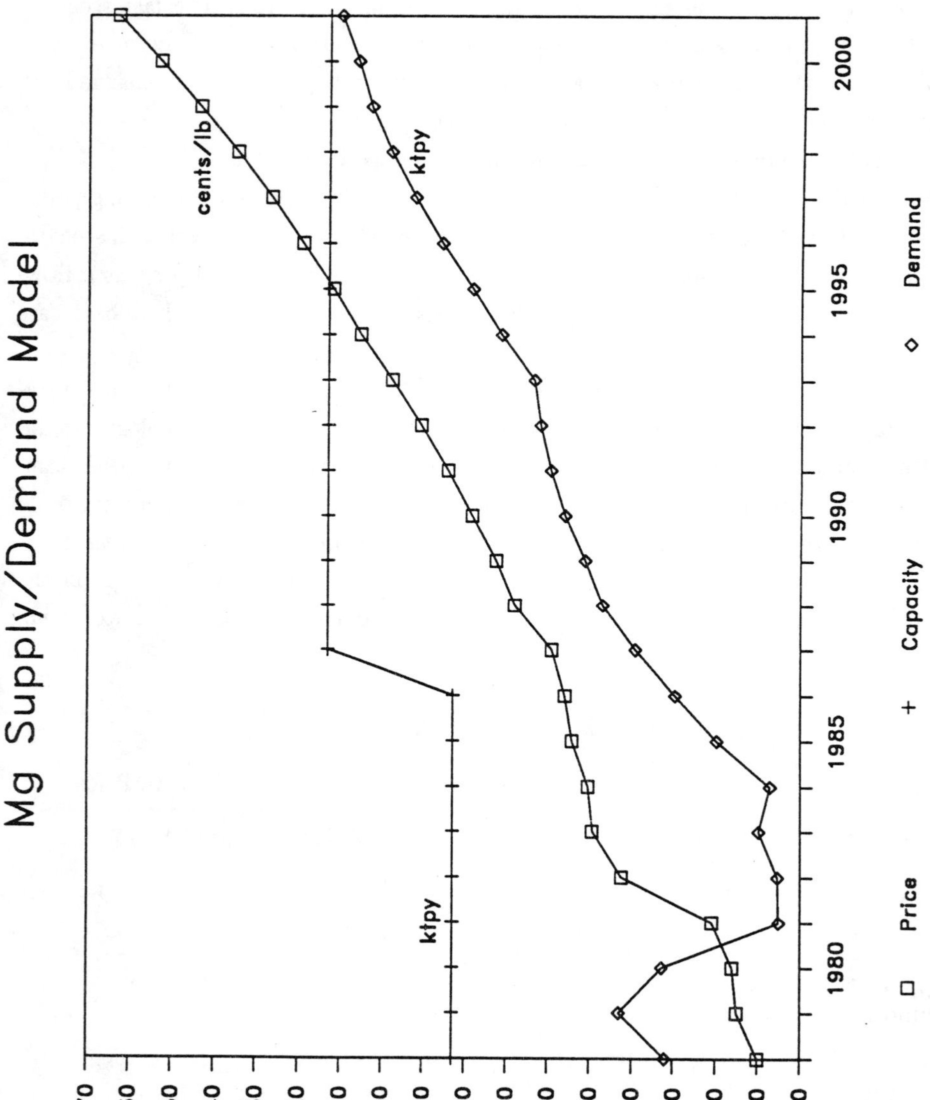

FIGURE 11. SCENARIO ANALYSIS – BASE CASE

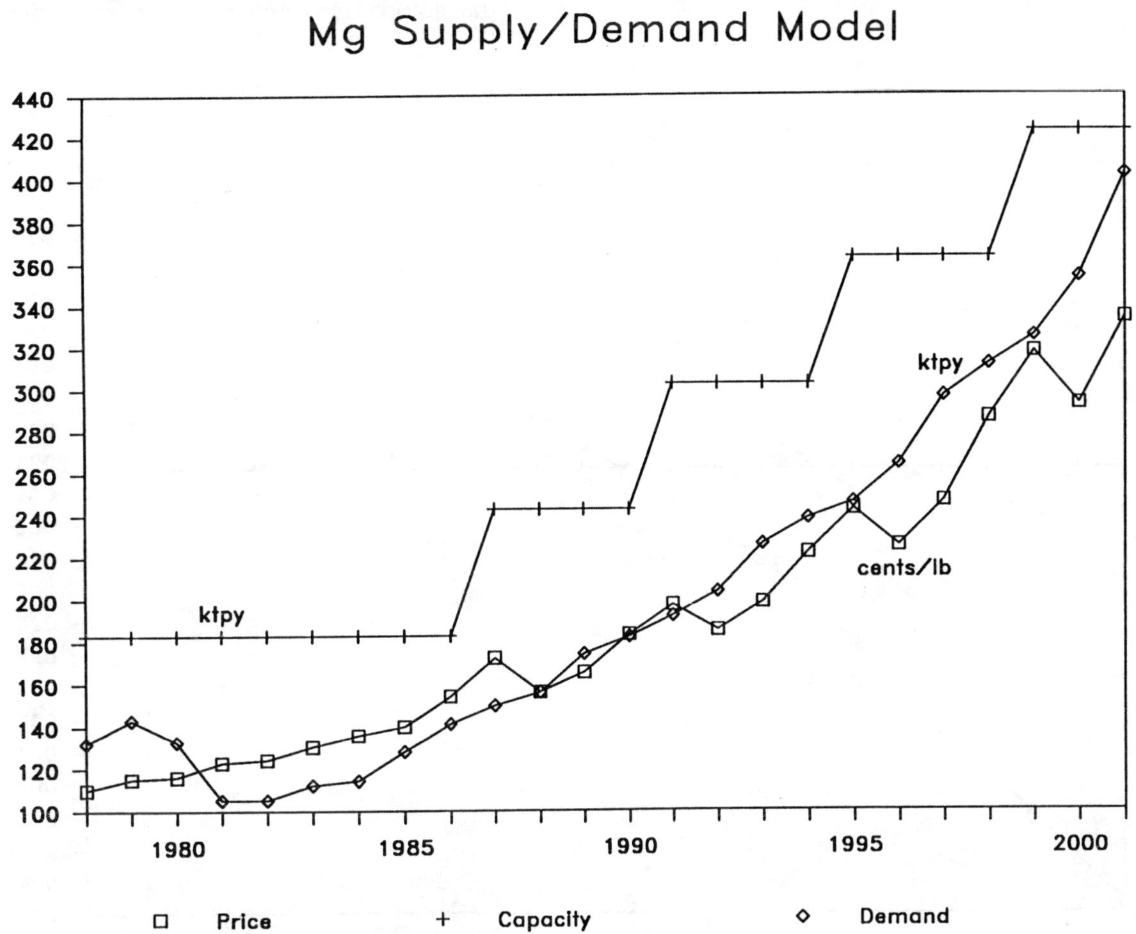

FIGURE 12. SCENARIO ANALYSIS – HIGH GROWTH

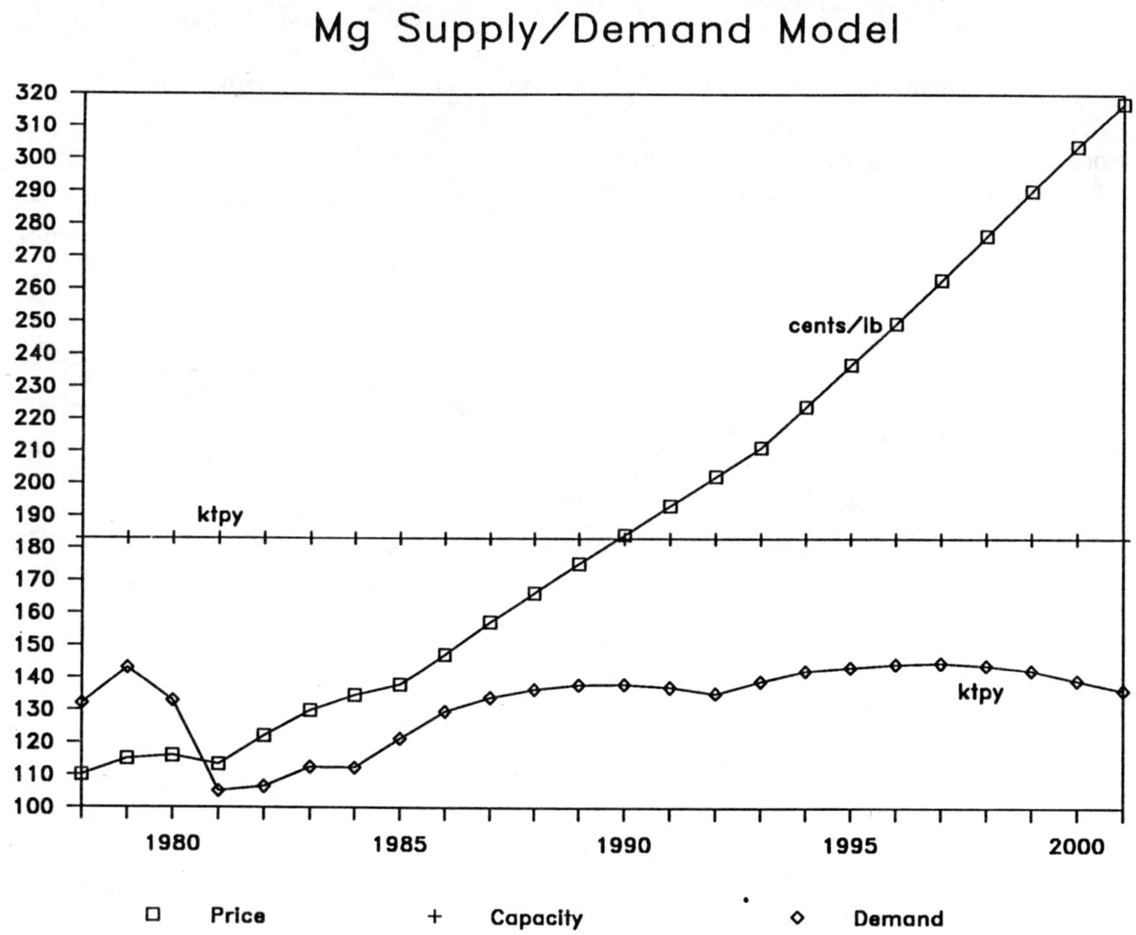

FIGURE 13. SCENARIO ANALYSIS – LOW GROWTH

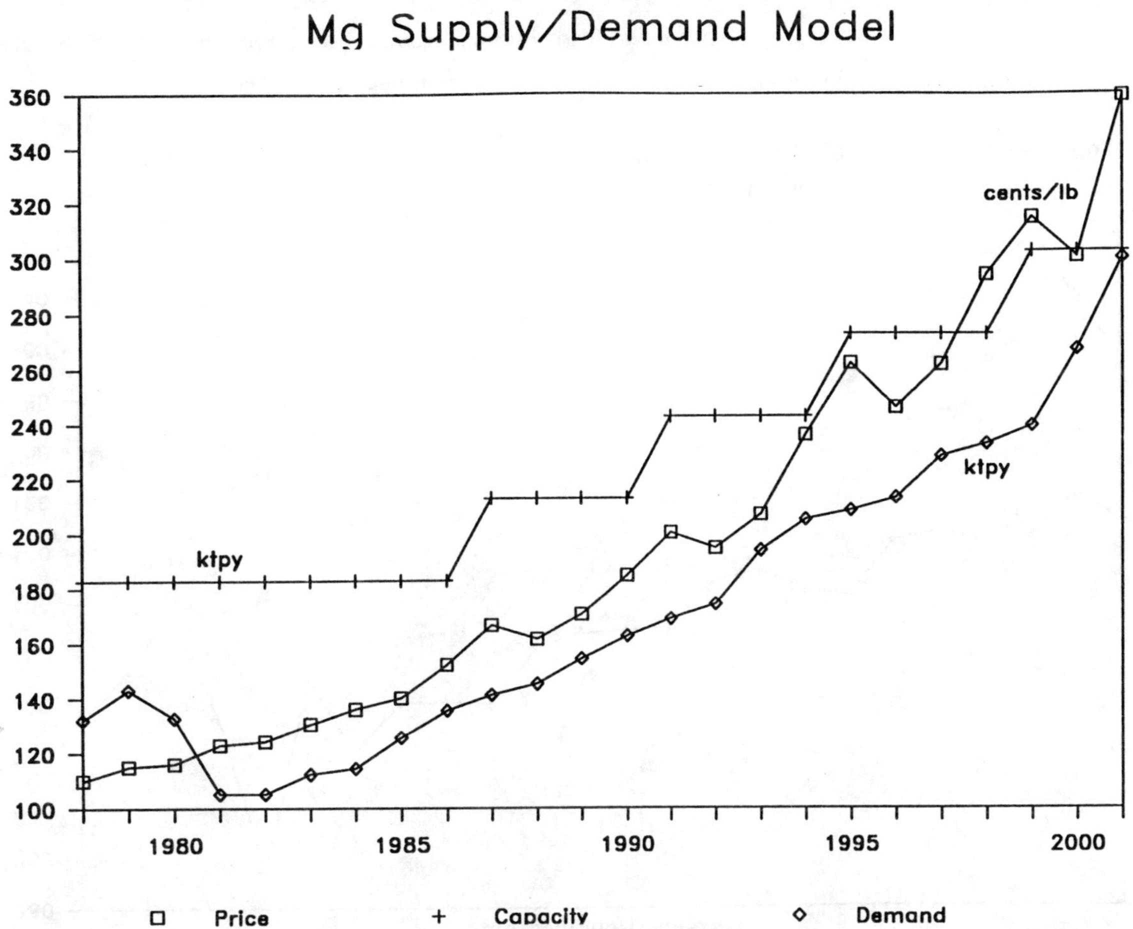

FIGURE 14. SCENARIO ANALYSIS – HIGH ALUMINUM PRICES

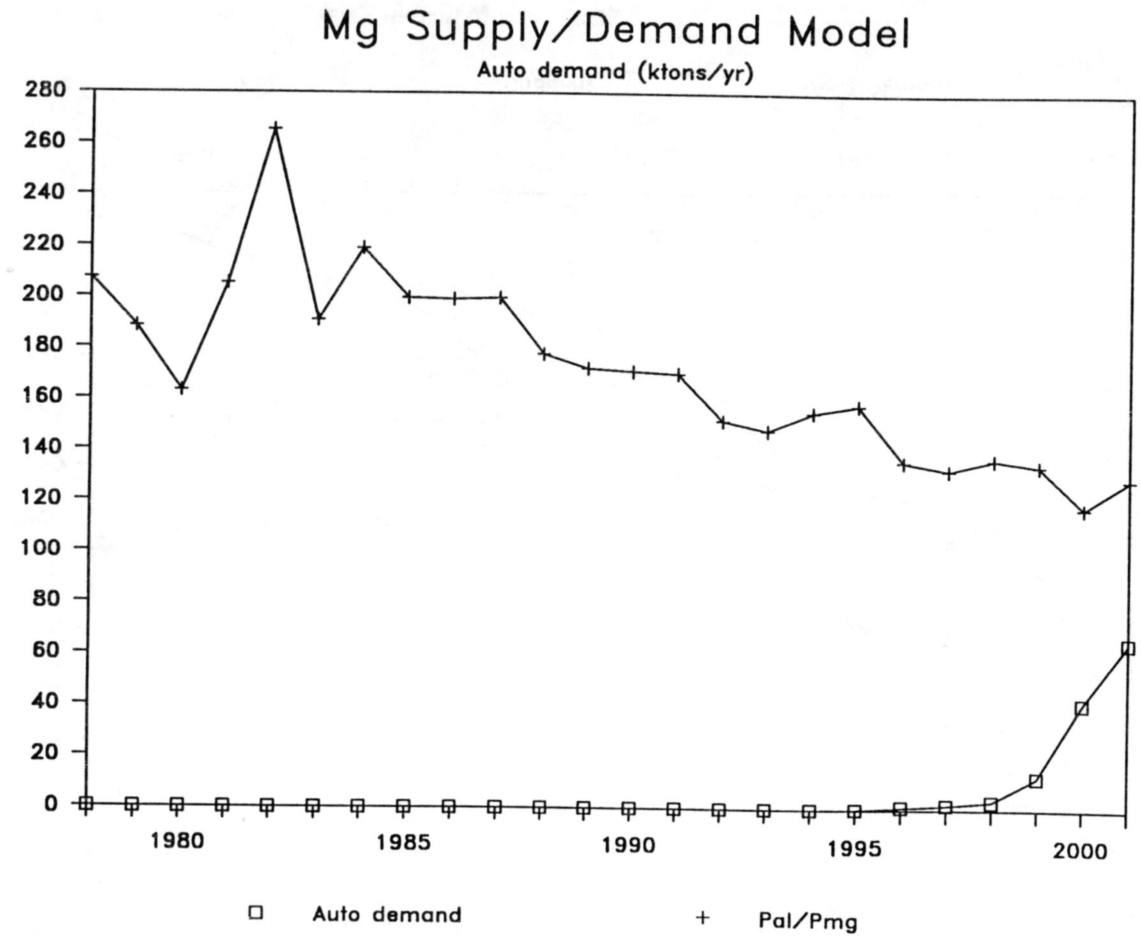

FIGURE 15. SCENARIO ANALYSIS – IMPACT OF HIGH ALUMINUM PRICES ON AUTOMOTIVE DEMAND

Base Case Scenario – In the base case, the consumption of magnesium increases 75.4% from 1985 to 2001; an average annual growth rate of 3.6%. The two market sectors with the largest increases in consumption are aluminium alloying, which grows by 139.7%, and external desulfurisation of steel, which grows 122% over the sixteen year period. The automotive sector, with its enormous growth potential, does not grow.

High Growth Scenario – In this scenario, magnesium consumption grows at 7.4% per year for a total growth from 1985 to 2001 of 213%. Growth is experienced in all market sectors, including aluminium alloying (9.6%/yr), aluminium cans (4.5%/yr), cathodic protection (5.2%/yr), exports (4.4%/yr), desulfurisation (5.1%/yr), and non–automotive die castings (5.1%/yr). Automotive use of magnesium reaches 6.8 lbs/car, consuming 47 ktpy in 2001.

Low Growth Scenario – In the low growth scenario, magnesium consumption increases only 12.4% from 1985 to 2001, corresponding to an annual growth rate of 0.7%. The consumption of magnesium by the aluminium industry increases 1%/yr. Use of magnesium for cathodic protection decreases 1.4%/yr. Magnesium is not used by the automotive industry.

High Aluminium Price Scenario – In the event of high aluminium prices, the consumption of magnesium is projected to increase 139.3%, for an average annual increase of 5.6%. Figure 15 shows the effect of these high prices on the consumption of magnesium for automotive applications. The price ratio (Mg/Al) that drives this demand is also presented. Consumption in the automotive sector is projected to grow to 66.7 ktpy by 2001. Because of the time lags built into the model and because of the high initial Mg/Al price ratio, significant consumption of magnesium in domestic automobiles will not begin until 1997.

6. CONCLUSIONS

In modelling both the supply and demand sides of an entire industry often no single modelling technique is adequate. Regression analysis, cost modelling, marginal cost pricing, etc., can be helpful tools, but none of them can stand alone. An alternative approach is to construct a simulation model that integrates these specific modelling techniques with engineering and judgmental assessments regarding potential technical and economic changes.

The world magnesium market model is a simulation model that can be separated broadly into supply, demand, and pricing sections. However, each of these sections is interconnected by a complex web of interactions. This aspect of the magnesium simulation model is intuitively compelling because, within the magnesium industry (as with most industries), changes on one side of the market are inevitably reflected on the other.

Using this model, it is possible to examine how a wide range of market forecasts will influence the magnesium industry. The model demonstrates that a rapid growth in the consumption of magnesium depends less upon penetration of the so–called 'evolutionary' markets than it does on the economic climate and pricing policies of producers of competitive materials. Growth in the industry depends as well on whether consumers perceive the price as stable.

The model also reveals the importance of non–structural uses of magnesium. If magnesium consumption increases in applications where recycling is feasible, the consumption of primary material decreases accordingly, following a time lag for recycling. Thus, while the automotive market is an attractive application of magnesium, in the long run, the volume of recycled magnesium can grow to equal that of a primary producer.

Depending upon the objectives of a magnesium producer, this model suggests a number of strategies. For producers interested in expanding their markets, the model suggests that long term supply contracts, with guaranteed prices and supplies, can lead to long term increases in consumption. Alternatively, those producers interested in high profitability should emphasise chemical applications and low volume market niches to prevent new entrants. Finally, potential entrants to the magnesium market should not attempt to 'go it alone' – rather, they should enter the market knowing who their customers will be, preferably with a contract in hand.

The greatest advantage of this type of model is that it allows the decision maker to incorporate his assumptions regarding the behaviour of the market in a consistent framework for analysis. Once his assumptions are made explicit, it is possible for him to identify the consequences of a wide range of situations in the market and to determine the strategy which best satisfies his ultimate goals, rather than a haphazard assessment of alternative strategies.

NOTES

* MIT, Cambridge, Mass.

+ IBIS Consultants, Cambridge, Mass.

CHAPTER 7

DEMAND FOR GASOLINE: AN APPLICATION OF A NEW SELECTION MODEL PROCEDURE

A. Aznar and P. Garcia Castrillo
University of Zaragoza, Spain

1. INTRODUCTION

In recent years there has been a growing number of efforts to model the demand for gasoline and its relationship to the underlying demand for transportation services. Many econometric models have been estimated using temporal data (Ramsey et al. (1975), Dahl (1979) and Tishler (1983)), cross section data (Wheaton (1982)), or pooling (Archibald and Gillingham (1980) and Baltagi and Griffin (1983)). One of the main objectives of these studies has been to determine the gasoline price elasticity; some summary results can be seen in Wheaton (1982) and Dahl (1979).

The purpose of this paper is to specify, estimate and select an econometric model in order to know the gasoline price elasticity using annual data for Spain from 1961 to 1981. In Section 2, we outline a simple theoretical model which forms the basis for econometric estimation. Section 3 outlines a methodology for the selection of an econometric model. Section 4 examines data, and the results are presented in Section 5.

2. MODEL SPECIFICATION

Following Wheaton (1982) and Baltagi and Griffin (1983), our approach to modelling gasoline consumption is to view consumption as composed of three separate determinants: the utilisation of the typical car, its gasoline efficiency, and the stock of cars. As Balgati and Griffin write:

$$\begin{matrix}\text{Gasoline} \\ \text{Consumption}\end{matrix} = \begin{matrix}\text{Miles driven} \\ \text{per car}\end{matrix} \times \begin{matrix}\text{Gasoline} \\ \text{consumption} \\ \text{per mile}\end{matrix} \times \text{Cars} \qquad (1)$$

$$\left(\text{Utilisation} \times \frac{1}{\text{Efficiency}} \times \text{Stock of Cars}\right)$$

O. Guvenen (ed.), International Commodity Market Models and Policy Analysis, 143–153.

Normally, a simultaneous equation model is proposed to explain the behaviour of each component. Since (1) is log linear, any elasticity of gasoline consumption is simply the sum of the three component elasticities.

Instead of estimating the structural relations, in this paper we estimate the reduced form relation corresponding to gasoline consumption. We employ the structural form to specify the exogenous variables to be used as explanatory variables in the reduced form. The list of exogenous variables considered is:

- Gasoline price
- Income
- Price of new cars
- Price index of transport services
- Index of transportation
- Population in urban area

In some cases, some components on the right of (1) were considered as exogenous variables.

3. SELECTION MODEL ECONOMETRIC TECHNIQUES[2]

The next question is: how many and which variables of the list are chosen in the last specification? In this paper we employ a selection process with the following three steps:

1) Determination of the set of admissible models;
2) Determination of the set of more informative models; and
3) Determination of the set of more corroborated models.

3.1 Set of Admissible Models

A model is said to be admissible if its random disturbance is what Hendry and Richard (1982) call a mean innovation process which implies that the random part of the model is, first, a white noise process and, second, is independent with respect to the explanatory variables.

To determine whether the random part is a white noise process we use the Durbin-Watson test, the test proposed by Berenblut and Webb (1973), and a non parametric test. This last test is based on the use of the recursive residuals; if these are white noise then we say that the disturbances are white noise as well.

The independence of the random part with respect to the explanatory variables is tested with the so–called test of exogeneity; we considered those proposed by Hausman (1978).

3.2 Set of More Informativ Models

We said before that our main objective is to choose a model which best estimates the gasoline price elasticity. Then we say that, between two models, M_1 and M_2, M_1 is more informative than M_2 if the variance of the estimator of the gasoline price elasticity using M_1 is smaller than the variance obtained using M_2. To determine the more informative models we use the AVE test developed in Aznar (1984c).

Consider the standard linear model with k explanatory variables and n observations:

$$y = x\beta + u \tag{2}$$

where we suppose that u is an innovation process.

Consider the following two models:

Model 1: $-y = x_1\beta_1 + U_1$

Model 2: $-y = x_2\beta_2 + U_2$

Suppose that both models include an explanatory variable, x_i, and that our objective is to estimate its parameter, β_i.

We take the first model as the true one and apply OLS; the variance of the estimator of β_i can be written as:

$$\mathrm{Var}\,(\hat{\beta}_{i1}) = \sigma_1^2/(1-R_{i1}^2)\Sigma x_i^2 \tag{3}$$

where R_{i1}^2 is the squared correlation coefficient between x_i and the rest of the k_{i-1} explanatory variables.

Consider now that the true model is the Model 2 and apply OLS; the variance of the estimator in this case is:

$$\mathrm{Var}\,(\hat{\beta}_{i2}) = \sigma_2^2/(1-R_{i2}^2)\Sigma x_i^2)$$

Model 1 is chosen in preference of Model 2 for the intended use of estimating β_i if:

$$\mathrm{Var}\,(\hat{\beta}_{i1}) < \mathrm{Var}\,(\hat{\beta}_{i2}) \tag{4}$$

$$\frac{\hat{\sigma}_1^2}{(1-R_{i1}^2)\Sigma x_i^2} < \frac{\hat{\sigma}_2^2}{(1-R_{i2}^2)\Sigma x_i^2}$$

where $\hat{\sigma}_1^2$ and $\hat{\sigma}_2^2$ are the respective OLS estimators of σ_1^2 and σ_2^2.

Equation (4) is equivalent to:

$$\frac{\hat{\sigma}_1^2}{\hat{\sigma}_2^2} < \frac{1 - R_{i1}^2}{1 - R_{i2}^2} \tag{5}$$

In the nested case in which x_2 has the same variables as x_1 minus q which have been suppressed in (5) is equivalent to:

$$F > \frac{n - k + q}{q} \cdot \frac{1 - R^2_{i2}}{1 - R^2_{i1}} - \frac{n - k}{q} \qquad (6)$$

where F is the test for $H_0: \beta_Q = 0$, β_Q being the vector of coefficients of the suppressed variables.

Note that the significance level depends on the sample size, the number of explanatory variables and the degree of collinearity. Results like these have been obtained with the tests proposed by Akaike (1973), Allen (1971), Mallows (1973), Sawa (1978) and Amemiya (1980).

3.3 Set of Corroborated Models

Corroboration is a concept related to how the model works with data not used to estimate the model. We say that M_1 is more corroborated than M_2 by a given 'new data' when this data is closer to M_1 than M_2. We know that $\hat{\beta}_i$ defines a probability distribution for the values of β_{ij} if we have an 'observed' value of β_i, we can determine how close it is to the estimate given by each model. By an observed value of β_i, say $\beta_{ij} \cdot j = 1,2$, we mean the following:

$$\beta_{ij} = (Y_0 - \sum_{k \neq i} X_{k0} \hat{\beta}_{kj}) / X_{0i} \qquad J = 1,2 \qquad (7)$$

where Y_0 and X_{k0} are observations not used to estimate the model. Here we identify the true values of β_{kj} with their estimates.

4. ANALYSIS OF DATA

In this section we do exploratory analysis. As Mayer (1980) indicates: 'Exploratory analysis is a set of methods designed to examine and describe the structure of data. The exploratory approach involves the use of descriptive techniques and the intuition of the analyst to investigate the structure of data'.

Figure 1 displays gasoline consumption (GG), stock of cars (SCO) and kilometres driven per car (UCO). Although they have a similar pattern there are some differences which are worth noting. First, the rate of growth is not the same; the stock of cars increases faster and gasoline consumption increases more slowly. Over the last five years, gasoline consumption changes its pattern and, even in two years, it decreases.

Price index of gasoline (PGD), national net product (R), price index of new cars (PCO), travellers on public transport (PTP) and population in urban areas (UR_1 and

UR_2) are displayed in Figure 2. It can be seen that the price index of gasoline and the price index of new cars decrease over the period of analysis and that a significant change occurred in 1974. In that year the first variable increased. National net product increases faster than the other variables except in the last two years in which it decreases. The other variables increase moderately over the period of analysis.

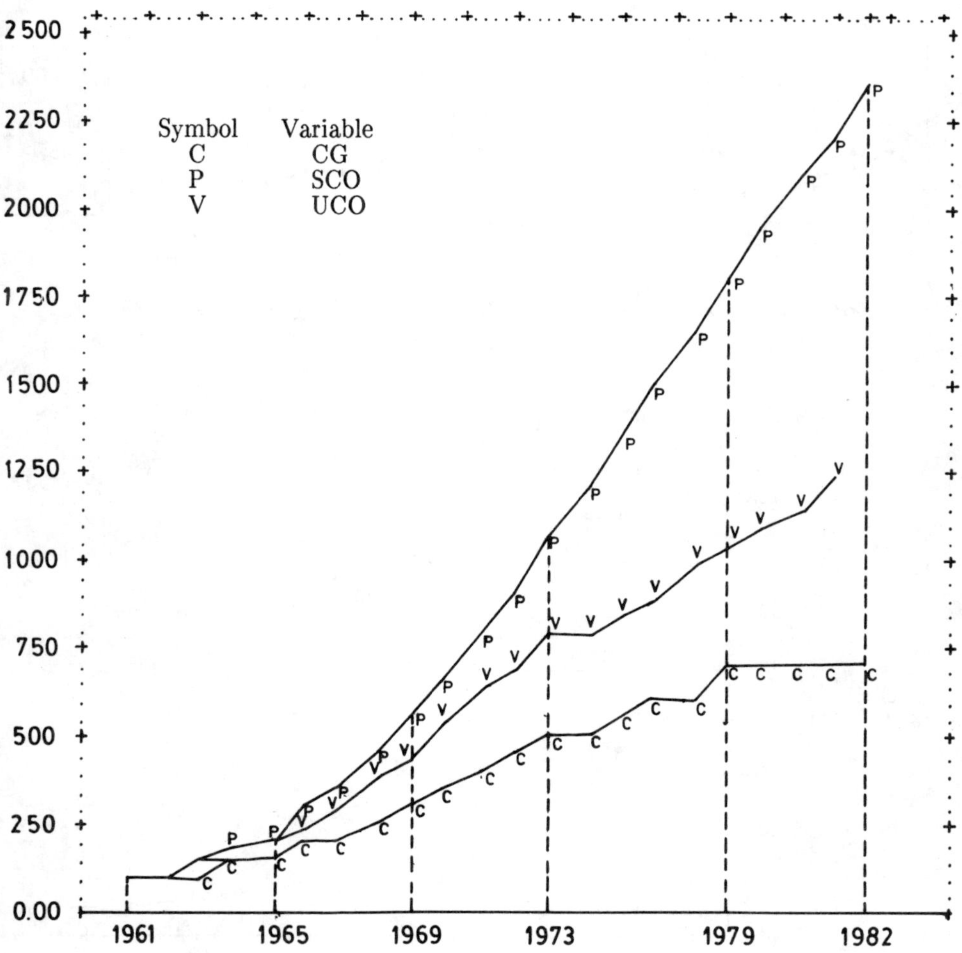

Figure 1

In Figure 3, gasoline consumption is plotted against the price index of gasoline with the years indicated. From 1961 to 1973 gasoline consumption increases as prices decrease. But from 1974 to 1982, the plot shows no pattern which indicates that the relation between those two variables is complex.

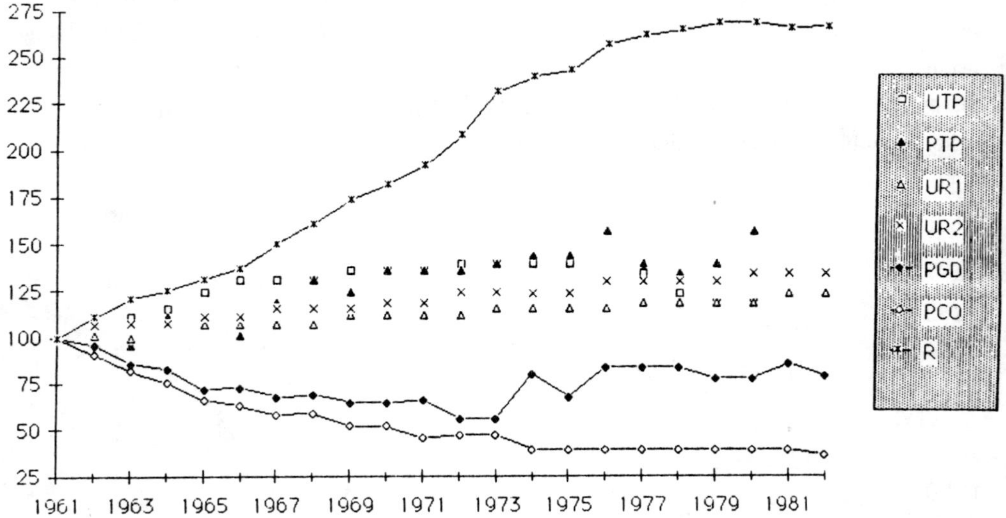

Figure 2

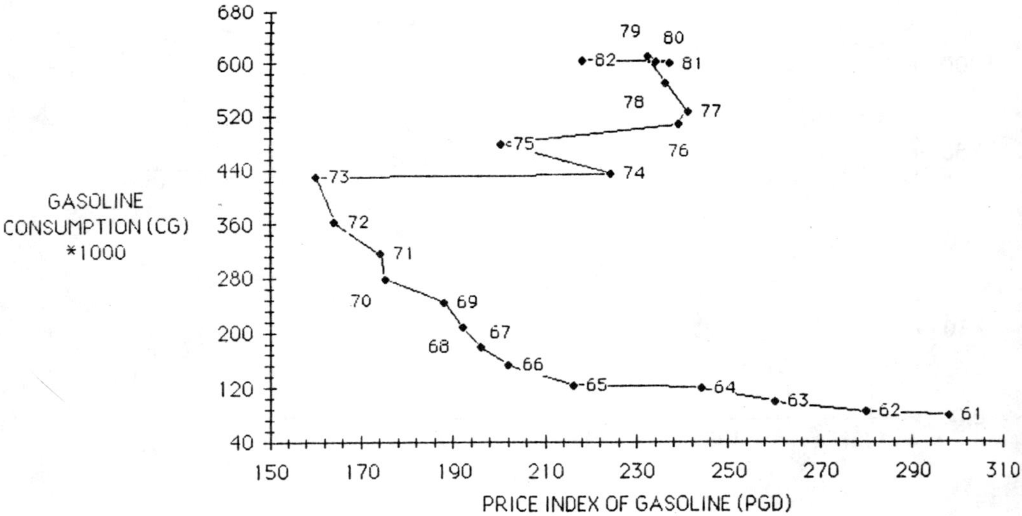

Figure 3

5. RESULTS

Following the process described in Section 3, the regression of GG on all possible combinations of the explanatory variables were calculated[2] with the values of the Durbin-Watson and Berenblut–Webb test. In Table 1 appear the equations values of the two tests indicating the white noise character of the corresponding disturbance. The null hypothesis of non–autocorrelation can be accepted using a level of significance of 1% or greater.

For the non–parametric test we calculate the recursive residuals and to test the white noise character of these residuals we use the turning points test, the difference sign test and the Rank test shown in Kendall (1976). All three tests indicate the white noise character of the disturbances of the ten equations.

The exogeneity test has been restricted to these ten equations and to only one variable, SCO. That is because in some works that variable has been treated as endogenous. As we said before, we use the Hausman test. This test is based on the comparison of any asymptotically efficient estimator and some consistent but asymptotically inefficien estimator. But as Hausman (1978), and Nakamura and Nakamura (1981) in more detail, show there are some equivalent forms of this test. The one we use here regresses the variable SCO on the accepted exogenous variables and the residuals of this regression form a new variable to be added to the original equation. If the null hypothesis that the coefficient of this new variable is zero is accepted, then the exogeneity character of the tested variable is accepted.

The best regression found for SCO is:

$$SCO = -102.2 - 0.706\ PCO - 0.355\ PGC + 0.488\ PTP + 11.45\ UR$$

$$R^2 = 0.999 \qquad \bar{R}^2 = 0.997$$

$$DW = 1.766 \qquad B\text{–}W = 0.948$$

Although the Berenblut–Webb test indicates some degree of autocorrelation, we were not able to find a better alternative for SCO. Then we use the residuals of this regression as a new explanatory variable in the ten equations shown in Table 1. The statistical significance of the coefficient of this new variable is tested by comparing the estimated standard errors of the price index of gasoline elasticity estimator before and after including that variable. The results are presented in Table 2. As can be seen in Table 2 the exogeneity character of SCO is rejected only in the first two equations.

Table 1. Autocorrelation test results

Equation Number	Explanatory Variables	Value of D–W	Value of B–W
1	PGD, R, SCO, PCO, PTP, UR	2.290	1.393
2	PGD, R, SCO, PCO, UR	2.208	1.109
3	PGD, R, SCO, PCO, PTP	2.183	1.393
4	PGD, R, SCO, PCO, UTP, PTP, UR	1.947	1.405
5	PGD, R, SCO, PCO, UTP, UR	1.805	1.299
6	PGD, R, SCO, PCO, UTP, PTP	2.068	1.430
7	PGD, R, SCO, PCO, UTP	1.736	1.179
8	PGD, R, SCO, PCO, UTP, UR	2.101	1.567
9	PGD, R, SCO, PCO, UR	2.017	1.393
10	PGD, R, SCO, PCO, UTP, PTP, UR	2.132	1.448

Table 2. Estimated Standard Errors

Equation Number	Original Equation	Residuals Included
1	0.04259	0.03875
2	0.04359	0.03824
3	0.04649	0.04783
4	0.05752	0.05963
5	0.05833	0.05988
6	0.06261	0.07532
7	0.06697	0.08045
8	0.07066	*
9	0.07369	0.09301
10	0.07388	*

* Extreme multicollinearity and it was not possible to calculate the values.

As a result of the application of these tests we can say that the set of admissible models is composed of equations (3) to (10). There is some evidence to say that the disturbances of these models are innovations.

Among these eight models we define the informative ones as those which have the smaller standard error of the price elasticity estimator. As can be seen in Table 2, the more informative regressions are numbers 3, 4, 5, and 6. Although the standard error of the last one was somehow greater, compared to the others, it was selected because of its good non–autocorrelation performance. Thus the set of more informative models is composed of equations (3) to (6).

To determine the set of more corroborated models we calculate the predicted elasticities as was shown in (6) under the hypothesis that the true values of coefficients or the variables other than the PGD coincide with the estimated values. We estimate the model with data until 1980, and use 1981 to calculate the predicted elasticities. Then we get the so–called corroboration critical level, which is the greater level of significance for which the null hypothesis that the value of the prices elasticity equals the corresponding predicted elasticity is not rejected. Then the set of the more corroborated models is composed of those models for which the corroboration critical level is greater. In our case these models are equations (4) to (6).

Table 3. Set of more corroborated models

Equation Number	Predicted Elasticity	Corroboration Critical Level
3	–0.122	40%
4	–0.175	42%
5	–0.190	46%
6	–0.135	41%

The finally accepted relation is equation (5). The estimated model using the data from 1961 to 1981 is:

$$\begin{aligned} CG = \ & \underset{\substack{(7.40)\\ \{1.68\}}}{12.439} - \underset{\substack{(0.06)\\ \{-3.18\}}}{0.1917}\ PGD + \underset{\substack{(0.19)\\ \{3.43\}}}{0.6621}\ R + \underset{\substack{(0.20)\\ \{5.66\}}}{1.1315}\ SCO \\ & + \underset{\substack{(0.17)\\ \{1.44\}}}{0.2520}\ PCO - \underset{\substack{(0.19)\\ \{-0.97\}}}{0.1892}\ UTP - \underset{\substack{(1.95)\\ \{-3.38\}}}{6.5834}\ UR \end{aligned}$$

$$R^2 = 0.999 \qquad \bar{R}^2 = 0.999$$

The figures in parentheses below each estimated coefficient are the estimated standard errors. The figures in braces below the standard errors are the t–ratios.

Since our model is a static model and involves the assumption that the gasoline market equilibrium is achieved within one year, it is useful to perform a test of the adequacy of the static model against an alternative dynamic formulation. To do that, the PGD lagged one and two periods were added to the list of explanatory variables and the process was repeated. The results show that these two lagged variables play no role in determining gasoline consumption.

The important question whether or not it is possible to estimate individual elasticities is not treated in this paper. In many cases, this univariate projection of multivariate evidence is doubtful (see Leamer (1978)). We suppose that, in our example, the univariate treatment is valid.

APPENDIX: List of Variables

CG : Gasoline consumption
PGD: Price index of gasoline deflated by consumer price index
R : National net product
SCO: Stock of cars
PCO: Price index of new cars deflated by consumer price index
UCO: Kms driven per car
UTP: Travellers on public transport
PTP: Price index of public transport deflated by consumer price index
UR : Population in urban areas

NOTES

1. A more developed version of the content of this section can be seen in Aznar (1984a, 1984b).
2. The log linear specification is used because constant elasticities are easier to work with as they are comparable to other work which also uses constant elasticities.

REFERENCES

Akaike, M. (1973), 'Information Theory and an Extension of the Maximum Likelihood Principle' in D. Koolemiai Kiodo (ed.), *Problems of Control and Information Theory*, Publishing House of the Hungarian Academy of Sciences, Budapest.

Allen, D.M. (1971), 'Mean Square Error of Prediction as a Cri– terion for Selecting Variables', *Technometrics*, 13, pp. 469–75.

Amemiya, T. (1980), 'Selection of Regressors', *International Economic Review*, 21, No. 2, pp. 331–54.

Archibald, R. and M. Gillingham (1980), 'An Analysis of the Short–Run Consumer Demand for Gasoline Using Household Survey Data', *Review of Economics and Statistics*, 62, pp. 622–28.

Aznar, A. (1984a), 'Propuesta de Estrategia para la seleccion de Modelos Econometricos', Ponencia presentada al IX Simposis de Teoria Economica y Econometrica, Barcelona, Sept. 1984.

Aznar, A. (1984b), 'Economistas Flexo, Economistas Bombilla, el contraste de lo Inesperado y la Simulacion de Politicas Alternativas', presentado al Cicolo de Conferencias Homenaje a Keynes organisado por la Universidad Autonoma de Madrid.

Aznar, A. (1984c), 'Buscando el Modelo Econometrico Util', *Estadistica Espanola*, No. 102, pp. 5–11.

Baltagi, B.H. and J.M. Griffin (1983), 'Gasoline Demand in the OECD', *European Economic Review*, 22, pp. 117–37.

Berenblut, J.J. and G.J. Webb (1973), 'A New Test for Autocor– related Errors in the Linear Regression Model', *Journal of the Royal Statistical Society*, Series B 35, pp. 33–50.

Dahl, C.A. (1979), 'Consumer Adjustment to a Gasoline Tax', *Review of Economics and Statistics*, Vol. LXI, 3, pp. 427–32.

Hausman, J.A. (1978), 'Specification Tests in Econometrics', *Econometrica*, 46, pp.

1251–71.

Hendry, D.F. and J.F. Richard (1982), 'On the Formulation of Empirical Models in Dynamic Econometrics', *Journal of Econometrics*, 20, pp. 3–33.

Kendall, M. (1976), *Time Series*, Charles Griffin, London.

Leamer, E.E. (1978), *Specification Tests in Econometrics*, John Wiley, New York.

Mallows, C.L. (1973), 'Some Comments on CP', *Techometrics*, 15, No. 4.

Mayer, L.S. (1980), 'The Use of Explanatory Methods in Economic Analysis: Analysing Residential Energy Demand' in J. Kmenta and J.B. Ramsey (eds.), *Evaluation of Econometric Models*, Academic Press, New York.

Nakamura, A. and M. Nakamura (1981), 'On the Relationships Among Several Specification Error Tests Presented by Durbin, Wu and Hausman', *Econometrica*, 49, pp 1583–88.

Ramsey, J., R. Rasche and B. Allen (1975), 'An Analysis of the Private and Commercial Demand for Gasoline', *Review of Economics and Statistics*, Vol. LVII, No. 6, pp.502–507.

Sawa, T. (1978), 'Information Criteria for Discriminating Among Alternative Regression Models', *Econometrica*, 46, No. 6, pp. 1273–93.

Tishler, A. (1983), 'The Demand for Gasoline', *European Economic Review*, 10, pp. 271–87.

Wheaton, W.C. (1982), 'The Long–run Structure of Transportation and Gasoline Demand', *Bell Journal of Economics*, 13, No. 2, pp. 439–54.

CHAPTER 8

COMPETITIVE TECHNOLOGIES, EQUIPMENT VINTAGES AND THE DEMAND FOR ENERGY

F. Carlevaro*

1. INTRODUCTION

Macroeconometric modelling of energy demand resorts to two approaches leading to models describing the reality from different points of view. The first approach specifies the demand of a group of consumers for a single form of energy, independent of the demand for other fuels. This approach leads to very flexible models which enable the specification of peculiarities of each fuel demand and which are easy to estimate and use. The most elaborate versions of these models focus upon the dynamics of energy demand and explicitly take into account the complementarity link between this demand and that of a stock of fuel burning equipments.[2] In this way, they enable the study of the lags with which energy demand reacts to the environmental changes and open the way to generalisations aimed at representing the part played by the equipment technological change.[2] Their main disadvantage concerns the specification of interfuel substitutions generated by changes in the pattern of energy prices. Indeed, when it is applied to modelling the demand for competitive fuels, this approach leads to a system of unrelated fuel demand functions. This lack of analytical integration leads, in general, to capture asymmetrical substitution effects by means of cross prices.

The second approach consists in deducing the demand system for the whole set of fuels from the assumptions of traditional producer and consumer microeconomic theory. This orientation leads to the specification of interdependent demand systems, giving a simultaneous description of the way by which economic agents choose the fuel mix they intend to use. While specifying the nature of the 'economic calculus' underlying energy demand, this approach analytically ensures the consistency of substitution price effects.

However, these models entail several drawbacks. Especially, to be feasible the estimation requires additional unrealistic assumptions and restrictions.[3] Therefore, it is not

O. Guvenen (ed.), International Commodity Market Models and Policy Analysis, 155–164.

surprising to find that several applications of these models have provided contradictory or inconsistent results.[4] What is more restrictive, for us, is the lack of reference to fuel burning equipment even when a link is established with the stock of capital. Indeed, this deficiency prevents differentiating short run from long run substitution possibilities. The former are those possible with the existing stock of equipments while the latter assume quantitative and technological change of this stock. Thus, these models are unable to describe the impact, on the level and pattern of energy demand, of technical change in the energy performance of equipment and of new technology penetrations.

One can very well understand the interest offered by a model combining the logic which determines the substitutions in the models of the second approach with the putty-clay mechanism governing the short and long term energy demand modelled by the first approach. Now, this merging seems feasible but it first requires a consistent conceptual framework in which these elements of explanation may hang together.

The purpose of this paper is to set up a conceptual framework fulfilling the above requirements. This framework goes back to the logic of a vintage energy demand model proposed by Carlevaro and Giovannini (1984) and generalises it in order to integrate the different equipment demands satisfying the same energy need, whatever the technology and fuel used may be. The equipments are distinguished by age and we assign a different energy efficiency to every equipment vintage. In this context, we notice that the technological change, by acting in a differentiated way on the energy efficiency of the different types of used equipments, modifies the level and pattern of energy demand for the same quantity of produced services. Thus, the technological change appears, together with the evolution of the market shares of the different types of disposable equipments, as a determinant of energy savings as well as of substitution between energy products.

This conceptual framework is presented in the following section. In section 3 we discuss the possibilities it offers to simulate the demand for energy.

2. THE CONCEPTUAL FRAMEWORK

The conceptual framework we consider retains a set of concepts and relations describing the final energy consumption in relation with the services it provides. This description concerns energy consumption changes for producing a specific service, for example, transportation. Therefore, we implicitly assume the possibility of disaggregating energy consumption by types of end use, even when the equipments which are tributary produce simultaneously several different services, as is the case for the joint transportation of people and goods.

Time will be represented by a discrete sequence of dates, denoted by $t = 0,1,2,...$, and by the corresponding sequence of unitary periods contained between two successive dates. Thus, we shall speak of period t to indicate that contained between dates t and t+1. It follows that date t indicates, at the same time, both the end of period t–1 and the beginning of period t.

The concepts we consider are of two types. Some are *stocks,* i.e. quantities expressing states, thus related to the dates. Others are *flows,* i.e. quantities expressing movements, thus related to the periods. When a discrete representation of time is assumed, as in our case, the linkage of these two types of quantities requires the adoption of conventions. Thus, we assume that stocks do not change during a unitary period. Changes are supposed to arise only at specific dates. It is worth noting that the impact of this convention on the precision of the adopted descriptions will be very limited if we choose the unitary period in a suitable way and if we measure the stocks at date t by their average level in the corresponding period.

For the needs of our description, an equipment is characterised by two quantities: its capacity and its specific consumption. The *capacity* of an equipment measures the maximum flow of energetic services which it can produce in a unit of time while its *specific consumption* measures the quantity of energy needed by the equipment to produce a unit of service. These quantities express the physical and technological constraints embedded in the equipment, which condition the transformation of energy into service. This transformation operates according to a proportionality rule defined by the specific consumption and the validity of the rule is limited by the capacity of the equipment.

Let us point out that the purely technological meaning assigned to the specific consumption requires the choice of a unit of measurement which may be very difficult to implement in practice. To measure the services provided by cars, for instance, using the conventional 'Km–vehicle' unit would lead to a notation of specific consumption varying also with driver's habits, like the speed and the load rate per vehicle.

At this point, it seems useful to put this description of the equipment together with the notion of production function used in economic theory. From this point of view, specific consumption defines the technical coefficient of a production function whose output is proportionally related to the level of energy input. More precisely, the reciprocal of specific consumption expresses the economic concept of *energy productivity.* It is, at the same time, both the average productivity and the marginal productivity, as we assume a strict proportionality relationship. Let us point out, however, that the relationship has a conditional nature if the functioning of the equipment requires other inputs. Thus, in the case of transportation, other inputs have to be considered, like the labour required for driving the means of transportation and the materials consumed during its running (lubricants, tyres, etc.). More precisely, the production function may be written, then, as follows:

$$s \leq \text{Min}\ \{\tfrac{q}{\eta}, f(x_1,...,x_m), S\}\ , \tag{1}$$

where:

s	services produced in a given period;
q	energy consumption of the corresponding period;
η	specific consumption of the equipment used;
$f(x_1,...,x_m)$	upper limit imposed on the production of services by the other m factors of production consumed in quantities $x_1,...,x_m$;
S	capacity of the equipment at the beginning of the period.

In the above expression of the production function, the inequality may be replaced by the equality sign if we also assume an optimal utilisation of the equipment leading to a non waste of production factors. Therefore, we observe that the proportionality relationship between energy consumption and production of energetic services implied by the notion of specific consumption:

$$q = \eta\, s\ , \tag{2}$$

has a meaning only if the other factors of production are available in sufficient quantities to have:

$$f(x_1,...,x_m) \geq \frac{q}{\eta}\ . \tag{3}$$

A similar relationship directly linking the energy consumption to the equipment capacity may be defined by means of the following ratio:

$$\alpha = \frac{s}{S}\ . \tag{4}$$

This ratio measures the *rate of use*[5] of capacity S, i.e. the intensity with which the potential production of the equipment is used during the period under consideration. Eliminating s from (2) by means of (4), we obtain:

$$q = \eta\, \alpha\, S\ . \tag{5}$$

This relationship linking the flow q to the stock S is at the centre of our conceptualisation as the justification of the aggregated approach we are going to adopt is based on it.

In fact, (5) may be directly transposed to the level of a stock of equipment if care is taken to split this stock into equipment classes homogeneous with respect to their specific consumption and intensity of use. The stock of equipments we consider is that used by a group of economic agents to produce a particular service during a given period, t. Economic agents will be grouped according to the criteria of similarity of energy service needs. As a rough approximation, one can therefore consider the categories of economic agents of applied macroeconomics.

To carry out this homogeneity, it is useful to split up, at first, this stock into sets of equipments using the same *energy technology.* By this expression we mean the technology used to transform the energy into services, for example, that using the gasoline engine or that using the Diesel engine, for transportation. Each one of these technologies will be indexed by $i = 1,2,...,n$. Then, it is useful to distinguish in each one of these equipment sets those put into service at the same time. Indeed, technological change acts, at first, when equipments are made. We will call these equipment classes *vintages*, each one being characterised by the date $\tau = 0,1,...,t$ at which is was put into service.

Therefore, the relationship linking the energy consumption of the equipments belonging to vintage τ and using the technology i, $q_{it\tau}$, to the capacity of these equipments, $S_{it\tau}$, by means of their specific consumption, $\eta_{it\tau}$, and their own rate of use, $\alpha_{it\tau}$, is written as follows:

$$q_{it\tau} = \eta_{it\tau}\,\alpha_{it\tau}\,S_{it\tau}\,. \tag{6}$$

The explanation of aggregated measures of energy consumption is easily obtained by adding up these relationships with respect to indices i and τ. One may be particularly interested in:

- energy consumption of the equipments using the technology i,

$$q_{it} = \sum_{\tau=0}^{t} q_{it\tau}\,, \tag{7}$$

- energy consumption of a given fuel used by the technologies $i \in E$,

$$q_{Et} = \sum_{i\in E} q_{it}\,, \tag{8}$$

- total energy consumption to produce the service we consider,

$$q_t = \sum_{i=1}^{n} q_{it}\,. \tag{9}$$

The condition enabling us to pass from the microeconomic relationship (5) to the aggregate equation (6) is the equality of the quantities η and α at each time and for all the equipments of the same vintage, provided, of course, that they use the same technology. This hypothesis may be refined by assuming a dispersion of values of η and α for equipments belonging to the same vintage. As far as the specific consumption is concerned, this distinction seems important especially when technological change may appear even for the old equipments by supplying modifications that improve their energy efficiency. Indeed, it is most unlikely that when this sort of improvement becomes possible it is simultaneously applied to every equipment of the same vintage. Therefore, the specific consumption $\eta_{it\tau}$ will be interpreted as an average:

$$\eta_{it\tau} = \sum_{j=1}^{N} f^j_{it\tau}\, \eta^j_{it\tau}\,, \tag{10}$$

where $\eta^j_{it\tau}$ is the j–th distinct value of the specific consumption of an equipment and $f^j_{it\tau}$ its relative frequency in the stock we consider.

Relationship (6) is a tool for a short run analysis of energy consumption as it is static. It is a Marshallian framework for short run analysis where the stock of fuel burning capital is kept constant. To tackle the analysis of this consumption from a long run point of view, a framework describing the evolution of variables $S_{it\tau}$, i = 1,...,n, has to be elaborated. The one we propose here is based upon new relationships that we are going to present now.

The first one of these relationships links the variable $S_{it\tau}$ to the initial number of equipments belonging to vintage τ by means of a survival law of equipments. Thus, it reflects the retirement process of the equipments belonging to a vintage, which is generated by wear and tear and by socio–economic obsolescence phenomena. This relationship is written as:

$$S_{it\tau} = c_{i\tau}\, \ell_{it\tau}\, z_{i\tau} \tag{11}$$

where:

- $z_{i\tau}$ number of new equipments using technology i, set up at date τ;
- $c_{i\tau}$ capacity of an equipment belonging to vintage τ, using technology i;
- $\ell_{it\tau}$ fraction of equipments belonging to vintage τ, using technology i and still in service at date t.

The main hypothesis we introduce here concerns per equipment capacity which is assumed to be equal and invariant for all units belonging to the same vintage. This simplification seems acceptable if, in practice, $c_{i\tau}$ expresses an average value of the capacity of sold equipments. As far as the sequence of $\ell_{it\tau}$, $t=\tau$, $\tau+1$,..., is concerned, it represents the *survival law* of equipments belonging to vintage τ. It is a decreasing sequence of non negative coefficients, with $\ell_{i\tau\tau}=1$. The double indexation, with t and τ, indicates that this law may change from one vintage to another. It is also specific to each energy technology.

The other relationships we introduce to analyse energy demand in the long run link the initial stock of equipments belonging to a vintage to the evolution of the demand for capacity. They express a two step logic of determination of installed capacity to the date t.

- In the first step, total capacity S_t to be installed at the date t is fixed without any reference to the equipments it requires. This is a *demand for capacity* that will always be assumed to be satisfied. Thus, we can write the following identity:

$$S_t = \sum_{i=1}^{n} \sum_{\tau=0}^{t} S_{it\tau} . \tag{12}$$

This demand for capacity implies that new equipment vintages adding up to the capacity

$$C_t = S_t - S_{t-1} \tag{13}$$

will be put into service at date t.

- In the second step, these vintages are determined by specifying their size according to the technology they use. By writing ω_{it} for the share of capacity C_t installed by resorting to technology i, we have:

$$c_{it}\, z_{it} = \omega_{it}\, C_t \tag{14}$$

with

$$\omega_{it} \geq 0 \quad \text{and} \quad \sum_{i=1}^{n} \omega_{it} = 1. \tag{15}$$

These relationships allow us to write a linear difference equation establishing a one-to-one mapping between the history of the demand for capacity and that of the capacity of new equipment vintages. In such a case, we can easily express energy consumption as a function of the history of variable S_t. This relationship is essential in every analysis where S_t is assumed to be exogenous.

This difference equation is obtained by first replacing, on the right hand side of equation (12), the variables $S_{it\tau}$ by their expression (11) and then replacing the products $c_{i\tau} z_{i\tau}$, appearing after this substitution, by their expression given on the right hand side of (14). So we have:

$$S_t = \sum_{\tau=0}^{t} \lambda_{t\tau}\, C_\tau \tag{16}$$

with:

$$\lambda_{t\tau} = \sum_{i=1}^{n} \ell_{it\tau}\, \omega_{i\tau} \tag{17}$$

The explicit solution of this equation with respect to C_t may be obtained by writing the first t+1 stages of this recurrence as a system of linear equations. In matrix notation, this system can be set out as follows:

$$\Lambda x = y , \tag{18}$$

with:

$$\Lambda = \begin{bmatrix} \lambda_{00} & & \\ \lambda_{10} & \lambda_{11} & 0 \\ \vdots & & \ddots \\ \lambda_{t0} & \cdots\cdots & \lambda_{tt} \end{bmatrix}, \quad x = \begin{bmatrix} C_0 \\ C_1 \\ \vdots \\ C_t \end{bmatrix}, \quad y = \begin{bmatrix} S_0 \\ S_1 \\ \vdots \\ S_t \end{bmatrix}.$$

The solution $x = \Lambda^{-1}y$ provides us with the expression of C_t as a function of S_τ, $\tau=0,\dots,t$:

$$C_t = \sum_{\tau=0}^{t} \lambda^{t\tau} S_\tau, \tag{19}$$

the coefficients $\lambda^{t\tau}$, $\tau=0,\dots,t$ being the elements of the last row of Λ^{-1}.

The following equations summarise the results of this section:

$$q_{it} = \sum_{\tau=0}^{t} \eta_{it\tau}\, \alpha_{it\tau}\, S_{it\tau}, \quad i=1,\dots,n \tag{20}$$

$$S_{it\tau} = c_{i\tau}\, \ell_{it\tau}\, z_{i\tau} \tag{21}$$

$$c_{i\tau}\, z_{i\tau} = \omega_{i\tau}\, C_\tau \tag{22}$$

$$C_t = \sum_{\theta=0}^{\tau} \lambda^{\tau\theta} S_\theta \tag{23}$$

It is a recursive system determining, as a function of the sequence of installed total capacities, S_θ, $\theta=0,\dots,t$, the history of variables C_t, z_{it}, $S_{it\tau}$ and q_{it}.

3. APPLICATION TO THE SIMULATION OF ENERGY DEMAND

The conceptual framework we have presented in the earlier section offers the possibility to simulate the impact on the demand for energy, of changes in the technology, in the composition or in the intensity of use of a stock of equipments. Thus we may evaluate, for instance, energy saving policies or policies aimed at substituting a given fuel by others.

This approach consists in comparing energy consumption calculated by assuming different hypotheses about the evolution of coefficients $\eta_{it\tau}$ (specific consumption), $\alpha_{it\tau}$ (rate of use of the equipments), $\ell_{it\tau}$ (survival rate of equipments) or ω_{it} (market shares of the different competing technologies), for the same prospect of evolution of capacity demand. In other words, a given evolution of the 'potential' of energy services to be made available to a community is first defined as a target. Then the approach consists of examining the consequences on fuel consumption of the choice of different energy 'options' characterising the stock of equipments to be set up and the quantity of energy services to be produced.

These simulations may be performed directly by means of the *final form* of the system of equations (20) – (23), i.e. by means of the relationship obtained by eliminating from these equations the variables $S_{it\tau}$, $z_{i\tau}$ and C_{τ}. This relationship:

$$q_{it} = \sum_{\tau=0}^{t} \eta_{it\tau}\, \alpha_{it\tau}\, \ell_{it\tau}\, \omega_{i\tau} \sum_{\theta=0}^{\tau} \lambda^{\tau\theta}\, S_{\theta} \tag{24}$$

directly links the energy consumption q_{it} to the evolution of the demand for capacity S_{θ}, $\theta=0,1,\ldots,t$.

Some examples borrowed from the sector of transportation by private cars will show the practical usefulness of these simulations.

- By lowering the value of the coefficient $\eta_{it\tau}$ as a function of τ, we may describe the reduction of specific energy consumption of new cars that has been observed recently, particularly after negotiations between several governments and their automobile industries. Thus we can simulate the gasoline savings which would result in a country from this technological change in cars. This kind of 'technological scenarios' of Swiss gasoline demand is presented in Carlevaro and Giovannini (1984).
- By lowering the specific consumption $\eta_{it\tau}$ and raising the survival rate $\ell_{it\tau}$ as a function of the difference $t-\tau$, we may describe legal rules imposing compulsory car servicing or reducing the official car checking intervals. Thus we can simulate the gasoline savings which would result from an energy policy imposing these sorts of requirements.
- If the duration of travel is included in the measure of transportation services, a change in speed of the travel will imply, for an equal distance, an opposite change in the intensity of car use. By lowering the rate of use of equipment, $\alpha_{it\tau}$ as a function of t, we may thus simulate an energy policy measure lowering the speed limits on the roads.
- A change in the motor fuel taxation policy modifies the competition conditions between the different technologies used for transportation by private cars, for example, between gasoline cars and Diesel cars. Thus, the market shares in these technologies are modified. By simulating a change of the coefficients $\omega_{i\tau}$ as a function of τ we can evaluate the impact of fiscal measures aimed at forcing the substitution of one motor fuel by another.

NOTES

* This research was supported by the Swiss National Science Foundation (Grant No. 4.476–0.81.4). I am grateful to Jayalakshmi Krishnakumar and Charles Spierer for their helpful comments and suggestions.

1) See Carlevaro and Spierer (1983).
2) See Carlevaro and Giovannini (1984).
3) See Fuss (1977).
4) Such results obtained by using Swiss data are presented by Spierer (1982, 1984).
5) If the unit of capacity refers to a unit of time different from the unitary period, α expresses the *duration* of use of the equipment. Thus if, in the case of passenger transportation, the unit of capacity is the 'passenger–Km per hour' and the unit of produced services is the 'passenger–Km per year', α is measured in 'hours per year'.

REFERENCES

Carlevaro, F. and B. Giovannini (1984), 'A Vintage Energy Demand Model', in M.H. Hamza (ed.), *Energy and Environmental Systems*, Acta Press, Anaheim–Calgary–Zurich.

Carlevaro, F. and C. Spierer (1983), 'Dynamic Energy Demand Models with Latent Equipment', *European Economic Review*, 23, pp. 161–94.

Fuss, M.A. (1977), 'The Demand for Energy in Canadian Manufacturing: An Example of the Estimation of Production Structures with Many Inputs', *Journal of Econometrics*, 5, pp. 89–116.

Spierer, C. (1982), *La demande d'énergie en Suisse*, Droz, Geneva.

Spierer, C. (1984), 'Interfuel Substitution and Concavity Constraints', *Cahiers du Département d'économétrie*, 84.06, University of Geneva.

PART III

STABILISATION POLICY

CHAPTER 9

ASYMMETRY AND ROBUSTNESS IN STABILISATION POLICY FOR IMPERFECT COMMODITY MARKETS

Jati K. Sengupta, *University of California, Santa Barbara*

1. INTRODUCTION

Recent theoretical discussions of commodity stabilisation policy through buffer fund and/or international commodity agreements have stressed three new aspects of the policy problem which are of great importance for the less developed countries (LDCs) and the North–South trade. The first aspect refers to the role of dominant producers in imperfect or cartelised markets, which may be significantly different from the competitive frameworks. Thus Newbery (1984) has developed the hypothesis that if demand is linear, then dominant producers find it optimal to undertake significantly more storage than is competitively justified and this storage policy increases price stability in proportion to the market share of the dominant producers. The second aspect deals with the risk sensitivity of buffer stock intervention rules and the extent to which conventional decision rules could be improved so as to protect the producers of primary commodities in LDCs against the uncertainty of future export earnings. Several features of this problem have been analysed by Brown (1975), Goreux (1978), Nguyen (1980) and Hughes Hallett (1986). The contributions by Nguyen (1980) and Hughes Hallett (1986) specifically introduce the need for minimising the variance of export earnings as a goal to be pursued by the buffer fund authority and in the framework of linear quadratic Gaussian (LQG) model of optimal control this introduces robustness into a buffer stock policy. This has been stressed by Whittle (1981) as a risk sensitive generalisation of the traditional LQG optimal control rule.

There is a third aspect of game theoretic conflict between rival suppliers in some commodity markets like coffee and cocoa, which implies that the competitive market models and their estimates of benefits and costs may not have here much of empirical realism and validity. As Geer (1971) and Sengupta and Sfeir (1983) have shown the International Coffee Agreements (ICAs) of 1962 and 1968 have been successful in estab-

O. Guvenen (ed.), International Commodity Market Models and Policy Analysis, 167–184.

lishing a regime of collusion among primary producers which prevented price instability due to oligopolistic price warfare. However in other times the ICAs did not prove very effective in their stabilisation objective. Thus, in 1964 when coffee prices rose, Brazil as the most dominant producer did not fulfil its quota obligation and the major importing countries like the U.S. faced severe problems of shortage and price rise. In 1970 when prices rose to an unprecedented high despite continuous increases in export quotas of producing countries, another major loophole of the ICA became apparent, e.g., price instability could occur as a result of high inventory accumulation of large buyers in anticipation of a future shortage of supply. Future uncertainty may thus aggravate the problem.

Our objective here is two–fold: to examine the relevance of the non–cooperative game model in world commodities like coffee and its implications for an integrated stabilisation policy on the lines of the Integrated Programme objectives of UNCTAD (1976). Two main theoretical issues are posed here. One is the difficulty of implementing a robust stabilisation policy in an oligopolistic stochastic market, where the role of supply uncertainty and market information is usually asymmetrical. The second is to evaluate the impact of instability associated with such non–cooperative game theoretic models, whereby the transmission of such instabilities to the LDCs may affect their development and diversification goals. This aspect of transmission of instability, when viewed in the light of the major primary commodities in world trade may be very substantial, as has been emphasised by the econometric simulation models of Adams and Behrman (1982).

2. WORLD COFFEE ECONOMY: A NON–COOPERATIVE GAME

The world coffee market, with its significant price and quantity fluctuations similar to that of copper provides in many ways a unique framework for testing the empirical realism of the hypothesis of dominant producers playing a significant role. Two major reasons are as follows. Historically the role of Brazil as a major producer has been very significant in world production and levels of inventory. Thus, Brazil has been and still is, the world's largest single coffee producing country although its share of the world market has been steadily declining from over 60% in the 1940's to around 30%in the late 1970's. The share of world inventories held by Brazil declined from 90% or more around 1962 and before, to about 35% or less around 1980. A second unique feature of the coffee economy is that Brazil has contributed very significantly to the year to year fluctuations in world production over the years 1946–1967 for which reliable estimates are available. According to one estimate (Sengupta and Sfeir (1983)), Brazil accounted for about 86% of total variability in world production measured by variance. It is no wonder that the

ICAssigned in 1940, 1968 and 1976 with the sole objective of stabilising the world coffee economy did not prove very effective. As Geer (1971) pointed out, efforts by Brazil to maintain her price policy led African and new exporters to go into price cutting for Robustas thus increasing excess capacity; also excess capacity was used as a weapon in oligopolistic price warfare between these Robusta producing countries and Brazil which is the largest producer of the Arabica variety.

These considerations lead very naturally to the specification of a game theoretic model with non–cooperative elements, which may be empirically tested. For this purpose two sample periods 1945–46 to 1961–62 and 1962–63 to 1979–80 have been considered for each coffee agricultural year (July to June). Sample I starts with the 1945 season in order to avoid the Second World War and 1962 was chosen to be the last year of Sample I, since an important ICA was signed then with a stronger enforcement of the export quota system. From a set of different forms of demand functions, the following turned out to be the best, in terms of R^2 and the plausible signs of the regression coefficients.

Sample I (1945–62)

$$p(t) = \underset{(0.90)}{29.42} - \underset{(-2.49)}{0.0026^{*}}\, x_1(t) + \underset{(2.01)}{1.988(10^{-8})^{*}}\, x_1^2(t) - \underset{(-0.25)}{0.0002}\, x_2(t) + \underset{(2.16)}{0.034^{*}}\, y(t) \tag{1}$$

$$R^2 = 0.87;\ DW = 2.15$$

Sample II (1962–80)

$$p(t) = \underset{(3.2)}{455.32^{**}} - \underset{(-2.15)}{0.0067^{*}}\, x_1(t) + \underset{(1.61)}{4.01(10^{-8})}\, x_1^2(t) - \underset{(-2.07)}{0.0040^{*}}\, x_2(t) + \underset{(1.34)}{0.012}\, y(t) \tag{2}$$

$$R^2 = 0.87;\ DW = 1.88$$

Here p(t) is the New York price of Brazilian coffee, $x_1(t)$, $x_2(t)$ are the supply quantities in year t of Brazil and the rest of the world (RW), where supply is defined as current production plus the inventory held at the beginning of the current year; y(t) is the U.S. gross national product per capita in real terms. The t–statistics are given in parentheses, one asterisk denoting significance at 5% level and two at 1% level. Some comments are in order about the two empirical estimates presented in (1) and (2). First, we note that these demand functions lead to Cournot–Nash reaction functions, if we add the usual profit maximisation assumption and zero conjectural variation. It is true there are more than two major producers in the world coffee economy, but Brazil being the largest producer can be assumed as one duopolist, while the rest of the world (RW) may be treated as a rival. The behaviour of all coffee producing countries other than Brazil may not exactly be similar to that of a single producer, but it seems reasonable to presume that Brazil may consider other producers as a potential threat to its dominant market share and thus consider them as a rival group. Moreover due to multi–collinearity, many rivals cannot easily be introduced in the supply equation estimation. Second, the role of lagged inventory is very important in each of the two demand equations. For example, if the supply quantity is replaced by production ($q_i(t)$) only, we obtain the following linear estimates (nonlinear terms were insignificant):

Sample I:
$$p(t) = \underset{(-0.76)}{-9.45} - \underset{(-1.98)}{0.0011}\, q_1(t) - \underset{(-2.12)}{0.0029^*}\, q_2(t) + \underset{(4.45)}{0.0691^{**}}\, y(t) \tag{3}$$
$$R^2 = 0.73;\ DW = 2.01$$

Sample II:
$$p(t) = \underset{(1.88)}{244.46} - \underset{(-1.32)}{0.0015}\, q_1(t) - \underset{(-2.08)}{0.0071^*}\, q_2(t) + \underset{(5.09)}{0.0372^{**}}\, y(t) \tag{4}$$
$$R^2 = 0.82;\ DW = 2.1$$

It is clear that Brazil's production level has no influence on price that is statistically significant at the 5% level, although it is a dominant producer in the world market.

To derive Cournot–Nash (CN) equilibrium solutions from the estimated demand functions (1) and (2), one needs annual average cost data for the two sample periods. Since this is unavailable, we take an average estimate of 2.5% as storage costs and 77.5% as production costs as percentages of wholesale price in 1945 and for subsequent years cost was adjusted at the same rate as wholesale prices. This method is consistent with the estimates made by Reynolds (1978) and Geer (1971), who noted that the additional production capacities created in RW in the 1960's reflected in part low production costs relative to the maintained price in world market. The optimal reaction curves satisfying the first order conditions of a CN equilibrium turn out as follows with k_i denoting the demand effect of y(t):

$$\text{Sample I:} \qquad x_1^* = 5{,}503 + k_1 - 0.0385\, x_2^* + 0.00001\, x_1^{*2} \tag{5}$$
$$x_2^* = 71{,}550 + k_2 - 6.5001\, x_1^* + 0.00005\, x_1^*$$

and

$$\text{Sample II:} \qquad x_1^* = 33{,}880 + k_1 - 0.2985\, x_2^* + 0.00001\, x_1^{*2} \tag{6}$$
$$x_2^* = 56{,}000 + k_2 - 0.8401\, x_1^* + 0.000005\, x_1^{*2}$$

The second order conditions for maximum profits require that $x_1^* < 43{,}000$ (Sample I) and $x_1^* < 53{,}600$ (Sample II). Two results are most significant here. One is that in sample period II the influence of RW on Brazil's optimal supply has increased – by almost eight times, i.e., $|\partial x_1^*/\partial x_2^*|_{II} = 7.75|\partial x_1^*/\partial x_2^*|_I$. The corresponding impact of Brazil on RW has declined considerably, e.g., by 0.13 times. Second, the nonlinear reaction functions show very clearly that in the space of optimal supply, x_1^* and x_2^* are not always negatively correlated. This implies that correlation of strategies may at times be deliberately utilised by Brazil as a tool to improve the non–cooperative CN equilibrium solution in such market games (Sengupta (1985)). In general however when the correlation of x_1^* and x_2^* is negative, the nonlinear elements in (5) and (6) augment the speed of convergence to a stable CN equilibrium solution. The final equilibrium solutions predicted by the optimal reaction curves (5) and (6) do however overestimate the average supply behaviour observed during the two sample periods. Two reasons for this discrepancy may be given. One is that the CN models above fail to incorporate future expectations about trends in supply and demand. Specifically, the regression coefficients of the demand functions in (1) and (2) do not allow any learning mechanism with respect to future trends and in terms of the recent theory of rational expectation applied to linear decision rules (Sengupta (1985)) this builds an element of inconsistency in the specification. One simple way to incorporate some consistency is to assume a value ρ of correlation between the two strategies x_1 and x_2 and incorporate this through correlated conjectural variations. Then the reaction functions (5) and (6) are modified as

$$x_1^*(\rho) = f_1(x_1^*, \rho)$$
$$x_2^*(\rho) = f_2(x_2^*, \rho)$$

Then we choose that value ρ^* of ρ within the range $-1 \leq \rho \leq 1$, which gives a minimum of the following distance statistic

$$D(\rho) = \sum_{i=1}^{2} (x_i^*(\rho) - x_i^a)^2$$

where x_i^a is the actual value observed. When this is applied to the reaction curves (5) and (6), the result improves substantially, the mean square error being reduced by 50% and 64% respectively for sample periods I and II.

The second limitation of the two reaction curves (5) and (6) is that they fail to incorporate both supply (yield) and demand (price) risks. This contributes in part to the overestimate of optimal supply in relation to the observed actual supply. Some idea of the commodity price cycles may be obtained from the estimates (1953–74) made by Reynolds (1978) as follows:

	complete cycle (peak to peak)		downsing only (peak to trough)	
	average length (months)	max. length	average length	max length
coffee	34	79	18	45
cocoa	17	33	8	15
sugar	13	26	7	20

Although no direct estimate of the yield risks are available along similar lines, the fluctuations in coffee production during the same period have been significantly high. According to one estimate (Nguyen (1980)) the fluctuation index computed as an average over 1953–74 of differences between annual observations and calculated trend values expressed as percent of trend value was as follows:

	Exports from LD	
	Indices of fluctuations	
	market price	value
coffee	22.1	15.7
cocoa	33.9	18.6
sugar	54.2	20.0

In addition to production fluctuations, world producer stocks of coffee show a long term cycle that fairly accurately mirrors the price cycle, with an all–time low in the mid–1950's, very high levels during the 1960's and lower in the early 1970's (Singh et al. (1977)). The main holder of coffee stocks among producers till 1970 has always been Brazil, due to the fact that it is the only country which could actually increase its export earnings by reducing its quantity of supply in the world market.

3. MODIFIED COURNOT–NASH MODEL AND STABILISATION POLICY

The modified CN model allows for a learning mechanism and the elements of risk aversion, when there are ($n \geq 2$) suppliers in a market. For the i–th supplier the profit $\Pi_i(t)$ at time t can be written as

$$\Pi_i(t) = R_i(t) - C_i(t) \tag{7}$$

where

$$
\begin{aligned}
R_i(t) &= (\hat{p} + u)x_i(t) && \text{(revenue)}\\
C_i(t) &= (c + v)x_i(t) && \text{(cost)}\\
\hat{p} &= E(p(t+1)\,|\,S(t-1)) && \text{(expected price)}\\
&= a_0 - bS(t-1) + \beta S^2(t-1) && \\
S(t) &= \sum_{j=1}^{n} x_j(t) && \text{(aggregate supply)}
\end{aligned}
\tag{8}
$$

Here the simplifying assumptions are that both expected price and expected marginal cost are similar across suppliers, u and v are random disturbance terms normally and independently distributed with zero means and finite variances σ_u^2, σ_v^2 which denote price and yield risks respectively. Each supplier is assumed to forecast $\hat{p}$, i.e. the level of expected price one period ahead and then choose his own optimal supply $x_i^*(t)$ by maximising the expected utility $f_i = EU(\Pi_i(t))$ of profit where the utility function is of the exponential form

$$U = 1 - \exp(-\alpha_i \Pi_i(t)), \quad \alpha_i > 0 \tag{9}$$

with a constant rate of absolute risk aversion denoted by α_i. This leads to the following maximand for each CN player

$$\max f_i = [a - bS(t-1) + \beta S^2(t-1)]x_i(t) - \tfrac{1}{2}\alpha\sigma^2 x_i(t) \tag{10}$$

$$\text{where } a = a_0 - c, \quad \sigma^2 = \sigma_u^2 + \sigma_v^2$$

Note that this maximand, though myopic in perspective seems to be consistent with the two–year coffee bearing cycle noted by Geer (1971) and others. Moreover, it provides a good approximation to an intertemporal profit function model in a certain sense discussed by Sengupta and Sfeir (1983), i.e., approximation to a dynamic limit pricing model. With an arbitrary lag τ say, ($\tau = 5$ seems to fit the empirical data on production very well), the maximand would appear as

$$f_i = [a - bS(t-\tau) + \beta S^2(t-\tau)]x_i(t) - \tfrac{1}{2}\alpha\sigma_i^2 x_i(t) \tag{11}$$

It is clear from (10) that the CN equilibrium solutions would satisfy the following nonlinear difference equation

$$S(t) = \theta_0 - \theta_1 S(t-1) + \theta_2 S^2(t-1) \tag{12}$$

$$\text{where} \theta_0 = (na)/(\alpha\sigma^2), \quad \theta_1 = (nb)/(\alpha\sigma^2)$$

$$\theta_2 = (n\beta)/(\alpha\sigma^2)$$

One has to note two important implications of the difference equation. First, consider a linear version by ignoring the nonlinear term: the solution then appears as

$$S(t) = [S(0) - (\theta_1)^{-1}\theta_0](-\theta_1)^t + (\theta_0/\theta_1)$$

The cycles represented by the range of $[(-\theta_1)^t$, t = odd, $(-\theta_1)^t$, t = even] clearly increases for increased $t > 1$, if either (nb) increases or $(\alpha\sigma^2)$ decreases. Since the increase of competition consequent on the decline in dominance of Brazil as the largest producer is most likely to lead to reduce $\alpha\sigma^2$, or increase (nb), it is clear that the range of fluctuations is likely to increase. Since the level of producer stocks held under competitive conditions would be much less than under imperfect competition under a dominant producer, the source of fluctuations may increase due to the existence of the so–called 'thin market' (Geer (1971)). Secondly, the impact of the nonlinear term $\theta_2 S^2(t-1)$ is to decrease the range of fluctuations, since by linearly approximating it as $2\theta_2\bar{S}S(t-1)$, where $\bar{S}$ is the mean value it changes the transient term $(-\theta_1)^t$ to $(-\theta_1 + 2\theta_2\bar{S})^t$. However the nonlinear element may contribute to oscillations due to complex roots of the associated quasi–polynomial (i.e., quasi–characteristic equation). To see its implication we may use the linearising approximations $\dot{S}(t) \simeq S(t) - S(t-1)$ and $S^2(t-1) \simeq \bar{S}^2 + [S(t-1) - \bar{S}](2\bar{S})$, whereby the homogeneous part of (12) reduces to the following system

$$\dot{S}(t) = \theta_3 S(t-1) + \theta_4 \tag{13}$$
$$\theta_3 = 2\theta_2\bar{S} - \theta_1 - 1$$
$$\theta_4 = \theta_0 - 2\bar{S}^2$$

On using another transformation $S(t) = z(t)\exp(rt)$ this finally reduces to the linear difference differential equation (homogeneous part only):

$$\dot{z}(t) + rz(t) + \theta_5 z(t-1) = 0 \tag{14}$$
$$\theta_5 = -\theta_3 \exp(-r)$$

The characteristic quasi–polynomial for (14) is

$$\phi(\lambda) = \lambda + r + \theta_5 \exp(-\tau\lambda), \quad \tau = 1 \tag{15}$$

with $\phi(\lambda) = 0$ being the characteristic equation. Various regions of the solution space characterised by the real and the complex values of λ may be characterised by the so–called Dpartition method. Thus the equation $\phi(\lambda) = 0$ clearly has a zero root for $r + \theta_5 = 0$, which is a straight line forming the boundary of one region of the D–partition. Now let the quasi–polynomial have the purely imaginary root iq:

$$iq + r + \theta_5 \exp(-\tau iq) = 0; \quad i = +\sqrt{-1}$$

or

$$iq + r + \theta_5(\cos \tau q - i \sin \tau q) = 0$$

On separating the real and imaginary parts and solving for r and θ_5 we get

$$\theta_5 = q(\sin \tau q), \quad r = (-q \cos \tau q)(\sin \tau q)^{-1} \tag{16}$$

where

$$C: \{r + \theta_5 \cos \tau q = 0, \ q - \theta_5 \sin \tau q = 0\} \tag{17}$$

defines a curve on which all roots λ of the quasi–polynomial (15) are purely imaginary. Clearly if $r > 0$ and $\theta_5 = 0$, then the degenerate quasi–polynomial (15) has no roots with positive real parts and hence the system (14) is then asymptotically stable. However there arises at least one root with a positive real part when $\theta_5\tau$ exceeds zero. Furthermore, if $\theta_5\tau$ exceeds unity, we get $\cos \tau q < 0$ on the curve C defined by (17). As a result we have unstable oscillations. It is clear that the Cournot–Nash equilibrium solutions in such cases would not possess any stability property that may be desirable by the players.

The above results on regions of asymptotic stability without oscillations and asymptotic instability with oscillations have two broad implications for stabilisation policies. One is that the nonlinear elements in the CN reaction curves contribute to oscillations due to complex roots, whenever the supply lag τ tends to increase above zero. The higher the lag, the greater the asymptotic instability along the curve C defined in (17). The role of producer stock level in smoothing out this incidence of production lags of 5 years or more for coffee becomes very critical. This also makes the case for a cooperative solution with an appropriate level of world buffer stock much stronger. Secondly, the existence of unstable regions in the space of eigenvalues explains in part the behaviour of Brazil, when it did not fulfill its export quota obligatition under ICA, although coffee prices started rising in 1964 and reached very high levels in 1969–0. During this period the share of African countries in world exportable production increased from 25% in 1960–61 to 25% in 1965–66 and to 38% in 1976–77. It is clear that the ICA of 1969 and 1976 sought, rather unsuccessfully, to bring about long term equilibrium between production and consumption through a system of variable export quotas. But the enforcement of quota control has posed a difficult problem due to two main reasons. One is that some producing countries invariably attempted to unload their surplus production to nonquota markets thus leading to a two–price system and defeating the overall stabilisation objective. Second, due to the lack of effective implementation of long term production control and diversification and very low price elasticity of demand (range: –0.105 to – 0.233 over 1960 to 1975), the producing countries participating in the ICAs could not rationally believe in the cooperative goal by which their total export earnings could increase.

It is clear therefore that for a world buffer stock programme to succeed, a long term program must be developed along with the short term stabilisation objectives. Since the export earnings from commodities like coffee, cocoa, etc. comprise a very significant share of total export revenues of the LDC and since this has sizeable impact on per capita national income and its growth in these countries (Adams and Behrman (1982)), it may be more economic and rational to support an integrated programme of common fund based on ten or so core commodities and then emphasise the quantum of gains to be obtained from a cooperative framework of stabilisation. First, consider a cooperative framework with x_j denoting world exports for commodity j (j=1,2,...,10), expressed as a proportion to total world exports of all the ten core commodities. Let $\tilde{r}_j$ be the net return (i.e., price minus cost) for commodity j in the world market, which may be assumed to have a fixed distribution with mean m_j and variance–covariance matrix $V = (v_{ij}) = \text{cov}(\tilde{r}_i, \tilde{r}_j)$. The buffer fund authority (BFA) may then adopt the following decision model for choosing the optimal export quotas x_j in the world market:

$$\begin{aligned} &\text{Min } \sigma^2 = \sum_{i=1}^{10} \sum_{j=1}^{10} x_i v_{ij} x_j = x'Vx \\ &\quad \text{subject to} \\ &\qquad m'x = \sum_{j=1}^{10} x_j m_j = c, \quad c > 0 \\ &\qquad e'x = \sum_{j=1}^{10} x_j = 1 \end{aligned} \tag{18}$$

Here m, e are vectors, prime denoting transpose, V is the variance–covariance matrix and the mean parameter is $m = (m_j)$. One could compute the optimal values $x^* = (x_j^*)$ as in the theory of efficient investment by diversified portfolios (Sengupta (1984)), except for two qualifications. The most important qualification is that the parameters m and V would not be purely random; they would depend among other things on the state of competition, cooperation or conflict, the extent of risk aversion and the policies towards producer stocks by the respective supplying countries. The task of a model builder is to develop a suitable specification in this respect, before an optimal scheme of international diversification can be achieved. It is clear however that a non–cooperative framework would tend to increase the overall variance $\sigma^2 = x'Vx$ and reduce the expected return $c = m'x$. A cooperative situation would have the opposite effect. One way to capture the contrasting impact is to assume bounds on the parameters as

$$c^- \le c \le c^+; \quad m^- \le m \le m^+; \quad V^- \le V \le V^+$$

and then associate (c^-, m^-, V^+) with the non–cooperative solution and (c^+, m^+, V^-) with the cooperative one. The difference in the optimal minimand in the two cases and their associated x values would measure the gains through cooperation, which avoid wasteful conflict.

The second qualification is that the BFA may find it economic to follow a partial stabilisation policy, e.g., not to intervene if $c_0 < c < c^0$, where (c_0, c^0) are the floor and ceiling levels of return. This is much less costly than a complete stabilisation policy, where with every change in c, the minimand $\sigma_*^2 = \min \sigma^2$ is to be monitored, for we have from (11) the following optimal relation between σ_*^2 and c:

$$\sigma_*^2 = (\alpha\gamma - \beta^2)^{-1}[\gamma c^2 - 2\beta c + \alpha] \tag{19}$$

$$x_* = \text{optimal vector } x = [(\alpha\gamma - \beta^2)V]^{-1}[(m\gamma - e\beta)c + (e\alpha - m\beta)]$$

where $\alpha = m'V^{-1}m$, $\beta = m'V^{-1}e$, $\gamma = e'V^{-1}e$ with e being a vector with each element unity. Since $(\alpha\gamma - \beta^2)$ would normally be positive and γ is necessarily positive by the positive definiteness of the variance–covariance matrix V, the minimum variance σ_*^2 is a strictly convex function of c; hence it can be further minimised by a choice of c, i.e. min σ_*^2 is given by a value c_* of $c = \beta/\gamma$, at which min σ_*^2 becmes $(1/\gamma)$.

Note however that this specification (18) of an allocation model for the BFA is only illustrative; many details of economic realism have to be filled in as follows. First, the dynamic aspect of change in the parameter value over time and a long run objective function has to be incorporated. Second, the role of specific countries or groups of countries has to be introduced. Thus $x_j = \sum_{k=1}^{N} x_{kj}$ may be viewed as the aggregate supply by N counntries; also supply may have to be separated as $x_{jt} = q_{jt} + h_{j,t-1}$ where q_{jt} is production in year t and $h_{j,t-1}$ is the stock level at the end of year t–1. Third, the buying and selling activities of the BFA have to be introduced. These technical details however can only serve to emphasise the important implications of the optimal risk–return relationship specified in (19). First, every attempt at increasing c has the effect of increasing the optimal risk level σ_*^2 and more so in a non–cooperative game theoretic world. Second, for any allocation vector x which is not optimal, the level of risk σ^2 would be higher. The difference $(\sigma^2 - \sigma_*^2)$ may be small or large depending on the type of non–optimal policies associated with the allocation vector x chosen, but it may have cumulative effects over time on the national income and growth performance of the LDCs. The potential gains to be achieved by reducing σ^2 to the minimum level σ_*^2 may therefore be one of the major objectives of the BFA, which has not been emphasised in the current literature (Labys (1975), Turnovsky (1978)). Such potential gains would exist even in a competitive framework, when the element of insurable risk could be minimised through diversification within a country or between countries.

One has to note however the importance of the two limit levels (c_0, c^0) for both producer and consumer countries. These can be associated with the target of keeping an appropriate maximum size of the buffer stock or fund, which would avoid or delay the use of export controls, thus makng the ICAs more effective in moderating short run price fluctuations. They would also benefit consumer nations by giving greater assurance of supply and reducing the probability of violating the price ceiling.

Two different methods may be suggested for determining the limit values of $c = (c_0, c^0)$. One is to use a truncated model for returns $y = \tilde{r}'x - c$, with $y \geq 0$, $c > 0$ and ask how its mean and variance denoted by $\mu(c)$, $\sigma^2(c)$ would change as the level of c is increased or decreased? The second method is to relate the BFA policy to a demand—supply model of a specific commodity or group of commodities for example:

$$\begin{aligned} x_d &= a - bp + u && \text{(demand)} \\ x_S &= \alpha + \beta p + v && \text{(supply)} \qquad (20) \\ x &= x_d = x_s && \text{(equilibrium)} \end{aligned}$$

Here x is the quantity supplied and p the price, u and v are random disturbance terms with zero–means. Under a fixed price stabilisation scheme, the BFA seeks to fix a level p^0 say in some optimal fashion. But under a partial price stabilisation scheme (Nguyen (1980)) the pricing rule is:

$$p = \begin{cases} \bar{p} + q, & \text{if } x_s > \alpha + \beta p,\ x_d < a - bp \\ \bar{p} - q, & \text{if } x_s < \alpha + \beta p,\ x_d > a - bp \end{cases} \qquad (21)$$

Here q is the positive level by which the mean market price ($\bar{p}$) has to be increased whenever supply exceeds ($\alpha + \beta p$), thus creating a pressure for the equilibrium market price below the mean level $\bar{p}$. The reverse holds when supply is too short, demand is high, thus creating a pressure for market price to rise much above the mean. These cases are now discussed in the next section.

4. ROBUST STABILISATION POLICIES

Considering the truncated model (Gbur (1981)), the mean return and variance can be explicitly computed as follows, if it is assumed that the return vector $\tilde{r}$ is normally distributed with mean m and variance–covariance matrix V:

$$\mu(c) = \left[-F\left[\frac{c-\mu}{\sigma}\right]\right]^{-1}\left[\mu + \sigma f\left[\frac{c-\mu}{\sigma}\right]\right] \qquad (22)$$

$$\sigma^2(c) = (\mu^2+\sigma^2) + (1-F)^{-1} f\left[\frac{c-\mu}{\sigma}\right][2\mu + \sigma c - \mu] - \mu^2(c)$$

where $F = F\left[\frac{c-\mu}{\sigma}\right]$ is the cumulative distribution function of a unit normal variate with a probability density $f = f\left[\frac{c-\mu}{\sigma}\right]$ and (μ, σ^2) denote the mean and variance of y when it is not truncated. Since F(t) and f(t) are positive for any finite t, it follows that

$$\mu(c) \geq \mu; \quad \sigma^2(c) \leq \sigma^2 \quad \text{for all c} \tag{23}$$

Furthermore, it can be shown from (22) that $\sigma^2(c)$ is strictly decreasing in c, as c is increased in the positive domain and this property holds for all gamma densities $f(y) = ky\exp(-\lambda y)$, $y \geq 0$, the double exponential and all Polya frequency densities. It follows from (23) that the truncated model is more stable in the sense that its coefficient of variation is lower, i.e.,

$$(\sigma(c)/\mu(c)) \leq (\sigma/\mu)$$

However there is a financial cost for the BFA in terms of storage and transaction costs for stocks carried for increasing the average return level c. Denote this cost by a strictly increasing function E(c), so that total cost T(c) of the BFA may be viewed as a weighted average

$$T(c) = wE(c) + (1-w)(\sigma^2(c)/\mu^2(c)) \quad 0 \leq w \leq 1 \tag{24}$$

Let $c^0 = c^0(w)$ be the value of c depending on the weight coefficient w, $0 \leq w \leq 1$ which minimises the total cost function T(c) in (24). This specifies a robust stabilisation policy, that is risk sensitive and cautious. This can be easily generalised in an intertemporal dynamic framework by following the simulation model of Goreux (1978); also the benefits in terms of reduced cost of operation of BFA and of increased export earnings and development for the producer countries may be directly evaluated. It would be interesting to compare this type of robust stabilisation policy with an alternative proposed by Whittle (1981) and empirically applied by Hughes Hallett (1986), where risk sensitive decision rules are derived by modifying the LQG framework.

Next we consider the fixed price policy in the linear market model (20), where supply responds to price p^0 set by the BFA. For simplicity we may assume u to be zero, so that we have supply disturbances only. The mean and variance of total revenue (R) in this case turn out to be:

$$\bar{R}: \text{ mean} = b^{-1}(k_0 + k_1 p^0 - k_2 p^{0^2}) \tag{25}$$

$$\sigma_R^2: \text{ variance} = b^{-2}(\alpha + \beta p^0)^2 \sigma_v^2$$

where: $\bar{p}$: mean price $= (b + \beta)^{-1}(a - \alpha) > 0$

k_0: $a\alpha - \alpha^2$, $k_1 = a - 2\alpha\beta$, $k_2 = \beta^2$

Two types of decision rules may be easily derived from (25), one being risk sensitive and the other non–sensitive. The optimal values of p^0 in these two cases are:

$$p^0 = [2bwk_2 + 2\beta(1-w)\sigma_v^2]^{-1}[bwk_1 - 2\alpha(1-w)\sigma_v^2] \tag{26}$$

(risk sensitive)

$$p^0 = (2\beta^2)^{-1}(a - 2\alpha\beta) \qquad \text{(non–sensitive)} \tag{27}$$

In the first case the optimising objective is the weighted average $(w\overline{R} - (1-w)\sigma_R^2)$ and in the second only $\overline{R}$. It is clear that the optimal price p^0 need not equal the mean price $\overline{p}$. For example in the risk non–sensitive case (27),

$$p^0 \gtreqless \overline{p}, \text{ as } a(b-\beta) - 2\alpha b \gtreqless 0$$

A dynamic version of this model with an intertemporal objective function can be easily set up as

$$\underset{p_t^0}{\text{Max}}\ J_T = \sum_{t=1}^{T} (1+\rho)^{-t}[w\overline{R}_t - (1-w)\sigma_{R_t}^2 - D_t] \tag{28}$$

where D_t is disbursement cost as defined in Goreux's model as follows:

$$D_t = cH_t + (H_t - H_{t-1})(1 - g\delta_t)\overline{p}_t$$

$$\delta_t = \begin{cases} 1, & \text{if } H_t > H_{t-1} \\ -1, & \text{if } H_t \leq H_{t-1} \end{cases} \qquad \rho\text{: discount rate}$$

$$cH_t = \text{storage cost;}\ \overline{p}_t = b^{-1}(a - \alpha - \beta p_t^0)$$

where $(H_t - H_{t-1})(1 - g\delta_t)\overline{p}_t$ is the cost of purchase (+) or sale (–) net of transactions fee. It is clear from this model that the limit price p_t^0 may change over time in an optimal sense, provided it maximises the discounted stream of profits for the BFA. This model can be numerically simulated with given parameter values. The risk sensitive rules $(w < 1)$ can then be compared with the non–sensitive rules $(w = 1)$ and the implicit cost of ignoring the time horizon T may be evaluated.

The next case is one of a price band rule defined in (21), where for simplicity we assume that the random element v has an equal probability of taking either a positive value $\theta(\theta>0)$ or, a negative value $-\theta$, $\theta > 0$. The mean and variance of total revenue can then be approximately calculated as

$$\overline{R} = \alpha\overline{p} + \beta(\overline{p}^2 + q^2) - \theta q$$

$$\sigma_R^2 \cong \overline{p}^2(\beta q - \theta)^2 + (\alpha + \beta\overline{p})^2 q^2 + T_1 \tag{29}$$

$$T_t = \text{all other terms not involving q}$$

Clearly σ_R^2 is strictly convex in q since β is positive. An optimal value q^0 of q can again be determined by using a risk sensitive objective function as

$$J = w\bar{R} - (1-w)\sigma_R^2 , \quad 0 \le w \le 1$$

The value of q^0 is

$$q^0 = [w\beta - (1-w)\{\beta^2\bar{p}^2 + (\alpha+\beta\bar{p})^2\}]^{-1}[\theta\{w - (1-w)\beta\bar{p}^2\}]$$

assuming of course that the second order condition for a maximum is satisfied. Hence we obtain for the two extreme cases: w = 0 and w = 1

$$q^0(w = 0) = [\beta^2\bar{p}^2 + (\alpha+\beta\bar{p})^2]^{-1}(\theta\beta\bar{p}^2)$$

$$q^0(w = 1) = \theta/\beta$$

In either case it is clear that the higher the value of θ, the higher is the required level of q. The cost of increasing q for the BFA would also rise. Thus it is clear that revenue could be stabilised at a low cost if the required level of q is low, but the cost of price stabilisation would increase substantially when the targets of stabilisation are increased, or when the range of fluctuation (i.e., 2θ) is raised. The implicit cost of risk aversion has also to be incorporated if there are private speculators in the market where the BFA's action are anticipated.

5. CONCLUDING REMARKS

By way of generalisation we may mention here a few other aspects of robustness not discussed before. First, consider the LQG framework with a quadratic loss function and a linear dynamic model with additive errors subject to a Gaussian distribution. This type of model has been frequently applied in formulating optimal stabilisation policies for commodity markets like coffee and cocoa using optimal control theory (Hughes Hallett (1986), Sengupta (1985), Turnovsky (1978)). Two types of robustness issues have been analysed and applied for the world cocoa market by Sengupta and Davutyan (1984) in this context: (a) the quadratic loss function is replaced by an absolute value or Chebyshev norm, and (b) the additive random errors follow a general Pareto–Levy class of symmetric stable distributions. Simulation experiments indicate that stabilisation policies based on LQG framework are not very robust (i.e., not insensitive) to such mis-specifications.

Another type of robustness issue arises when the parameters of the demand and supply functions for example (20) are either unknown or likely to change after the stabilisation policy is introduced. Such issues call for some types of adaptive control methods with a learning mechanism built into it. In this dynamic framework future information structure and its availability play important roles. Although there exist methods of optimal control, discussed by Sengupta (1985) in its economic applications, they tend in general to lead to nonlinear optimal decision rules with some computational complexity. Much more applied empirical work is needed before the trade–off issue between improved nonlinear DR and increased computational costs can be settled.

REFERENCES

Adams, F.G. and J. Behrman (1982), *Commodity Exports and Economic Development*, D.C. Heath, Lexington, Massachusetts.

Brown, C.P. (1975), *Primary Commodity Control*, Oxford University Press, London.

Gbur, E.E. (1981), 'The Effects of Constraints on the Response Variable in Regression', *Journal of Statistical Computation and Simulation*, 13, pp. 115–30.

Geer, T. (1971), *The World Coffee Economy and Stabilisation Schemes*, Dunellen, New York.

Goreux, L.M. (1978), 'Optimal Rule of Buffer Stock Intervention', Mimeographed Report, IMF Research Department DM/78/7, Washington, D.C.

Hughes Hallett, A.J. (1986), 'Commodity Market Stabilisation and North–South Income Transfers: An Empirical Investigation', *Journal of Development Economics*, 24, pp. 294–313.

Labys, W.C. (1975), *Quantitative Models of Commodity Markets*, Ballinger, Boston.

Nappi, C. (1979), *Commodity Market Controls*, D.C. Heath, Lexington, Massachusetts.

Newbery, D.M.G. and J.E. Stiglitz (1981), *The Theory of Commodity Price Stabilisation*, Oxford University Press, Oxford.

Newbery, D.M.G. (1984), 'Commodity Price Stabilisation in Imperfect or Cartelised Markets', *Econometrica*, 52, pp. 563–78,

Nguyen, D.T. (1980), The Effects of Partial Price Stabilisation on Export Earnings Instability and Level: Implications for the North–South Negotiations, in *Commodities, Finance and Trade: Issues in North–South Negotiations*, Greenwood Press, Westport, Connecticut.

Reynolds, P.D. (1978), *International Commodity Agreements and the Common Fund*, Praeger Publishers, New York.

Sengupta, J.K. and R.E. Sfeir (1983), 'Control Theory Models in World Coffee: Some Empirical Tests', *International Journal of Systems Science*, 14, pp. 811–27.

Sengupta, J.K. (1984), 'A Theory of Portfolio Revision: Robustness and Truncation Problems', *International Journal of Systems Science*, 15, pp. 804–25.

Sengupta, J.K. and N. Davutyan (1984), 'Stabilisation Policies in Commodity Markets: How Robust are They?', Paper prepared for the Western Social Science Conference, San Diego.

Sengupta, J.K. (1985), 'Stochastic Models in Dynamic Economics: Problems of Time Inconsistency, Causality and Estimation' in: J.K. Sengupta, *Information and Efficiency in Economic Decision*, Martinus Nijhoff Publishers, Boston.

Sengupta, J.K. (1985), 'Correlated Equilibria and Rayleigh Quotient in Cournot–Nash Games', Working Paper, Department of Economics, University of California, Santa Barbara.

Singh, S. et al. (1977), *Coffee, Tea and Cocoa: Market Prospects and Development Lending*, John Hopkins University Press, Baltimore.

Turnovsky, S.J. (1978), 'The Distribution of Welfare Gains from Price Stabilisation' in F.G. Adams and S.A. Klein (eds.), *Stabilising World Commodity Markets*, D.C. Heath, Lexington, Massachusetts.

UNCTAD (1976), 'Integrated Programme for Commodities', Report No. ID/RES/ 93(IV), Geneva.

Whittle, P. (1981), 'Risk–Sensitive Linear Quadratic Gaussian Control', *Advances in Applied Probability*, 13, pp. 764–77.

CHAPTER 10

COMMODITY MARKET STABILISATION WITH SPECULATIVE ACTIVITY: AN EXAMPLE FROM THE WORLD COPPER MARKET

A.J. Hughes Hallett, *University of Newcastle, England*

1. INTRODUCTION

The purpose of this paper is to examine the costs and benefits of market stabilisation schemes when the behaviour of speculators and other agents depends on forward looking (rational) expectations about future states of the market. Stabilisation agreements are (or have been) in operation in five commodity markets – coffee, cocoa, tin, rubber, and sugar – and they have been proposed for a further eleven core commodity markets in the integrated Commodity Market Stabilization Program (UNCTAD (1976)). Stabilisation agreements are also widely used elsewhere; for example in the EMS currency stabilisation scheme, or price support schemes for stabilising agricultural incomes. All of these schemes have specified buffer stock interventions triggered by price movements (although some have kept production controls as a reserve instrument). But their chief difficulty has been the selection of an appropriate buffer stock size and/or price support level. In practice these quantities have been estimated from observations of market responses made *before* the proposed stabilisation scheme was in place (see, e.g., UNCTAD (1977)). Normally one would expect that to underestimate the size of the buffer stock needed since the introduction of a market authority strong enough to influence the state of the market will itself alter the behavioural responses of these agents. In particular the creation of a buffer stock would lead consumers and producers to carry lower working stocks since part of their function (providing protection from price fluctuations) will be taken over by the buffer stock.

Thus one reason for studying the performance of price stabilisation schemes under rational expectations is to discover how much the markets responses would be altered by forward lookig behaviour, to what extent those altered responses would erode the market authorities' ability to control prices, and how much larger the buffer stock would therefore have to be. In fact the academic literature already contains several studies of price

O. Guvenen (ed.), International Commodity Market Models and Policy Analysis, 185–204.

stabilisation schemes[2], but agents' behaviour is postulated to be invariant to the buffer stock activities. Although no work has been done on these issues, the Lucas critique suggests that they could be an important difficulty for the design of price stabilisation programmes.

A second, and closely related, reason for studying stabilisation schemes in markets with forward looking behaviour is that agents will tend to increase their speculative stocks as future prices become more predictable (but not necessarily more stable) and hence more vulnerable to speculative attack. Such changes will increase the role of the buffer stock since it will have to overcome increased speculative activity – including speculative attacks on the stock itself (Salant (1983)). Stabilisation schemes which ignore speculation would therefore eventually break down. Buffer stocks do appear to have been too small in practice; all the stabilisation schemes mentioned above have foundered or become ineffective because of insufficient stock level. The recent collapse of the tin agreement was perhaps the most dramatic example.

A third reason for studying stabilisation in markets with rational expectations is to investigate whether we should follow the orthodox time consistent but suboptimal decision rules, or whether it would be better to adopt optimal but predictably time inconsistent intervention sequences at each moment. This is a question which has been extensively and inconclusively debated in theoretical models, but which has never been subjected to empirical examination. This paper stresses that the two strategies can always be computed and compared, even if there is no theoretical resolution to that debate. If, as happens here, the suboptimality is large but the time inconsistent deviations of the intervention paths are small (or vice versa), then the appropriate form of decision rule is quite clear, at least for the problem in hand.

2. A MODEL OF THE WORLD COPPER MARKET

The focus of commodity market models is the price at which the commodity is exchanged. Models of commodity markets are therefore built round a simple structure reflecting the determination of prices through the interaction of supply and demand:

$$\begin{aligned} Q_t &= f(\alpha(L)P_t, X_t) \\ C_t &= g(\beta(L)P_t, X_t) \\ S_t &= h(\gamma(L)P_t, P_t^e, X_t) \\ \Delta S_t &= Q_t - C_t \end{aligned} \tag{1}$$

where Q_t is production, C_t consumption, and S_t stockholdings in period t. Here P_t is the market price; P_t^e is a vector of expected prices as formed at t; X_t is a vector of exogenous variables; and $\alpha(L)$, $\beta(L)$, $\gamma(L)$ denote distributed lags in the lag operator L. This model is complete once the expectations mechanism is specified. If stockholders form adaptive expectations, the stock relationship becomes

$$S_t = h^*(\gamma^*(L)P_t, \gamma(L)X_t) \tag{2}$$

and the price will clear the market period by period. However it is generally found that, due to unobserved stockholding, predicted prices have to play too large an equilibriating role in the model. Predicted prices are then more variable than the corresponding historical series. Previous models have therefore usually replaced the market clearing identity by an explicit price formation mechanism (see, for example, Fisher, Cootner and Bailey (1972)):

$$\Delta P_t = k(Z_t, X_t) \tag{3}$$

where $Z_t = Q_t - C_t - \Delta S_t$ is the market's excess supply.

However it is also possible that the assumption of mechanistic expectations is the source of this problem. An alternative model can be built up from the intertemporal price relation $(1+r_t)P_t = P_{t+1|t}$ (where $P_{t+1|t}$ is the price expected, in period t, to prevail in period t+1) which must hold under competitive storage conditions at an interest rate r_t. This relationship defines the entire path of currently expected future prices, and consequently the entire path of expected excess supplies $Z_{t+} = Q_{t+j} - C_{t+j}$, $j \geq 0$, which follow from the first two equations in (1). The market clearing mechanism $\Delta S_t = Q_t - C_t$ can now be used to solve for the stock levels which would be expected to clear the market over an interval of h periods. Having obtained an expression for stocks in terms of expected excess supplies, this can be used in place of the equation for S_t in (1) and the resulting system solved to determine prices as a function of excess supplies and exogenous variables. That provides the rational expectations price relation of the form $\Delta P_t = f(r_t, Z_{t+1|1}, \gamma(L)P_t)$ to replace both (3) and the explicit stocks equation which we wished to avoid. Thus, in effect, by assuming efficient storage and consequently the intertemporal price expectation, we solve (1) for stock values rather than prices, and *then* use that result to substitute the stock variables out of (1). The system can then be solved in terms of prices. The derivation and precise specification of this model is given in Ghosh, Gilbert and Hughes Hallett (1987), but the estimated equations are summarised in the Appendix.

At this stage we have two alternative forms of the copper market model: one with rational expectations terms in the price equation (denoted 'RE base' in the empirical exercise) and one without such expectations ('No RE' in the empirical section). Moreover introducing adaptive expectations for the excess supply terms in the RE base model would also give a price equation such as (3) with lags in Z_t. So either form of the price equation is nested within a common specification with a complete set of leads and lags in Z_t. Non–nested encompassing tests rejected the 'No RE' model when the RE model was the alternative (the Cox–Pesaran test) and came close to doing so when the unrestricted specification was the alternative (a Mizon–Richard (1986) test)[2]. Since the former test appears to have higher power in small samples (Pesaran (1974)), these results suggest that the RE model is appropriate while the other version describes what would happen when forward looking expectations are ignored. The next stage is to show how speculative activity would lead the buffer stock manager to set up a rational expectations model specification.

3. SOLVING RATIONAL EXPECTATIONS MODELS

Consider a dynamic model with rational expectations terms:

$$y_t = Ay_{t-1} + Bx_t + C_0 y_{t|t} + C_1 y_{t+1|t} + u_t \tag{4}$$

where $y_{t+j|1} = E(y_{t+j}|\Omega_t)$, for $j \geq 0$, is an expectation conditioned on the information available at the start of period t. There are m endogenous variables, y_t; n policy instruments, x_t; and the exogenous random variables, u_t. A, B, C_0, and C_1 are matrices of known coefficients. Each information set, Ω_t, contains certain information on y_{t-j}, x_{t-j}, u_{t-j} and $u_{t+j-1|1}$ for $j \geq 1$, in addition to the coefficients in (4).

Each expectation in (4) is the same as the forecast obtained by solving the model for period t+1, conditional on the information set Ω_t. But these expectations are linked forward in time, so that to solve (4) also requires solutions for $y_{t+j|t}$ where j=1,2,... . Thus, in period 1, the expectation of each y_t, up to a horizon t=1...T, is obtained from[3]:

$$\begin{bmatrix} y_{1|1} \\ \vdots \\ \vdots \\ y_{T|1} \end{bmatrix} = \begin{bmatrix} (I-C_0) & -C_1 & & 0 \\ -A & \ddots & \ddots & \\ & \ddots & \ddots & -C_1 \\ 0 & & -A & (I-C_0) \end{bmatrix}^{-1} \left\{ \begin{bmatrix} B & & 0 \\ & \ddots & \\ 0 & & B \end{bmatrix} \begin{bmatrix} x_{1|1} \\ \vdots \\ x_{T|1} \end{bmatrix} + \begin{bmatrix} u_{1|1} \\ \vdots \\ u_{T|1} \end{bmatrix} + \begin{bmatrix} A \\ 0 \\ \vdots \\ 0 \end{bmatrix} y_0 \right.$$

$$+\begin{bmatrix}0\\ \vdots\\ 0\\ C_1\end{bmatrix} y_{T+1|1} \Bigg] = \begin{bmatrix}R_{11} & \cdots & R_{1T}\\ \vdots & & \vdots\\ R_{T1} & \cdots & R_{TT}\end{bmatrix}\begin{bmatrix}x_{1|1}\\ \vdots\\ x_{T|1}\end{bmatrix} + \begin{bmatrix}s_{1|1}\\ \vdots\\ s_{T|1}\end{bmatrix} = Rx + s \tag{5}$$

where $u_{t|1}$ is taken from Ω_1, and $x_{t|1}$ are the instrument values to be determined. We can regard $x_{1|1}$ as a decision intended for immediate implementation, and $x_{t|1}$ as the currently expected future decisions ($t \geq 2$). To construct this solution, the user must *either* supply expected terminal values $y_{T+1|1}$ (Chow (1980)) *or* check that the terminal values have no impact on the solutions of interest, $y_{1|1} \ldots y_{1|t}$ say, when T is large. The latter may be done by verifying the saddlepoint property (Blanchard and Khan (1980)); or numerically (see Fair and Taylor (1983)) by checking that the first t submatrices in the final column of the inverse matrix in (5) vanishes as $T \to \infty$[4]. It is important to emphasise that in practice the system's multipliers, $R_{tj} = \partial y_{t|1}/\partial x_{j|1}$, would be evaluated numerically rather than by direct matrix inversion. A number of techniques for doing that are now available, and the procedures summarised in Fisher et al. (1986), for example, provide a cheap way of evaluating (5) numerically for large non-linear models.

4. MULTIPERIOD CERTAINTY EQUIVALENT DECISION RULES

4.1. Optimal Loop Decisions

We start from the solved out model given by (5). Stack up the decision variables as $z' = (y'_{1|1} \ldots y'_{T|1}, x'_{1|1} \ldots x'_{T|1})$, where each $y_{t|1}$ may be understood to be a subset of targets from the endogenous variables of (1). Hence, deleting any equations in (5) which correspond to nontargets, the constraints are

$$H\tilde{z} = b \quad \text{where } H = [I \vdots -R] \text{ and } b = s - Hz^d \tag{6}$$

Now let z^d be the ideal (but infeasible) decision values. We use the quadratic objective function

$$w = \tfrac{1}{2}\tilde{z}'Q\tilde{z} + q'z \tag{7}$$

where $\tilde{z} = z - z^d$, and Q is symmetric and positive definite. Optimal (open loop) decisions are then defined by

$$z^* = \min_z \, [E(w) - \mu'(H\tilde{z} - b) \,|\, Q_1] \tag{8}$$

where μ is a vector of Lagrange multipliers. We can now apply the conventional certainty equivalence theorem to (8) and minimise

$$\frac{1}{2}\begin{bmatrix}\tilde{z}\\ \\ \mu\end{bmatrix}'\begin{bmatrix}Q & -H'\\ \\ -H & 0\end{bmatrix}\begin{bmatrix}\tilde{z}\\ \\ \mu\end{bmatrix}+\begin{bmatrix}q\\ \\ E_1(b)\end{bmatrix}'\begin{bmatrix}\tilde{z}\\ \\ \mu\end{bmatrix}. \tag{9}$$

The optimal decisions are therefore

$$\begin{bmatrix}\tilde{z}^*\\ \\ \mu^*\end{bmatrix}=-\begin{bmatrix}Q & -H'\\ \\ -H & 0\end{bmatrix}^{-1}\begin{bmatrix}q\\ \\ E_1(b)\end{bmatrix} \tag{10}$$

If uncertainty is indeed confined to u_t, then $\tilde{z}^*$ contains the current rational expectations of the optimal policy choices and their outcomes given Ω_1.

4.2 Information Innovations

In order to update the conditioning information in successive solutions, the components of (5) may be partitioned with respect to the past and future. Thus, for some $t \geq 2$, (5) is written

$$\begin{bmatrix}y_{1|1}\\ \\ y_{T|1}\end{bmatrix}=\begin{bmatrix}R^{(o)} & R^{(2)}\\ \\ R^{(1)} & R^{(t)}\end{bmatrix}\begin{bmatrix}x_{1|1}\\ \\ x_{T|1}\end{bmatrix}+\begin{bmatrix}S^{(o)} & S^{(2)}\\ \\ S^{(1)} & S^{(t)}\end{bmatrix}\begin{bmatrix}u_{1|1}\\ \\ u_{T|1}\end{bmatrix}+P_1y_o+P_2y_{T+1|1} \tag{11}$$

where

$$R^{(o)}=\begin{bmatrix}R_{11}\cdots\cdots R_{1,t-1}\\ \vdots \qquad \vdots\\ R_{t-1,1}\cdots R_{t-1,t-1}\end{bmatrix},\quad R^{(1)}=\begin{bmatrix}R_{t1}\cdots\cdots R_{t,t-1}\\ \vdots \qquad \vdots\\ R_{T1}\cdots\cdots R_{T,t-1}\end{bmatrix},$$

$$R^{(2)}=\begin{bmatrix}R_{1t}\cdots\cdots R_{1T}\\ \vdots \qquad \vdots\\ R_{t-1,t}\cdots R_{t-1,T}\end{bmatrix},\quad R^{(t)}=\begin{bmatrix}R_{tt}\cdots\cdots R_{tT}\\ \vdots \qquad \vdots\\ R_{tT}\cdots\cdots R_{TT}\end{bmatrix}.$$

The submatrices $S^{(o)}$, $S^{(1)}$, $S^{(2)}$ and $S^{(t)}$ correspond to an analogous partitioning of the inverse matrix of (5). Now, given Ω_t:

$$\begin{bmatrix} y_{t|t} \\ \vdots \\ y_{T|t} \end{bmatrix} = R^{(1)} \begin{bmatrix} x_1 \\ \vdots \\ x_{t-1} \end{bmatrix} + R^{(t)} \begin{bmatrix} x_{t|t} \\ \vdots \\ x_{T|t} \end{bmatrix} + S^{(1)} \begin{bmatrix} u_1 \\ \vdots \\ u_{t-1} \end{bmatrix} + S^{(t)} \begin{bmatrix} u_{t|t} \\ \vdots \\ u_{T|t} \end{bmatrix}$$

$$P_1^{(1)} y_o + P_2^{(t)} y_{T+1|t} \tag{12}$$

where $P_1^{(t)}$ and $P_2^{(t)}$ are the lower m(T–t+1) rows of P_1 and P_2. Thus (12) involves no more than a different partitioning of the coefficient matrices already obtained for (5).

4.3 Revised Optimal Conditions

The remaining problem is to determine how to revise the decision values (for $t \geq 2$) given unanticipated shocks ($s_{t-j} \neq s_{t-j|t-1}$ for $j \geq 1$), past achievements (the realisations for y_{t-j}, $j \geq 1$), and changed expectations of the future ($s_{t+j|1} \neq s_{t+j|t-1}$ for $j \geq 0$). The decision variables are partitioned between past realisations and future choices.

$$\tilde{y}' = (\tilde{y}_o^{*\prime}, \tilde{y}_{(t)}') \text{ and } \tilde{x}' = (\tilde{x}_o^{*\prime}, \tilde{x}_{(t)}') \tag{13}$$

where $\tilde{y}_o^{*\prime} = (\tilde{y}_1^{*\prime} \ldots \tilde{y}_{t-1}^{*\prime})$ and $\tilde{x}_o^{*\prime} = (\tilde{x}_1^{*\prime} \ldots \tilde{x}_{t-1}^{*\prime})$ are fixed realisations. We write $\tilde{z}_o^{*\prime} = (\tilde{y}_o^{*\prime}, \tilde{x}_o^{*\prime})$. Meanwhile $\tilde{z}_{(t)}' = (\tilde{y}_{t|t}' \ldots \tilde{y}_{T|t}', \tilde{x}_{t|t}' \ldots \tilde{x}_{T|t}')$ must be reoptimised at t. First we must partition the parameters of the objective function with respect to past and future. If $Q = \begin{bmatrix} L & M' \\ M & N \end{bmatrix}$ conforms to the partitioning of z, let $L = \begin{bmatrix} L_o & L_1 \\ L_1' & L_{(t)} \end{bmatrix}$, $N = \begin{bmatrix} N_o & N_1 \\ N_1' & N_{(t)} \end{bmatrix}$, and $M = \begin{bmatrix} M_o & M_1 \\ M_2 & M_{(t)} \end{bmatrix}$ conform to the partitioning in $\tilde{y}$ and $\tilde{x}$ defined by (13). Then expanding $\frac{1}{2}\tilde{z}'Q\tilde{z}$ and collecting terms,

$$\tfrac{1}{2}\tilde{z}'Q\tilde{z} = \tfrac{1}{2}\tilde{z}_o^{*\prime} Q_o \tilde{z}_o^* + \tilde{z}_o^{*\prime} Q_1 \tilde{z}_{(t)} + \tfrac{1}{2}\tilde{z}_{(t)}' Q_{(t)} \tilde{z}_{(t)} \tag{14}$$

where $Q_o = \begin{bmatrix} L_o & M_o' \\ M_o & N_o \end{bmatrix}$, $Q_{(t)} = \begin{bmatrix} L_{(t)} & M_{(t)}' \\ M_{(t)} & N_{(t)} \end{bmatrix}$ and $Q_1 = \begin{bmatrix} L_1 & M_2' \\ M_1 & N_1 \end{bmatrix}$

Similarly $q'\tilde{z} = q_o'\tilde{z}_o^* + q_{(t)}'\tilde{z}_{(t)}$. The constant in this modified objective function may be ignored in the reoptimisations; but the linear term contains $(q_{(t)}' + \tilde{z}_o^{*\prime} Q_1)$ in place of the original $q'_{(t)}$, and the quadratic term involves only $Q_{(t)}$. In exactly the same way the constrained objective, (9), becomes

$$\frac{1}{2}\begin{bmatrix}\tilde{z}_{(t)}\\ \\ \mu_{(t)}\end{bmatrix}'\begin{bmatrix}Q_{(t)} & -H^{(t)'}\\ \\ -H^{(t)} & 0\end{bmatrix}\begin{bmatrix}\tilde{z}_{(t)}\\ \\ \mu_{(t)}\end{bmatrix}+\begin{bmatrix}q_{(t)}+Q_1'\tilde{z}_o^*-H^{(2)'}\mu_o^*\\ \\ b_{(t)}-H^{(1)}\tilde{z}_o^*\end{bmatrix}'\begin{bmatrix}\tilde{z}_{(t)}\\ \\ \mu_{(t)}\end{bmatrix} \tag{15}$$

where $\mu' = (\mu_o^{*\prime}, \mu'_{(t)})$ is also partitioned with respect to the past and the future; and $H^{(t)} = [I\vdots-R^{(t)}]$, $H^{(2)} = [0\vdots-R^{(2)}]$ and $H^{(1)} = [0\vdots-R^{(1)}]$ are all derived from

$H = \begin{bmatrix}I & 0\vdots -R^{(o)} & -R^{(2)}\\ & \vdots & \\ 0 & I\vdots -R^{(1)} & -R^{(t)}\end{bmatrix}$. Finally $b_{(t)}$ contains the lower m(T–t+1) elements of b.

Thus we have an optimisation problem of precisely the same form as (9), but with Q replaced by $Q_{(t)}$ and H by $H^{(t)}$. In addition, since $-H^{(1)}\tilde{z}_o^* = R^{(1)}\tilde{x}_o^*$, we must replace

$$q \text{ by } Q_1'\tilde{z}_o^* + (0{:}R^{(2)})'\mu_o^* + q_{(t)} \tag{16}$$

and

$$b \text{ by } R^{(1)}\tilde{x}_o^* + E_t(b_{(t)}). \tag{17}$$

Finally, certainty equivalence has been reapplied to (15) to complete the latter's conditioning on Ω_t. Therefore the optimally revised policies are given by (10) with Q, H, q and $E_1(b)$ replaced, respectively, by $Q_{(t)}$, $H^{(t)}$, and the quantities in (16) and (17). Of course only $x^*_{t|t}$ itself will be implemented (with the expectation of achieving $y^*_{t|t}$) before the next revision. Thus each subvector $x^*_{t|t}$ is therefore multiperiod certainty equivalent and innovations dependent.

4.4 Time Consistency

Should economists recommend policies which are time consistent, on a period–by–period basis, but suboptimal? Or should they recommend policies which are optimal but predictably will not be carried out? There are a number of possible responses to this dilemma. Kydland and Prescott (1977) recommend consistent (but suboptimal) decisions, while Buiter (1981) favoured the optimal (but potentially inconsistent) decision rule. Others (e.g. Backus and Driffil (1985), Currie and Levine (1985)) have introduced additional features, such as the cost of a lost reputation or the threat of retaliatory action by other agents, which would restrain policy makers from attempting time inconsistent behaviour. Indeed retaliatory action, if policy makers fail to convince the market that they will stick to their announced policies, would typically cost the policy makers more (through being forced back on to the inferior time consistent solution) than they forego by not reneging on an open loop optimal strategy (Hughes Hallett (1987)). That, being predictable in advance, would in itself ensure that policy makers would maintain the policies computed from (10) in the absence of information changes.

Thus, having got the model into the conventional rational expectations form, it is comparatively easy to develop decision rules for the market authority (or buffer stock manager). First, there is an optimal sequence of decisions based on the initial period's information; the optimal open loop decisions at (10). Then a sequence of optimally revised values can be computed, following the procedure in (15)–(17), in order to incorporate any new information which becomes available during the stabilisation period. These revisions may be time inconsistent; decision makers may discover that even in the absence of information changes they can still gain by revising their decisions during the course of the stabilisation period from their initial (open loop) announcement.

In this paper we simply compute the time inconsistent sequence and show it to be virtually identical to the optimal open loop one so that difficulty is of no practical interest in this case.

5. THE STABILISATION EXERCISE

5.1 Measures of Costs and Benefits

The orthodox specification of the objective of market stabilisation is the maximisation of a discounted sum of producers' and consumers' surplus (Just et al. (1978), Newbery and Stiglitz (1982)). However Cochrane (1980), among others, has attacked that formulation, arguing that consumers and producers are more concerned with price levels because they identify prices, and hence revenues, with welfare. Consumers are typically concerned about price increases which can substantially alter real income levels, while producers worry about low prices which could lead to bankcruptcy and the interruption of development funds. A plausible goal for policy is therefore the stabilisation of market prices – at least to the extent of removing peaks, troughs, or sudden changes in prices. Most authors (e.g. Arzac and Wilkinson (1979), Dixon and Chen (1982)) have in fact concentrated on price levels in empirical work.

A second reason for focusing on the stabilisation of prices is that economic surplus has its limitations as a measure of social welfare in stochastic or nonlinear contexts (Turnovsky (1978)). Indeed, producers' surplus only gives a satisfactory measure of producers' benefits from stabilisation if producers' marginal utilities of income are constant; and that holds only under risk neutrality. Similarly, consumers' surplus only provides an adequate measure of their benefits if consumers' marginal utilities of income are independent of the commodity price. The latter condition might be satisfied approximately, but the former is implausible for many and perhaps most commodity producers. A major benefit of commodity price stabilisation might therefore be a reduction in the risks faced by producers and producing countries (Hughes Hallett (1986)). In principle one should analyse the variations of producers' marginal utilities directly, but that is difficult to do because it involves imposing explicit utility functions (or risk aversion coefficient values) in order to be operational. Instead we use a very simple objective function (involving just market prices and the buffer stock levels) as a means of generating conditionally optimal market interventions. The resulting stabilisation programme can then be judged by whichever measures of financial cost, stability, transfers, or general welfare that are considered appropriate to the case.

In what follows, three measures of agggate operating costs were used:

(i) the expected Net Present Value of the programme, in 1975\$b, allowing for transactions, warehousing and overhead costs at the rates assumed by Bhaskar, Gilbert and Perlman (1978);

(ii) the expected maximum finance (1975\$b) required by the programme, defined as the maximum (outward) cash flow implied by transactions in (i);

(iii) the expected maximum buffer stock (m tonnes).

Three measures of net benefits were also used:

(iv) the expected root mean square error of prices about the trend;

(v) the mean deviation of prices about that trend;

(vi) a measure of the transfer benefit to the Third World (the 'South') from the developed countries (the 'North'). For each country there is:

- (a) the benefit to producers, measured by the discounted deflated change in their profits. If prestabilisation production is q_0 and stabilised production is q_1 , then the change in profits is approximately $\frac{1}{2}(q_0+q_1)\Delta p$ where Δp is the change in the price resulting from stabilisation;
- (b) the benefit to consumers, measureed by the discounted deflated change in consumers' surplus, approximated as $-\frac{1}{2}(c_0+c_1)\Delta p$;
- (c) the discounted deflated revenues of the buffer stock.

Summing these by countries within a group gives the (risk neutral) North–South transfer.

5.2 An Endogenised Price Support Level

An important practical problem is to determine the path about which prices should be stabilised. Most studies use the historical price trend although the market authority cannot know that trend in advance and the stability lost by using a trend estimated in advance can be substantial (Ghosh, Gilbert and Hughes Hallett (1987)). The alternative is to estimate the underlying equilibrium path by setting the ideal values, y_t^d, equal to the target projections generated by the mean stochastic simulation of the model without instrument interventions (Just et al. (1978)). But there are three drawbacks to using that to define the ideal stabilisation path. First, model projections supply no incentive to smooth the dynamics of market price fluctuations. Second, if the projections fluctuate, it may prove very expensive to make actual prices track those fluctuations. Third, if the exogenous random variables (or the model's parameters) have large variances, then interventions designed to track those ideal values can actually end up increasing the target fluctuations (Just et al. (1978)).

In this paper, the ideal (price) path is generated by the following extrapolation scheme:

$$y_t^d = e_t + d_1 y_{t-1}^d + d_2 y_{t-1} \tag{18}$$

This scheme contains three components: (i) preassigned elements, e_t, describing the initial trend or model projections; (ii) updating elements, $d_2 y_{t-1}$, to revise the ideal path as shocks or information innovations cause the targets to deviate from their projected values; and (iii) smoothing elements, $d_1 y_{t-1}^d$, to damp out any fluctuations induced by the preassigned elements or random shocks in the updating elements. Each e_t was set equal to the increment in the prestabilisation price trend. Then $d_1 = (1-d_2)$ ensures y_t^d stays on trend so long as y_{t-1} remains on trend. Finally (18) was inserted into the market authorities objective function (7) so that the stabilisation agency can select that combination of interventions and ideal stabilisation levels which yields the best expected results. The best value of d_2 was determined by numerical search.

5.3 The Information Set

We controlled the copper model over a period of 40 quarters, from 1971.1 to 1980.4. The instrument available to the stabilisation agency was purchases or sales of a buffer stock maintained by the agency. The target variables are deviations of the market (LME) price from an initial predetermined trend, and deviations of the buffer stock level from a constant level set at 1.5 million tonnes. The relative priorities on all decision variables were specified to be constant, within a quadratic objective function, throughout the stabilisation period. The relative penalties were 100 on the squared deviations of (log) prices, 1 on squared buffer stock deviations, and 0.1 on squared buffer stock purchases or sales.

These stabilisation exercises assume historical values for the non–controllable exogenous variables, with the exception that net sales by the United States (GSA) strategic stockpile of copper were set at zero and the total amount sold (225,000 tonnes) over the period was transferred to the stabilisation authority at the start of the exercise. Sales by the GSA (or at least the timing of these sales) have in practice been motivated by price stabilisation, even if this has not always been the result. We therefore assume that had the United States been a signatory of a stabilisation agreement of the type envisaged, then its stockpile sales would have been coordinated with the activities of the buffer stock.

If the stabilisation rules are not fully stochastic in taking historical values for non-controllable variables it is because we have no satisfactory model for forecasting the important variables – industrial production in the OECD countries, plus monetary and trade variables. Unlike the copper market model, such an auxiliary forecasting model would be an impressionistic attempt to capture the relationships between the exogenous variables. It is naive to suppose that an auxiliary model of a few simple equations would be an adequate model for the entire world economy. Moreover market agents are subjected to a battery of forecasts generated by the financial community, and they are therefore much better informed than an agent obliged to rely on such a simple auxiliary model. So for the purposes of comparison we have used historical exogenous values. However, all the results quoted below are for closed loop stochastic control exercises with respect to the remaining disturbances terms. We assume that the buffer stock authority knows only the current and past prediction errors in y_t; future random disturbances are forecasted at their expected values.

6. THE EFFECT OF SPECULATIVE ACTIVITY

In Table 1, the first five of our summary measures of cost and performance (benefits) show that speculative activity could be expected to have remarkably little impact on the ability of buffer stock interventions to stabilise world copper prices – given that the Lucas critique will be satisfied in the sense that the rational expectations model reflects the changes in decision rules, and hence in market responses, which are caused by both the speculators and the stabilisation authority anticipating each others reactions when making their own policy adjustments. Table 1 shows that allowing for rational expectations effects in the standard (informationally infeasible) exercise means that financial requirements for stabilisation would rise 17% and the maximum stock level would increase by 19%; but profitability would also rise 10%. Such increases are perhaps significant, but as absolute changes they are rather small.

The second, and more interesting, feature is that speculative activity appears to be mildly stabilising although the mean price level falls under stabilisation. Direct evidence is given by the fact that the price variability measure (RMSE) actually falls 5.5% when speculative attacks are allowed for. Thus the activities of self–interested speculators need not offset the stabilising efforts of the buffer stock manager – provided that enough funds are made available to support the necessary interventions. Indeed if sufficient supporting funds are made available, then the buffer stock manager can make interventions which are strong enough to convince the speculators that the buffer stock will indeed succeed in stabilising prices. In that case they will speculate on that outcome, with the result that their activities start to add to the stabilising power of the buffer stock. Naturally a larger buffer stock, and more vigorous sequence of interventions, will be needed; and the sharp jump of 170% in the objective function evaluation w_d^*, which reflects buffer stock movements *in addition* to the price movements, emphasises the extent of the extra work needed to achieve this result.

The result that speculative activity is stabilising, provided that the buffer stock can demonstrate a capacity and willingness to intervene vigorously enough, is the main conclusion of this paper. The intuition here is that speculators need to be convinced that the market will actually be stabilised. In that case, they will perceive that it is in their interest to go along with the stabilisation authority and help reduce the price fluctuations. But in order to convince them in the first place, the buffer stock interventions must be large enough for speculators to *anticipate* that there is no chance (or at least a substantially smaller chance) of large price variations appearing in future periods; and to demonstrate that change in the probabilities will require a capacity for more vigorous interventions in the current period. Hence speculative activity does not necessarily imply losses in stabilising performance, but it may well mean that it is a good deal more expensive to operate a buffer stock to ensure that result. For this reason we go on to look at the vigour of the buffer stock interventions under rational expectations in more detail in the next section.

7. THE VIGOUR OF THE BUFFER STOCK INTERVENTIONS

The results so far suggest that the summary measures of cost and stabilising performance can be rendered insensitive to the effects of speculation, given sufficient finance for a larger buffer stock. But the pattern and size of the interventions may vary considerably when speculative behaviour is allowed for, compared to when it is not. Table 2 illustrates that conclusion. In fact the average intervention rises in size by60% on allowing for speculative activity in the standard exercises. Although varying the terminal condition can modify the average interventions a bit, that increase remains over 30% in part (b) of this table. The measures of the variability of the interventions show similar increases once speculative behaviour is accommodated; the standard deviation of the buffer stock intervention values rises 30%, and the number of times the direction of the intervention strategy has to be reversed jumps from 10 to 18 out of the 40 decision periods. Thus speculation has the effect of destroying any continuity in the intervention sequence, and it makes larger and more active movements in the buffer stock necessary.

8. THE IMPACT OF 'NONCAUSALITIES' AND TIME INCONSISTENCY

We turn now to the degree of suboptimality implied by using (time consistent) recursive programming techniques to determine the buffer stock interventions under rational expectations. There are two parts to this question. First, how serious are the consequences of ignoring the 'noncausal' elements which arise from the forward looking expectations? The results marked 'Noncausality Ignored' in Table 1, part (c), show what happens to the standard (RE base) stabilisation exercise when the noncausal multipliers, R_{tk} for $t \geq k$ in (5), or $R^{(2)}$ in (11) to (16), are set to zero throughout the decision process.

However Brandsma and Hughes Hallett (1984) show that the inclusion of the noncausal multipliers is a necessary but not sufficient condition for optimal decisions in a multiperiod framework. The second part of the question is how to maintain the optimality of the performance index. If that is done following the updating procedure given in section 4 (specifically (15) to (17)) we get the results market 'RE base' in Tables 1 and 2. But if, on the other hand, this is done simply by reoptimising the remaining part of the plan at each t (i.e. from t to T) conditional on the realisations of past decision variables (but not on any expectations for those variables which may have been held in the past) we get the usual time inconsistent decision sequence.[5] Those results are marked as time inconsistent in Tables 1 and 2. The reason why the time inconsistent solution produces a worse outcome than the optimal time consistent one is that in the former both sets of agents (the buffer stock manager and the speculators) attempt to gain by time inconsistency. If either one managed to do that individually, then he would necessarily be better off than by maintaining the previously announced solution. But, in

Table 1 : The Impact of Speculative Activity on Price Stabilisation

Exercise	NPV (1975$b.)	Max. Finance (1975$b.)	Max. Stock (m.tonnes)	Mean Price Deviation (c/lb)	Price RMSE (c/lb)	Gains to South (1975$m.)	w^*_d
(a) Standard Exercises							
No RE	-.26	7.15	3.14	-0.89	10.44	-171.4	24.47
RE base	-.23	8.39	3.74	-3.62	9.86	-137.9	66.75
row 2/row 1 % increase	+10.7	+17.3	+19.1	-307.0	-5.5	-19.5	+172.7
(b) Variations in the terminal condition							
RE "high"	-.23	8.39	3.74	-3.64	9.87	-122.9	66.80
RE "low"	-.23	8.39	3.74	-3.60	9.86	-124.6	66.70
(c) The impacts of noncausality and time-consistency							
Noncausality Ignored	-.22	8.12	3.67	-3.49	10.03	-114.7	67.58
Time-inconsistent	-.21	7.94	3.61	-3.61	10.08	-109.2	66.76

Table 2 : The Vigour of the Buffer Stock Interventions

Exercise	Standard (a)		(b) Terminal Condition		(c)	
Vigour	No RE	RE Base	RE "high"	RE "low"	Non-causality Ignored	Time Incon-sistent
Average Inter-vention (m.tonnes)	.0361	.0577	.0510	.0473	.0476	.0483
S.D. of Inter-ventions (m.tonnes)	.2781	.3679	.3773	.3627	.3793	.3613
No of sign changes in interventions	10	18	17	17	17	17

doing so, he automatically makes the other agents worse off. Thus, if all agents try to be time inconsistent simultaneously, the individual gains vanish in the *net* outcome. This still happens in a rational expectations model with only one set of policy instruments because speculators must insert their *own* expectations for future buffer stock purchases/sales to determine their expectations of the future state of the market which in turn influence current behaviour and hence current decisions. The point here is that the temptation to be time inconsistent is predictable *ex ante* for a given sequence of information sets.

In this exercise it appears that ignoring noncausality is not serious; there is a 1.7% loss in stabilising performance (RMSE), but a 3% saving in financial requirements, compared to the RE base case (Table 1, row 6). There are corresponding marginal reductions in the physical stock level and average price deviation. On the other hand the average interventions are quite a lot smaller (Table 2), although the vigour of the buffer stock interventions has scarcely changed. Thus ignoring noncausality could not be expected to cause significant problems for the stabilisation authority, nor serious losses in performance. But the power of multiperiod certainty equivalent decision making for controlling random fluctuations in market prices is sharply reduced if the anticipations effects are ignored in decision making. That is an important result because it shows that, despite their theoretical differences, any of the standard decision procedures will produce approximately optimal results for the open loop problem. Hence it is their ability to produce the appropriate policy revisions in the face of stochastic shocks (or model errors) which distinguishes rules that successfully allow for anticipations effects from those which do not.

Time inconsistent decisions produce slightly less stability (2.25% worse than the RE base case) for a yet smaller financial commitment (5% down); Table 1, row 7. In all other respects the time inconsistent results are hardly distinguishable from the standard exercise – see also Table 2.

9. CONCLUSION

The conslusion here is clearly that the time inconsistency debate in this example has no empirical significance, and that finding corroborates similar conclusions reached (in a rather different application) by Holly and Zarrop (1983). Since previous sections of this paper showed that the introduction of rational expectations did make an appreciable difference to the stabilisation results, the effect of forward looking expectations and speculative activity is to modify the maket's dynamic responses rather than to cause policy design problems through the noncausal influences. That means the controversies raised by Kydland and Prescott (1977), and by Buiter (1981), about the appropriate form of decision rule are unimportant here. The crucial issue turns out to be one of making sure that the market's dynamic structure is modelled correctly.

NOTES

1. For example, Pindyck (1978), Dixon and Chen (1982), Newbery and Stiglitz (1982), Hughes Hallett (1984a, 1986). An example which does show that the quality of stocks held will change as a function of market structure is in Newbery (1984).
2. These test results are reported in Ghosh, Gilbert and Hughes Hallett (1987).
3. The inverse exists provided C_0 and $A(1-C_0)^{-1}C_1(I-C_0)$ have no unit roots.
4. A relatively simply check on the coefficients of (4) is given in Fisher and Hughes Hallett (1986).
5. Comparison of this updating procedure given in section 4.3 with the equivalent procedure for a standard (strictly causal) model, where there is no question of gains from time inconsistent behaviour, shows that the *only* modification under rational expectations is the addition term involving $R^{(2)\prime}\mu_0^*$ in (16). Hence we can indentify the usual time inconsistent choices with ignoring that additional term. That gives a simple way of generating the choices generated when both sets of agents are time inconsistent.

REFERENCES

Arzac, E.R. and M. Wilkinson (1979), 'Stabilisation Policies for United Feedgrain and Livestock Markets', *Journal of Economic Dynamics and Control*, 1, pp.39–58.

Backus, D. and E.J. Driffil (1985), 'Inflation and Reputation', *American Economic Review*, 75, pp. 530–38.

Bhaskar, K.N., C.L. Gilbert and R.A. Perlman (1978), 'Stabilisation of the International Copper Market: A Simulation Study', *Resources Policy*, 4, pp. 13–24.

Blanchard, O.J. and C.M. Kahn (1980), 'The Solution of Linear Difference Models under Rational Expectations', *Econometrica*, 48, pp. 1305–11.

Brandsma, A.S. and A.J. Hughes Hallett (1984) 'Economic Conflict and the Solution of Dynamic Games', *European Economic Review*, 26, pp. 13–32.

Buiter, W.H. (1981), 'The Superiority of Contingent Rules over Fixed Rules in Models with Rational Expectations', *Economic Journal*, 91, pp. 647–70.

Cochrane, W.W. (1980), 'Some Nonconformist Thoughts on Welfare Economics and Commodity Stabilisation Policy', *American Journal of Agricultural Economics*, 72, pp. 508–11.

Currie, D.A. and P. Levine (1985), 'Credibility and Time Inconsistency in a Stochastic World', PRISM Discussion Paper 36, Dept. of Economics, Queen Mary College, University of London.

Dixon, B.L. and W.H. Chen (1982), 'A Stochastic Control Approach to Buffer Stock Management in the Taiwan Rice Market', *Journal of Development Economics*, 10, pp. 187–207.

Fair, R.C. and J.B. Taylor (1983), 'Solution and Maximum Likelihood Estimation of Dynamic Nonlinear Rational Expectations Models', *Econometrica*, 51, pp. 1169–86.

Fisher, F.M., P.H. Cootner and M.N. Bailey (1972), 'An Econometric Model of the

World Copper Industry', *Bell Journal of Economics and Management Science*, 3, pp. 568–601.

Fisher, P.G., S. Holly and A.J. Hughes Hallett (1986), 'Efficient Solution Techniques for Dynamic Nonlinear Rational Expectations Models', *Journal of Economic Dynamics and Control*, 10, pp. 139–45.

Fisher, P.G. and A.J. Hughes Hallett (1986), 'An Efficient Strategy for Solving Nonlinear Rational Expectations Models', Discussion Paper, Dept. of Economics, University of Newcastle upon Tyne.

Ghosh, S., C.L. Gilbert and A.J. Hughes Hallett (1987), *Stabilising Speculative Commodity Markets*, Oxford University Press, Oxford.

Holly, S. and M.B. Zarrop (1983), 'On Optimality and Time Consistency when Expectations are Rational', *European Economic Review*, 20, pp. 23–40.

Hughes Hallett, A.J. (1984), 'Optimal Stockpiling in a High Risk Commodity Market: The Case of Copper', *Journal of Economic Dynamics and Control*, 8, pp. 211–38.

Hughes Hallett, A.J. (1986), 'Commodity Market Stabilisation and 'North–South' Transfers: An Empirical Investigation', *Journal of Development Economics*, 24, pp. 293–316.

Hughes Hallett, A.J. (1987), 'Is Time Inconsistent Behaviour Really Possible?', Discussion Paper 138, Centre for Economic Policy and Research, London.

Just, R., E. Lutz, A. Schmitz and S.J. Turnovsky (1978), 'The Distribution of Welfare Gains from Pure Stabilisation: An International Perspective', *Journal of International Economics*, 8, pp. 551–63.

Kydland, F. and E.C. Prescott (1977), 'Rules Rather Than Discretion: The Inconsistency of Optimal Plans', *Journal of Political Economy*, 85, pp. 473–91.

Mizon, G.E. and J.F. Richard (1986),' The Encompassing Principle and its Application to Testing Non–nested Hypotheses', *Econometrica*, 54, pp. 657–78.

Newbery, D.M.G. (1984), 'Commodity Price Stabilisation in Imperfect or Cartelised Markets', *Econometrica*, 52, pp. 563–78.

Newbery, D.M.G. and J.E. Stiglitz (1982), 'Optimal Stockpiling Rules', *Oxford Economic Papers*, 34, pp.403–27.

Pesaran, M.H. (1974), 'On the General Problem of Model Selection', *Review of Economic Studies*, 41, pp. 153–71.

Pindyck, R.S. (1978), 'Gains to Producers from the Cartelisation of Exhaustible Resources', *Review of Economics and Statistics*, 50, pp. 238–51.

Salant, S.W. (1983), 'The Vulnerability of Price Stabilisation Schemes to Speculative Attack', *Journal of Political Economy*, 91, pp.1–38.

Turnovsky, S.J. (1978), 'The Distribution of Welfare Gains from Price Stabilisation: A Survey of Some Theoretical Issues', in F.G. Adams and S.A. Klein (eds.), *Stabilising World Commodity Markets*, Lexington Books, Lexington, Mass.

UNCTAD (1976), 'Integrated Program for Commodities', UN Doc ID/RES/93 (IV), Geneva.

UNCTAD (1977), 'Identification of Possible Economic Elements of an International Arrangement on Copper – The Feasibility of Copper Price Stabilisation Using a Buffer Stock as Supply Restrictions', UN Doc ID/IPC/COPPER/AC/L42, Geneva.

APPENDIX: A Model of the World Copper Market

(i) Aggregate Production:

$$PR_t = \alpha_0 + \alpha_1 t + \alpha_2 PR_{t-1} + \alpha_3 CXS_{t-1} + \sum_{i=1}^{41} \alpha_{4i}(\ln LME - \ln USWHP)_{t-i}$$
$$+ \alpha_5 USST_t + \alpha_6 DUM73_t + \text{seasonals}$$

where PR_t = aggregate copper production; CXS_t = cumulated excess supply; LME_t = free market (London Metal Exchange) price of copper; $USWHP_t$ = US wholesale price index; $USST_t$ = US miners' strike dummy (1 in quarter of a strike, 0 elsewhere); $DUM73_t$ = 1 in third and fourth quarters of 1973.

(ii) Aggregate Consumption:

$$CR_t = \beta_0 + \beta_1 t + \beta_2 CR_{t-1} + \sum_{i=0}^{5} \beta_{3i} OEIP_{t-i} + \beta_4(\ln LME^a - \ln ALPP^a)_{t-5}$$
$$+ \beta_5 USST_t + \beta_6 USST_{t-1} + \text{seasonals}$$

where CR_t = aggregate copper consumption; $OEIP_t$ = industrial production index for OECD economies; $ALPP_t$ = aluminium producers price; $\ln X_t^a = \sum_{i=0}^{11} w_i \ln X_{t-i}$ with $w_i = .0625$ for i=0...3,8...11 and $w_i = .125$ for 1=4...7.

(iii) Consumer Stocks:

$$CRS_t = \gamma_0 + \gamma_1 t + \gamma_2 CRS_{t-1} + \gamma_3 CRS_{t-2} + \gamma_4 USINT_t + \gamma_5 \Delta USST_t^e$$
$$+ \gamma_6 \Delta \ln LME_t + \gamma_7 \Delta \ln LME_{t-1} + \text{seasonals}$$

where CRS_t = aggregate stock; $USINT_t$ = US commercial bank prime interest rate; $USST_t^e$ = anticipated U strike dummy (1 in quarter prior to a strike, 0 elsewhere).

(iv) Socialist Countries Net Imports from World Market:

$$SONMR_t = \sigma_0 + \sigma_1 t + \sigma_2 SONMR_{t-1} + \sigma_3 SONMR_{t-2} + \text{seasonals}$$

(v) Identities:

(a) Producers' Stocks = Excess Supply ($AGXS_t$)

$$= PR_t - CR_t - CRS_t - SONMR_t$$

(b) Cummulated Excess Supply $CXS_t = \sum_{i=0}^{3} AGXS_{t-i}$

(vi) Aluminium Price:

$$\ln ALPP_t = \epsilon_0 + \epsilon_1 t + \epsilon_2(\ln ALPP - \ln USENP)_{t-1} + \sum_{i=1}^{5} \epsilon_{3i} USPP_{t-i} + \text{seasonals}$$

where $USPP_t$ = US energy price index; $USPP_t$ = US copper producers' price.

(vii) Copper Prices:

(a) With rational expectations:

$$\begin{aligned}\Delta \ln LME_t = \Phi_0 + \Phi_1 t + .25USINT_{t-1} + \Phi_2 AGXS_{t+1|t} + \Phi_3 AGXS_{t|t-1} \\ + \Phi_4(\ln LME - \ln USWHP)_{t-1} + \Phi_5(\ln LME - \ln USWHP)_{t-4} \\ + \Phi_6 \Delta_4 \ln USWHP_{t-1} + \text{seasonals}\end{aligned}$$

(b) Without rational expectations:

As above but with $\Phi_2^* AGXS_t$ and $\Phi_3^* AGXS_{t-1}$ replacing the terms involving Φ_2 and Φ_3 respectively.

(viii) The Estimates:

The estimates were obtained from quarterly data from 1956–78 using Generalised Instrumental Variables Techniques (GIVE), and were subjected to a range of diagnostic checks (including post sample residual tests, structural stability, identification restrictions, and LM autocorrelation tests).

Table 3. Model Estimates

Equation	Coefficien 0	1	2	3	4	5	6	7
PR	1012.2	7.05	.120	–.139	576.2*	–217.8	–96.8	–
CR	169.9	–2.25	.421	9.02*	–40.7	–66.7	–13.5	–
CRS	–58.5	3.82	.533	–.233	–921.6	.221	–126.5	114.9
SONMR	18.3	–.234	.415	.242	–	–	–	–
ln ALPP	–.118	–.003	–.234	.335*	–	–	–	–
(a) ln LME	1.078	–.020	–.156	–.833	–.482	–.369	3.467	–
(b) ln LME	1.093	–.021	–.344	–.271	–.508	–.492	3.302	–

* The sum of distributed lag coefficients estimated by Almon techniques. Long run price elasticity estimated at the sample mean; of production = .33, and of consumption = –.05.

(a) Rational expectations version

(b) Without rational expectations

PART IV

TRADE ASPECTS

CHAPTER 11

OIL AND THE NORTH–SOUTH TERMS OF TRADE

A. Gonzalez–Romero, *University of Essex and Complutense Madrid University*
S.M.R. Kanbur, *University of Essex and Princeton University*

1. INTRODUCTION

The terms of trade between manufactures and primary commodities have been a major topic of research at least since the inter– war period. Keynes's worries regarding the instability of commodity prices (see his collected works, Vol. XXVII) were supplemented, in the post–Second World War concern with development, with worries about a secular decline in the purchasing power of commodities vis–a–vis manufactures. The classic work here is of course that of Prebisch (1950) and Singer (1950), but the debate about trends in these terms of trade is as lively as ever (see, for example, Spraos (1980)). In the 1970s the case for a New International Economic Order saw the manufactures/ commodities terms of trade problem as being a problem of the North–South terms of trade (Brandt (1980)). But the oil price shocks of the mid and late 1970s, after the initial euphoria about 'commodity power' had subsided, forced a distinction between the oil producers and the (poorer) countries of the world selling other commodities. The 'South' is of course defined to exclude the oil rich countries, and is seen as having suffered particularly badly from the oil price hikes. A new dimension is thus added to the determination of the North–South terms of trade – the price of oil. The recent dramatic falls in the price of oil further emphasise the need for such an analysis.

The object of this paper is thus to analyse the impact of the price of oil on the terms of trade between North and South. The existing literature is characterised by two main approaches to the problem. The first approach is one of employing large models of the world economy, with high degrees of disaggregation, to simulate the impact of an increase in the price of oil (see, for example, papers in Hickman (1983)). The second approach is one of using a small model with a minimum of disaggregation in order to derive analytical expressions for the effects of changes in the price of oil – see Taylor

O. Guvenen (ed.), International Commodity Market Models and Policy Analysis, 207–219.

(1981) and Adams and Marquez (1983). The present paper is a contribution to this second strand of the literature. It is an attempt at a tractable representation of the world economy in terms of a model which is nevertheless rich enough to enable some interesting questions to be asked.

The plan of the paper is as follows. Section 2 presents a three regional model of the world economy with full employment. One of the regions specialises in the production of oil while the other two, North and South, specialise in manufactures and primary commodities, respectively. The impact of the price of oil on the North–South terms of trade are seen to depend crucially on the supply responses in the two regions, which is not surprising in a world of fully employed resources. Section 3 moves closer to the spirit of 'structuralist' models of Taylor (1983) and Kanbur and Vines (1984), by introducing wage rigidity and Keynesian unemployment in the North. The effective demand consequences of a change in the price of oil are now seen to be crucial. Section 4 concludes the paper.

2. A NEOCLASSICAL THREE REGION MODEL

We suppose that the North specialises in the production of a single commodity, 'steel', which is produced using labour and oil. The two inputs are required in fixed proportions; the per unit requirement of labour for this industrial product is denoted by ℓ_I, and the per unit oil (or resource) requirement by a_{RI}. The South also specialises in the production of a single commodity, 'corn', and this agricultural commodity also requires labour and oil in fixed proportions in production, the coefficients being ℓ_A and a_{RA}, respectively. Competitive pricing in both North and South gives the following price equations

$$p_I = w_I \ell_I + p_R a_{RI} \quad (1)$$

$$p_A = w_A \ell_A + p_R a_{RA} \quad (2)$$

where p_I, p_A, and p_R are the prices of steel, corn, and oil, respectively, and w_I and w_A are the wages in the two regions. We are thus abstracting from capital requirements, the introduction of which causes no problems in principle, but would reduce the tractability of the model.

This description of production in the two regions differs from that of Chichilnisky (1981) in excluding capital and assuming specialisation. It differs from the model of Findlay (1980) in excluding capital, in assuming fixed coefficients and in assuming a neoclassical South (whereas in the Findlay models it operates as a Lewisian dual economy). Of course the major difference between our model and those of Chichilnisky and Findlay is that we introduce oil as an intermediate input, thereby enabling us to ask and answer questions which cannot be asked in the other two models. The special assumptions we have introduced, in order to maintain tractability, is the price that has to be paid in return.

The production of oil is assumed to be costless – the introduction of such costs would be a routine exercise that would not illuminate the analysis. The entire revenue from oil is spent, a proportion α_R on corn, and the remaining $1-\alpha_R$ on steel. A similar proportional expenditure demand system is assumed for the other two regions – labour income here is entirely spent (profits are zero). A fraction $\alpha_A(\alpha_I)$ of labour income is spent on corn by workers in the South (North) and the remaining $1-\alpha_A(1-\alpha_I)$ is spent on steel.

Finally, we model labour supply in the two regions as depending on the real wage. With nominal wage in the North (South) at $w_I(w_A)$, and the ideal cost of living index for the proportional expenditure system being $p_A^{\alpha_I} p_I^{1-\alpha_I}\left[p_A^{\alpha_A} p_I^{1-\alpha_A}\right]$, the real wage is given by $w_I/p_A^{\alpha_I} p_I^{1-\alpha_I}\left[w_A/p_A^{\alpha_A} p_I^{1-\alpha_A}\right]$. We assume a constant elasticity labour supply function in the two regions, so that labour supply in the North (L_I) and labour supply in the South (L_A) are given by[2]

$$L_I = \beta_0\left[w_I/p_A^{\alpha_I} p_I^{1-\alpha_I}\right]^{\beta_1} \tag{3}$$

$$L_A = \gamma_0\left[w_A/p_A^{\alpha_A} p_I^{1-\alpha_A}\right]^{\gamma_1} \tag{4}$$

Denoting steel output by Q_I and corn output by Q_A, the labour market equilibrium conditions are given by

$$\ell_I Q_I = L_I \tag{5}$$

$$\ell_A Q_A = L_A \tag{6}$$

The three market clearing equations for steel, corn, and oil, are, respectively:

$$Q_I = w_I \ell_I Q_I\left[\frac{1-\alpha_I}{p_I}\right] + w_A \ell_A Q_A\left[\frac{1-\alpha_A}{p_I}\right] + p_R Q_R\left[\frac{1-\alpha_R}{p_I}\right] \tag{7}$$

$$Q_A = w_I \ell_I Q_I\left[\frac{\alpha_I}{p_A}\right] + w_A \ell_A Q_A\left[\frac{\alpha_A}{p_A}\right] + p_R Q_R\left[\frac{\alpha_R}{p_A}\right] \tag{8}$$

$$Q_R = a_{RI} Q_I = a_{RA} Q_A \tag{9}$$

where Q_R is the quantity of oil supplied and equation (9) says that this is equal to the intermediate input demand for oil from steel and corn production.

Equations (1) – (9) represent our three region model of global interaction. The variables of the model are p_I, p_R, p_A, w_A, w_I, L_A, L_I, Q_I, Q_A, Q_R. Moreover, inspection of (7), (8), and (9) shows that they are linearly dependent, so that we have a system of eight independent equations in ten unknowns. Now it can be checked that the system (1) – (9) is homogeneous of degree zero in p_I, p_R, p_A, w_I and w_A. We will normalise by setting $p_A = 1$, so that all prices and wages are measured in terms of corn, but this still leaves us eight independent equations in nine unknowns. Thus, if one of the unknowns is fixed exogenously, the eight equations will determine the eight unknowns. The procedure we adopt is of fixing p_R and determining the other unknowns. The assumption, then, is that oil producers fix the price of oil and supply whatever is demanded. Our interest is in investigating how changes in p_R influence p_I (which measures the North–South terms of trade when $p_A = 1$).

To solve the model, substitute (8) and (9) into (7) to give

$$Q_I[1 - w_I \ell_I \frac{(1-\alpha_I)}{p_I} - a_{RI} \frac{p_R}{p_I} (1-\alpha_R)]$$
$$= Q_A[w_A \ell_A \frac{(1-\alpha_A)}{p_I} + a_{RA} \frac{p_R}{p_I} (1-\alpha_R)] \tag{10}$$

The left hand side is the supply of steel after Northern workers' demands, and that part of oil producers' steel demand which arises from oil sales to the North, have been netted out. The right hand side is just the Southern workers' demand for steel and that part of oil producers' demand which arises from oil sales the the South. Using (1) and (2) in (10) we get

$$Q_I\left[\alpha_I + a_{RI} \frac{p_R}{p_I} (\alpha_R - \alpha_I)\right] = Q_A\left[(1-\alpha_A) \frac{p_A}{p_I} + a_{RA} \frac{p_R}{p_I} (\alpha_A - \alpha_R)\right] \tag{11}$$

From now on we apply the normalisation $p_A = 1$. Substituting for Q_I and Q_A from (5) and (6), for L_I and L_A from (3) and (4), and for w_I from (1) and (2), we get an expression which implicitly solves for p_I:

$$(\beta_o/\gamma_o)\ell_I^{-(1+\beta_1)} \ell_A^{(1+\gamma_1)} (1-a_{RA}p_R)^{-\gamma_1} \times$$
$$(p_I - a_{RI}p_R)^{\beta_1} p_I^{[\gamma_1(1-\alpha_A)-\beta_1(1-\alpha_I)]} = \frac{[1-\alpha_A] + a_{RA}p_R[\alpha_A - \alpha_R]}{\alpha_I p_I + a_{RI}p_R[\alpha_R - \alpha_I]} \tag{12}$$

Taking logarithms of both sides of (12) and differentiating with respect to p_I shows that while the right hand side is decreasing in p_I the left hand side is increasing in p_I. Hence, a solution to (12) exists and is unique (for further details see Gonzalez–Romero (1985)). Given the solution for p_I we can solve for w_I and w_A from (1) and (2), then for L_I and L_A from (3) and (4), and finally for Q_I, Q_A, and Q_R from (5), (6), and thence (9). We can now ask various comparative static questions about the impact of the price of oil on the equilibrium values of the endogenous variables.

Does an increase in the price of oil improve the Northern terms of trade vis–a–vis the South, or worsen them? Differentiating (12) with respect to p_R, and after some manipulation, we get

$$\left\{\frac{\beta_1}{p_I-a_{RI}p_R}+\frac{\gamma_1(1-\alpha_A)-\beta_1(1-\alpha_I)}{p_I}+\frac{\alpha_I}{\alpha_I p_I+a_{RI}p_R(\alpha_R-\alpha_I)}\right\}\frac{dp_I}{dp_R}$$
$$=\frac{\beta_1 a_{RI}}{p_I-a_{RI}p_R}-\frac{\gamma_1 a_{RA}}{1-a_{RA}p_R}+\frac{a_{RA}(\alpha_A-\alpha_R)}{(1-\alpha_A)+a_{RA}p_R(\alpha_A-\alpha_R)}-\frac{a_{RI}(\alpha_R-\alpha_I)}{\alpha_I p_I+a_{RI}p_R(\alpha_R-\alpha_I)} \tag{13}$$

Notice that $\beta_1/(p_I-a_{RI}p_R) > \beta_1(1-\alpha_I)/p_I$, so that the term in curly brackets on the left hand side of (13) is positive. Hence, the sign of dp_I/dp_R depends entirely on the right hand side of (13).

The response of the North–South terms of trade to a change in the price of oil is thus seen to depend on a complex set of supply and demand side factors. While the general expression (13) is useful, we need further simplification to gain insight. Let us first of all make the simplest assumption, of identical consumption preferences. Then we get the following proposition:

If $\alpha_A = \alpha_R = \alpha_I$,

$$\frac{dp_I}{dp_R} \lesseqgtr 0 \text{ according as } \beta_1 0_1 \lesseqgtr \gamma_1 0_A \tag{14}$$

where

$$0_I = \frac{a_{RI}p_R}{p_I-a_{RI}p_R}$$

$$0_A = \frac{a_{RA}p_R}{1-a_{RA}p_R}$$

Thus if the supply elasticity of labour and/or the ratio of the fuel bill to the wage bill is large in the North relative to the South, then the Northern terms of trade will improve. But if we suppose that ϕ_I is equal to ϕ_A, then the conventional assumption that $\gamma_1 > \beta_1$ (because of 'surplus labour' in the South) will give us the result that an increase in the price of oil will worsen Northern terms of trade vis–a–vis the South. To see the intuition behind this, take the extreme assumption that $\beta_1 = 0$. Then Northern output of steel remains unchanged and the increase in the price of oil is a straight transfer of spending power from the workers of the North to the oil producers. But with the assumption of identical demand patterns ($\alpha_R = \alpha_I$) this has no impact on the demand for steel. Similarly, if Southern output were to remain constant, the assumption $\alpha_A = \alpha_R$ would ensure that there was no change in the demand for steel through this channel. However, with $\gamma_1 > 0$ Southern output does fall and the world demand for steel falls with it. There is now excess supply in the steel market and given Walrasian stability (which, it can be shown, is the same as the term in the curly brackets on the left hand side of (13) being positive) the price of steel will fall. If the assumption $\phi_I = \phi_A$ is relaxed then the result is ambiguous. A priori we would expect manufactures to be relatively energy intensive, i.e., $\phi_I > \phi_A$, so that this factor would tend to improve Northern terms of trade vis–a–vis the South.

Of course the assumption that $\alpha_A = \alpha_R = \alpha_I$ is very special. A more plausible assumption would be $\alpha_A > \alpha_R > \alpha_I$, so that the expenditure proportion on corn (which can be thought of as 'necessities') is greatest in the low income countries of the South and least in the advanced countries of the North, with the oil producers taking the middle place. As can be seen from (13), with this general specification of demand the sign of dp_I/dp_R is ambiguous. However, if we simplify be setting $\beta_1 = \gamma_1 = 0$ then it can be shown that

$$\frac{dp_I}{dp_R} \lesseqgtr 0 \text{ according as } p_I \lesseqgtr \frac{(1-\alpha_A)}{\alpha_I} \frac{(\alpha_R-\alpha_I)}{(\alpha_A-\alpha_R)} \frac{a_{RI}}{a_{RA}} \tag{15}$$

The intuition behind these can be developed from (11). Since $\beta_1 = \gamma_1 = 0$, both Q_I and Q_A are constant. An increase in the price of oil increases the net supply of steel (since the increase in p_R leads to a transfer of income from the North to the oil producing region, i.e., from a region with a high propensity to consume steel to a region with a low propensity to consume steel). But an increase in the price of oil also increases the demand for steel as shown in the right hand side of (11), since income is transferrèd from the South to the oil producing region. If the income transfer from the South to the oil region is large enough, relative to the income transfer from the North to the oil region then the world demand for steel will fall and Northern terms of trade will tend to deteriorate. Similarly, for a given transfer from both regions to the oil region, if the differential impact on steel demand is much larger for the South/oil region transfer than for the North/oil region transfer, i.e., $\alpha_A - \alpha_R << \alpha_R - \alpha_I$, then Northern terms of trade will again tend to deteriorate. The net effect depends, therefore, on how 'close' the consumption preferences of the oil region are to the preferences of the North or of the South. If $\alpha_R = \alpha_I$ is a plausible assumption, then in this full employment world Northern terms of trade will tend to improve.

If the supply elasticities are not zero, or the demand parameters α_A, α_R, and α_I are not equal to each other, then the situation is more complex and a clear cut result is less likely. However, we can establish the following proposition:

$$\alpha_A > \alpha_R > \alpha_I \,;\quad \gamma_1 < \frac{1 - a_{RA}p_R}{\dfrac{1-\alpha_A}{\alpha_A-\alpha_R} + a_{RA}p_R} \,;\ \beta_1 > \frac{\alpha_R-\alpha_I}{\alpha_I} \tag{16}$$

$$\rightarrow \frac{dp_I}{dp_R} > 0$$

Thus, a large elasticity of supply in the North and a small elasticity of output supply in the South are seen to favour an improvement in the North's terms of trade when the price of oil increases.

This brings us to the conclusion of the 'neoclassical' analysis of oil and the terms of trade. The expressions we derive highlight the parameters that will be crucial in determining comparative static results (for other exercises see Gonzalez–Romero (1985)). However, while the analysis is complicated, the overall impression is that such full employment analysis tends not to generate for us, under plausible assumptions, a deterioration in the South's terms of trade vis–a–vis the North when the price of oil goes up. In fact, the assumptions which produce this result – particularly those on the supply side – tend to be in opposition to the stylised facts. We now turn to an alternative framework of analysis to see if that can produce a more plausible scenario.

3. A STRUCTURALIST THREE REGION MODEL

It has been argued by Taylor (1983) and others that the full employment framework is not an appropriate one in which to study global interactions. Keynesian rigidities in Northern economies mean that involuntary unemployment is a prominent feature, and that the effective demand consequences of any change have to be taken into account. Kanbur and Vines (1984) have applied a North–South model of this structuralist' variety to analyse the benefits from commodity price stabilisation schemes. In this section we extend the analysis of Taylor (1983) and Kanbur–Vines (1984) by introducing oil as an intermediate input, and the oil producing region as a source of demand. In fact, the model we study is a variant of that in Taylor (1981).

As in the previous section, the North is assumed to specialise in the production of steel, using labour and oil. But now the North is a 'fix–price' economy with excess capacity. The price of steel is determined by a stable markup over variable cost:

$$p_I = (1+\pi)(a_{RI}p_R+\ell_I\overline{w}_I) \tag{17}$$

where π is the markup rate and $\overline{w}_I$ is the fixed money wage in the North. The South specialises in the production of corn using labour and oil under competitive conditions, so that we have the pricing equation

$$p_A = a_{RA}p_R + \ell_A w_A \tag{18}$$

While the output of steel will be determined by effective demand, the output of corn is determined by supply – indeed, we simplify matters by assuming this supply to be fixed. The price of corn will then adjust to clear the market for corn.

Turning to the demand side, we assume propensities to spend out of income of c_A for the South and c_I for the North. Profits and wages are not distinguished for this purpose; although it would be relatively straightforward to introduce this complication it will not add greatly to the analysis. The oil region's propensity to consume is denoted by c_R. Out of total consumption, each region is assumed to spend a given fraction on corn and the rest on steel. As in the previous section, let the proportion of consumption expenditure allocated to corn be α_A, α_R, and α_I in the three regions. On top of these consumption demands, we assume autonomous demand for steel in the North of G.. This can be interpreted as investment, or a combination of investment and government expenditure.

With this specification, we can write the equilibrium conditions for the markets in steel, corn, and oil as follows:

$$Q_I = c_I(1-\alpha_I)(p_I-a_{RI}p_R)Q_I/p_I + G + c_A(1-\alpha_A)(p_A-a_{RA}p_R)Q_A/p_I$$

$$+ c_R(1-\alpha_R)p_R(Q_R/p_I) \tag{19}$$

$$Q_A = c_I\alpha_I(p_I-a_{RI}p_R)Q_A/p_A + c_A\alpha_A(p_A-a_{RA}p_R)Q_A/p_A$$

$$+ c_R\alpha_R p_R(Q_R/p_A) \tag{20}$$

$$Q_R = a_{RI}Q_I + a_{RA}Q_A \tag{21}$$

Given p_R, $\overline{w}_I$ and hence p_I, and Q_A these three equations determine Q_I, p_A, and Q_R. We are particularly interested in Northern output and the North–South terms of trade. Substituting (21) into (19) and (20) and solving the resulting pair of equations in Q_I and p_A gives us, after some manipulation:

$$Q_I = \frac{G + a_{RA} \frac{p_R}{p_I} \cdot \frac{Q_A}{1-c_A\alpha_A} \psi_1}{\frac{1}{1-c_A\alpha_A} \{\psi_2 + a_{RI}(p_R/p_I)\psi_3\}} \tag{22}$$

$$\frac{p_A}{p_I} = \frac{G[c_I\alpha_I + a_{RI} \frac{p_R}{p_I}(c_R\alpha_R - c_I\alpha_I)] + a_{RA} \frac{p_R}{p_I} Q_A\psi_4 + a_R \frac{p_R}{p_I} a_{RA} \frac{p_R}{p_I} Q_A\psi_5}{Q_A(\psi_2 + a_{RI} \frac{p_R}{p_I} \psi_3)} \tag{23}$$

where

$$\psi_1 = c_R(1-\alpha_R) - c_A(1-\alpha_A) - c_Rc_A(\alpha_A-\alpha_R)$$

$$\psi_2 = [1-c_I(1-\alpha_I)](1-c_A\alpha_A) - c_I\alpha_Ic_A(1-\alpha_A)\ ; \quad \psi_2 > 0 \text{ always}$$

$$\psi_3 = c_I(1-\alpha_I) - c_R(1-\alpha_R) - c_A[c_I(\alpha_A-\alpha_I) - c_R(\alpha_A-\alpha_R)]$$

$$\psi_4 = c_R\alpha_R - c_A\alpha_A - c_I[c_A(\alpha_A-\alpha_I) - c_R(\alpha_R-\alpha_I)]$$

$$\psi_5 = c_R\alpha_R(c_I-c_A) - c_I\alpha_I(c_R-c_A) - c_A\alpha_A(c_I-c_R)$$

While complicated, expressions (22) and (23) are in fact exact generalisations of the corresponding expressions in the tworegion model of Kanbur and Vines (1984). Thus, if $a_{RA} = a_{RI} = 0$, equations (22) and (23) collapse to equations (5) and (6) in the Kanbur–Vines paper. As in Kanbur–Vines, it can also be shown that the Northern multiplier when terms of trade repercussions are suppressed is smaller than when they are not. The new feature here, and the feature we wish to concentrate on, is the price of oil.[2]

How does a change in the price of oil affect Northern output and the North–South terms of trade? Differentiating (22) and (23) with respect to p_R we get

$$\frac{dQ_I}{dp_R} = \tag{24}$$

$$\frac{\frac{d(p_R/p_I)}{dp_R}\left[\frac{a_{RA}Q_A}{1-c_A\alpha_A}\right]\cdot\psi_1\psi_6\,\frac{1}{1-c_A\alpha_A} - a_{RI}\psi_3\,\frac{1}{1-c_A\alpha_A}(G+a_{RA}\,\frac{p_R}{p_I}\,\frac{Q_A}{1-c_A\alpha_A}\,\psi_1)\Big]}{\frac{1}{1-c_A\alpha_A}\,\psi_6^2}$$

$$\frac{d(p_A/p_I)}{dp_R} = \frac{d(p_R/p_I)}{dp_R}\ \ x$$

$$\frac{[Ga_{RI}(c_R\alpha_R-c_I\alpha_I) + a_{RA}Q_A\psi_4 + \frac{d(p_R/p_I)}{dp_R}\cdot a_{RI}a_{RA}Q_A\psi_5]\cdot\psi_6Q_A}{Q_A^2\ \psi_6^2}$$

$$-\frac{\frac{d(p_R/p_I)}{dp_R}\cdot a_{RI}Q_A\psi_3\ \cdot\ (\text{numerator of }(p_A/p_I))}{Q_A^2\ \psi_6^2} \tag{25}$$

where

$$\psi_6 = \psi_2 + a_{RI}(p_R/p_I)\psi_3 > 0$$

Clearly the expressions in (24) and (25) are extremely complicated, reflecting the myriad of interacting factors that influence the result. But some insight can nevertheless be obtained with perseverance. Thus, we know from the definition of p_I that

$$\frac{d(p_R/p_I)}{dp_R} = \frac{p_I - a_{RI}p_R(1+\pi)}{p_I^2} > 0$$

from which it follows that the sign of (24) is determined by the sign of the term in square brackets. Moreover, using the positivity of ψ_6 we can derive the proposition that

$$\psi_1 < 0 \ \text{ and } \ \psi_3 > 0 \rightarrow \frac{dQ_I}{dp_R} < 0$$

$$\tag{26}$$

$$\psi_1 > 0 \ \text{ and } \ \psi_3 < 0 \rightarrow \frac{dQ_I}{dp_R} > 0$$

Similarly, from (25) we can derive

$$c_R\alpha_R < c_I\alpha_I,\ \psi_4 < 0,\ \psi_5 < 0,\ \psi_3 > 0 \rightarrow \frac{d(p_A/p_I)}{dp_R} < 0$$

$$c_R\alpha_R > c_I\alpha_I,\ \psi_4 > 0,\ \psi_5 > 0,\ \psi_3 < 0 \rightarrow \frac{d(p_A/p_I)}{dp_R} > 0 \qquad (27)$$

To develop some intuition behind these propositions, let us first of all assume that $\alpha_A = \alpha_R = \alpha_I$. Then (26) and (27) collapse to

$$c_R < c_A,\ c_R < c_I \rightarrow \frac{dQ_I}{dp_R} < 0$$

$$c_R > c_A,\ c_R > c_I \rightarrow \frac{dQ_I}{dp_R} > 0 \qquad (28)$$

$$c_R < c_A,\ c_R < c_I \rightarrow \frac{d(p_A/p_I)}{dp_R} < 0$$

$$c_R > c_A,\ c_R > c_I \rightarrow \frac{d(p_A/p_I)}{dp_R} > 0 \qquad (29)$$

In other words, assuming identical demand patterns in the world, if the oil region's propensity to consume out of income is below that of the North and of the South, then an increase in the price of oil will induce a recession in the North *and* lead to a worsening of the South's terms of trade. The intuition behind this result is obvious. Given the demand assumptions the transfer of income from the non–oil regions to the oil region leads to an excess supply in the market for steel and for corn. Given that the steel market adjusts by quantity changes and the corn market adjusts by price changes, the recession in the North and the worsening of Southern terms of trade follows.

The above argument gives us the clue as to how the model works, and the relevance of the demand side requirements in (26) and (27). The key issue is whether, at given Q_I and p_A, the reallocation of income that an increase in p_R brings about will lead to excess supply or excess demand in the markets for steel or corn. The previous argument was based on assumptions which led to excess supply in both markets given the oil region's low propensity to consume out of its newly acquired income. If the propensity to spend on steel out of total consumption is higher in the oil region than in either of the other two regions, then this further reallocation would exacerbate the excess supply in the market for corn but mitigate the excess supply in the market for steel. The recession in the North would be less severe, but the deterioration in the South's terms of trade would be worse. If the consumption proportions are in the relation $\alpha_A > \alpha_R > \alpha_I$, as assumed in the previous section, the net impact of income reallocation is ambiguous.

Another important feature which this argument illustrates is that the interests of the North and South are in conflict with each other, at least if these are measured by Northern output and Southern terms of trade. Depending on the oil region's consumption preferences vis–a–vis the outputs of the two regions, for a given total reduction in world demand the depth of recession in the North is inversely related to the deterioration in Southern terms of trade.

4. CONCLUSION

It has been argued that the oil price rises of the 1970s, while affecting all non–oil producers adversely, had a worse affect on the poor countries of the South than on the industrialised countries of the North. In this paper we have attempted to explore this argument in the context of a specific measure, the North–South terms of trade. We develope and explore the impact of oil prices on the North–South terms of trade in two alternative frameworks, neoclassical and structuralist. While the three region models of global interaction investigated here lead to some intractabilities, simplifications can nevertheless provide insights. The two types of models emphasise different aspects of responses to an oil price increase. The neoclassical model emphasises supply elasticities, while the structuralist model emphasises the reallocation of effective demand within the world economy. The latter is capable of generating for us, under plausible assumptions, a recession in the North as well as a deterioration in the South's terms of trade vis–a–vis the North as the consequence of an oil price increase. This seems to represent the stylised facts of the response of the world economy after OPEC I and OPEC II. The neoclassical model cannot, of course, generate recessions, but its predictions on the terms of trade are ambiguous and do not necessarily, under plausible assumptions, imply a deterioration in the South's terms of trade.

NOTES

1) The choice–theoretic foundations of these equations cannot lie in the proportional expenditure system extended to include leisure, since that implies a constant labour supply. Rather, we have to assume further that the reservation real wage has a distribution in the population which generates supply functions (3) and (4).

See Gonzalez–Romero (1985).

2) We are also assuming positive solutions to exist, and that the equilibrium is stable. For a detailed treatment of these issues, see Gonzalez–Romero (1985).

REFERENCES

Adams, G. and J. Marquez (1983), 'The Impact of Petroleum and Commodity Prices in a Model of the World Economy', in B. Hickman (ed.), *Global International Economic Models*, North–Holland, Amsterdam.

Brandt, W. (1980), *North–South: A Programme for Survival*, Pan Books, London.

Chichilnisky, G. (1981), 'Terms of Trade and Domestic Distribution: Export–led Growth with Abundant Labour', *Journal of Development Economics*, 8, pp. 163–92.

Findlay, R. (1980), 'The Terms of Trade and Equilibrium Growth in the World Economy', *American Economic Review*, 70, pp. 291–99.

Gonzalez–Romero, A. (1985), 'North–South–OPEC: A Theoretical Analysis of Three Region Models of Global Interaction', unpublished Ph.D. thesis, University of Essex.

Hickman, B. (ed.) (1983), *Global International Economic Models*, North–Holland, Amsterdam.

Kanbur, S.M.R. and D. Vines (1986), 'North–South Interaction and Commodity Control', *Journal of Development Economics*, 22, pp. 371–87.

Keynes, J.M. (1981), *The Collected Works of J.M. Keynes, Vol. XXVII*, MacMillan, London.

Prebisch, R. (1950), 'The Economic Development of Latin America and its Principal Problems', *Economic Bulletin for Latin America, 1962* (first published as a booklet in 1950).

Singer, H. (1950), 'The Distribution of Gains Between Investing and Borrowing Countries', *American Economic Review*, 40, pp. 473–85.

Spraos, J. (1980), 'The Statistical Debate on the Net Barter Terms of Trade Between Primary Commodities and Manufactures', *Economic Journal*, 90, pp. 107–28.

Taylor, L. (1981), 'South–North Trade and Southern Growth', *Journal of International Economics*, 11, pp. 589–602.

Taylor, L. (1983), *Structuralist Macroeconomics*, Basic Books, New York.

CHAPTER 12

MODELLING COMMODITY PRICES IN A WORLD MACROECONOMIC MODEL

G.H. Holtham*, *OECD, Paris, France*

INTRODUCTION

This paper describes work in progress to endogenise commodity prices in the OECD's world macro–model INTERLINK. Part I gives the purpose of the work and an overview of the model and describes the modelling strategy. Part II gives results of empirical work on commodity price equations. Long run properties of estimated equations are reported, together with short run forecast performance. Simulation testing of the full model system incorporating the equations is still in progress at the time of writing and only preliminary results are available.

PART I. COMMODITY PRICES IN INTERLINK

1. INTERLINK AND ITS USES

INTERLINK consists of 23 country models and eight sub–models of non–OECD zones grouped around a trade model. Trade is disaggregated into five categories, with separate equations and accounting for imports and exports of: manufactured goods, services, food, energy, and other raw materials. Imports are determined by domestic demand and relative prices, and the model ensures globally consistent exports. Unit value equations for exports treat exporters as monopolistic competitors setting prices on the basis of domestic costs and the prices of competitors. Export prices are then translated by the model into a consistent set of import prices for all goods. For a single country in the model, therefore, import prices, at least in dollars, are exogenous though endogenous to the system as a whole.

The country models are fairly standard macroeconomic models of an income-expenditure type. For the larger OECD countries they are econometrically estimated incorporating money demand and supply relations and a real supply side. The latter

O. Guvenen (ed.), International Commodity Market Models and Policy Analysis, 221–258.

includes consistent factor–demand equations derived from an aggregate production function and has all price deflators determined in a behavioural wage/price system reflecting capacity utilisation. Price linkages are discussed below. For the smaller OECD countries the models are simpler and frequently have imposed coefficients, set so as to approximately reproduce the properties of models maintained in the country concerned.

For the non–OECD zones the models are extremely simple, merely determining imports as a function of available finance, the latter being determined by lagged foreign exchange earnings (exports) plus any change in net credit availability.

Different countries and zones in the model are linked by consistent capital flows as well as by trade and this permits seventeen exchange rates to be endogenously determined.[2]

The model is used for two purposes. One is to ensure the international consistency of the OECD's twice yearly forecast. The model is 'locked' on to baseline forecasts produced by country specialists, through the calculation of relevant addfactors. It is then solved to get an internationally coherent forecast taking all linkages into account. A baseline forecast of commodity prices is made 'off–model' and is used to inform forecasts of export unit values for food and raw materials of the OECD and non–OECD. The model locks on these too by calculation of necessary add–factors. Energy prices are dealt with by 'technical assumption' in the forecast – they are normally assumed to remain unchanged. The present work does not encompass energy prices.

The second purpose of the model is simulation analysis, particularly of policy changes. Clearly, the impact of changes in OECD activity and inflation on world commodity prices and their feedback on the OECD economy is an important linkage mechanism in a world model. In the past versions of INTERLINK it was dealt with by specifying export unit values for food and raw materials as functions of OECD GDP at constant prices and of OECD inflation. The equations were identical for all countries and non–OECD regions. Other explanatory variables or empirically based dynamics were lacking.

The inadequacy of that approach became evident some time ago. A number of academic commentators have come to assign an increasing importance to commodities in the world economy. A 'hog cycle' of commodity prices whereby supply and investment respond negatively to low prices, ensuring higher prices later at any swift increase of world demand, has been alleged to be an important source of glocal economic instability.[2] The steep decline of commodity prices in recent years has also been credited with the major role in slowing OECD inflation.[3] The debt crisis affecting many less developed countries who are primary product exporters has made their terms of trade (and hence the level of real commodity prices) a matter of concern for OECD policy makers and the effect of OECD policies on them has become an urgent topic of analysis.

2. THE STRATEGY FOR ENDOGENISING COMMODITY PRICES

The aim was to endogenise commodity prices in INTERLINK as simply and economically as possible, permitting simulation analysis of such issues. It is evident from those issues that the focus was very aggregate and macroeconomic. The operation of individual commodity markets or their stabilisation was not the focus of concern. The essential task was to get some quantitative indication of how commodity prices as a set interact with the world economy in broad terms. This is clearly work where a world model is necessary. Commodity prices are likely to remain substantially exogenous in even the largest national macro model. Furthermore, refined models of individual commodity markets in all their institutional detail will miss out the feedback effects of those commodity prices on the world economy.[4]

The approach followed was to model a series of 'world' prices for groups of commodities. A reduced form equation for each price was derived from a simple theoretical model of a storable commodity market. Commodities have been grouped into four sets: agricultural raw materials, food, metals and minerals, and tropical beverages. Price indices for these groups of commodities, determined in a separate block of the model, are then passed to the models for different countries and zones in the system. The 'world' prices become explanatory variables in the export unit value equations of individual countries. The trade model transmits the effect of commodity price variations into import prices. Domestic wage/price blocks further transmit them into domestic costs and prices. These in aggregate influence the commodity price equations directly and the circle is complete. Figure 1 is a flow chart showing the main influences in the model.

The specification and estimation of the reduced form commodity price equations are dealt with in the next section. They are linked to the rest of the model by certain aggregate variables for OECD activity, inflation and monetary conditions which enter them as explanatory variables. Three remaining parts of the linkage system remain to be described in a little more detail here:

a) The influence of commodity prices on export unit values;
b) The effect of export unit values on import prices;
c) The influence of import prices on domestic prices and costs and thence on commodity prices in further rounds of reaction.

a) For OECD countries export unit value equations are estimated for raw materials in which the indices for prices of agricultural raw materials and minerals and metals

Figure 1

INTERLINK TRADE AND FINANCIAL LINKAGES

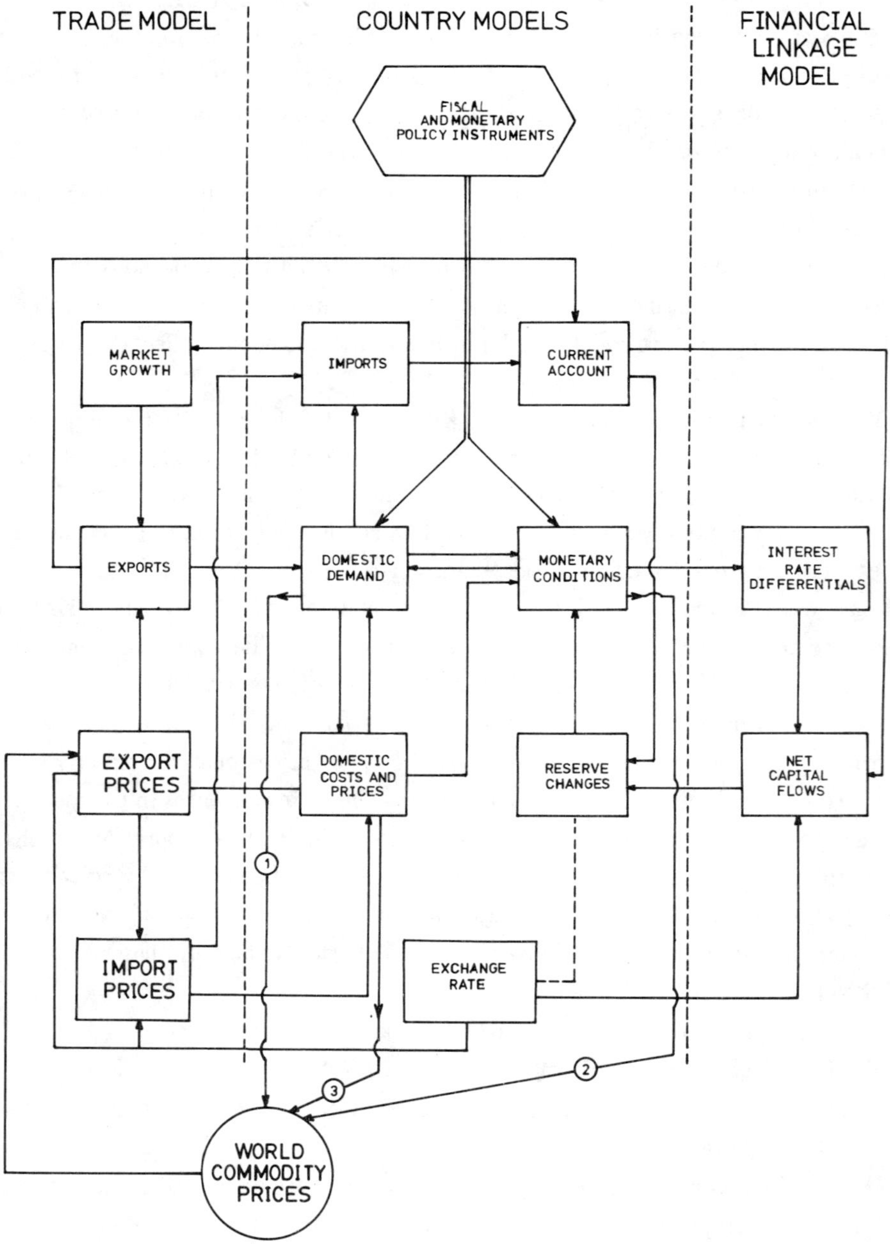

enter as explanatory variables. Unit value equations for food exports use the world food price index. Domestic costs, usually proxied by a distributed lag in the GDP deflator, are the other explanatory variable in both sets of equations.[5]

In principle, if commodity prices are indeed equilibrium prices for approximately homogeneous commodities (as the implicit commodity price models imply), the export unit values for individual countries should simply be distributed lag functions of the world prices where the lags are generated because some trade is according to contracts reflecting past spot prices. There are, however, a number of reasons why the relationship may be looser between commodity price indices and export unit values.

One is the possibility of some product differentiation on the basis of quality differentials or security of supply. Probably more important is the question of coverage. There will not in general be an identically weighted set of commodities in the exports of any country and in the world price index. Unit values in any case use a current, variable, weighting scheme unlike that of the world price indices which have fixed weights. This means unit values will generally be less volatile than world prices. Data limitations mean a strict accounting relationship between world prices and export unit values of individual countries cannot be established and a looser regression based relationship is used.

Given the discrepancies between economic–theoretic concepts and the data actually used, relatively few restrictions were imposed on the equations for export unit values. The specification adopted, however, does not allow the growth of raw material export unit values to diverge indefinitely from the growth of the commodity price indices. It does not constrain the relative levels of the two measures to any particular value; in general the ratio will be a function of the average rate of commodity price inflation and, where domestic costs are significant in the export unit value equation, of the domestic inflation rate.

b) Export prices are translated into import prices by the INTERLINK trade model according to the formula:

$$\%\Delta PM_{jk} = g(L)\sum_{i} w_{ijk}^{t-1}\ \%\Delta PX_{ik} + \lambda[\%\Delta PGDP/\%\Delta WPGDP],\ \ \lambda = 0.1$$

where:

PX_{ik} = export unit value of country i, US dollar index for goods in class k,
PM_{jk} = import price of country j, US dollar index for goods in class k,
w_{ijk}^{t-1} = market share weights as of previous periods for k goods
$g(L)$ = distributed lag function,
PGDP = domestic cost variable, GDP deflator in country j, local currency,

WPGDP = world cost variable, OECD GDP deflator in dollars divided by the exchange rate of country j.

c) Import prices affect domestic inflation via several channels in the larger country models of INTERLINK. The deflator for each expenditure aggregate is modelled separately; import prices as well as domestic producer prices enter each such equation. The coefficient on import prices reflects the direct import content of that expenditure aggregate (e.g. generally higher in the case of private consumption than in the case of government consumption). Domestic producer prices are derived from the cost dual of a three factor production function and reflect unit costs of labour, 'normal' capital, and energy. They are also influenced by import prices as the prices and margins of domestic suppliers reflect import competition. Energy prices in any country model depend on trade energy prices and government policy rules which are both treated as exogenous. The energy price does not directly enter value added deflators but affects domestic producer prices, which are derived from a pseudo gross output measure (value added plus energy inputs). As energy is a substitute for capital and labour in production an increase (decrease) in its price leads to greater (less) demand for labour and/or capital at a given output level raising (lowering) the price of these factors. (The fact that such a price change also alters world demand and the output level is a considerable complication.) Energy prices therefore affect domestic costs through factor substitution as well as entering expenditure deflators directly through the direct imported energy content of the latter. No doubt a substitution effect exists in the case of raw materials inputs too but this is not explicitly modelled. Nonetheless, if imported commodity prices rise, this feeds into wage and capital costs via its effect on expenditure deflators, especially consumption. And to the extent that domestic producers of energy and raw materials have to follow a world price this effect is captured in principle by the import price term in the aggregate domestic producer price equation.

The procedure adopted is in some respect an *ad hoc* one adapting to the current structure of the model, but it echoes some features of reality. For many commodities, recorded prices are those established on 'world' spot markets. These are in practice residual markets, while much trade takes place on the basis of long lived bilateral contracts between purchaser and supplier. The free market prices are established between those suppliers and buyers whose requirements have not been met by such contracts and by the activities of speculators. Such market prices will therefore reflect unexpected developments in supply or in demand (owing to higher or lower activity than anticipated, for example), as well as speculative buying and selling. The prices established in such markets are very often used as the basis for pricing of bilateral contracts. For this reason, it may not be unreasonable to make actual export prices derivative of current and past 'world' commodity prices.

PART II. MODELLING COMMODITY PRICE INDICES

1. DATA AND THE APPROACH TO SPECIFICATION

As noted, four commodity groupings were selected as the basis for the price indices to be modelled. Obviously, different indices can be obtained with different weightings of individual commodities. Two published sets of indices were used. One is the UNCTAD price indices which weights commodities according to the exports of less developed countries.[6] These indices are directly relevant to the export prices of the non–OECD zones in INTERLINK. Another set of published indices is those of the Hamburg Institut fuer Wirtschaftsforschung (HWWA); these weight commodities according to their position in imports of OECD countries.[7] Given intra–OECD commodity trade, these are more useful in explaining OECD export prices of commodities than the UNCTAD indices. Table 1 gives the weights of different commodities in the indices used so far.

A necessary assumption in what follows is that a price index of one of those groupings can be modelled like the price of a homogeneous storable commodity in a single market. Aggregation biases are ignored. The starting point is a simple model or real price formation in a storable materials market with three behavioural equations: consumption demand, inventory demand (ending stocks minus beginning stocks) and supply. Demand and supply are treated as functions of price and a set of exogenous variables. Storage demand depends on the expected capital gain (expected future price minus today's price both relative to a general price index minus carrying costs, chiefly interest rates) and exogenous variables. Stock equilibrium is assumed and the equilibrium condition ensures that inventory and consumption demand equal supply:

$$D_t = d[(L)P_t, (L)S_t, (L)Y_t, T, u_t]$$

$$Q_t = q[(L)P_t, (L)X_t, T, v_t]$$

$$I_t = i[(P^e_{t+1} - P_t), r_t, T_{t-1}, (L)W_t, z_t]$$

$$D_t = \Delta I_t = Q_t.$$

P_t = current spot price in dollars relative to an index of the overall price level ('real' price),

P^e_{t+1} = expected 'real' spot price for period t+1

Table 1. Comparison of UNCTAD and HWWA Indices

	UNCTAD weights: dollar value of LDC exports		HWWA weights: import trade of industrialised countries
Food	100	Food	100
Sugar	39.3	Maize	32.9
Rice	11.1	Soyabeans	26.3
Maize	11.2	Wheat	19.7
Soymeal	10.6	Barley	5.3
Bananas	8.3	Rice	3.9
Beef	7.1	Coconut, palm, sunflower oil	9.2
Wheat	5.9	Others	2.7
Others	6.5		
Tropical beverages	100	Tropical beverages	100
Coffee	71.4	Sugar	39.8
Cocoa	18.4	Coffee	30.1
Tea	10.0	Cocoa	10.8
		Tea	4.8
		Tobacco	15.7
Agricultural raw materials 100		Agricultural raw materials 100	
Tropical timber	33.7	Wood pulps	36.6
Cotton	32.5	Sawn wood	28.7
Rubber	25.3	Cotton	12.9
Others	8.6	Rubber	7.9
		Others	13.9
Minerals	100	Minerals	100
Copper	33.3	Copper	28.7
Iron ore	21.0	Iron ore	34.3
Aluminium	13.1	Aluminium	10.2
Tin	12.1	Tin	4.6
Phosphate rocks	10.9	Steel scrap	9.3
Others	6.4	Nickel	5.6
		Lead	2.8
		Zinc	4.6

The endogenous variables are:

D_t = consumption demand,

Q_t = production,

I_t = inventories,

The exogenous variables are:

Y_t = consumers' income or activity level,

D_t = real price vector of substitute products,

T = time trend representing technical change in the supply equation and technical change and/or trends in taste in the demand function,

X_t = other variables which are relevant to supply such as interest rates, productivity capacity, cost of inputs, etc.,

r_t = interest rates,

W_t = exogenous variables relevant to the market for storage such as insurance rates,

u_t, v_t, z_t = error terms assumed to be normally distributed with zero mean,

(L) indicates a distributed lag in the relevant variable

The expected signs of steady state partial derivatives with lags worked through are as follows:

$d_p < 0$, $d_y > 0$, $d_s > 0$, $q_p > 0$, $q_T > 0$, $i_{p^e} > 0$, $i_I < 0$, $i_{\Delta r} < 0$, while q_x, i_w and d_T are indeterminate. The system can be solved to yield a reduced form equation in the price:

$$P_t = p((L)Y_t, (L)P_{t-1}, (L)X_t, T, \Delta P^e_{t+1}, (L)S_t, \Delta r_t \\ (L)W_t, I_{t-1}, u_t, v_t, z_t) \tag{1}$$

where expected signs are: $P_Y > 0$, $P_{\Delta p^e} > 0$, $P_{\Delta r} < 0$, $P_I < 0$, $P_s > 0$ and other partial derivatives are indeterminate.

Several unobservable variables appear in these equations – price expectations, productive capacity, existing stocks and costs of production. Productive capacity, and existing stocks are both unobservable because data are not collected at the necessary level of aggregation. They are a function of current and past investment activity and as such may exhibit cyclical as well as secular movements.

To the extent that the unobservable supply related variables are correlated with other variables appearing in the model, the estimated coefficients will be biased. Even more probable is that some of the omitted variables (in the vector X_t for example) are stock variables reflecting capacity levels and hence the course of past fixed investment, just as the omitted variables in lagged inventory investment. That investment was no doubt a function of then current price expectations and profitability. Low prices implying low profits could retard inventory and capacity creation leading to higher prices later and vice versa. When the stock variables in X_t are omitted owing to data constraints, it is therefore probable that an equation using low frequency data (e.g. annual) should be supplemented by more terms in lagged values of the dependent and independent variables, reflecting the investment cycle. Failure to specify the appropriate, probably lengthy, lag structures will generally lead to high order autocorrelation in estimated residuals.

On the other hand, these influences may be relatively unimportant where speculation dominates the market and will be invisible in high frequency data. Many commodity markets are dominated by inventories which can represent more than a year's production. Changed willingness to hold inventories (which themselves change relatively slowly) may then be responsible for most variation prices. If that willingness is mainly a function of expectations about future prices, altering as a function of randomly arriving bits of news, price movements will have a large random element and may show little autocorrelation at least in the case of high frequency data (e.g. monthly). Whether there are long cycles or autocorrelations in semi–annual data was treated as an empirical matter.

Two assumptions were made about real price expectations. The chief one, discussed now, is that they may be represented as a forecast based on a view of prices as a general stochastic process on a stationary series with q moving average terms in an hypothesised white noise error series, e_t, and r autoregressive terms. The expectation of e_{t+1} is zero and past forecasting errors are known values so the expectation of P_{t+1} is

$$P^e_{t+1} = \phi 1.P_t + \phi 2(B)P_{t-1} - \theta 1(B)e_t \tag{2}$$

where (B) indicates a polynomial function of the backward shift operator.

The distributed lag term in the dependent variable of the reduced form price equation (1) (derived from lagged adjustment of demand and, particularly, supply to price) thus is overlaid with other autoregressive elements related to the assumed process of expectation formation. In addition, the equation could acquire a moving average error process $\theta 1(B)e_t$ as well as the hypothesised white noise error, $u_t + v_t + z_t$.

The other assumption that can be made is that expectations are 'rational', so that $P^e = P + \epsilon_t$ where ϵ is a white noise error process and $E(\epsilon_{t+1}) = 0$. The reduced form equation then becomes:

$$P_t = p((L)Y_t, T, (L)P_{t-1}, (L)X_t, P_{t+1}, \Delta r_t, (L)W_t, \\ (L)S_t, I_{t-1}, u_t\ v_t, z_t, \epsilon_t \tag{3}$$

This can be estimated by an errors–in–variables approach using the value of the real price with a one period lag.[8] Work is proceeding on this approach (which parallels the methods used to estimate exchange rate equations). Results so far are not particularly promising but analysis is at an early stage and is not reported in this paper.

Equations like (1) determine the real price. However, it is necessary to take account of the fact that real prices can vary with the inflation rate in the short run. This could represent temporary money illusion due to information or learning lags, or the influence of contracts fixed in nominal terms, or it could reflect aggregation problems when dealing with aggregate price indices; it could also result from the influence of omitted variables correlated with inflation.

There is another nominal or 'numeraire' effect to be considered. Commodity price indices reflect prices in dollars. These would be expected to change with the exchange rate of the dollar. In other words, the 'real' price is the price in a basket of currencies where the basket weights depend on the share in world commodity trade of various countries and on production and consumption elasticities.[9] This real price, being determined by the 'real' factors specified in (1) should be invariant to exchange rate movements except insofar as those imply real changes in the market. Consequently, for the real price to be unaltered when dollar exchange rates change, prices in dollars must change too. However, there is some belief in a 'numeraire effect' whereby dollar prices do not adjust instantly to changes in the exchange rate so that, for a period of some months at least, exchange rate movements are not fully offset and hence affect the real price. In addition, the weights of different currencies in the aggregate OECD general price index are given by GDP and in general are not those appropriate to deflation of commodity prices.

It is appropriate to define the general price level in terms of a dollar price index. This is done by calculating an OECD GDP price deflator in dollars. Nominal GDP of each OECD country is converted to dollars at the current exchange rates. These nominal GDPs are summed and divided by the sum of constant price GDPs (GDPV) converted to dollars at the exchange rate of the base year of the index; i.e.:

$$PG = \frac{\Sigma_i \, GDP_{ti} \cdot Exch_{ti}}{\Sigma_i \, GDPV_{ti} \cdot Exch_{oi}}$$

where PD is the OECD price level, i is an index of all OECD countries, t is a time subscript and t = 0 indicates base year. $Exch_i$ is the exchange rate of country i expressed as US dollars per unit of local currency. This is equivalent to:

$$\sum_i PGDP_{ti} \cdot Exch_{ti} \cdot w_{ti}$$

where the weight $w_{ti} = \frac{GDPV_{ti} \cdot Exch_{oi}}{\Sigma_i \; GDPV_{ti} \cdot Exch_{oi}}$ and $PGDP_{ti}$ is the GDP deflator $GDP_{ti}/GDPV_{ti}$.

This price index will clearly vary with the dollar exchange rate. If the dollar appreciates ($Exch_i$ falls for all i ≠ USA), then PG declines. If homogeneity between the nominal commodity price and PG is enforced, the theoretically appropriate long run behaviour of commodity prices, without money illusion, is assured – abstracting from weighting questions. Temporary numeraire effects could be reflected in a lagged adjustment of commodity prices to the general price index. This could be reflected by changes in inflation appearing in the real price equation. If the response differs as between inflation changes owing to exchange rate movements and those owing to other things or if numeraire effects last longer than other forms of money illusion this can be tested by including the change in effective exchange rate of the dollar as a separate explanatory variable. Results of such tests are reported in Section 2.3.

It is clear, unfortunately, that the type of reduced form price equation to be estimated will not permit the identification of the parameters of the hypothesised structural system. In particular, it will not be possible to disentangle dynamic adjustment in the supply and demand equations from expectation formation processes. Where the same variable occurs in supply and demand equations e.g. TIME) there are further identification problems.

2.2 Estimation Methods

There is reason to believe that the dependent variable may be correlated with long lags on itself yet the length and structure of the lags are not known *a priori*. Moving average errors may also be present. In general, it seem improbable that any parsimonious regression equation would have white noise errors. A strategy of over–parameterisation, of specifying a most general equation embodying many lags, is likely to fail because of multi–collinearity and general instability. Because of this a mixed procedure was followed of attempting to combine the classical regression analysis with techniques of causality analysis. The procedure is not optimal but is partly forced by computing constraints at OECD. Vector autoregression techniques, which may be preferable, are not possible for the requisite number of explanatory variables with existing software.

The estimation of equations like (1) therefore used regression techniques. However, time series techniques were used for three purposes:

– Filtering and cross correlation of time series was used in an attempt to get some idea of the causal influences at work and to aid in identifying the appropriate lags in the subsequent regression equation; these cross correlations are of some interest in their own right;

- Box–Jenkins techniques of model identification were used on the regression residuals of equations; this was to find any regularities not explained by the explanatory variables and in particular to identify any long cycles (autocorrelations at long intervals) in the residuals that would point to omitted supply effects, particularly investment cycles;
- ARIMA models of real commodity prices were also constructed as a benchmark; to ensure that the regression equation contained all the information captured in the ARIMA model, fitted values of the latter were included as additional explanatory variables in regression equations; forecasts of ARIMA and regression equations were also compared.

The next section gives results of empirical work. The first part reports the tests for 'Granger causality' in the system. The second part reports regression results for selected equations and gives a summary of alternative specifications which were not preferred. The third part gives long run properties and out–of–sample forecast results.

2.3 Empirical Results

a) ARIMA models of real commodity prices and tests for Granger causality

One possibility is that as many commodity prices are determined on speculative markets, these will turn out to be speculatively efficient and the prices will generally follow a Martingale process (i.e. price changes will not be serially correlated). This may hold for daily quotations of actual commodity prices. Period average prices may show a moving average structure as a result of time aggregation and it is unclear how aggregation across commodities into indices would affect the time series. At any rate, for all indices examined a model was found which dominated the random walk. ARIMA models were constructed for the real commodity price indices and also for seven independent variables. All the variables are semi–annual and, except for interest rates, are measured in natural log form. The variables with the appropriate differencing to achieve stationarity are the following.

Real price indices (UNCTAD and HWWA) in US dollars:

i) Agricultural raw materials (AGRM, LHAR), log level.
ii) Food (FOOD, LHMR), log level.
iii) Minerals (MINO, LMHR), log level.
iv) Tropical beverages (TBEV, LHTR), log level.

Independent variables:

i) Industrial production for the seven largest OECD economies, commodity import weights (B7IP), first difference.

ii) GDP of the seven largest OECD countries, 1980 prices and dollars, (B7GDPV), first difference.

iii) GDP price deflator in dollars of the seven largest OECD economies, weighted by GDP shares (WPGDPD), first difference.

iv) US three month Treasury bill real interest rate (nominal rate minus inflation rate) (USAIRSREAL), first difference.

v) US effective exchange rate in dollars, MERM weights, second difference (EFFEX).

vi) Volume of private consumption in the seven largest OECD economies (OECDCPV), GDP weights, first difference.

vii) Money stock (M1) of the seven largest OECD economies, (OECDM1), second difference.

Graphs of the price indices are in Figure 2. Some exceptional events have affected the variables being analysed. A few observations of the food price and tropical beverages price time series were therefore adjusted before estimation of the ARIMA model, so that estimates of the model parameters would be unaffected by the events. The adjustment was done by regressing the dependent variable against time and a number of dummy variables. Dummy variables were used for FOOD in 1973 and 1974 representing effects of the earlier Soviet harvest failure and poor weather conditions and in 1980I–1980II because of the coffee frost in Brazil in 1975.[21] The adjustment was then added back to the residuals of the ARIMA process being treated *a priori* as part of the irregular component of the series and being used in cross correlations.

The ARIMA estimation results are presented in Table 2. The parameter estimates and standard errors indicate significance in all parameters except in the models for industrial production and OECD inflation. In the industrial production (IP) model the second order autoregressive operator is not quite significant, but the t–value is high enough to include it in the model.

The residual autocorrelation functions contain no significant correlations, and the Box–Pierre statistic which tests the autocorrelations collectively[22], was always below the 90 per cent level for the chi–squared distribution. This suggests that the residuals are random and the models need no further elaboration.

The residuals of the ARIMA models for commodity prices were cross correlated with those of the other variables for which models were fitted and which are reported in

Figure 2

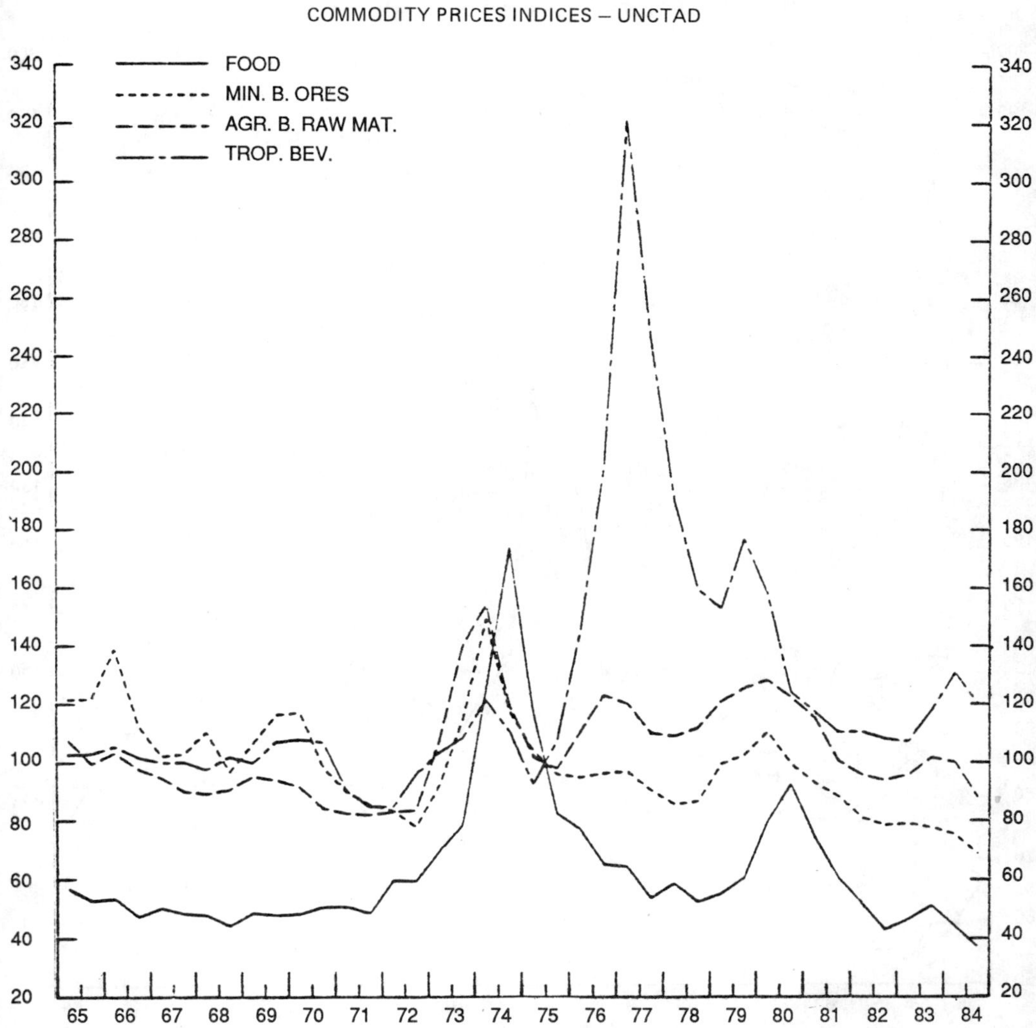

<u>Note</u>: Real prices (nominal index deflated by OECD prices), base year = 1975.

Figure 2 cont.

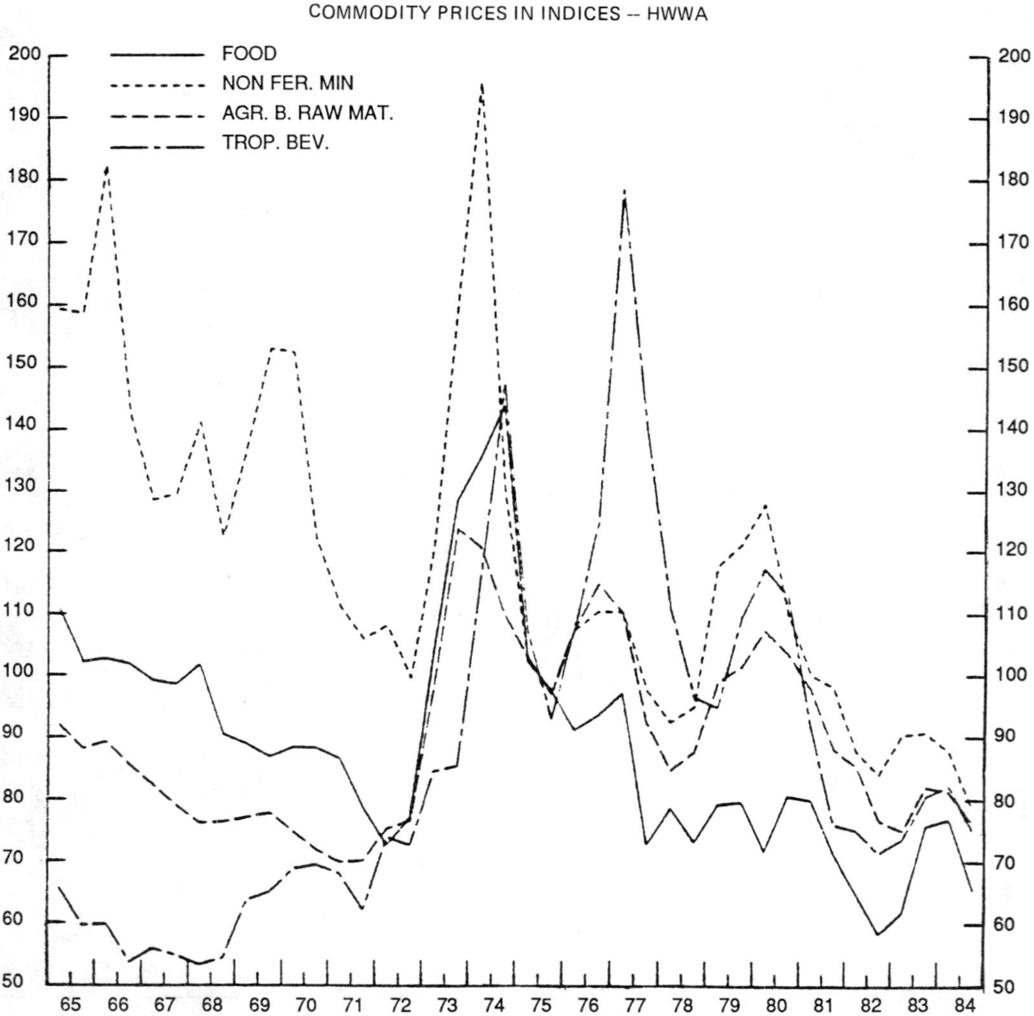

Table 2. The results are graphed in Figure 3. Significant cross autocorrelations can be taken to indicate that one variable is Granger–causing another. This form of causality test, proposed by Haugh and Pierce[22], is in some sense more severe than those proposed by Granger and Sims as independent filtering of each variable has been carried out[23]. Several writers have argued that the causality test applied in this form is prone to the error of not finding a relationship between two variables, even when one exists; the test is only unbiased when a given variable, X, is uncorrelated with all other variables determining the other variable being tested, Y[24]. The test is therefore powerful in establishing that series are not independent but the finding that series are independent cannot be treated with great confidence.

Figure 3, showing cross correlation between commodity price residuals and those of six of the explanatory variables, should be interpreted in the light of these warnings. The sample size of 36 is also small for this type of analysis. There is generally an identifiable effect of OECD economic activity on commodity prices with broadly similar effects on both indices. Depending on commodity group the effect ranges from contemporaneous to a lag of two or three half years later. Aggregate consumption appears to affect food prices with a three period lag. Innovations in agricultural raw materials prices are significantly negatively correlated with those in real GDP and in industrial production up to three periods later and with real aggreate consumption one period later; mineral prices are also negatively correlated with real GDP and industrial production two periods later. Food is negatively correlated with GDP one period later. This result may, of course, owe much to the particular experience of recession in 1974 following on the immediately preceding rise in commodity prices. On the other hand, it may be seen as providing some confirmation of the importance of commodity prices and terms of trade changes for OECD activity.

Interest rates are found to influence most prices negatively, with a lag of two semesters in the case of food, more slowly in the case of minerals (four semesters). The correlation with the effective exchange rate of the dollar is significant at the same interval. This presumably reflects the effect of interest rates on exchange rates rather than a genuine effect of exchange rates on minerals and food prices. Another explanatory variable tried in these tests was the real spot oil price, as oil is an input both into the production of other commodities and into the production of synthetic substitutes. The clearest impact was found on food prices, contemporaneously and with a one period lag.

Further examination of possible money illusion was carried out by running an equation on the nominal commodity price index with lagged values of the dependent variable and the current level of the OECD GDP deflator (dollar terms) as explanatory vari-

Table 2 : Estimated ARIMA Equations For Commodity Price Equation Variables

1966I to 1983II	Constant (2)	ϕ_1	ϕ_2	θ_1	θ_2	R^2 (3)	Box-Pierce X^2	d.f
AGRM, log level, AR1 MA2	0.52 (3.08)	0.47 (2.73)		-1.24 (10.07)	-0.79 (6.27)	0.84	3.88	3
MINO, log level, MA2	0.96 (22.41)			-1.23 (18.63)	-0.89 (15.75)	0.65	1.95	4
FOOD, log level, AR1 MA1		0.93 (29.65)		-0.38 (2.41)		0.69	2.27	5
TBEV, log level, AR1 MA1	0.24 (1.86)	0.77 (6.50)		-0.54 (3.43)		0.80	5.31	4
LHAR, log level, AR2	1.12 (2.95)	1.37 (9.21)	-0.59 (3.97)			0.82	3.57	3
LHMR, log level, AR2	2.10 (3.33)	1.09 (6.82)	-0.50 (3.07)			0.61	4.04	3
LHFR, log level, AR1	0.87 (1.71)	0.82 (8.02)				0.64	7.28	4
LHTR, log level, AR2		1.94 (22.27)	-0.95 (11.24)			0.51	9.25	4
B7IP, 1.diff., AR2		0.77 (4.71)	-0.28 (1.71)			0.17	4.41	5
USAIRSREAL, Δ%, MA1				0.57 (4.08)		0.23	1.53	6
EFFEX, 2.diff., AR2		-0.63 (3.93)	-0.45 (2.65)			0.30	4.74	4
OECDCPV, 1.diff., AR1		0.88 (16.09)				0.30	6.18	6
OECDM1, 2.diff., MA1				0.97 (34.98)		0.32	3.91	5
B7GDPV, 1.diff., AR1	0.008 (2.61)	0.51 (3.41)				0.25	5.69	5
WPGDPD, 1.diff., AR1	0.019 (2.77)	0.38 (2.28)				0.10	3.13	5
POILR, 1.diff., random walk	-	-	-	-	-	-	2.88	7

Notes

1. Semi-annual data 1966-1983, for HWWA commodity prices 1967II to 1983II. Statistics in parentheses are t-values. For variable definitions see main paper, p.231/2.

2. To ensure that the residuals (a_t) of the ARIMA models in log-transformed form have a mean not significantly different from zero, a constant was introduced where necessary, as the mean of the original log-transformed series (μ) was significantly different from zero.

   i.e. $\mu > 2 \sigma N$

   where μ = mean of the log-transformed series,
   σ = standard deviation,
   N = number of observations.

3. For the models, the statistic R^2 is defined as: $1 - \hat{V}(a_t)\ \hat{V}(Z_t)$.
   where $\hat{V}(a_t)$ and $\hat{V}(Z_t)$ denote estimated variances of a_t and Z_t. It is comparable with R^2 in standard multiple regression.

Independent variables (all in logs except the interest rate):

B7IP:	Industrial production of the seven largest economies
USAIRSREAL:	U.S. three-month Treasury Bill real interest rate (nominal rate minus actual inflation rate), first difference.
EFFEX:	U.S. effective exchange rate in dollars, MERM weights, second difference.
OECDCPV:	OECD consumption in volume terms.
OECDM1:	Money stock (MO) of seven largest OECD economies, second difference.
B7GDPV:	GDP of the seven largest OECD countries, 1980 prices and dollars, first difference.
WPGDPD:	GDP price deflator in dollars of the seven largest OECD economies, weighted by GDP shares, first difference.
POILR:	Spot price for oil in Rotterdam market, deflated by OECD price deflator, first difference.

Figure 3: Cross–Correlation of Commodity Prices and Explanatory Variables

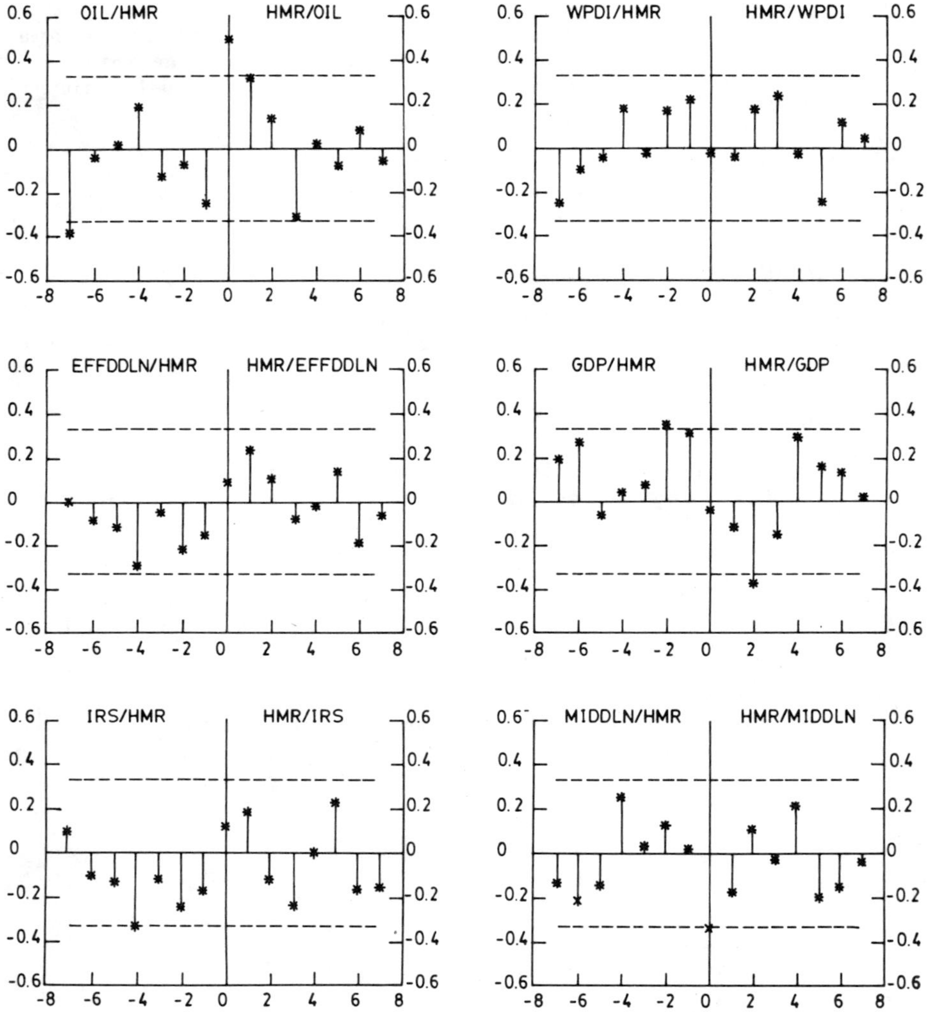

Figure 3 cont.

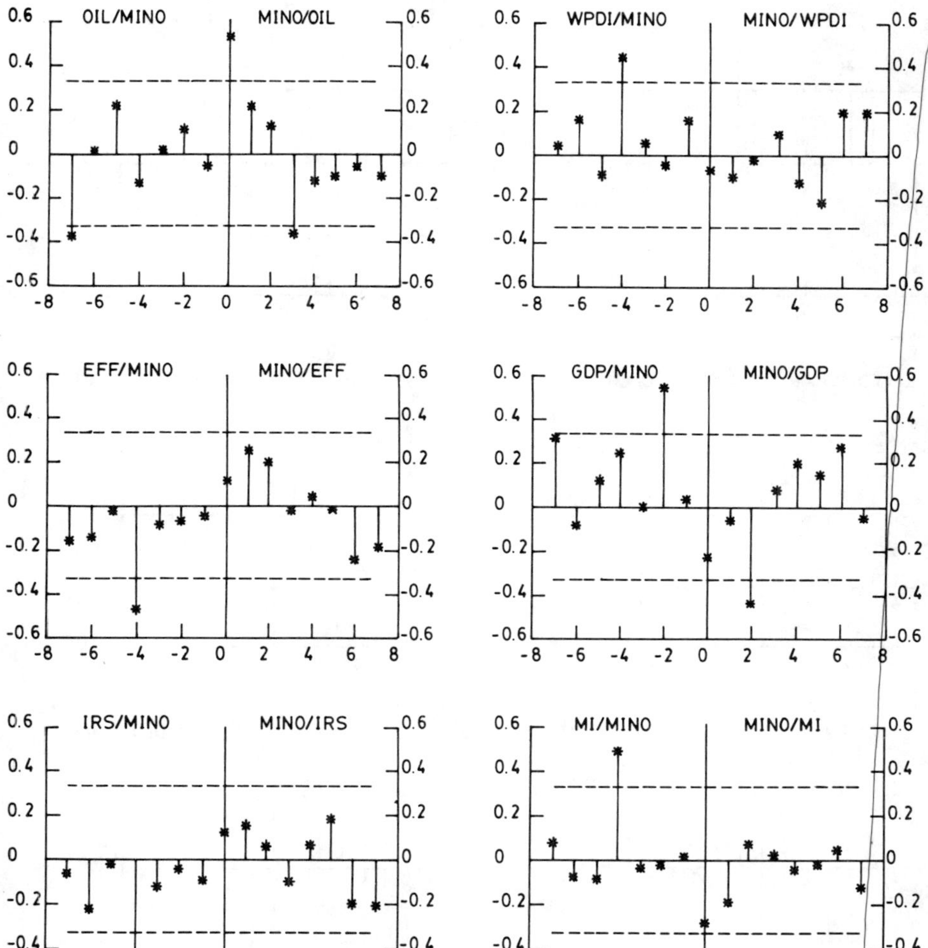

Figure 3 cont.

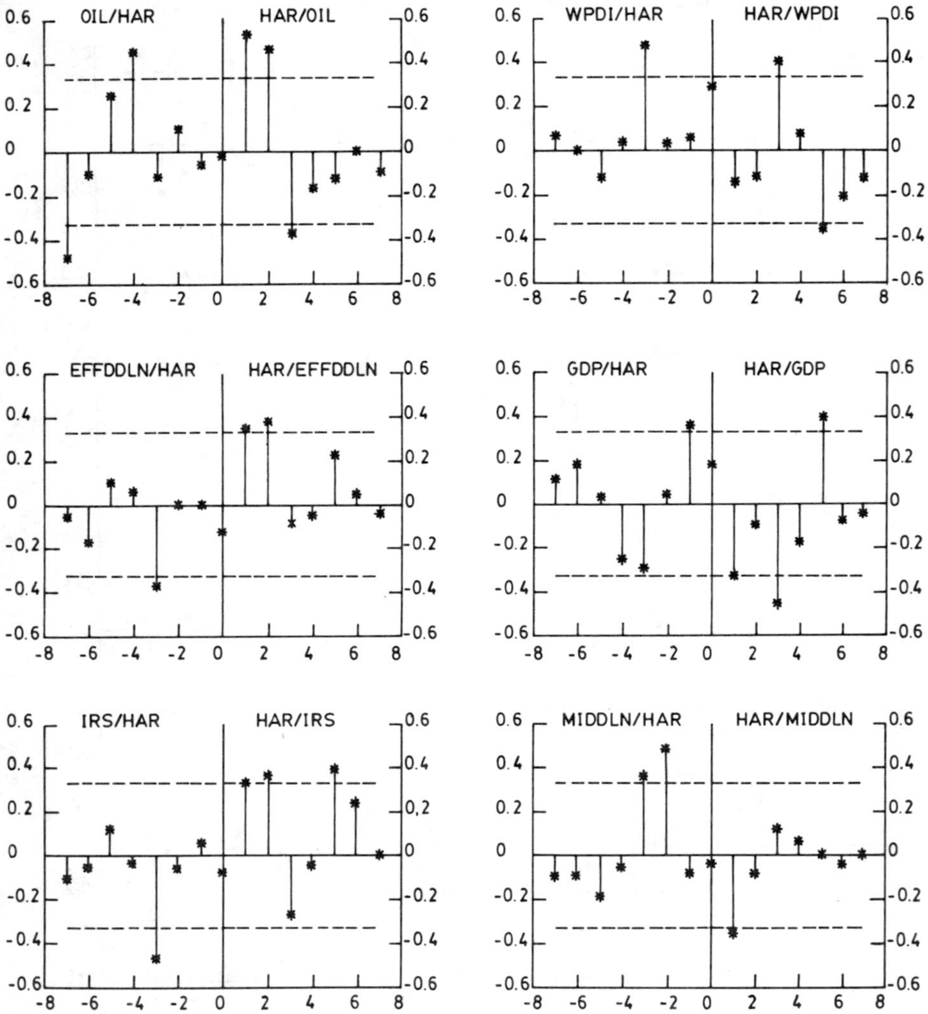

Figure 3 cont.

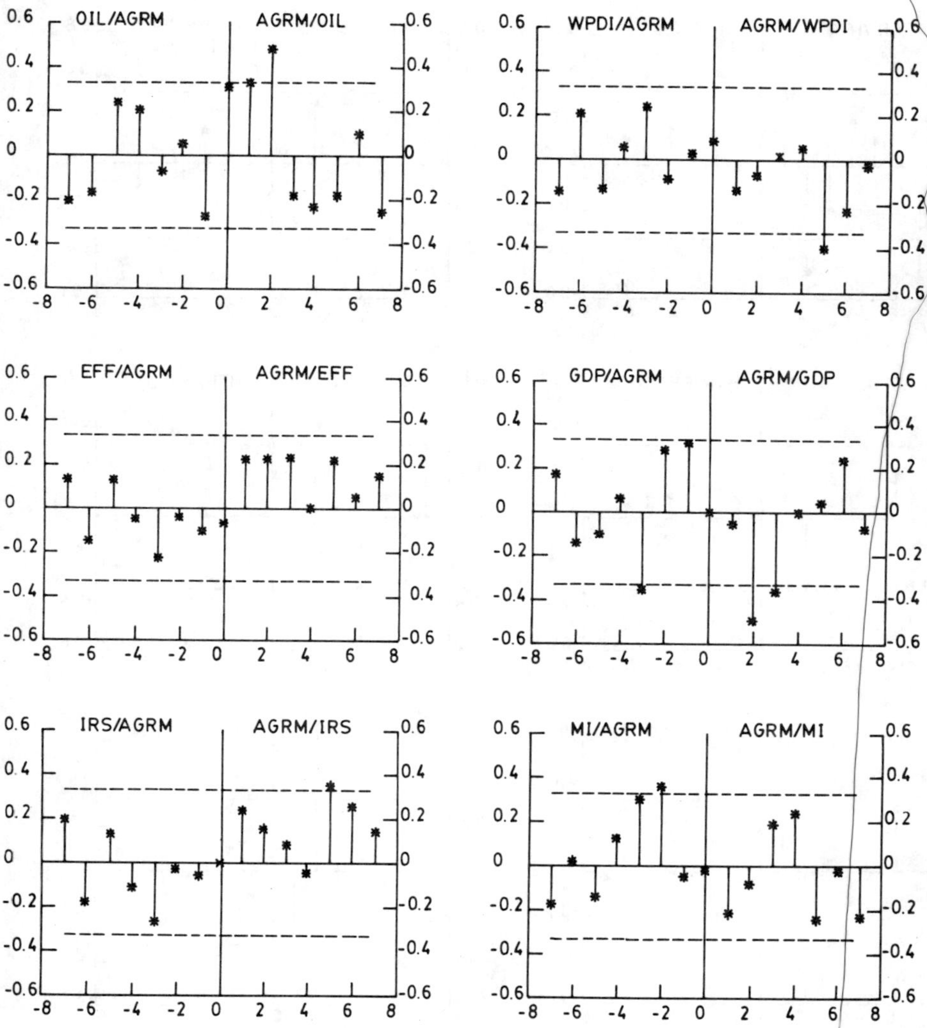

Figure 3 cont.

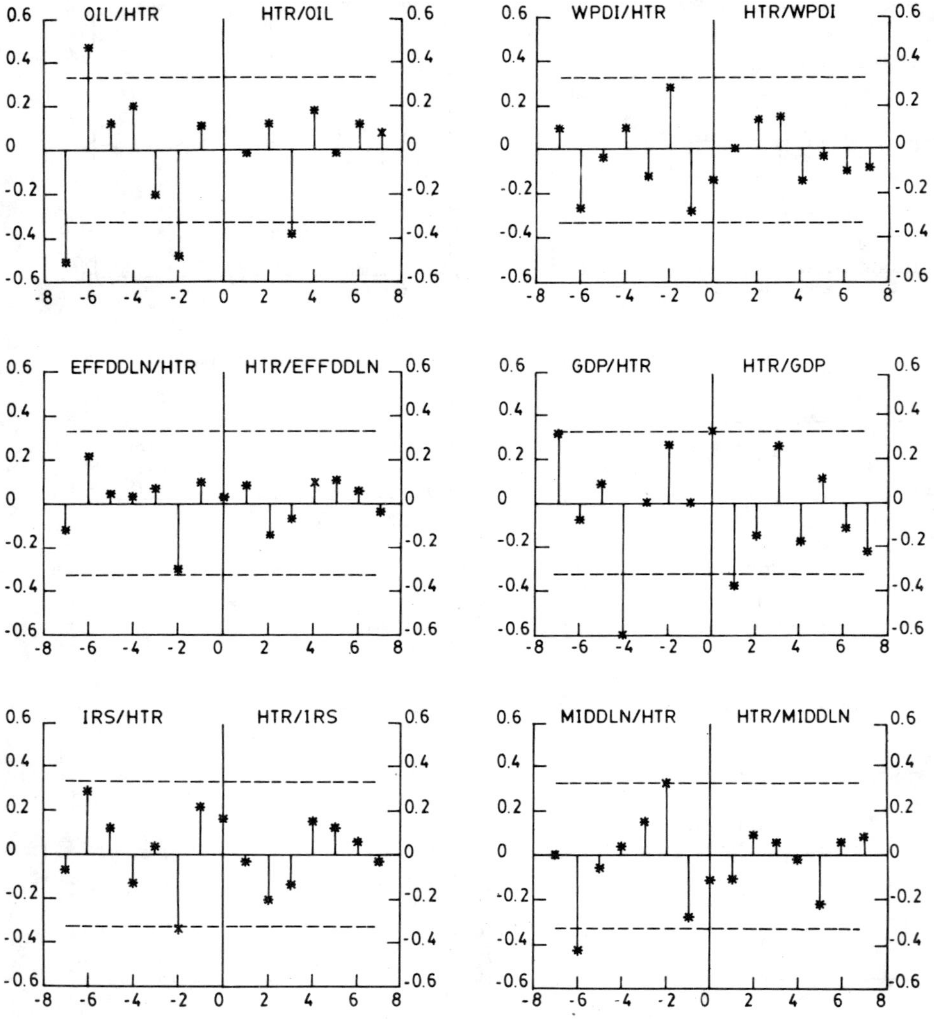

Figure 3 cont.

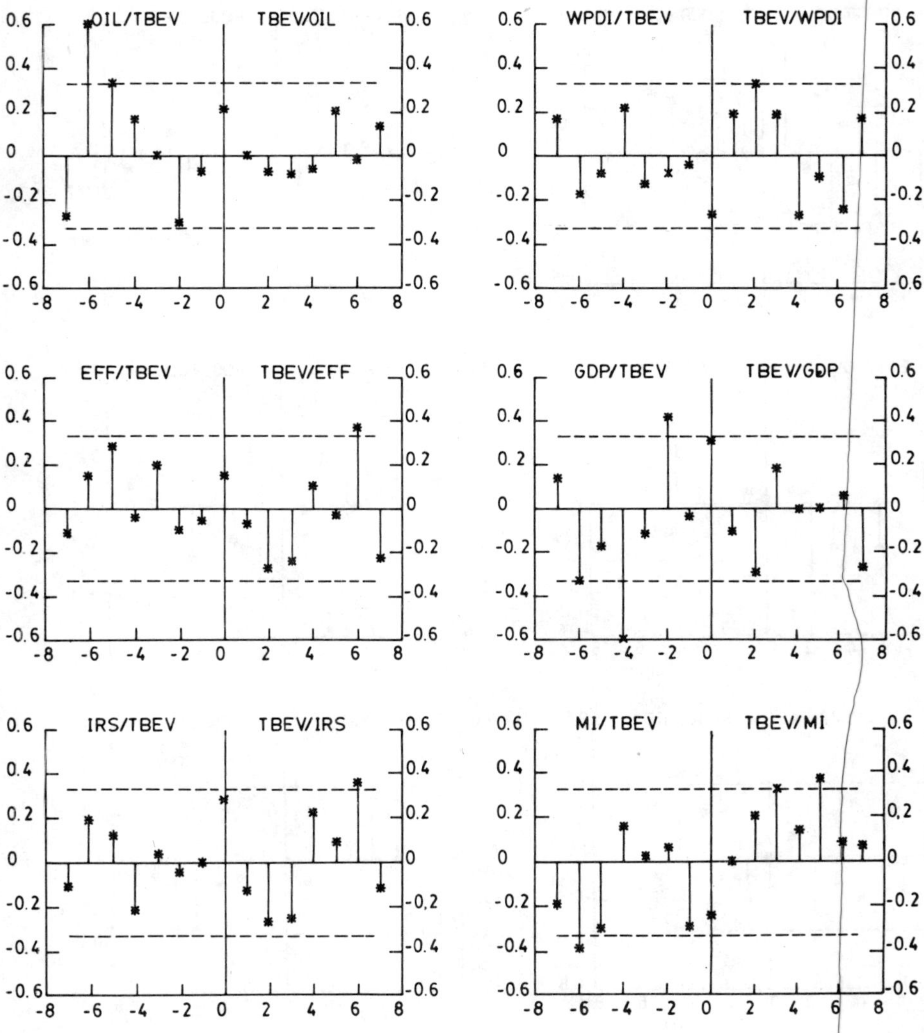

Figure 3 cont.

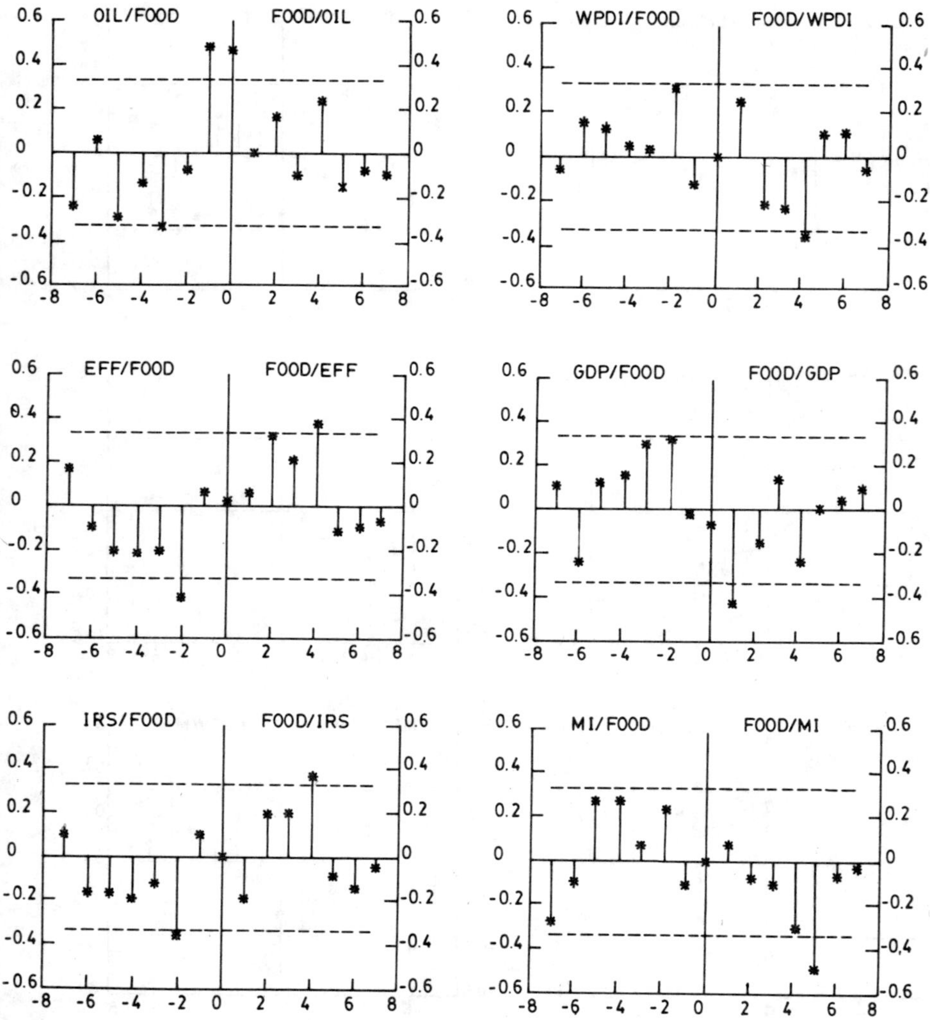

Figure 3 cont.

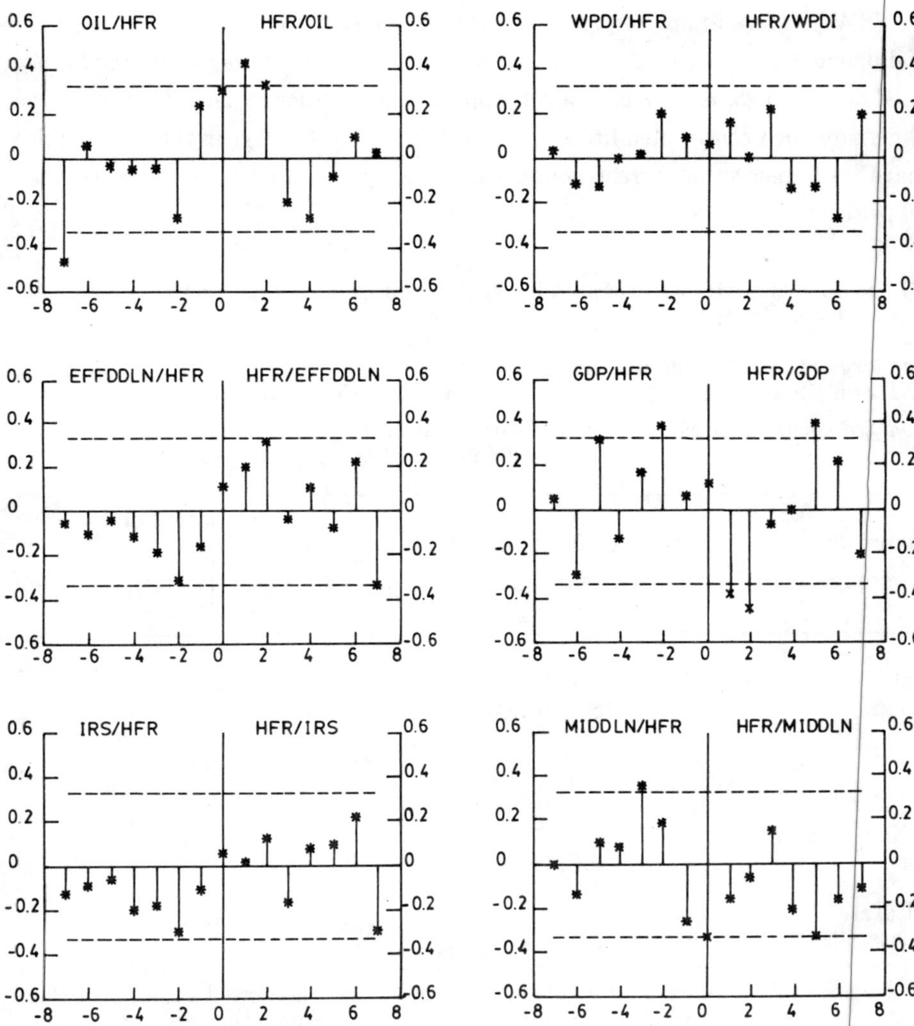

ables. In the absence of money illusion, the coefficient on the general price level should be insignificantly different from unity. The results for UNCTAD indices only are in Table 3. HWWA results are very similar. They show that the coefficient is insignificantly different from one in all cases, although for tropical beverages the coefficient, estimated at only 0.25, is very poorly determined. The addition of lagged values of the OECD deflator then contributed little. The null hypothesis that lags in the general price level have no influence on current nominal commodity prices could never be rejected with 90 per cent confidence.

Table 3. Effects of OECD Prices (WP) on Nominal Commodity Prices (NP)

Standard equation for nominal commodity price:
$\ln NP = a_0 + a_1 dumm + a_2 \ln NP(-1), + \ldots a_6 \ln NP(-5) + a_7 \ln WP$
Modified equation: standard equation with addition of
$+ a_8 \ln WP(-1) + \ldots a_{12} WP(-5)$

Commodity group	a_7, coefficient of WP (standard equation)	Significance of coefficients $a_8 \rightarrow a_{12}$ (lags in WP): 'F' statistic
Tropical beverages	0.25 (S.E. 0.49)	1.48
Food	0.85 (S.E. 0.37)	1.85
Metals and minerals	1.05 (S.E. 0.34)	1.14
Agricultural raw materials	1.32 (S.E. 0.37)	1.44

Note: The F statistic reflects a test of the hypothesis that the lagged values of WP do not Granger–cause the dependent variable. It relates the residual sum of squares in the standard and modified equations, corrected for degrees of freedom. See text for details. The 95% significance level is 2.77.

The Haugh–Pierce tests were carried out sequentially in a bivariate manner. Their results were used as the starting point for the usual sort of specification search with regression equations. Running multivariate regressions produced results broadly compatible with the results of the tests although some interaction between explanatory variables tended to alter initial specifications as final results show.

b) Regression results

Table 4 reports the estimation results of the finally preferred specification for the eight price indices considered. Estimation was by ordinary least squares for the period 1967:2 to 1984:2.

The equations are of differing quality with relatively large standannnerrors for tropical beverages and for food prices, especially when account is taken of the fact that dummy variables were included representing 1973 harvest failures and the 1980 sugar crop failure.

Different activity variables were tried: OECD industrial production for six of the indices and OECD consumption for food prices. Effects on the equations were marginal. OECD GDP was also calculated using import weights in aggregation and this variable used in estimation to investigate suggestions that the current weakness of commodity prices is owing to the regional distribution of demand and activity within the OECD, with the United States, which is nearer commodity self sufficiency than other OECD countries, providing much demand growth. Again, the effect on equations of this change was marginal.

The appropriate functional specification of the activity variable was the subject of considerable experimentation. Various formulations could be found yielding a reasonable fit and forecasting ability including the level and the change of OECD GDP at various lags. No particular formulation dominated in all equations, however. Deviations of GDP from its trend appear to have the closest association with real price movements overall and were adopted as the best all–round specification. In the tropical beverages equations trend GDP appears as well as the deviation. For the other equations, the long run elasticity of real prices with respect to GDP is zero as deviations of GDP from trend cannot persist indefinitely by construction; eventually the trend, defined as a moving average, adapts to actual developments. This property, which distinguishes these equations from other work in the field, implies that a shift in commodity demand has a temporary effect on price but that the long run supply curve is perfectly elastic.

Interest rate effects are frequently identified though not always statistically well determined. Inflation was tried as an explanatory variable in all the equations and appeared to be significant, lagged three periods, in the Hamburg agricultural raw materials equation and in first difference (acceleration) form with a negative sign in the minerals equation. Lagged inflation terms appeared for those prices also in the cross correlation tests. However their interpretation is problematic. They were treated as spurious and dropped from final equations.

The equations for the HWWA real commodity price indices are broadly similar to

Table 4. Commodity Price Equations

$$LHMR = \underset{}{7.02^{**}} + \underset{(0.15)}{0.43^{*}}\,LMHR(-1) - \underset{(0.14)}{0.54^{**}}\,LMHR(-2) - \underset{(0.11)}{0.21}\,LMHR(-5)$$

$$+ \underset{(1.37)}{3.64^{**}}\,MA.DEV(-1) + \underset{(0.04)}{0.15^{**}}\,LPOILR - \underset{(0.005)}{0.03^{**}}\,TIME$$

$SEE = 0.077$, $\bar{R}^2 = 0.86$, $H = 1.61$

$$LMINR = -0.14^{**} + \underset{(0.14)}{0.33^{*}}\,LMINR(-1) - \underset{(0.13)}{0.29^{*}}\,LMINR(-2)$$

$$- \underset{(0.09)}{0.19^{*}}\,LMINR(-5) + \underset{(0.95)}{2.63^{**}}\,MA.DEV(-1) + \underset{(0.04)}{0.20^{**}}\,LPOILR$$

$$- \underset{(0.004)}{0.025^{**}}\,TIME$$

$SEE = 0.057$, $\bar{R}^2 = 0.87$, $H = 1.39$

$$LHAR = 1.63^{**} + \underset{(0.15)}{1.10}\,LHAR(-1) - \underset{(0.16)}{0.44}\,LHAR(-2) + \underset{(0.96)}{1.33}\,MA.DEV$$

$$+ \underset{(0.01)}{0.03^{*}}\,LPOILR(-2) - \underset{(0.20)}{0.62^{**}}\,IRS(-3)$$

$SEE = 0.062$, $\bar{R}^2 = 0.87$, $H = 2.35$

$$LAGRR = -0.19^{**} + \underset{(0.19)}{1.09^{**}}\,LAGRR(-1) - \underset{(0.18)}{0.57^{**}}\,LAGRR(-2) + \underset{(1.04)}{1.10}\,MA.DEV$$

$$+ \underset{(0.05)}{0.13^{**}}\,LPOILR - \underset{(0.07)}{0.22^{**}}\,LPOILR(-1) + \underset{(0.06)}{0.13^{*}}\,LPOILR(-2)$$

$$- \underset{(0.19)}{0.54^{**}}\,IRS(-3)$$

$SEE = 0.059$, $\bar{R}^2 = 0.87$, H statistic cannot be calculated

$$LHTR = \underset{}{-9.0^{*}} + \underset{(0.14)}{0.87^{**}} LHTR(-1) - \underset{(0.14)}{0.31^{*}} LHTR(-2) + \underset{(1.40)}{2.23} MA.DEV(-1)$$

$$+ \underset{(0.17)}{0.38^{*}} MA.TREND - \underset{(0.32)}{0.92^{**}} IRS(-2) + 0.31^{**} DUM.1$$

$$SEE = 0.103,\ \overline{R}^2 = 0.88,\ H = -1.69$$

$$LTBR = -5.81 + \underset{(0.12)}{0.84^{**}} LTBR(-1) - \underset{(0.12)}{0.15}\ LTBR(-2) + \underset{(1.09)}{2.45^{*}} MA.DEV$$

$$+ \underset{(0.12)}{0.20}\ MA.TREND - \underset{(0.25)}{0.23}\ IRS(-1) + 0.42^{**} UDUM.1$$

$$SEE = 0.086,\ \overline{R}^2 = 0.92,\ H = -1.11$$

$$LHFR = 1.78^{*} + \underset{(0.10)}{0.63^{**}} LHFR(-1) + \underset{(1.25)}{2.55}\ MA.DEV - \underset{(0.25)}{0.34}\ IRS(-1)$$

$$+ 0.26^{**} DUM.2$$

$$SEE = 0.095,\ \overline{R}^2 = 0.78,\ H = 0.088$$

$$LFOOR = -0.18 + \underset{(0.05)}{0.67^{**}} LFOOR(-1) + \underset{(1.16)}{0.67}\ MA.DEV - \underset{(0.21)}{0.43}\ IRS$$

$$+ 0.63^{**} UDUM.2$$

$$SEE = 0.086,\ \overline{R}^2 = 0.93,\ H = -0.28$$

Note: The real price indices in US dollars (log level) are denoted by:

HWWA		*UNCTAD*	
LHMR:	Non–ferrous metals	LMINR:	Minerals
LHAR:	Agricult. raw materials	LAGRR:	Agricult. raw materials
LHTR:	Tropical beverages	LTBR:	Tropical beverages
LHFR:	Food	LFOOR:	Food

Explanatory variables:
MA.DEV: deviation from trend of constant price GDP of the seven largest OECD economies
LPOILR: spot price of oil in Rotterdam market, deflated by OECD GDP deflator
IRS: US three month Treasury bill rate minus actual inflation rate
MA.TREND: trended series of constant price, GDP of the seven largest OECD economies
For explanation of dummy variables, see text.

those for the UNCTAD indices, even in the case of the tropical beverages equations where the coverage is different: HWWA includes sugar and tobacco in tropical beverages while sugar is in the UNCTAD food group. This difference is reflected in the relative importance of the dummy variable. Both equations include a trend GDP variable which does not appear in the equations for the other commodity groups. However, the HWWA equation responds less to trend GDP and more strongly to deviations from trend GDP than does the UNCTAD equation. Interest rate effects appear in both, with a larger and much better determined coefficient in the case of Hamburg. In spite of the difference in coverage, the same lags on the dependent variable were found to be significant for both indices.

Dynamics were also similar for the two indices in the agricultural raw materials equations (two lags on the dependent variable) and the minerals equations. In the latter, a lag at minus five could not be excluded for either the HWWA or the UNCTAD price index. The net effect is an endogenous cycle in mineral prices whereby they overshoot in response to a disturbance and the equilibrium elasticity of mineral prices with respect to all explanatory variables is less than the impact elasticity.

Both minerals equations feature the current oil price but the effect is weaker for the HWWA index. Regressions on the Hamburg price with the sample period split in two (1967:2 – 1975:2; 1976:1 – 1983:2) indicate that the oil price had a much stronger influence in the latter period (coefficient 0.4 as opposed to 0.1). Both real minerals prices respond to the deviation of GDP from trend with one lag, with a larger coefficient in the Hamburg case. Split period regressions on this equation showed a smaller effect of changes in activity in the second period. Recursive regressions also indicated that the influence of activity decreased even more markedly within the latter period. This suggests coefficients estimated over the full sample period may not be optimal for forecasting or simulation. The equations were reestimated by discounted least squares. Comparative forecasts showed, however, that this gave little improvement (see below).

The current deviation of GDP from trend appears in both agricultural raw materials equations. The real oil price plays a much lesser role in the Hamburg than in the UNCTAD agricultural raw materials equation, where the current and lagged prices appear. Removal of the lagged oil prices causes the equation to deteriorate markedly.

Both food equations also feature the current deviation of GDP from trend. In the UNCTAD equation the coefficient is lower and poorly determined but the variable was retained to prevent simulation properties of the two food price equations diverging excessively. Interest rate effects are comparable (stronger for UNCTAD). The dummy variables are important reflecting the poor Russian grain harvest in 1973/74 and in the case of UNCTAD, the sugar crop failure of 1980.

A feature of the equations for minerals is the marked time trends. As estimated these have strong implications for the steady state properties of the equations when taken in conjunction with the absence of long run activity effects. As the equations are estimated on semestrial data, the annual rates of decline of prices are double the coefficients on the time variable, hence some 6 per cent. If real oil prices and interest rates are constant therefore these commoditiy price indices would fall at 5–6 per cent a year. In effect, the equation implies a trend fall in mineral prices quite apart from cyclical weakness, perhaps due to technical change and shifts in demand patterns.

The estimated equations cannot be rigorously compared to other reduced form estimates of aggregate commodity price indices in the literature because of differences in coverage, sample period and specification. Nonetheless, some broad comparison may be helpful. Distinguishing features of these equations, compared with the equations of Chu and Morrison and Grilli and Young[25], are: the negative coefficients on real interest rates, though not often well determined, and the substantial long run interest rate semi elasticity; the only temporary positive effect of OECD activity except on tropical beverages prices. This latter may owe something to the different time periods over which the equations were estimated as there is some evidence that the effect of OECD activity on prices has declined over time, especially in the case of minerals. The other specifications do not allow for oil price effects, whether as a cost or as a substitute raw material, while here significant coefficients were found for the oil price in minerals and in agricultural raw materials. Long run elasticities, however, are small. The OECD equations seem to fit relatively well in sample, but for food and tropical beverages this may be owing to the more precise specification of dummies for supply shocks. A common difficulty is the multicollinearity of explanatory variables. More detailed comparisons are not very informative as the commodity groupings are different.

c) Equation properties and forecasts

The long run and dynamic properties of the equations are shown in Table 5, which gives long run elasticities, mean lags in non–oscillating equations and the phase of the price cycle in the case of oscillating processes. Mean lags are generally short, around 2 periods. In oscillating equations the phase of cycles is usually 8 to 10 periods (4 to 5 years) except in the case of the minerals prices which have a phase of 5.5 periods.

In–sample forecasting of the equations was generally satisfactory. An out–of–sample test was conducted by estimating the equations to 1983 and using them to forecast for 1984. Firm data were available for the first half of the year but some explana-

Table 5. Long Run Properties of Commodity Price Equations

	Nature of adjustment	Long Run Elasticity with respect to : GDP (1)	OIL	IRS (2)	Mean Lag (3)	Phase (3)
LMINR	oscillating	0	0.17	-	-	5.5*
LHAR	oscillating	0	0.07	-1.82	-	10.6
LAGRR	oscillating	0	0.09	-1.13	-	8.3
LHTR	oscillating	0.86	-	-2.09	-	9.4
LTBR	non-oscillating	0.64	-	-0.74	2.2	-
LHFR	non-oscillating	0	-	-0.92	1.7	-
LFOOR	non-oscillating	0	-	-1.30	2.0	-

1. The GDP variable in all equations is a deviation from trend. The trend is a moving average function of GDP so the long run elasticity of prices with respect to GDP is zero by construction (given that the equations' dynamic properties are stable). However, for tropical beverages equations the level of trend GDP itself appears as an explanatory variable and the elasticity is calculated with respect to trend GDP.

2. Semi-elasticity.

3. In half years.

* Both mineral equations are fifth order autoregressive processes, making analytic solution for the phase impossible. This estimate is approximate, based on simulation experiments.

tory variables had to be estimated for the second half. (Even official data for a recent period are, of course, subject to large revisions.) In general the equations fail to capture the precipitate decline in commodity prices early in the second semester of 1984. Results are shown in Table 6. In view of the large and generally unexpected decline in commodity prices the test is a severe one and it remains to be ascertained whether the equations would do any better when used to forecast for other periods.

The raw materials and the UNCTAD food equations fail the chi–squared test of parameter stability at the 99 per cent level. The food equation does particularly poorly and it alone is outperformed by the ARIMA model.

In view of this, it and the other equations were reestimated with the fitted values of the ARIMA model added as an explanatory variable. This was never significant, the 't'–values being 1.4, 1.4, 0.3 and 0.7 for the four indices ordered as in Table 6. In general the equations were also robust to this modification with the coefficients on explanatory variables (apart from lags on the dependent variable) hardly changing. This procedure could be seen as a rough and ready way to take account of moving average errors in the regression equation. A mixed equation for food with the ARIMA fitted values in place of the lagged dependent variable was also used for forecasting. This produced some improvement for 1984II, no doubt because of the moving average error term, but the prediction error was slightly greater for 1984I than the simple regression equation and the mixed equation still did not outperform the simple ARIMA specification, for this particular forecast period.

A comparison is also made with the same equations estimated by Discounted Least Square to take account of possible shifts in parameters over time. In general this did not improve forecasting (Table 6). An interesting observation is that for most of the indices a longer forecast starting from an earlier base gives more accurate terminal level forecasts for 1984.

4. CONCLUSION

Empirical work is at an early stage. Estimated equations appear to have standard errors at least as low as other similar ones in the literature. Nonetheless, results do not suggest that the use of such aggregate equations would be much improvement on current judgemental methods of forecasting aggregate commodity price indices.

Simulation testing is equally at an early stage. However some remarks are possible. There are generally modest estimated coefficients on OECD activity in these equations. When combined with the damping implicit in converting commodity prices to export unit values, these would imply that the simulated inflationary effect of an increase in

Table 6 : Real Commodity Price Forecasts (Percentage Changes 1984I - 1984II in log-differences)

		UNCTAD					HWWA				
		Actual	Univariate ARIMA Model	OLS	DLS	$X^2_2(2)$ (a)	Actual	Univariate ARIMA Model	OLS	DLS	$X^2_2(2)$ (a)
Agricultural	83II	6.3	-	-	-	-	9.5	-	-	-	-
Raw Materials	84 I	-2.1	8.0	4.4	4.5	-	-1.3	10.6	5.0	5.9	-
	84II	-12.6	0.9	5.3	5.5	26.82	-6.2	9.2	7.0	7.4	12.38
s.e.e.				0.049					0.051		
Minerals	83II	-1.7	-	-	-	-	0.5	-	-	-	-
	84 I	-2.9	1.5	-3.2	-2.0	-	-3.8	7.3	-8.1	-5.6	-
	84II	-8.7	9.7	0.8	-0.2	2.93	-11.0	7.7	-0.4	-1.0	0.97
s.e.e.				0.056					0.077		
Food	83II	9.8	-	-	-	-	20.2	-	-	-	-
	84 I	-15.1	-1.3	-0.9	0.0	-	1.3	2.1	0.1	-2.4	-
	84II	-16.7	-5.5	-1.9	-0.5	18.98	-15.6	1.7	-0.7	0.4	2.67
s.e.e.				0.076					0.093		
Tropical	83II	9.6	-	-	-	-	9.0	-	-	-	-
Beverages	84 I	10.1	-4.3	2.4	4.9	-	1.8	3.7	12.1	12.2	-
	84II	-8.2	-0.6	1.5	3.8	0.85	-9.0	-1.3	2.6	3.0	5.47
s.e.e.				0.086					0.103		

a. Chi-squared statistic of parameter stability defined as :

$$\sum_{e=1\to m} e^2_{t+1}/(SSQ/N-1-k) \text{ with n degrees of freedom}$$

where e_t are forecast errors, SSQ is the sum of squared regression residuals, N observations in regression sample, k number of regressors. The joint hypothesis of parameter stability and equation adequacy can be rejected with 95 per cent confidence if the statistic exceeds 6 in this case. The X^2-statistics refer to the OLS forecasts for the period 1984I to 1984II.

b. DLS refers to forecasts of identically specified equations estimated by discounted least squares.

<u>Note :</u> Forecasts for 1984 were static extrapolations from a base of actual data for 1983II.

OECD activity would not be qualitatively different as a result of endogenising commodity prices in this way. Financial effects are also small.

In some applications it would be a drawback of the equations that they use the real oil price as an explanatory variable when this itself may not be easy to predict. When the projected oil price is made a technical assumption underlying a forecast, however, (as at the OECD) the inclusion of this variable is conductive to forecast consistency. The finding that this is a significant explanatory variable for raw materials and minerals is intuitively reasonable. The findings that real commodity prices are not affected by inflation, so nominal prices adjust to OECD prices within a half year, and that dollar numeraire effects are equally short lived also accord with economic intuituion. An implication is that dollar prices should rise if there is a decline in the dollar, which, however, has not been the experience in 1985, an out–of–sample year.

The equations clearly imply that current low prices for minerals and metals are more than cyclical or owing to exchange rate or financial considerations (indeed, oddly, interest rates could be found to play no role in these equations). For reasons lying beyond the aggregate statistical analysis presented here, these particular prices appear to be on a long term declining trend.

NOTES AND REFERENCES

* This paper owes its existence to the encouragement of Orhan Guvenen. Empirical work was carried out by OECD colleagues, Mr. Tapio Saavalained and Ms. Helen Sutch, who also contributed many comments on substance and method. The point of departure was some work on commodity prices carried out at the OECD by Ms. Katie Gordon. Any views expressed are those of the author and do not necessarily represent the opinions of the OECD or its member governments.

1. See G.H. Holtham (1984), 'Multinational Modelling of Financial Linkages and Exchange Rates', OECD *Economic Studies*, 2, for a description of this part of the system. It has subsequently been revised but the approach remains similar.
2. See Kaldor, N. (1976), 'Inflation and Recession in the World Economy', *Economic Journal*, 86, No. 344, pp. 703–14; and 'The Role of Commodity Prices in Economic Recovery', *Lloyds Bank Review*, 1983.
3. Beckerman, W. and T. Jenkinson, 'Commodity Prices, Import Prices and the Inflation Slowdown: A Pooled Cross–country Time Series Analysis', unpublished mimeo.
4. A previous attempt to endogenise commodity prices in the context of a world model was the COMLINK project. A series of 28 commodity market models ranging from two to over 30 equations were integrated into the Project Link system. This was a more elaborate and ambitious approach than the present one. See F.G. Adams, 'Integrating Commodity Markets into LINK' in I.A. Sawyer (ed.) (1979), *Modelling the International Transmission Mechanism*, North Holland, New York.
5. This work, by Mr. Paul Saunders of OECD, is reported in a forthcoming OECD Economics Department Working Paper, 'Commodity Prices in INTERLINK'.

6. See *Monthly Commodity Price Bulletin*, UNCTAD, Geneva and Supplement TD/B/C.1/CPB/L.24/ADD.1, April 1983. These monthly prices are calculated from daily or weekly quotations. They have been averaged to give semestrial series.
7. See H.J. Timm (1980), 'A New HWWA Raw Material Price Index', Hamburg. Monthly prices are based on daily computations and they are averaged to give semestrial series. The HWWA has kindly agreed to supply the OECD with an unpublished index weighted according to OECD exports, and this may be used in future developments.
8. See Wickens, M.R. (1982), 'The Efficient Estimation of Econometric Models with Rational Expectations', *Review of Economic Studies.*
9. See D. Ridler and C.A. Yandle (19), 'A Simplified Method for Analysing the Effects of Exchange Rate Changes on Exports of Primary Commodity', *IMF Staff Papers*, 19.
10. Although the frost was in mid–1975 its full effects on supply were not realised until they affected Brazilian production in the 1976–77 season – roughly March to March. For FOOD the estimated .value of the dummy was 0.3 for 1973I and II, 1 for 1974I and II and 0.4 for 1980I and II, 0 otherwise; for TBEV it was 1 for 1976I to 1977I, 0 otherwise.
11. Box, G.E.P. and D.A. Pierce (1970), 'Distribution of Residual Autocorrelations in Autoregressive–Integrated Moving Average Time Series Models', *Journal of the American Statistical Association*, 65, No. 332, p. 1509.
12. Pierce, D. and L. Haugh (1977), 'Causality in Temporal Systems: Characterisations and a Survey', *Journal of Econometrics*, 5, pp. 265–93.
13. Alternative regression basd techniques were first proposed by Granger, C.W.J. (1969), 'Investigating Causal Relationships by Econometric Methods and Cross Spectral Methods', *Econometrica*, 36, and Sims, C. (1972), 'Money, Income and Causality', *American Economic Review*, 62.
14. Sims, C. (1977) in 'Comment on Pierce' *Journal of the American Statistical Association*, 72, No. 357, pp. 23–24.
15. Chu, Ke–Young and T.K. Morrison (1984), 'The 1981–82 Recession and Non–oil Primary Commodity Prices', *IMF Staff Papers* (March). Grilli, E.R. and Maw-Cheng Yang (1981), 'Real and Moneatry Determinants of Non–oil Price Movements', Division Working Paper No. 1981–6, Commodities and Export Projections Division, The World Bank.

CHAPTER 13

THE ECONOMETRICS OF COMMODITIES IN INTERNATIONAL ECONOMIC LINKAGES

F.Gerard Adams, *University of Pennsylvania*
CADE/Economics Research Unit

1. INTRODUCTION

International economic interrelations have come increasingly into the foreground as internationally linked economic instability has mounted since the early 1970s, as a result of broad movements in prices of fuels and other commodities. It is fortunate that economists are also increasingly better able to handle global econometric systems and to integrate commodity price impacts into these models. In this paper we ask how far econometric approaches have been developed to deal with commodities in international economic linkages.

We conclude that great progress has been made in modelling international economic linkages related to the business cycle. The focus has been on trade flows and import prices, particularly as a result of the pioneering work of the University of Pennsylvania's Project LINK. Commodity markets have been integrated into global model systems. Ongoing work promises to deal further with commodity trade flows, exchange rates, financial flows and debts which have increasingly become sources of instability. The description of some long term changes affecting commodity producers and consumers, in particular those related to industrial policies, technical change, and transfer of technology, are still a challenge to econometric modellers.

2. ECONOMETRIC APPROACH TO WORLD MODELLING

It has been more than twenty years that econometric models, originally oriented towards description of the economies of separate countries, have been extended to the linkage between country economies and to coverage of the global world economy. The econometric approach is analogous whether one is building a model system describing

O. Guvenen (ed.), International Commodity Market Models and Policy Analysis, 259–273.

behaviour within a country or between countries. But unless a world model is greatly aggregated, the complexity of developing such a system, programming it for solution, testing it and applying it for forecasting and simulation is, of course, very much greater.

Project LINK is an example, perhaps an extreme one, of the size of such a system, it contains 79 country models, and embodies approximately 10 thousand behavioural equations. Typically, such systems begin with models describing the economies of the underlying countries using as appropriate Keynesian or growth model structures. Then linkages are provided between the countries reflecting trade flows, price linkages, commodity price determination, and most recently capital flows and current financial flows. The objective is a comprehensive model system which will give solutions for economic activity within countries which are consistent with the relationship between them. The objective is also to provide a useful multipurpose system, one which can be applied to a variety of problems affecting the global economy. In this section we will examine the typical linkages between country models in greater detail.

2.1 The Trade Flow Linkages

The simplest and most obvious linkage between country economies is by way of the merchandise trade flows, exports and imports between countries. Recognising that net exports (X–M) enter into the GNP demand identity in the simplified Keynesian model suggests a linked theoretical system. The basic interrelationship through trade flows is the heart of trade models like Project LINK, the OECD'S various model systems, the Japanese world model at Tsukuba, the EPA, and the new Elsa model, the Wharton Econometrics World Model and other models. Like in Project LINK, most of these models determine imports as a classical demand function on the basis of income and domestic price relative to import price. Exports are determined in relation to imports of the market countries and a relative competitiveness variable for example:

$$M_i = m(Y_i, P_i/P_{\neq i})$$

$$X_i = x(\sum_i w_{ijo} M_j, P_i/P_{\neq i})$$

where w_{ijo} is market share of country i in country j's imports in base year o. This weight is the appropriate element of a base year trade matrix. This matrix can be held fixed or its elements can themselves be endogenised to move with respect to competitiveness or technological trends. Trade can (and is typically) broken down into a number of product categories. There is no need in this formulation to identify country to country flows; only aggregate exports and imports for each country are shown, though models with country–to–country trade flows have also been developed.

An alternative approach to trade flow linkage is through input–output. The input-output approach postulates a considerably finer breakdown of product flows between countries and is able to recognise the composition of the product as it leaves the i–o matrix of the producer country and as it enters the i–o matrix of the importer. This has some significant advantages, but also suffers from some disadvantages. On the positive side is the fact that specific industry/product categories are fed through the i–o system. In a more general trade matrix formulation only broad categories of exports and imports are tracked whereas the i–o system permits the impact of exports or imports of particular products to affect directly the appropriate industries in the importing and exporting countries. This is particularly important for studies of trade policy or of the international impact of industrial policies. On the other hand, the i–o approach poses considerable difficulties at handling the shifts in the import parameters over time and it requires a much greater degree of disaggregation in the trade flows as well as in the domestic economy models.

2.2 The Price Linkages

The second traditional linkage between country models is by way of export and import prices. Given a set of exchange rates and transportation markups, import prices should be closely linked (indeed identical except for transportation and exchange rate translation) to export prices. Each country's import prices (unit values) are an appropriately weighted average of the export prices (unit values) of its suppliers, e.g.,

$$P_{mj} = \Sigma\, w_{jio}\, P_{xi}$$

where weights w_{jio} are again based on the trade matrix.

The key here is that export prices are dominant and are determined in the exporting countries. Exchange rates are assumed given. It is clear that this type of export price determination is most suited for large industrial countries, where the assumptions of a Keynesian domestic model apply and where prices are determined within the country for locationally diverse products (Armington (1969)) through a markup on costs of production of domestically produced and imported inputs. Each importing country is then essentially a price taker and each exporter a price maker though the presence of price terms in the import equations and the exports equations and the simultaneous solution of the system means that prices are jointly determined with all the other variables. This approach applies more meaningfully to industrial products with markup pricing by monopolistic producers where Armington's assumption of origin diverse product applies than to primary commodity markets where pricing might be determined in a world commodity market with competition or under the pressure of a cartel as in the case of petroleum. Consequently, the price mechanism described here has traditionally been used only for manufactures. Other prices have frequently been treated as exogenous.

2.3 Primary Commodity Linkages

In recent years, we have become increasingly aware of the potential for disturbance to the world economy from abrupt changes in prices of primary commodities, the two oil shocks and the swings of the prices of other raw materials, for example. The impact of these developments has highlighted the differences between the industrial countries which are largely consumers of these products, the petroleum producers and the other less developed countries which are consumers of oil and producers of primary products. In the industrial countries the increase of primary material and fuel prices has caused inflation, and recession. In the economies of the producer countries increases in primary product prices have fuelled rapid expansion, and a variety of other less desirable consequences. The changed terms of trade between fuels and prices of manufactures and the price volatility have been major contributors to international economic instability. Yet, the traditional linked international model system lacked the ability to recognise these phenomena.

The determination of primary commodity prices is best handled with a commodity market model which determines price as a reconciliation between forces on the demand and on the supply sides. The commodity prices are then introduced into the linked country model system using the trade matrix as a basis for allocating the prices to the importing countries. It is important to note here that commodity exports serve as an important source of foreign exchange revenues to the producing countries and that the growth of many of the less developed countries depends on their earnings of foreign exchange which are closely tied to the price of primary commodities. This linkage must, of course, be recognised in the model system. A more difficult question is how to deal with quantitative flows of commodities. On the import side, this is relatively straightforward since quantities of imports of commodities are closely linked with economic activity in the consuming country. But on the exporting side, exports are often dependent on harvest conditions or on decisions by producer companies and must frequently be explained on the basis of exogenous forces.

2.4 Other Linkages

A number of other linkages relate the world's national and regional economies. These include flows of services, short term and long term capital flows, exchange rate determination, international migration, technological transfers etc. These relationships are now being integrated into world models.

3. MODELLING APPLICATIONS – SOME EXAMPLES

In this section we describe some applications of modelling the international domestic economic interactions. The first example is the work on modelling export instability and economic growth by Adams and Behrman (1982). Another example is a global block model system by Adams and Marquez (1982). The final one is the Project LINK world trade interaction model system of Klein and his associates. (Ball (1973) and Sawyer (1979)).

3.1 Export Instability and Economic Growth – Econometric Model Studies

Despite the fact that the evidence on the impact of export instability is quite 'mixed', the developing countries have pushed substantial initiatives on commodity price stabilisation in the framework of the New International Economic Order, the so–called 'integrated programme for commodities' and 'common fund' proposals of UNCTAD (Cline (1979), Behrman (1977)).

The question of the impact of export instability on economic growth has had a long history in empirical economics, particularly in the form of cross section studies (McBean (1966), Kenen and Voivodas (1972)), and simple models (Rangarajan and Sundararajan (1976)).

A series of studies by Adams and Behrman and their associates[2] were intended to view the interactions of instability in international commodity markets and the development of the producing economies from a different perspective. The approach is that of integrating econometric models of the world markets for primary commodities with econometric models of the commodity producing sector and of the economy of the producing country. The studies completed include a world model of the copper market linked to the economies of Zambia and Chile, and a model of the world market for coffee linked to the economies of Brazil, Central America, and the Ivory Coast, and a study of commodity exports from Malaysia. Other country studies are in progress.

We will discuss here the essential components of the linked model system using the 'coffee market–Brazil country' model as a typical example. The model of the world coffee market follows traditional lines of such models for primary agricultural commodities (Adams and Behrman (1976) and Labys (1980)). The essentials of such models are:

- demand functions which relate consumption of the commodity to industrial activity (Y) in the consuming country and to price (P), relative to the price of alternatives (P_s).

  $D = f(Y, P, P_s)$

- supply functions based on the assumption of profit maximisation by producers and consequently relating supply to price relative to production costs (C) usually with a long time lag and often time trends (T).

  $S = f(P, C, T)$

- inventory supply functions which are based on the identity relationship between production and consumption and official stockpile purchases (ΔI_0).

  $I_s = I_{s-1} + S - D - \Delta I_0$

- And finally, price functions which relate price to available stocks relative to consumption requirements for stocks, and to price expectations (P^e). The price function may reflect long run costs, (C), it may represent equilibrium in the market for inventories or it may take the form of a disequilibrium formulation based on the difference between supply and demand.

  $P = f(I_s, D, P^e, D)$.

In the case of coffee, the consumption and production structure follows this pattern closely. One should note particularly the long lags in the coffee supply and the impact of frosts in the Brazilian producing areas. Price stabilisation efforts through stockpile purchases and export controls also influence coffee prices. Regional coffee prices, which determine the share of various areas in the world coffee market, are influenced by the world price and by regional production. The operation of the Brazilian coffee sector is thus closely linked with the world commodity model.

The micro model of the coffee sector in the Brazil economy involves the determination of production in Brazil, the inputs of labour and other materials into the production of coffee, and the generation of revenues to the producers, to the wage earners, and to the Brazilian government in the form of export taxes and other tax revenues, and the foreign exchange receipts of Brazil from coffee exports.

The Brazilian country econometric model combines supply and demand side considerations in the tradition of recent models of developing economies (Behrman and Hanson (1979)). Real GDP is determined as the sum of output in the various sectors of the economy with feedbacks to consumption, investment and government spending through the revenue flows generated for the private and public sectors. Price determination rests on a mixed strategy, a monetary approach, minimum wage regulation, import prices, and structural considerations. Important linkages from the earnings of primary commodity exports to the monetary system are through the effect of commodity export earnings on money supply and from commodity tax revenues on the budget surplus/deficit.

Such a model system has extensive potentials for modelling the impact of world primary commodity markets on the economic development of Brazil. On the one hand, it is possible to hypothesize changes in the world price of coffee and to evaluate the short term and long term impacts on various dimensions of Brazilian economic goal attainment. What is the effect of coffee prices on Brazilian economic activity, money supply and price level? What would be the impact of price stabilisation? Alternatively, one may hypothesize developments in the coffee sector in Brazil on Brazilian earnings from coffee and on Brazilian economic performance.

The calculation for Brazil, and for most of the other countries considered, show that fluctuations in international commodity markets can produce important movements in the many aspects of the domestic economies of the producing ecnomies. But there is only limited evidence that fluctuations in commodity markets and foreign exchange earnings, as contrasted to a stabilised price path, have important effects on the long term growth of the producing countries. An important aspect of this work has been the role that active domestic commodity policies and fiscal and monetary policies can play, as constrasted to passive policy inaction, to ease the impact of fluctuations in international commodity markets. In this respect, as in others to be discussed below, world model systems must recognise explicitly the policy posture of each participating country.

4. A GLOBAL MODEL OF OIL PRICE IMPACTS

Another approach to global econometric modelling is a simple model system treating the developed countries, the OPEC countries, and the non oil producing LDC's as separate blocks.[2] This system assumes that the industrial countries can be modelled largely in terms of a Keynesian system. The developed country models are demand dominated but we can allow for supply side shifts in production capacity as a result of oil shocks or as a result of new technologies for example. The non oil LDC's are modelled on the basis of a production function approach constrained by internal and external savings gaps. This is a growth theory view where capital investment is influenced by a country's ability to export and earn foreign exchange. The OPEC countries are modelled simply in terms of recycling the oil revenues.[3]

The model deals with trade flows of raw materials, purchased by the DCs from the

LDCs, manufactures exported to OPEC and the LDCs, and petroleum sold by OPEC to both DCs and LDCs. Price determination focuses on the export price of manufactures of the DCs, which is determined endogenously and is significantly affected by the movements of the petroleum price.

The essential of this system is to investigate the impact of oil prices (and of optimal utilisation of OPEC's oil revenues) on economic activity, growth, and inflation in the industrial countries and non oil LDCs. Exogenous increases in oil prices affect the rest of the world through various feedback channels:

- The increased imports of the oil producers;
- The reduced real income and greater inflation in the developed countries;
- The reduced foreign exchange revenues, higher import prices, and lower growth of the non oil developing countries.

These studies illustrate how responses by the developed economies can partially offset the burden of oil price increases for the developed economies and how the impact of higher oil prices has fallen particularly on the non oil LDCs. By reducing GNP in the developed countries, higher oil prices increase the elasticity of demand for OPEC oil and limit its ability to raise prices (Adams and Marquez (1984)). Policy responses by the developed economies, which may have increased the adverse real impact of the oil price shock, as well as concessional aid transfers to the LDCs are also investigated.

5. THE PROJECT LINK WORLD MODEL SYSTEM

Our third example of international modelling is Project LINK developed by Lawrence R. Klein and his associates at research centres all over the world. LINK, as the name suggests, is a linked system of country models encompassing the major developed market economies, models of the centrally planned countries, and models of regional groupings of the developing world. The primary linkages between the countries are through trade flows in one dimension and through prices in the other. The country models, described in Waelbroeck (1976)[5], are a mixture of models specifically designed for each country by the various participating country model centres. These are predominantly of the Keynesian type, with emphasis on modelling short term business cycle phenomena. Each model explains imports for four commodity categories (SITC 0,1, food; SITC 2,4, raw materials; SITC 3, fuels; and SITC 5–9, manufactures) typically as a function of domestic activity variables and of relative prices. These demands for imports are then translated by way of a trade matrix into exports of the exporting countries and fed into their respective models. With respect to import prices a similar solution is followed. Each of the country models explains export prices endogenously as a function of conditions in the exporting countries. In turn, the trade matrix provides the appropriate weights to aggregate the export price indices into the import price indices of the importing countries. Iterations between the models proceed until economic activity and prices in each of the country models are consistent with all others.

Numerous studies using this system have been carried out for purposes of forecasting, for testing the price and activity multiplier interrelationships between countries (Hickman (1975)), and for examining the impact of alternative policy scenarios, for example, the well–known 'locomotive and boxcars' ideas of economic stimulus in the 1970s. A LINK simulation of protectionism, with import restrictions imposed by the major industrial countries concluded that 'There are apparent gains for individual countries, but taken as a whole, the world loses, ... and, worst of all, the developing countries, which can least afford it, stand to lose.' (Klein and Su (1979), p. 34). A recent study, Klein, Bollino, and Fardoust (1981), investigated the impact of industrial incentive policies, first in the United States alone and then in all the industrial countries together under conditions of stable and flexible exchange rates. This study showed that significant improvement in world economic performance could be achieved by such policies, particularly if the industrial countries participated in a joint effort of providing additional incentives to industrial investment.

The LINK system has substantial potentials for modelling the questions related to the international monetary system and the relationships to the LDCs. Important questions can be modelled either in the model system as it stands, as we have noted above, or through adjustments and modifications. Thus, for example, it is possible to introduce the impact of capital transfers in favour of the LDCs, to recognise the impact of shock from the high price of oil (Klein (1978)), or to deal with adjustments in exchange rates (Johnson and Klein (1974)).

The LINK project is a live effort with significant ongoing work on the models, system expansion and improvement. Among the current efforts are, for example:

– full endogenisation of exchange rates recognising elements of purchasing power parity over the long run and of balance of payments disequilibrium in the short run. In the past the models simply assumed exchange rates as fixed, an assumption which was appropriate to the Bretton Woods period fixed exchange rate situation. But with the turn towards floating rates came the need to make exchange rates endogenous. This has proved difficult because the exchange rate depends not only on commodity trade, but on the entire current account and on capital movements. Moreover, there are significant speculative components to exchange rate determinats.

- modelling of service flows in the balance of payments. The most important item here is the interest payments on the outstanding debt and the other payments to foreign factors.
- elaboration of the LDC countries by endogenisation of separate country models for LDCs, for example, Pacific Basin countries, India, Brazil, Egypt, Indnesia, etc.
- modelling of country external debts. Problems of international debt are an important matter of concern. The difficulties of the debtor countries, and their impact on international economic instability. There have been a number of debt simulation models (Adams, Sanchez, and Adams (1983)) but so far they have not been integrated into the world model systems. Moreover, the problem is that the kind of instability which a failure of a particular country to meet its obligations would evoke is difficult to integrate into the model. A panic situation which would impact on the banks holding the debt is hard to model econometrically. However, simulations dealing with international financial crisis scenarios have been carried out (Wharton Econometrics (1983)).

These projects involve significant new challenges in many cases. New theoretical underpinnings must be created, important new data sources must be exploited, and new empirical relationships specified and estimated.

6. COMMODITIES IN MODELS OF THE WORLD ECONOMY

In this section we consider examples of the integration of commodities in a world model system.

6.1 The Comlink Version of LINK

The integration of commodity market modes into Project LINK (Adams (1978)) called Comlink, represented a significant step forward to recognise the impact of fluctuations in the prices of primary commodities on the world economy.

The mechanisms for integrating commodity prices were quite simple. To determine the prices of principal commodities in international trade, simple commodity market models, like those discussed above, were built to cover 23 commodities. These models were linked to the country models of LINK on the input side through the economic activity variables which affected commodity demands and through the world GDP deflator which established a worldwide price numeraire. The commodity models predicted the export prices of the major commodities (UN commodity export price indices). In turn linkage equations for each exporting country translated these commodity prices into export price indices for commodity categories SITC 0,1 and 2,4, food and industrial raw materials respectively. Category 3, fuels, could be altered exogenously in this system. The further linkages from export prices to import price indices, and from export price indices to the earnings of the LDC country blocks was left to procedures already in the LINK system. Estimation and application of the Comlink system showed the following features important for further work in this area.

- Commodity market models can be used to explain commodity price movements, though frequently the wide speculative swings of commodity prices observed on the commodity exchanges (London Metals Exchange, for example), are greatly attenuated in model simulations.
- The linkage between commodity prices and the prices in international trade (export price indices for SITC categories) show further attenuation of variability and some price lags. This is probably a realistic result since world trade in commodities is not generally at spot market prices (though it may be linked to them) and since contract prices often move with less volatility and with lags behind the spot prices.
- The commodity prices feed through into import prices of consuming countries and with further time lags affect the domestic and export price level. The degree to which this feed–through occurs depends greatly on the importance of the commodities in the imports and production of the consuming countries (petroleum price movements are obviously more important than price movements in commodities like coffee and cocoa).
- Unless one were to introduce very violent price movements like the oil shocks of the 1970s, the GNPs of the industrial countries are affected only slightly by changes in commodity prices. But large swings in demand, perhaps the result of synchronisation of the world business cycle phase, or large movements in supply could and do affect worldwide economic conditions. (The implications for everyday forecasting with a world model system, however, are that as long as swings in the world economy are mild, the impact of commodity price movements on the industrial economies is likely to be small).
- The impact of fluctuations of commodity prices on the producing countries is typically more marked than on the consuming countries since the former are in many cases developing countries with great dependence on one or a small number of export commodities.
- Policy steps at the level of the consuming and producing economies can have significant impacts on the effect of commodity market changes on the world economy. In the developed countries anti–inflationary responses to commodity price upswings have exacerbated the effect of oil price shocks. Policy at the level of the producing

countries also has potential for moderating the internal impact of commodity market developments.

6.2 Other Commodity Linkages

The scheme described above integrates the commodity prices and the revenues obtained from commodity exports into the model system, it fails in a number of respects to recognise important characteristics of the commodity sector.

- There is no attempt to force correspondence between the quantitative imports of consuming countries and exports of producing countries as measured in the trade statistics and predicted in the country models, with the flows of commodities as observed in the commodity models. Such a reconciliation would be a serious challenge. Clearly, the commodity flows themselves should correspond to trade flows, a factor which is particularly important in the countries which have only a limited variety of export products. But it would be difficult statistically to maintain the correspondence. And it is not clear that except in a few of the commodity exporters, reconciliation between commodity flows would significantly alter the result.
- The volatility of commodity markets, partly the result of changing expectations is difficult to capture in the world model systems. While we have noted that some attenuation of price movements is to be expected, it would be interesting to integrate speculative markets operating on a much smaller time dimension (daily or monthly) into econometric systems of the world economy which are typically based on annual data.
- Technological changes are likely particularly to affect the consumption of industrial raw materials and the production side of many primary products. Yet, while technological change frequently shifts technical or behavioural relations it is seldom adequately represented in econometric models. This is not to say that technological change is not represented altogether. Many aspects of technological change are responses to changes in relative prices and are thus recognised. Trend variables often account for longer term gradual changes. But it must be recognised that technological factors such as the Green Revolution, the substitution of plasnonferrous and ferrous materials, and the improvements in energy utilisation efficiency are only imperfectly recognised in the models. This is an important omission in a world where technological transfers are occurring with increasing rapidity and where industrial policies are being expressly aimed towards accelerating technological and economic change.

7. CONCLUSION

The scheme utilised to integrate commodity models into Project LINK offers a good starting point for further work. Commodity market models are being constructed and updated. These should be comprehensive but simple to make possible straightforward integration into a world model system. The linkages from these models to the models of the commodity producing countries are particularly important since the well–being of these countries is closely linked to the value of their commodity exports. Finally, the global linkages from the prices of commodities to the imports of the consuming countries and to their domestic economic conditions must be fully elaborated. The pattern of the Comlink studies represents a practical and useful precedent.

NOTES

1) The work is summarised in Adams and Behrman (1982). The individual studies are Priovolos (1981), Lasaga (1981), Obidegwu and Nziramasanga (1981), Adams and Priovolos (1981), and Siri (1984), Ho (1983). An earlier study using a similar approach for cocoa in Ghana is Acquah (1972).

2) Adams and Marquez (1982) and Adams and Marquez (1983). There are also a number of other global regional block studies such as Klein and Yeh (1979), etc. The advantage of modelling regional blocks rather than individual countries lies in the simplicity and small size of such a system, particularly for pedagogical or demonstration purposes.

3) The centrally planned economies might have been modelled as well, but have been omitted to make the system simple. In any case, trade with the centrally planned block would not be sufficient to make a significant difference on the simulation results at the world aggregate level.

4) There are numerous descriptions of Project LINK and of its applications. Particularly relevant here are Ball (1973) and Sawyer (1979).

5) All models in the system have been updated and many new ones added since the publication of the Waelbroeck volume. But the general nature of the models has not changed.

REFERENCES

Acquah, P. (1972), 'A Macroeconomic Analysis of Export Instability and Economic Growth: The Case of Ghana and the WORLD COCOA MARKET', Ph.D. Dissertation, University of Pennsylvania, Philadelphia.

Adams, F.G. and J.R. Behrman (1976), *Econometric Models of World Agricultural Commodity Markets*, Ballinger, Cambridge.

Adams, F.G. (1978), 'Primary Commodity Markets in a World Trade System', in F.G. Adams and S.A. Klein (eds.), *Stabilising World Commodity Markets*, D.C. Heath, Lexington, Mass.

Adams, F.G. and T. Priovolos (1981), *Coffee and Brazil*, D.C. Heath, Lexington, Mass.

Adams, F.G. and J.R. Behrman (1982), *Commodity Exports and Economic Development*, D.C. Heath, Lexington, Mass.

Adams, F.G. and J.R. Marquez (1982), 'A Global Model of Oil Price Impacts', in F.G. Adams and B.G. Hickman (eds.), *Global Econometrics*, (1983), MIT Press, Cambridge.

Adams, F.G. and L.R. Klein (eds.) (1983), *Industrial Policies for Growth and*

Competitiveness, D.C. Heath, Lexington, Mass.

Adams, F.G. and J.R. Marquez (1984), 'Petroleum Price Elasticity Income Effects, and the OPEC's Pricing Policy', *Energy Economics*, 52 (1), pp. 115–28.

Adams, F.G., E.P. Sanchez, and M.E. Adams (1983), 'Can Latin America Carry Its International Debt?', *Journal of Policy Modeling*, 5 (3), pp. 419–41.

Armington, P. (1980), 'New Exchange Rate Model for Forecasting and Analysis of Multilateral Stabilisation Policies', SRI/ WEFA, World Economic Programme, Discussion Paper 6, April.

Ball, R.J. (ed.) (1973), *International Linkage of National Economic Models*, North Holland, Amsterdam.

Behrman, J.R. (1977), *International Commodity Agreements: An Evaluation of the UNCTAD Integrated Commodity Programme*, Overseas Development Council, Washington.

Behrman, J.R. and J.A. Hanson (1979), 'The Use of Econometric Models in Developing Countries', in J.R. Behrman and J.A. Hanson (eds.), *Short Term Macroeconomic Policy in Latin America*, Ballinger, Cambridge.

Cline, W.R. (ed.) (1979), *Proposals for a New Economic Order*, Praeger, Washington.

Hickman, B.G. (1975), 'Project LINK in 1972: Retrospect and Prospect', in G.A. Renton (ed.), *Modelling the Economy*, Heinemann, London.

Hickman, B.G. and L.T. Lau (1973), 'Elasticities of Substitution and Export Demands in a World Trade Model', *European Economic Review*, 4, pp. 347–80.

Hickman, B.G. (1975), 'International Transmission of Economic Fluctuations and Inflation', in A. Ando (ed.), *International Aspects of Stabilisation Policies*, Federal Reserve Bank, Boston.

Ho, Ting–Seng (1983), 'An Econometric Study of Export Fluctuations and Stabilisation Policies in Malaysia', Ph.D. Dissertation, University of Pennsylvania, Philadelphia.

Johnson, K.N. and L.R. Klein (1974), 'LINK Model Simulations of International Trade: An Evaluation of the Effects of Currency Realignment', *Journal of Finance*, Papers and Proceedings, 29, pp. 617–30.

Kenen, P. and C. Voivodas (1972), 'Export Instability and Economic Growth', *Kyklos*, 25, pp. 791–804.

Klein, L.R. (1976), 'Five Year Experience of Linking National Econometric Models and of Forecasting International Trade', in H. Glejser (ed.), *Quantitative Studies of International Economics*, North Holland, Amsterdam.

Klein, L.R. (1978), 'Disturbances to the International Economy', in *After the Phillips Curve*, Federal Reserve Bank, Boston.

Klein, L.R. and V. Su (1979), 'Protectionism: An Analysis from Project LINK', *Journal of Policy Modeling*, 1, pp. 5–35.

Klein, L.R. and B. Yeh (1979), 'A Global Economic Model', International Institute for Applied Systems Analysis, Laxenburg, Austria.

Klein, L.R., A. Bollino, S. Fardoust (1982), 'Industrial Policy in the World Economy Medium Term Simulations with the LINK System, 1982– 1990', *Journal of Policy Modeling*, 4 (2), pp. 175–89.

Labys, W. (1973), *Dynamic Commodity Models*, D.C. Heath, Lexing– ton, Mass.

Labys, W. (1980), 'Commodity Price Stabilisation Models: A Review and Appraisal', *Journal of Policy Modeling*, 2, pp. 121–36.

Lasaga, M. (1981), *The Copper Industry in the Chilean Economy*, D.C. Heath, Lexington, Mass.

McBean, A. (1966), *Export Instability and Economic Deveopment*, Harvard University Press, Cambridge.

Obidegwu, C. and M. Nziramasanga (1981), *Copper and Zambia*, D.C. Heath, Lexington, Mass.

Priovolos, T. (1981), *Coffee and the Ivory Coast*, D.C. Heath, Lexington, Mass.

Rangarajan, C. and V. Sundararajan (1976), 'Impact of Export Fluctuations on Income: A Cross Country Analysis', *Review of Economics and Statistics*, 58, pp. 368–72.

Sawyer, J.A. (ed.) (1979), *Modelling the International Transmission Mechanism*, North Holland, Amsterdam.

Siri, G. (1984), *El Salvador and Economic Integration in Latin America*, D.C. Heath, Lexington, Mass.

Waelbroeck, J. (ed.) (1976), *The Models of Project LINK*, North Holland, Amsterdam.

Wharton Econometrics (1983), 'World Economy at a Cross Roads: International Financial Crunch, Crisis or Crash?', Special Report.

ADVANCED STUDIES IN THEORETICAL AND APPLIED ECONOMETRICS

1. Paelinck J.H.P. (ed.): Qualitative and Quantitative Mathematical Economics, 1982. ISBN 90 247 2623 9.
2. Ancot J.P. (ed.): Analysing the Structure of Economic Models, 1984. ISBN 90 247 2894 0.
3. Hughes Hallett A.J. (ed.): Applied Decision Analysis and Economic Behaviour, 1984. ISBN 90 247 2968 8.
4. Sengupta J.K.: Information and Efficiency in Economic Decision, 1985. ISBN 90 247 3072 4.
5. Artus P. and Guvenen O., in collaboration with Gagey F. (eds.): International Macroeconomic Modelling for Policy Decisions, 1986. ISBN 90 247 3201 8.
6. Vilares M.J.: Structural Change in Macroeconomic Models, 1986. ISBN 90 247 3277 8.
7. Carraro C. and Sartore D. (eds.): Developments of Control Theory for Economic Analysis, 1987. ISBN 90 247 3345 6.
8. Broer D.P. (ed.): Neoclassical Theory and Empirical Models of Aggregate Firm Behaviour, 1987. ISBN 90 247 3412 6.
9. Italianer A. (ed.): Theory and Practice of International Trade Linkage Models, 1986. ISBN 90 247 3407 X.
10. Kendrick D.A.: Feedback, 1988. ISBN 90 247 3593 9 (HB). ISBN 90 247 3650 1 (PB).
11. Sengupta J.K. and Kadekodi G.K. (eds.): Econometrics of Planning and Efficiency, 1988. ISBN 90 247 3602 1.
12. Griffith D.A.: Advanced Spatial Statistics, 1988. ISBN 90 247 3627 7.
13. Guvenen, O.: International Commodity Market Models and Policy Analysis, 1988. ISBN 90 247 3768 0.